Neuro-Fuzzy Pattern Recognition

Neuro-Fuzzy Pattern Recognition

Methods in Soft Computing

SANKAR K. PAL
SUSHMITA MITRA
Indian Statistical Institute
Calcutta

A Wiley-Interscience Publication
JOHN WILEY & SONS, INC.
New York • Chichester • Weinheim • Brisbane • Singapore • Toronto

This text is printed on acid-free paper. ⊖

For ordering and customer service, call 1-800-CALL-WILEY.

Library of Congress Cataloging-in-Publication Data:

Pal, Sankar K.
    Neuro-fuzzy pattern recognition : methods in soft computing /
Sankar K. Pal, Sushmita Mitra.
        p.   cm.
    Includes bibliographical references and index.
    ISBN 0-471-34844-9 (alk. paper)
    1. Soft computing.   2. Pattern recognition systems.   3. Neural networks (Computer science)   4. Fuzzy systems.   I. Mitra, Sushmita, 1962– .   II. Title.
    QA76.9.S63P35   1999
    006.3—dc21   99-24974

Printed in the United States of America

10 9 8 7 6 5 4 3 2

To our parents

Contents

Foreword

The treatise by Drs. S. K. Pal and S. Mitra, *Neuro-Fuzzy Pattern Recognition: Methods in Soft Computing*, is a work whose importance is impossible to exaggerate. Authored by two of the foremost authorities in pattern recognition, it reflects the highly influential role of the Machine Intelligence Unit at the renowned Indian Statistical Institute as one of the world's leading centers of research in recognition technology. In the tradition of earlier pioneering work by Drs. S. K. Pal and D. Dutta Majumder, *Fuzzy Mathematical Approach to Pattern Recognition*, the Pal-Mitra treatise is a model of expository skill, insight, authority, and relevance to real-world problems. It covers a vast array of concepts, methods, and techniques in ways that clarify their interconnections and highlight their roles within the partnership of methodologies that form the core of soft computing.

Pattern recognition is not a new subject. Recognition systems of one kind or another – among them character recognition systems, speech recognition systems, handwriting recognition systems, target recognition systems, and diagnostic systems – have been around for a long time. But what we are beginning to see today are recognition systems that are capable of performing tasks that could not be done in the past. Among examples of such systems are: computer virus detection systems; eyeprint identification systems; supermarket checkout scanners which use scent sensors; molecular breath analyzers for medical diagnosis; and password authentication systems using typing biometrics.

The quantum jump in the capabilities of today's recognition systems reflect three converging developments: (a) major advances in sensor technology; (b) major advances in sensor data processing technology; and (c) the use of soft computing techniques to infer a conclusion from observed data.

The employment of soft computing – a consortium of fuzzy logic, neuro-computing, evolutionary computing, and probabilistic computing – is a key factor in the enhanced capabilities of recognition systems. The basic idea underlying soft computing is that its constituent methodologies are for the most part complementary and synergistic – rather than competitive. What this means is that in almost all cases better results can be obtained by employing the constituent methodologies of soft computing in combination rather than in a stand-alone mode. This is particularly true of so-called neuro-fuzzy systems – systems that play a central role in the Pal-Mitra treatise. The constituent methodologies of soft computing, their synergism, and their roles in pattern recognition are discussed at length and with incisive insight in the Pal-Mitra work. In what follows, I will take the liberty of adding a few thoughts of my own.

Traditionally, pattern recognition has been formulated and approached as a problem in statistical classification, based on the assumption that data are noisy but the underlying classes are crisp and have precisely defined boundaries. The problem with this assumption is that most real-world classes are fuzzy rather than crisp. A typical example is: diseases and their symptoms. Thus, as was pointed out in an earlier paper by Bellman, Kalaba, and Zadeh (1966), the basic problem in pattern recognition may be viewed as that of estimating from observed data the grade of membership of an object in a fuzzy set rather than that of deciding whether or not a given object belongs to a crisp set. This is one of the reasons why fuzzy set theory and, more particularly, fuzzy logic, are so closely linked to the basic conceptual structure of pattern recognition.

In my recent work, I have suggested a new direction in fuzzy logic that may have a substantial impact on the ways in which problems in pattern recognition are formulated and solved in coming years. Specifically, the direction in question relates to what is referred to as the computational theory of perceptions (CTP).

The computational theory of perceptions is inspired by the remarkable human capability to perform a wide variety of physical and mental tasks – recognition tasks among them – without any measurements and any computations. Everyday examples of such tasks are parking a car, driving in city traffic, playing golf, understanding speech, and recognizing similarities. Underlying this capability is the brain's crucial ability to manipulate perceptions – of time, distance, force, weight, shape, color, taste, number, intent, likelihood, and truth, among others.

Recognition and perception are closely related. In a fundamental way, a recognition process may be viewed as a sequence of decisions. Decisions are based on information. In most realistic settings, decision-relevant information is a mixture of measurements and perceptions; for example, Michelle is 21 and Michelle is slim. In existing theories, perceptions are converted into measurements. The problem is that in many cases, such conversion is infeasible, unrealistic or counterproductive. An alternative suggested by the computational theory of perceptions is to convert perceptions into propositions expressed in a natural language. Simple examples of perceptions expressed in a natural language are: "it is a warm day," "Robert is very honest," "it is very unlikely that there will be a significant increase in the price of oil in the near future."

Perceptions are intrinsically imprecise. More specifically, perceptions are f-granular, that is, both fuzzy and granular, with a granule being a clump of elements of a class that are drawn together by indistinguishability, similarity, proximity or functionality. F-granularity of perceptions reflects the finite ability of sensory organs and, ultimately, the brain, to resolve detail and store information. In effect, f-granulation is a human way of achieving data compression.

F-granularity of perceptions puts them well beyond the meaning representation capabilities of predicate logic and other available meaning representation methods. In CTP, meaning representation is based on the use of so-called constraint-centered semantics, and reasoning with perceptions is carried out by goal-directed propagation of generalized constraints. In this way, the computational theory of perception adds to existing theories the capability to operate on and reason with perception-based information.

To some extent, this capability is already provided by fuzzy logic and, in particular, by the concept of a linguistic variable and the calculus of fuzzy if-then rules, both of which are discussed in the Pal-Mitra treatise. The computational theory of perceptions extends this capability much further and in new directions. In application to pattern recognition, the computational theory of perceptions opens the door to a much wider and more systematic use of natural languages in the description of patterns, classes, perceptions and methods of recognition, organization, and knowledge discovery. In my view, this is what lies ahead.

There is so much that we can do today in marshaling the combined resources of fuzzy logic, neurocomputing, evolutionary computing, probabilistic computing, and related methodologies. How this can be done is the principal contribution of the Pal-Mitra treatise – a work that is truly outstanding by all criteria that matter. The authors and the publisher deserve our profound thanks and congratulations for producing a text that is a must reading for anyone who is concerned with any aspect of recognition technology and its real-world applications.

July 21, 1999   Lotfi A. Zadeh

Preface

Fuzzy set theory provides an approximate but effective and flexible way of representing, manipulating and utilizing vaguely defined data and information, and of describing the behaviors of systems that are too complex or too ill-defined to admit of precise mathematical analysis by classical methods and tools. Successful use of fuzzy logic to create many commercial products has been made in Japan. This, in turn, has increased interest among engineers, researchers, and company executives to understand and further explore this technology. Although the approach tries to model the human thought process in a decision-making system, it has no relation with the architecture of the human neural information processing system, nor does it take into consideration the information storage technique of human beings, and sometimes it is computationally intensive.

Human intelligence and discriminating power, on the other hand, are mainly attributed to the massively connected network of biological neurons in the human brain. *Artificial neural network* models are attempts to emulate electronically the architecture and information representation scheme of the biological neural network. The collective computational abilities of the densely interconnected nodes or processors may provide a natural technique, at least to a great extent, for solving highly complex real life problems in a manner analogous to humans.

It therefore appears that a judicious integration of the merits of these two technologies can provide more intelligent systems (in terms of generic advantages like parallelism, fault tolerance, adaptivity, and uncertainty management) by evolving synergism between them, to handle real life ambiguous situations and recognition problems. These promises have motivated (during the last 7–10 years) a large number of researchers to exploit these modern concepts for solving real world problems, leading to the development of a new paradigm called *neuro-fuzzy* computing. Besides the generic advantages, the neuro-fuzzy paradigm sometimes provides application specific advantages. One may note that the neuro-fuzzy approach is a key component of today's *soft computing* research, which provides the foundation for the conception and design of high-MIQ (machine IQ) systems and forms the basis of future-generation computing technology.

The aim of the book is to discuss the contribution of neuro-fuzzy computing to the development of methodologies for pattern recognition problems, with an application-oriented approach. The different tasks considered here are classification, feature evaluation, rule generation, knowledge extraction, and hybridization with other soft computing tools. We have provided extensive experimental results along with comparison to various real life data, *e.g.*, speech, medical (hepatobiliary disorders and kala-azar [1]) and fingerprints.

Sizable portions of the material presented in the book are unified from our published work, which has been presented and discussed in different seminars, conferences, and workshops. The book may be used either in a graduate-level course as a part of the subject of pattern recognition, machine learning, and artificial intelligence, or as a reference book for professionals and researchers in fuzzy set theory, artificial neural networks, soft computing, and their application to pattern recognition and image processing problems. It is assumed that the readers have adequate background in college-level mathematics and introductory knowledge of statistics and probability theory.

We have kept the presentation concise and included a comprehensive bibliography for the convenience of readers. Some material in related areas may have been inadvertently omitted because of our oversight or ignorance.

The text is organized in nine chapters. The preliminaries of pattern recognition along with application areas, various approaches, relevance of fuzzy sets and artificial neural networks to pattern recognition problems, and the need for neuro-fuzzy computing are introduced in Chapter 1. Chapter 2 is devoted to the introduction of fuzzy set theory, different fuzzy pattern recognition techniques, basic neural networks, various ways of fuzzy–neural integration along with mathematical formulations, development of fuzzy knowledge-based networks, hybridization with other tools, and the emergence of soft computing.

In Chapter 3 we have presented various neuro-fuzzy models for pattern classification. These are followed by detailed descriptions of a fuzzy multilayer perceptron (MLP), fuzzy logical MLP, and fuzzy Kohonen network, with experimental results. Some more real life applications of the aforesaid fuzzy

---

[1] A form of visceral leishmaniasis

MLP for certain problems of medical diagnosis and fingerprint classification are described in Chapter 4.

The problem of self-organization, pixel classification, and object extraction for noisy images in neuro-fuzzy framework is discussed in Chapter 5. Here the effectiveness of different fuzziness measures for making an MLP work in unsupervised mode is demonstrated. This is followed by a judicious hybridization of three soft computing components, *e.g.*, fuzziness in a set, cellular networks, and genetic algorithms. Methodologies for feature selection and feature extraction under both supervised and unsupervised modes are discussed in Chapter 6. Various connectionist models for optimization of fuzzy feature evaluation indices are described, along with theoretical analysis and experimental results.

Chapter 7 deals with the task of rule generation. Here various methodologies for inferencing, querying, and linguistic rule generation are described. The use of the fuzzy MLP, fuzzy logical MLP, and fuzzy Kohonen network (as described in Chapter 3) in this regard, is explained in detail along with experimental results.

Chapter 8 introduces the development of knowledge-based networks, elucidates the incorporation of fuzziness at different stages, and demonstrates the use of fuzzy knowledge-based MLP for both classification and rule generation. Finally, an integration of fuzzy neural networks with rough sets, for designing a knowledge-based system in a stronger soft computing paradigm, is demonstrated in Chapter 9. The merits of using rough sets for knowledge extraction are experimentally justified for the classification problem.

We take this opportunity to thank Dr. Albert Zomaya of University of Western Australia, and Ms. Lina Lopez and Ms. Angioline Loredo of John Wiley & Sons, Inc., for their initiative and encouragement. We owe a vote of thanks to all our colleauges, particularly Dr. M. K. Kundu, Dr. C. A. Murthy, Dr. A. Pal and Mr. Rajat K. De for their helpful discussions. We are grateful to Mr. B. Uma Shankar, Mr. Pabitra Mitra, and Ms. Amy Hendrickson for their tireless endeavors while preparing the camera-ready manuscript. The valuable secretarial assistance rendered by Ms. Maya De, Mr. Sanjoy Das, and Mr. Indranil Dutta is also acknowledged.

Sankar K. Pal

Sushmita Mitra

December 1998

List of Figures

1

Introduction

1.1 INTRODUCTION

Patterns are the means by which we interpret the world. Pattern is the language of nature. We are performing the task of pattern recognition at every instant of our working lives. We recognize the objects around us, and move and act in relation to them. Typical examples include recognizing the voice of a friend over the phone, or the flavor of an icecream, reading a newspaper, driving a car, diagnosing a disease, and distinguishing a piece of music played on a *sitar* from that on a *sarod*. How a new-born baby learns to recognize patterns gradually makes an interesting study. Initially it learns to recognize its parents and other near and dear ones, and to detect whether someone is a stranger to it or not. It can then identify its feeding bottle. As it grows older, it refines its recognition process and acquires the ability to discriminate between different types of direct (concrete) and indirect (conceptual) patterns.

The recognition of concrete patterns includes visual and aural recognition of spatial (character, picture, fingerprint) and temporal (waveform, speech, ECG) patterns for which one needs sensory aids (*e.g.*, ears, eyes, nose). The recognition of abstract items such as concepts and ideas, on the other hand, can be done without the help of sensors. These may be accordingly termed sensory recognition and conceptual recognition. We shall restrict our discussion to sensory recognition.

Let us now discuss various approaches to pattern recognition with their relevance. Consider, for example, the problem of recognizing speech sound corrupted with noise. Here the theory of probability may be used to model uncertainty arising from randomness of patterns and a decision can be taken under minimum risk. On the other hand, the letter H can be structurally represented as two vertical lines connected by a horizontal line; thereby enabling its recognition syntactically. We can recognize a chair or a table from any direction, orientation or color, even at a long distance. The concept "chair" which appears as a visual pattern and stimulates our vision, seems to be not very clear, but it bears a rational interrelationship with the actual data entering our eyes. One can also perceive patterns even when they are grossly distorted, ambiguous, incomplete, occluded, or severely affected by "noise". For example, if we have a distorted letter Ⱶ, this could be an A, an H, or a new letter. But if it appears as "ⱵAT" then the letter is H, and if it is "CⱵAT", then it is A. So context is of crucial importance in pattern recognition.

We are continuously having to recognize people, objects, handwriting, voice, images, and other patterns, using distorted or unfamiliar, incomplete, occluded, fuzzy, and inconclusive data, where a pattern should be allowed to have membership or belongingness to more than one class. This is also very significant in (say) medical diagnosis, where a patient afflicted with a certain set of symptoms can be simultaneously suffering from more than one disease. Again, the symptoms need not necessarily be strictly numerical. It would be in *natural* terms, defined as linguistic and/or set variables such as *very high, more or less low, between* $50°C$ *and* $55°C$. This is how the concept of *fuzziness* comes into the picture.

Let us explain the concept of membership with an example. You ask a friend to meet you at 10 a.m. tomorrow. It is highly likely that your friend will arrive *any* time *around* 10 a.m., say, from 9.55 a.m. to 10.05 a.m. This defines the concept of a membership function along the time axis, with a peak (membership of 1) at 10 a.m. sharp having a bandwidth of 10 min. As you move away either side from the peak, the membership approaches the value 0. The bandwidth, again, is problem- and context-dependent. Hence if your friend is a German, the bandwidth would be less, whereas if this person is an Indian, the bandwidth would usually be more! Thus we see that although 10 a.m. is a *crisp* concept with $\{0,1\}$ *hard* characterizing function, in reality it becomes fuzzy with $[0,1]$ graded membership function. One may note that the membership value reflects the degree of compatibility/similarity of an event with an imprecise concept representing a fuzzy set, whereas the probability of an event is related to the number of times it occurs.

The concept of fuzzy sets can be used to describe situations in which there is imprecision due to vagueness rather than randomness. For example, the handwritten letters denoting B constitute a fuzzy set where the ambiguity is created due to imprecision in writing. This vagueness, instead of using the probability concept of badly written characters, can be described by a fuzzy membership function that assigns the degree of similarity between the imperfect and perfect ones. Analogously, one can use the notion of fuzziness to suitably handle patterns like speech sounds, where the variability or uncertainty arises mainly from the speaker's health, age, sex, mood, dialect, and so on.

The notion of multiple membership also shows considerable promise in the interpretation of satellite imagery. Let us consider, for defense interests, the problem of identifying a road shaded with trees and adjacent to a stream. Here each element of the image (pixel) may represent the signature of all the three regions – concrete, vegetation, and water body – because of its resolution. Consequently, during interpretation/recognition, a pixel may have membership to all these classes with varying degrees. Here lies the relevance of making a *soft* decision by not enforcing a strict belongingness to only one class.

Another important point about pattern recognition is concerned with the part played by memory and learning in the recognition process. There are two aspects of the memory to be considered: (1) the part that holds the information we can recall, such as a poem, a face, a vocabulary, or a theorem and (2) the information that we have gained and that presumably is stored somewhere, because we make use of it, but that we cannot retrieve. For example, we cannot describe how we balance when we walk, how we recognize a speech, how we drive a car, or similar aspects of pattern processing, although the information must be stored somewhere in our brain and nervous system.

There are millions and millions of very simple processing elements or *neurons* in the brain, linked together in a massively parallel manner. This is believed to be responsible for the human intelligence and discriminating power. All information is stored in a distributed fashion among the connection weights. There is also a large amount of redundancy inherent among the connections, leading to a *graceful degradation* of performance in case of any damage. *Artificial neural networks* provide crude emulation of the brain. These connectionist models implement certain important aspects of a pattern recognition system: robustness, adaptivity, speed, and learning. A neural network can learn through examples the discriminating characteristics among various pattern classes, by automatically discovering the inherent relationship among them in a data-rich environment. No rules need to be specified beforehand. This bears an analogy to how a baby learns to recognize objects, or perhaps learns to speak.

Note that fuzzy set theory tries to mimic the human reasoning and thought processes, while the neural networks attempt to emulate the architecture and information representation scheme of the human brain. One may therefore naturally think of judiciously integrating them by augmenting each other in order to build a more intelligent/information system, in *neuro-fuzzy computing* paradigm, with recognition performance better than those obtained by the individual technologies. For example, one can have a neural classifier that can learn even with linguistic, incomplete, imprecise, or vague examples; or, a fuzzy classifier with the capability of learning intractable classes more accurately and rapidly through neural networks. Efficient searching or retrieval of information can also be accomplished in the said framework even when the complexity of the input space is high with or without noise/distortion, or when too many parameters are involved. *Genetic algorithms*, another biologically inspired tool, come in here. This provides suitable adaptive, robust, and fast search techniques for designing efficient pattern recognition systems through evolution based on the mechanism of natural genetics. Similarly, one can incorporate the domain knowledge (about class structures) into this system for enhancing its learning ability (rate) and efficacy further. Here lies the significance of using *rough set* theory, which can perform the task of knowledge encoding into network parameters efficiently. This theory approximates a rough (vague) concept, arising from the limited discernibility of objects in the domain of discourse, in terms of two exact concepts.

The challenge is, therefore, to devise powerful recognition methodologies and systems by symbiotically combining these tools. The systems should have the capability of flexible information processing to deal with real life ambiguous situations and to achieve tractability, robustness, and low-cost solutions.

1.2 MACHINE RECOGNITION OF PATTERNS

Pattern recognition and machine learning form a major area of research and development (R&D) activity that encompasses the processing of pictorial and other nonnumerical information obtained from the interaction betwccn science, technology, and society. A motivation for the spurt of activity in this field is the need for people to communicate with the computing machines in their natural mode of communication. Another important motivation is that the scientists are also concerned with the idea of designing and making intelligent machines that can carry out certain tasks that we human beings do. The most salient outcome of these is the concept of future generation computing systems.

Machine recognition [1, 2] of patterns can be viewed as a twofold task, consisting of learning the invariant and common properties of a set of samples characterizing a class, and of deciding a new sample as a possible member of the class by noting that it has properties common to those of the set of samples. In other words, pattern recognition by computers can be described as a transformation from the measurement space M to the feature space F and finally to the decision space D [1]:

$$M \to F \to D.$$

Here, the mapping $\delta : F \to D$ is the decision function and the elements $d \in D$ are termed as decisions.

Pattern recognition, by its nature, admits many approaches, sometimes complementary, sometimes competing, to provide the appropriate solution of a given problem. Various approaches so far proposed and experimented with for the design of pattern recognition systems can be broadly categorized into decision theoretic approach (both deterministic and probabilistic), syntactic approach, and connectionist approach. In the decision theoretic approach [1]–[3], once a pattern is transformed through feature selection to a vector in the feature space, its characteristics are expressed only by a set of numerical values. On the other hand, when a pattern is rich in structural information (*e.g.*, picture recognition, character recognition, scene analysis), *i.e.*, the structural information plays an important role in describing and recognizing the patterns, it is convenient to use syntactic approaches [4] that deal with the representation of structures via sentences, grammars, and automata.

For any pattern recognition system, one desires to achieve robustness with respect to random noise and failure of components and to obtain output in real time. It is also desirable for the system to be adaptive to changes in environment. Moreover, a system can be made artificially intelligent if it is able to emulate some aspects of the human processing system. Connectionist approaches [5]–[10] to pattern recognition are attempts to achieve these goals. The architecture of the network depends on the goal one is trying to achieve. There is a close relationship between some of the popular artificial neural network models (ANNs) and statistical pattern recognition [11]–[14]. Specifically, ANNs have provided architectures on which many classical pattern recognition algorithms (like tree classifiers, principal-component analysis, k-means clustering) can be mapped to facilitate hardware implementation. Similarly, ANNs can derive benefit from some wellknown results in statistical pattern recognition, such as Bayes' decision theory, nearest neighbor rules, and curse of dimensionality. Besides pattern classification, another important application of neural networks is rule generation for discriminating and identifying different classes. Such models use the set of connection weights and/or node activations of a *trained* neural net for generating the antecedent and consequent parts of the rules.

In each and every phase of a pattern recognition system, uncertainty can arise either implicitly or explicitly. This results from the incomplete or imprecise or ambiguous input information, the ill-defined and/or overlapping boundaries among the classes or regions, and the indefiniteness in defining and extracting features and relations among them. Any decision taken at a particular level will have impact on all other higher-level activities. It is therefore required for a pattern recognition system to have sufficient provision for representing these uncertainties involved at every stage, so that the ultimate output of the system can be obtained with least uncertainty. Hence the methods and technologies developed under the aforesaid categories (*viz.*, decision theoretic, syntactic, and connectionist) may again be fuzzy set theoretic in order to handle various uncertainties. Accordingly, fuzzy decision theoretic, fuzzy syntactic, and fuzzy connectionist approaches have been developed.

The significance of fuzzy set theory in the realm of pattern recognition [15]–[27] is adequately justified in

- Representing input patterns as array of membership values denoting the degree of possession of certain properties

- Representing linguistically phrased input features for processing

- Providing an estimate (representation) of missing information in terms of membership values

- Representing multiclass membership of ambiguous patterns and in generating rules and inferences in linguistic form

- Extracting ill-defined image regions, primitives, and properties and describing relations among them as fuzzy subsets

Several attempts were made during the 1990s to evolve different hybrid approaches to pattern recognition by combining the merits of individual techniques. An integration of neural network and fuzzy theory, commonly known as *neuro-fuzzy computing*, is one such hybrid paradigm that has been adequately investigated. This allows one to incorporate the generic advantages of artificial neural networks and fuzzy logic–like massive parallelism, robustness, learning, and handling of uncertainty and impreciseness, into the system. Moreover, some application specific merits can also be incorporated. For example, in the case of pattern classification and rule generation, one can exploit the capability of neural nets in generating highly nonlinear decision boundaries, and model the uncertainties in the input description and output decision by the concept of fuzzy sets. Often the neuro-fuzzy model is found to perform better than either a neural network or a fuzzy system considered individually.

This book provides an insight into various neuro-fuzzy approaches to certain pattern recognition tasks, along with extensive application and comparison on various real life problems. The preliminaries of pattern recognition are briefly discussed in Section 1.3. This includes a short description of Bayes' classifier and the k nearest neighbor classifier, whose performance is provided for comparison in Chapter 3. Section 1.4 describes the relevance of fuzzy set theory. Section 1.5 deals with the usefulness and characteristic features of artificial neural networks for pattern recognition, including rule generation. The need for integrating fuzzy sets and ANNs and the significance of the neuro-fuzzy approach is described in Section 1.6. This is followed by the contents of the remaining part of the book (*i.e.*, Chapters 2–9), which deal with different aspects of neuro-fuzzy pattern classification, feature evaluation and rule generation, development of fuzzy knowledge-based networks and hybridization in soft computing paradigm.

1.3 PRELIMINARIES OF PATTERN RECOGNITION

In a general setting the process of pattern recognition [3, 17], [28]–[30] is visualized as a sequence of few steps: (1) data acquisition, (2) feature selection, and (3) classification. At the first step, depending on the environment within which the objects are to be classified, data are gathered via a set of sensors. Afterward, a feature space is constituted in order to reduce the space dimensionality. However, in a broader perspective this stage significantly influences the entire recognition process. Finally, at the third stage of the scheme the classifier is constructed, or in other words, a transformation relationship is established between features and classes. This can be, for instance, a Bayesian rule of computing *a posteriori* class probability, linear or nonlinear discriminant function, nearest neighbor rule, or a nearest prototype (mean) classification rule [1]–[3], [15, 16, 19, 31]. Let us now describe, in brief, the tasks of data acquisition and feature selection, and a few techniques of traditional decision theoretic classification.

1.3.1   Data acquisition

Pattern recognition techniques are applicable in a wide domain, where the data may be qualitative, quantitative, or both; they may be numerical, linguistic, pictorial, or any combination thereof. Generally, the data structures that are used in pattern recognition systems are of two types: object data vectors and relational data. *Object data*, sets of numerical vectors of n features, are represented as $\mathbf{x} = \{\mathbf{x}_1, \mathbf{x}_2, \ldots, \mathbf{x}_N\}$, a set of N feature vectors in the n-dimensional measurement space $\mathcal{R}^n$. The ith object, $i = 1, 2, \ldots, N$, observed in the process has vector $\mathbf{x}_i$ as its numerical representation; x_{ij} is the jth, $(j = 1, 2, \ldots, n)$ feature associated with the object i.

Relational data are a set of N^2 numerical relationships, say, $\{r_{ii'}\}$, between pairs of objects. In other words, $r_{ii'}$ represents the extent to which object i and i' are related in the sense of some binary relationship ρ. If the objects that are pairwise related by ρ are called $O = \{o_1, o_2, \ldots, o_N\}$, then $\rho : O \times O \to \mathbb{R}$.

Sometimes, the data acquisition phase includes some preprocessing tasks such as noise reduction, filtering, encoding, and enhancement for extracting pattern vectors. For example, if the input pattern is an image, these preprocessing operations play a crucial role for extracting salient features for its recognition.

1.3.2   Feature selection

Feature selection is one of the major tasks in any automatic pattern recognition system. The main objective of *feature selection* [32]–[34], is to retain the optimum salient characteristics necessary for the recognition process and to reduce the dimensionality of the measurement space $\mathcal{R}^n$ so that effective and easily computable algorithms can be devised for efficient classification. The problem of feature selection has two aspects: the formulation of a suitable criterion to evaluate the goodness of a feature and the selection of optimal subset from the available features.

The major mathematical measures so far devised for the estimation of feature quality are mostly statistical in nature, and can be broadly classified into two categories:

- Feature selection in the measurement space

- Feature extraction in the transformed space

The techniques in the first category generally reduce the dimensionality of the feature set by discarding redundant information carrying features. On the other hand, those in the second category utilize all the information contained in the pattern vectors, and map a higher-dimensional pattern vector to a lower-dimensional one.

Feature selection is the process of selecting a map of the form $\mathbf{x}' = f(\mathbf{x})$, by which a sample $\mathbf{x}$ $(=x_1, x_2, \ldots, x_n)$ in an n-dimensional measurement space $\mathcal{R}^n$ is transformed into a point $\mathbf{x}'$ $(=x'_1, x'_2, \ldots, x'_{n'})$ in an n'-dimensional feature space $\mathcal{R}^{n'}$, where $n' < n$.

The pioneering research on feature selection deals mostly with statistical tools. Later, the thrust of the research shifted to the development of various other approaches to feature selection, including fuzzy and neural approaches [19, 35, 36].

1.3.3   Classification

The problem of classification is basically one of partitioning the feature space into regions, one region for each category of input. Thus it attempts to assign every data point in the entire feature space to one of the possible (say, l) classes. Classifiers are usually, but not always, designed with labeled data, in which case these problems are sometimes referred to as *supervised classification* (where the parameters of a classifier function D are learned). Some common examples of the *supervised* pattern classification techniques are the nearest neighbor rule, Bayes' maximum likelihood classifier and perceptron rule. Many clustering algorithms (*e.g.*, k-means, ISODATA) are used as precursors to the design of a classifier when the only data available are unlabeled data. In such cases, the problems are sometimes referred to as *unsupervised classification* [37].

In real life, the complete description of the classes is not known. We have, instead, a finite and usually smaller number of samples that often provide partial information for optimal design of feature extractor or classifier. Under such circumstances, it is assumed that these samples are representative of the classes (usually consisting of an infinite number of samples). Such a set of typical patterns is called a *training set*. On the basis of the information gathered from the samples in the training set, the pattern recognition systems are designed, *i.e.*, one decides the values of the parameters of various pattern recognition methods. Details of different aspects of pattern recognition – data acquisition and preprocessing, classifier design, cluster analysis, feature

selection/extraction, learning, scene analysis, and their various applications –
are available in the literature [1, 2], [15]–[17], [19]. A good pattern classifier
should possess several properties: online adaptation, nonlinear separability,
handling of overlapping classes, fast decision making, generation of soft and
hard decisions, verification and validation mechanisms for evaluating its performance, and minimizing the number of parameters in the system that have
to be tuned.

Let $C_1, C_2, \ldots, C_i, \ldots, C_l$ be the l possible classes in an n-dimensional feature space. Let $\mathbf{x} = [x_1, x_2, \ldots, x_j, \ldots, x_n]'$ be an unknown pattern vector.
In deterministic classification approach, it is assumed that there exists only
one unambiguous pattern class corresponding to each of the unknown pattern
vectors.

If the pattern $\mathbf{x}$ is a member of class C_i, the *discriminant (decision) function*, $D_i(\mathbf{x})$ associated with the class C_i, $i = 1, 2, \ldots, l$ must then possess the
largest value. In other words, classificatory decision would be as follows:

$$\text{Decide} \quad \mathbf{x} \in C_i, \qquad \text{if} \ \ D_i(\mathbf{x}) > D_j(\mathbf{x}) \tag{1.1}$$

$(\forall \ i, j)$ in $(1, \ldots, l)$ and $i \neq j$. Ties are resolved arbitrarily. The decision
boundary in the feature space between regions associated with the classes C_i
and C_j would be governed by the expression

$$D_i(\mathbf{x}) - D_j(\mathbf{x}) = 0. \tag{1.2}$$

Many different forms satisfying eqn. (1.2) can be selected for $D_i(\mathbf{x})$. The
functions that are often used are linear discriminant functions, quadratic discriminant functions, and polynomial discriminant functions.

The k nearest neighbor classifier and the Bayes maximum likelihood classifier, whose performance is used for comparison in Chapter 3, are now briefly
described.

1.3.3.1 *k nearest neighbor classifier* Pattern classification by distance func-
tions [2] is one of the earliest concepts in pattern recognition. Here the proximity of an unknown pattern to a class serves as a measure for its classification.
A class can be characterized by single or multiple prototype pattern(s). The
k nearest neighbor classifier considers multiple prototypes while making a
decision. It uses a piecewise linear discriminant function.

Let us consider a set of sample patterns of *known* classification $\{\mu_1, \mu_2, \ldots,$
$\mu_{N'}\}$, where it is assumed that each pattern belongs to one of the classes
$C_1, C_2, \ldots, C_l$. A *nearest neighbor* (NN) classification rule assigns a pattern
$\mathbf{x}$ of unknown classification to the class of its nearest neighbor. Here $\mu_i \in$
$\{\mu_1, \mu_2, \ldots, \mu_{N'}\}$ is a nearest neighbor to $\mathbf{x}$ if

$$D(\mu_i, \mathbf{x}) = \min_j \{D(\mu_j, \mathbf{x})\}, \quad j = 1, 2, \ldots, N', \tag{1.3}$$

where D is any distance measure definable over the pattern space. This scheme
can be termed the 1-NN rule since it employs only the classification of the
nearest neighbor to $\mathbf{x}$.

Analogously, a k-NN rule consists of determining the k nearest neighbors to $\mathbf{x}$, and using the *majority* of equal classifications in this group as the classification of $\mathbf{x}$. The k-NN classifier is reputed to be able to generate piecewise linear decision boundaries.

1.3.3.2 Bayes' classifier In most practical problems, the features are usually noisy and the classes in the feature space are overlapping. In order to model such systems, the feature values $x_1, x_2, \ldots, x_j, \ldots, x_n$ are considered as random values in the probabilistic approach. The most commonly used classifier in such probabilistic systems is the *Bayes maximum likelihood classifier* [1, 2]. It considers likelihood functions in order to arrive at a decision. The decision-making process is considered as a two-person game against nature. This classifier minimizes the total expected loss with respect to all decisions.

Let $P(C_j)$ and $p(\mathbf{x}|C_j)$ denote the *a priori* probability and class-conditional density respectively, corresponding to the class C_j ($j = 1, 2, \ldots, l$). If the classifier decides $\mathbf{x}$ to be from class C_j when it actually belongs to C_k, it incurs a loss of L_{kj}. The expected loss (conditional average loss or risk) incurred in assigning an observation $\mathbf{x}$ to class C_j is given by

$$r_j(\mathbf{x}) = \sum_{k=1}^{l} L_{kj} p(C_k|\mathbf{x}), \qquad (1.4)$$

where $p(C_k|\mathbf{x})$ represents the probability that $\mathbf{x}$ is from C_k. Using Bayes' relation [1],

$$r_j(\mathbf{x}) = \frac{1}{p(\mathbf{x})} \sum_{k=1}^{l} L_{kj} p(\mathbf{x}|C_k) P(C_k), \qquad (1.5)$$

where $p(\mathbf{x}) = \sum_{k=1}^{l} p(\mathbf{x}|C_k) P(C_k)$. The pattern $\mathbf{x}$ is assigned to the class with the smallest expected loss. This is called *Bayes' classifier*.

Let us assume that the loss (L_{kj}s) is nil for correct decisions, and is the same for all erroneous decisions. In such cases, the expected loss of eqn. (1.5) becomes

$$r_j(\mathbf{x}) = 1 - \frac{p(\mathbf{x}|C_j) P(C_j)}{p(\mathbf{x})}. \qquad (1.6)$$

Since $p(\mathbf{x})$ is independent of class, Bayes' decision rule boils down to the implementation of the decision functions

$$D_j(\mathbf{x}) = p(\mathbf{x}|C_j) P(C_j) \qquad (1.7)$$

for $j = 1, 2, \ldots, l$, where a pattern $\mathbf{x}$ is assigned to class C_j iff $D_j(\mathbf{x}) > D_i(\mathbf{x})$ for all $j \neq i$.

If one assumes $p(\mathbf{x}|C_j)$ to be a Gaussian density with mean vector $\mathbf{m}_j$ and covariance matrix $\sum_j$, i.e.,

$$p(\mathbf{x}|C_j) = \frac{1}{(2\pi)^{n/2} |\sum_j|^{1/2}} \exp\left[-\frac{1}{2} (\mathbf{x} - \mathbf{m}_j)' \sum_j^{-1} (\mathbf{x} - \mathbf{m}_j) \right] \qquad (1.8)$$

for $j = 1, 2, \ldots, l$, then $D_j(\mathbf{x})$ becomes

$$D_j(\mathbf{x}) = \ln P(C_j) - \frac{1}{2} \ln \left| \sum_j \right| - \frac{1}{2}(\mathbf{x} - \mathbf{m}_j)' \sum_j^{-1} (\mathbf{x} - \mathbf{m}_j) \qquad (1.9)$$

for $j = 1, 2, \ldots, l$.

The decision functions in eqn. (1.9) are hyperquadrics. This is apparent, as there are no terms higher than the second degree in the components of $\mathbf{x}$. Thus a Bayes' classifier for normally distributed patterns in reality defines second-order decision surfaces between each pair of pattern classes. If the pattern classes are truly characterized by normal densities, no other surfaces can yield results better than that of Bayes on average. In fact, the Bayes classifier designed over known probability distribution functions provides, on average, the minimum probability of misclassification over all decision rules.

1.3.4 Applications

Pattern recognition research is driven mostly by the need to process data and information obtained from the interaction between human society, science, and technology. Researchers in this area are concerned with the idea of designing and making intelligent machines that can carry out certain tasks with skills comparable to human performance. Some of the application areas of pattern recognition are in

- *Medicine:* medical diagnosis, image analysis, and disease classification

- *Natural resource study and estimation:* agriculture, forestry, geology, and environment

- *Human–machine communication:* automatic speech recognition and understanding, natural-language processing, image processing, and script recognition

- *Vehicular:* automobile, airplane, train, and boat controllers

- *Defense:* automatic target recognition, guidance, and control

- *Police and detective:* crime and criminal detection from analysis of speech, handwriting, fingerprints, and photographs

- *Remote sensing:* detection of human-made objects and estimation of natural resources

- *Industry:* computer-assisted design and manufacturing (CAD, CAM), product testing and assembly, inspection, and quality control

- *Domestic systems:* appliances

1.4   RELEVANCE OF FUZZY SET THEORETIC APPROACH

Fuzzy sets were introduced in 1965 by Zadeh [38] as a new way of representing vagueness in everyday life. This theory provides an approximate and yet effective means for describing the characteristics of a system that is too complex or ill-defined to admit precise mathematical analysis [39, 40]. Fuzzy approach is based on the premise that key elements in human thinking are not just numbers but can be approximated to tables of fuzzy sets, or, in other words, classes of objects in which the transition from membership to nonmembership is gradual rather than abrupt. Much of the logic behind human reasoning is not the traditional two-valued or even multivalued logic, but logic with fuzzy truths, fuzzy connectives, and fuzzy rules of inference. This fuzzy logic plays a basic role in various aspects of the human thought process.

The relevance of fuzzy set theoretic methods to pattern recognition problems has adequately been addressed in the literature [15]–[19], [22, 27], [41]–[45]. Fuzzy set theory is reputed to handle, to a reasonable extent, uncertainties (arising from deficiencies of information) in various applications particularly in decision-making models under different kinds of risk, subjective judgment, vagueness, and ambiguity. The deficiencies may result from various reasons, *viz.*, incomplete, imprecise, not fully reliable, vague, or contradictory information depending on the problem. Since this theory is a generalization of the classical set theory, it has greater flexibility to capture various aspects of incompleteness or imperfection in information about a situation.

Some of the uncertainties that one encounters while designing a pattern recognition system are discussed here in short. Let us consider, first, the case of the decision theoretic approach to pattern classification. With the conventional probabilistic and deterministic classifiers [1]–[3], [31], the features characterizing the input patterns are considered to be quantitative (numerical) in nature. The pattern vectors having imprecise or incomplete specification are usually ignored or discarded from the design and test sets. The impreciseness (or ambiguity) may arise from various reasons. For example, instrumental error or noise corruption in the experiment may lead to partial or partially reliable information available on a feature measurement. Again, in some cases the expense incurred in extracting a very precise exact value of a feature may be high, or it may be difficult to decide on the most salient features to be extracted.

For these reasons, it may become convenient to use the linguistic variables and hedges (*e.g., low, medium, high, very, more or less*) in order to describe the feature information. In such cases, it is not appropriate to give exact representation to uncertain feature data. Rather, it is reasonable to represent uncertain feature information by fuzzy subsets.

The use of linguistic variables may be viewed as a form of data compression, that can be termed *granulation* [46]. The same effect can also be achieved by conventional quantization. However, in the case of quantization the values are intervals, whereas in the case of granulation the values are overlapping fuzzy sets. The advantages of granulation over quantization are that

- It is more general.

- It mimics the way in which humans interpret linguistic values.

- The transition from one linguistic value to a contiguous linguistic value is gradual rather than abrupt, resulting in continuity and robustness.

Again, the uncertainty in classification or clustering of patterns may arise from the overlapping nature of the various classes. This overlapping may result from fuzziness or randomness. In the conventional classification technique, it is usually assumed that a pattern belongs to only one class. This is not necessarily realistic physically, and certainly not mathematically. A pattern can and should be allowed to have degrees of membership in more than one class. It is therefore necessary to convey this information while classifying a pattern or clustering a data set.

Similarly, consider the problem of determining the boundary or shape of a class from its sampled points (*i.e.*, training samples). There are various approaches [47, 48] described in literature that attempt to estimate an exact shape for the area in question by determining a boundary that contains (*i.e.*, passes through) some or all of the sample points. This is not necessarily true in practice. It may be necessary to extend the boundaries to some extent to represent the possible uncovered portions by the sampled points. The extended portions should have lower possibility to be in the class than the portions explicitly highlighted by these points. The size of the extended regions should also decrease with an increase in the number of sample points. This leads one to define a multivalued or fuzzy shape and boundary of a pattern class.

Let us now consider the problem of processing and recognizing a gray tone image pattern. In a conventional vision system, each operation in low level, middle level and high level involves crisp decision to make regions, features, primitives, relations, and interpretations crisp. Since the regions in an image are not always crisply defined, uncertainty can arise at every phase of recognition tasks. Therefore it becomes convenient, natural, and appropriate to avoid committing ourselves to specific (hard) decision by allowing the segments or contours to be fuzzy subsets of the image; the subsets being characterized by the possibility (degree) of a pixel belonging to them. Similarly, for describing and interpreting ill-defined structural information in a pattern, it is natural to define primitives (line, corner, curve, *etc.*) and relations among them using labels of fuzzy sets. The production rules of a grammar may similarly be fuzzified to account for the fuzziness in physical relation among the primitives, thereby increasing the generative power of a grammar for syntactic recognition of a pattern.

From the aforementioned examples, we see that the concept of fuzzy sets can be used at the *feature level* in representing input data as an array of membership values denoting the degree of possession of certain properties;

in representing linguistically phrased input features for their processing; in weakening the strong commitments for extracting ill-defined image regions, properties, primitives, and relations among them; and at the *classification level,* for representing class membership of objects, and for providing an estimate (or representation) of missing information in terms of membership values. In other words, *fuzzy set theory provides a notion of embedding; we find a better solution to a crisp problem by looking in a large space at first, which has different (usually less) constraints and therefore allows the algorithm more freedom to avoid errors forced by commission to hard answers in intermediate stages.*

Various methods and methodologies for pattern recognition using the fuzzy set theoretic approach are described in the next chapter (Section 2.3).

1.5   CONNECTIONIST APPROACH: RELEVANCE AND FEATURES

Modern digital computers outperform humans in the domain of numeric computation and related symbol manipulation. However, humans can effortlessly solve complex perceptual problems (*e.g.,* recognizing a person in a crowd from a mere glimpse of the face) at such a high speed and extent as to dwarf the world's fastest computer. Why is there such a remarkable difference in their performance? The biological neural system architecture is completely different from the VonNeumann architecture. This difference significantly affects the type of functions each computational model can best perform.

In the human body, cells die all the time without affecting the performance of the system. This robustness is possibly achieved by the massive connectivity of the biological neural network. The death or malfunctioning of a few cells is not expected to influence overall system behavior. This suggests that computational neural nets may also be made to achieve this property with massive interconnection and parallel processing. Note that in a VonNeumann kind of machine, error in one bit can severely affect the final outcome.

Biological neurons are believed to be the structural constituents of the brain, and they are much slower than silicon logic gates. But inferencing in biological neural nets is faster than the fastest computer available today. The brain compensates for the relatively slower operation by a really large number of neurons with massive interconnections between them. A biological neural network enjoys the following characteristics:

- It is a nonlinear device that is highly parallel, robust, and fault-tolerant.

- It has a built-in capability to adapt its synaptic weights to changes in the surrounding environment.

- It can easily handle imprecise, fuzzy, noisy, and probabilistic information.

- It can generalize from known tasks or examples to unknown ones.

Artificial neural networks (ANNs) are an attempt to mimic some or all of these characteristics.

During the mid-1950s and early 1960s a class of machines called *perceptron*, proposed by Rosenblatt [49, 50], seemed to offer what many researchers thought was a natural and powerful model of machine learning. However, interest in these tapered off when Minsky and Papert [51] proved that the simple single-layer networks were not capable of discriminating between linearly nonseparable classes. Work continued on linear and piecewise linear machines, providing the mathematical foundation for further research. In 1986, Rumelhart *et al.* [52] presented the generalized delta rule, which provided a practicable means of training even multilayer perceptrons, and removed the one major stumbling block. The advent of this algorithm rejuvenated a stagnating area of research and lead to a veritable surge of interest in neural network models.

Artificial neural networks (ANNs) [5]–[10], [53]–[63] are signal processing systems that try to emulate the behavior of biological nervous systems by providing a mathematical model of combination of numerous neurons connected in a network. These can be formally defined as *massively parallel interconnections of simple (usually adaptive) processing elements that interact with objects of the real world in a manner similar to biological systems*. The origin of artificial neural networks can be traced to the work of Hebb [64], where a local learning rule was proposed. This rule assumed that correlations between the states of two neurons determined the strength of the coupling between them. Subsequently, a synaptic connection that was very active grew in strength and vice versa.

The benefit of neural nets lies in the high computation rate provided by their inherent massive parallelism. This allows real-time processing of huge data sets with proper hardware backing. All information is stored distributed among the various connection weights. The redundancy of interconnections produces a high degree of robustness, resulting in a *graceful degradation* of performance in case of noise or damage to a few nodes or links.

Neural network models have been studied for many years with the hope of achieving human like performance (artificially), particularly in the field of pattern recognition, by capturing the key ingredients responsible for the remarkable capabilities of the human nervous system. For any pattern recognition system, it is always desirable for a model to possess characteristics such as adaptivity, speed, robustness, ruggedness, and optimality. As these are easily possible with neural network models, the usefulness of such networks becomes evident. Moreover, there exists some direct analogy between the working principles of many pattern recognition tasks and neural network models. However, all such models are extreme simplifications of the actual human nervous system.

Some researchers view ANNs as mechanisms to study intelligence [7], but most literature in the area sees ANNs as a tool to solve problems in science and engineering. Most of these problems involve pattern recognition in one form or another—everything from speech recognition to image recognition to sonar data classification to stockmarket tracking, and so on.

The task of pattern recognition in real life problems involves searching a complex decision space. This becomes more complicated, particularly when there is no *a priori* information on class distribution. Neural-network-based systems use nonparametric adaptive learning procedures, learn from examples and attempt to find a relation between input and output, however complex it may be, for decision-making problems. Neural networks are also reputed to model complex nonlinear boundaries and discover important underlying regularities in the task domain. These characteristics demand that methods are needed for constructing and refining neural network models for various recognition tasks.

For example, consider the case of supervised classification. Here each pattern is characterized by a number of features. Different features usually have different weights in characterizing the classes. A collective decision, taking into account all the features, is made for assignment of class labels to an input. A multilayer perceptron in which the input layer has neurons equal to the number of features and the output layer has neurons equal to the number of classes can therefore be used to tackle this classification problem. Here the importance of different features will automatically be encoded in the connection links during training. The nonlinear decision boundaries are modeled, and class labels are assigned by taking collective decisions.

Again, the tasks of image processing and analysis in the spatial domain mainly employ simple arithmetic operations at each pixel site in parallel. These operations usually involve information of neighboring pixels (cooperative processing) in order to reduce the local ambiguity and to attain global consistency. An objective measure is required (representing the overall status of the system), the optimum of which represents the desired goal. The system thus involves collective decisions. We notice that neural network models are also based on parallel and distributed working principles (all neurons work in parallel and independently). The operations performed at each processor site are also simpler and independent of the others. The overall status of a neural network can also be measured. Let us consider, in particular, the case of pixel classification. A pixel is normally classified into different classes depending on its gray value, positional information, and contextual information (collected from the neighbors). Pixels at different sites can be classified independently. The mathematical operations needed for this task are also simple. A neural network architecture in which a single neuron is assigned to a pixel and is connected to its neighbors can therefore be applied for this task. The neurons operate in parallel and are independent of each other. The local interconnections provide the contextual information (which can be adaptive or dynamic) for classification.

In short, neural networks are natural classifiers having resistance to noise, tolerance to distorted images or patterns (ability to generalize), superior ability to recognize partially occluded or degraded images or overlapping pattern classes or classes with highly nonlinear boundaries, and potential for parallel processing.

Some of the commonly known neural networks generally used for pattern recognition and optimization tasks include the single-layer perceptron [50], Boltzmann machine [65], multilayer perceptron (MLP) using backpropagation of errors [52, 66, 67], Hopfield network [68], Hamming network [54], Grossberg–Carpenter network (ART) [69]–[72], Kohonen's self-organizing feature map [8, 73], radial basis function network [74], counterpropagation network [75, 76], X-tron [77, 78], PsyCOP [79], and neocognitron [80, 81]. The Hopfield and Hamming nets are used primarily with fixed weights for optimization tasks, while the single- and multilayer perceptrons undergo supervised learning, basically for classifier design. On the other hand, the Grossberg–Carpenter net and Kohonen's feature map perform unsupervised learning or clustering. In addition, the Kohonen net has a good application to feature analysis because of its self-organizing ability. Combinations of the different neural algorithms have also been attempted, to design connectionist systems [82, 83] for pattern recognition.

X-tron [77, 78] is a highly structured connectionist model with supervised and unsupervised learning algorithms for perception of mixed objects by integrating structural description of objects on a new connectionist framework. Here the competition process is confined only within the feature–object associations, thereby enhancing the capability of tolerating a high degree of overlap. Its ability for building a psychologically motivated system, called "PsyCOP" [79], (by employing two different channels for "identification" and "localization") for occluded object recognition has been established both theoretically and experimentally.

Applications of the various neural network models have been made in diverse spheres of pattern recognition. Good surveys can be found elsewhere in the literature [84]–[87]. Details of some of the basic ANN models are given in the next chapter (Section 2.4).

An impediment to a more widespread acceptance of ANNs is the absence of a capability to explain to the user, in a human-comprehensible form, how the network arrives at a particular decision. Neither can one say something about the *knowledge* encoded within the *blackbox*. Recently there has been widespread activity aimed at redressing this situation, by extracting the embedded knowledge in trained feedforward ANNs in the form of symbolic rules [88]–[93]. This serves to identify the attributes that, either individually or in a combination, are the most significant determinants of the decision or classification.

Often an ANN solution with good generalization does not necessarily imply involvement of hidden units with distinct *meaning* [94]. Hence any individual unit cannot essentially be associated with a single concept or feature of the problem domain. This is typical of connectionist approaches, where all information is stored in a distributed manner among the neurons and their associated connectivity. In certain situations, one can extract causal factors and functional dependencies from the data domain for initial encoding of the ANN [94, 95] and later extract refined rules from the trained network.

In general, the primary input to a connectionist rule generation algorithm is a representation of the trained ANN, in terms of its nodes and links, and sometimes the data set. One interprets one or more hidden and output units into rules, which may later be combined and simplified to arrive at a more comprehensible rule set. The use of ANN helps in (1) incorporating parallelism and (2) tackling optimization problems in the data domain. The models are usually suitable in data-rich environments and seem to be capable of overcoming the problem of the *knowledge acquisition bottleneck* faced by knowledge engineers while designing the knowledge base of traditional expert systems.

The trained link weights and node activations of the ANN are used to automatically generate the rules, either for later use in a traditional expert system or for providing justification or explanation in the case of an inferred decision. This automates and also speeds up the knowledge acquisition process.

1.6   NEED FOR INTEGRATING FUZZY LOGIC AND ARTIFICIAL NEURAL NETWORKS

Both neural networks and fuzzy systems are trainable dynamic systems that estimate input–output functions. They estimate a function without any mathematical model and *learn from experience* with sample data. A fuzzy system adaptively infers and modifies its fuzzy associations from representative numerical samples. Neural networks, on the other hand, can *blindly* generate and refine fuzzy rules from training data [96]. Fuzzy systems and neural networks also differ in how they estimate sampled functions, the kind of samples used and how they represent and store these samples. Fuzzy systems estimate functions with fuzzy set samples (A_i, B_i), while neural systems use numerical point samples (x_i, y_i) where both kinds of samples reside in the input–output product space $X \times Y$. Hence the input–output mapping corresponds to $f : X \to Y$ in both cases.

Fuzzy sets are considered to be advantageous in the logical field, and in handling higher order processing easily. The higher flexibility is a characteristic feature of neural nets produced by learning, and hence this suits data-driven processing better [97]. Fuzzy systems and neural networks are now established as universal approximators [98]–[100]. This implies that fuzzy systems and neural networks can approximate each other. This leads to a symbiotic relationship, in which fuzzy systems provide a powerful framework for knowledge representation, while neural networks provide learning capabilities and exceptional suitability for computationally efficient hardware implementations.

Fuzzy logic and neural systems have very contrasting application requirements. For example, fuzzy systems are appropriate if sufficient expert knowledge about the process is available, while neural systems are useful if sufficient process data are available or measurable. Both approaches build nonlinear systems based on bounded continuous variables, the difference being that neural systems are treated in a numeric, quantitative manner whereas fuzzy systems are treated in a symbolic, qualitative manner. Fuzzy systems, however, exhibit both symbolic and numeric features. For example, when treated as collections of objects encapsulated by linguistic labels they lend themselves to symbolic processing via rule-based operations, while by referring to the definitions of the linguistic labels their membership functions are also suitable for numeric processing. Therefore, the integration of neural and fuzzy systems offers a facility that can bridge the demarcation between symbolic knowledge processing and connectionist learning. The significance of this integration becomes even more apparent by considering their disparities. Neural networks do not provide a strong scheme for knowledge representation, while fuzzy logic controllers do not possess capabilities for automated learning.

Neuro-fuzzy computing, which is a judicious integration of the merits of neural and fuzzy approaches, enables one to build more intelligent decision making systems. As mentioned in Section 1.2, this incorporates the generic advantages of artificial neural networks like massive parallelism, robustness, and learning in data-rich environments into the system. The modeling of imprecise and qualitative knowledge as well as the transmission of uncertainty are possible through the use of fuzzy logic. Besides these generic advantages, the neuro-fuzzy approach provides some application specific merits in the following way. For example, in the case of pattern classification one is typically interested in exploiting the capability of neural nets in generating the required (linearly nonseparable) decision regions. The uncertainties involved in the input description and output decision can be taken care of by the concept of fuzzy sets. Similarly fuzziness measures can be used as the target output vector of an MLP for unsupervised classification, while exploiting its capability of generating highly nonlinear decision boundary.

The neuro-fuzzy approach, which provides flexible information processing capability by devising methodologies and algorithms on a massively parallel system for representation and recognition of real life ambiguous situations, forms at this juncture, a key component of what is called soft computing. (In fact, the concept "soft" originated from fuzzy set theory.) The details of soft computing and its relevance to real world computing (RWC) systems, which form the kernel of sixth-generation computing technology, are described in Section 2.7.

Chapter 2 introduces some of the basic operations and models of fuzzy sets and artificial neural networks, used for pattern recognition. This is followed by different methodologies of neuro-fuzzy integration along with their key features, and a mathematical formulation of different relations in this framework. Next, we explain the characteristic features of knowledge-based networks and their integration with fuzzy sets. Finally, the concept of soft computing, which encompasses neuro-fuzzy computing and other hybridizations, is described.

In Chapter 3 we provide description of various fuzzy–neural network models for pattern classification. This includes fuzzy MLP, fuzzy logical MLP, and the fuzzy Kohonen network, along with their implementation results on both real life and synthetic data. Their comparison with Bayes' maximum likelihood classifier, k-NN rule, and the conventional connectionist models are also given.

Some other applications of the fuzzy MLP to the medical domain and for selective partitioning of the feature space are provided in Chapter 4. Results on noisy fingerprint classification, using MLP and fuzzy geometric features, are also included.

Chapter 5 describes the problem of pixel classification and object extraction. Here two methodologies using various fuzziness measures are explained. The first one involves a self-organizing multilayer network, while the second considers a cellular network model with genetic algorithms.

Chapter 6 deals with supervised and unsupervised neuro-fuzzy feature evaluation algorithms. This includes both feature selection and extraction. Theoretical analysis and comparative results are also provided.

In Chapter 7 we describe various neuro-fuzzy approaches for inferencing, querying, and rule generation. This includes those developed based on the fuzzy MLP, fuzzy logical MLP, and fuzzy Kohonen network (as described in Chapter 3). The querying and justification phases of these models, along with detailed results on both real life and synthetic data, are provided. Adequate comparison of the performance with those of other related methods is also given.

Different knowledge-based nets, and the incorporation of fuzzy set theoretic concepts and genetic algorithms in this framework, are described in Chapter 8. Details about the classification and rule generation aspects of a knowledge-based network (designed using the fuzzy MLP of Chapter 3) along with some comparative results are included.

Finally, in Chapter 9 we show a method of integrating rough sets with a neuro-fuzzy system to result in a stronger soft computing paradigm, where all the tools act synergetically. The concept of rough sets, and their role in designing fuzzy knowledge-based networks by extracting crude domain knowledge from the data and determining an appropriate network architecture, are described. Comparative results of classification of the rough–fuzzy MLP are provided.

REFERENCES

1. R. O. Duda and P. E. Hart, *Pattern Classification and Scene Analysis*. New York: Wiley, 1973.

2. J. T. Tou and R. C. Gonzalez, *Pattern Recognition Principles*. London: Addison-Wesley, 1974.

3. P. A. Devijver and J. Kittler, eds., *Pattern Recognition Theory and Applications*. Berlin: Springer-Verlag, 1987.

4. K. S. Fu, *Syntactic Pattern Recognition and Applications*. London: Academic Press, 1982.

5. S. Haykin, *Neural Networks: A Comprehensive Foundation*. New York: Macmillan, 1994.

6. J. Hertz, A. Krogh, and R. G. Palmer, *Introduction to the Theory of Neural Computation*. Reading, MA: Addison-Wesley, 1994.

7. D. E. Rumelhart and J. L. McClelland, eds., *Parallel Distributed Processing: Explorations in the Microstructures of Cognition*, Vol. 1. Cambridge, MA: MIT Press, 1986.

8. T. Kohonen, *Self-Organization and Associative Memory*. Berlin: Springer-Verlag, 1989.

9. S. Grossberg, ed., *Neural Networks and Natural Intelligence*. Cambridge, MA: MIT Press, 1988.

10. P. D. Wassermann, *Neural Computing: Theory and Practice*. New York: Van Nostrand Reinhold, 1990.

11. "Special issue on artificial neural networks and statistical pattern recognition," *IEEE Transactions on Neural Networks*, vol. 8, 1997.

12. I. K. Sethi and A. K. Jain, eds., *Artificial Neural Networks and Statistical Pattern Recognition: Old and New Connections*. Amsterdam: North Holland, 1991.

13. B. D. Ripley, *Pattern Recognition and Neural Networks*. New York: Cambridge University Press, 1996.

14. A. Joshi, N. Ramakrishnan, E. N. Houstis, and J. R. Rice, "On neurobiological, neuro-fuzzy, machine learning, and statistical pattern recognition techniques," *IEEE Transactions on Neural Networks*, vol. 8, pp. 18–31, 1997.

15. J. C. Bezdek, *Pattern Recognition with Fuzzy Objective Function Algorithms*. New York: Plenum Press, 1981.

16. J. C. Bezdek and S. K. Pal, eds., *Fuzzy Models for Pattern Recognition: Methods that Search for Structures in Data*. New York: IEEE Press, 1992.

17. A. Kandel, *Fuzzy Techniques in Pattern Recognition*. New York: Wiley-Interscience, 1982.

18. A. Kandel, *Fuzzy Mathematical Techniques with Applications*. Reading, MA: Addison-Wesley, 1986.

19. S. K. Pal and D. Dutta Majumder, *Fuzzy Mathematical Approach to Pattern Recognition*. New York: Wiley (Halsted Press), 1986.

20. R. R. Yager, ed., *Fuzzy Set and Possibility Theory*. New York: Pergamon Press, 1982.

21. J. M. Kickert, *Fuzzy Theories on Decision-making*. London: Martinus Nijhoff Social Sciences Division, 1978.

22. D. Dubois and H. Prade, *Fuzzy Sets and Systems: Theory and Applications*. Boston: Academic Press, 1980.

23. A. Kaufmann and M. Gupta, *Introduction to Fuzzy Mathematics*. New York: Van Nostrand Reinhold, 1985.

24. L. A. Zadeh, K. S. Fu, K. Tanaka, and M. Shimura, eds., *Fuzzy Sets and Their Applications to Cognitive and Decision Processes*. London: Academic Press, 1975.

25. E. Sanchez and L. A. Zadeh, eds., *Approximate Reasoning in Intelligent Systems, Decision and Control*. Oxford: Pergamon Press, 1987.

26. D. Dubois and H. Prade, *Possibility Theory*. New York: Plenum Press, 1988.

27. H. -J. Zimmermann, *Fuzzy Set Theory and Its Applications*. Boston, MA: Kluwer, 1991.

28. P. W. Becker, *Recognition of Patterns*. Vienna: Springer-Verlag, 1978.

29. L. Kanal, "Patterns in pattern recognition," *IEEE Transactions on Information Theory*, vol. 20, pp. 697–722, 1974.

30. G. S. Sebestyen, *Decision Making Processes in Pattern Recognition*. New York: Macmillan, 1962.

31. K. Fukunaga, *Introduction to Statistical Pattern Recognition*. New York: Academic Press, 1972.

32. R. Battiti, "Using mutual information for selecting features in supervised neural net learning," *IEEE Transactions on Neural Networks*, vol. 5, pp. 537–550, 1994.

33. M. Ben-Bassat, "Use of distance measures, information measures and error bounds in feature evaluation," in *Handbook of Statistics 2. Classification, Pattern Recognition and Reduction of Dimensionality*, P. R. Krishnaiah and L. N. Kanal, eds., pp. 773—792. Amsterdam: North-Holland, 1982.

34. P. A. Devijver and J. Kittler, *Pattern Recognition, A Statistical Approach*. London: Prentice–Hall, 1982.

35. S. K. Pal, "Fuzzy set theoretic measures for automatic feature evaluation: II," *Information Sciences*, vol. 64, pp. 165–179, 1992.

36. D. W. Ruck, S. K. Rogers, and M. Kabrisky, "Feature selection using a multilayer perceptron," *Neural Network Computing*, vol. 20, pp. 40–48, 1990.

37. E. H. Ruspini, "A new approach to clustering," *Information and Control*, vol. 15, pp. 22–32, 1969.

38. L. A. Zadeh, "Fuzzy sets," *Information and Control*, vol. 8, pp. 338–353, 1965.

39. L. A. Zadeh, "The concept of a linguistic variable and its application to approximate reasoning: Parts 1, 2, and 3," *Information Sciences*, vols. 8, 8, 9, pp. 199–249, 301–357, 43–80, 1975.

40. L. A. Zadeh, "Fuzzy sets as a basis for a theory of possibility," *Fuzzy Sets and Systems*, vol. 1, pp. 3–28, 1978.

41. A. Kaufmann, *Introduction to the Theory of Fuzzy Subsets–Fundamental Theoretical Elements*, Vol. 1. New York: Academic Press, 1975.

42. G. J. Klir and B. Yuan, *Fuzzy Sets and Fuzzy Logic: Theory and Applications*. Englewood Cliffs, NJ: Prentice-Hall, 1995.

43. J. C. Bezdek, ed., *Analysis of Fuzzy Information*, Vols. I–III. Boca Raton: CRC Press, 1987.

44. R. R. Yager and L. A. Zadeh, eds., *An Introduction to Fuzzy Logic Applications in Intelligent Systems*. Boston: Kluwer Academic Press, 1992.

45. W. Pedrycz, "Fuzzy sets in pattern recognition: Methodology and methods," *Pattern Recognition*, vol. 23, pp. 121–146, 1990.

46. L. A. Zadeh, "Fuzzy logic, neural networks, and soft computing," *Communications of the ACM*, vol. 37, pp. 77–84, 1994.

47. H. Edelsbrunner, D. G. Kirkpatrick, and R. Seidel, "On the shape of a set of points in a plane," *IEEE Transactions on Information Theory*, vol. 29, pp. 551–559, 1983.

48. C. A. Murthy, *On Consistent Estimation of Classes in R^2 in the Context of Cluster Analysis*. Ph.D. thesis, Indian Statistical Institute, Calcutta, India, 1988.

49. F. Rosenblatt, "The perceptron: A probabilistic model for information storage and organization in the brain," *Psychological Review*, vol. 65, pp. 386–408, 1958.

50. F. Rosenblatt, *Principles of Neurodynamics, Perceptrons and the Theory of Brain Mechanisms*. Washington DC: Spartan Books, 1961.

51. M. Minsky and S. Papert, *Perceptrons: An Introduction to Computational Geometry*. Cambridge, MA: MIT Press, 1969.

52. D. E. Rumelhart, G. E. Hinton, and R. J. Williams, "Learning internal representations by error propagation," in *Parallel Distributed Processing: Explorations in the Microstructures of Cognition*, D. E. Rumelhart and J. L. McClelland, eds., Cambridge, MA: MIT Press, 1986.

53. R. Rosenfeld and J. Anderson, eds., *Neuro Computing*. Cambridge, MA: MIT, 1988.

54. R. P. Lippmann, "An introduction to computing with neural nets," *IEEE Acoustics, Speech and Signal Processing Magazine*, vol. 4, pp. 4–22, 1987.

55. J. Dayhoff, *Neural Network Architectures: An Introduction*. New York: Van Nostrand Reinhold, 1990.

56. P. Simpson, *Artificial Neural Systems: Foundations, Paradigms, Applications and Implementations*. Elmsford, NY: Pergamon Press, 1990.

57. J. M. Zurada, *Introduction to Artificial Neural Systems*. Boston, MA: PWS, 1992.

58. D. R. Hush and B. G. Horne, "Progress in supervised neural networks," *IEEE Signal Processing Magazine*, pp. 8–39, January 1993.

59. A. K. Jain and J. Mao, "Artificial neural networks: A tutorial," *IEEE Computer*, pp. 31–44, March 1996.

60. S. K. Pal and P. K. Srimani, eds., *Special Issue on Neural Networks: Theory and Applications, IEEE Computer*, vol. 29, no. 3, 1996.

61. S. K. Pal, ed., *Special Issue on Neural Networks, Journal of the Institute of Electronics and Telecommunications Engineers*, vol. 42, nos. 4, 5, 1996.

62. S. K. Pal and P. K. Srimani, "Neurocomputing: Motivation, models and hybridization," *IEEE Computer*, vol. 29, pp. 24–28, 1996.

63. J. A. Freeman and D. M. Skupura, *Neural Networks Algorithms, Applications and Programming Techniques*. New York: Addison-Wesley, 1991.

64. D. O. Hebb, *The Organization of Behaviour*. New York: Wiley, 1949.

65. D. H. Ackley, G. E. Hinton, and T. J. Sejnowski, "A learning algorithm for Boltzmann machine," *Cognitive Science*, vol. 9, pp. 147–169, 1985.

66. D. Parker, Learning logic, Technical Report TR-87, Center for Computational Research in Economics and Management Science, MIT, Cambridge, MA, 1985.

67. Y. Le Cun, "Learning processes in an asymmetric threshold network," in *Disordered Systems and Biological Organization*, E. Bienenstock, F. F. Souli, and G. Weisbuch, eds., Berlin: Springer-Verlag, 1986.

68. J. J. Hopfield, "Neurons with graded response have collective computational property like those of two-state neurons," *Proceedings of National Academy of Sciences, USA*, vol. 81, pp. 3088–3092, 1984.

69. G. A. Carpenter and S. Grossberg, "A massively parallel architecture for a self-organising neural pattern recognition machine," *Computer Vision, Graphics and Image Processing*, vol. 37, pp. 54–115, 1987.

70. G. A. Carpenter and S. Grossberg, "ART2: Self-organization of stable category recognition codes for analog input patterns," *Applied Optics*, vol. 26, pp. 4919–4930, 1987.

71. G. A. Carpenter and S. Grossberg, "ART3: Hierarchical search using chemical transmitters in self-organizing pattern recognition architectures," *Neural Networks*, vol. 3, pp. 129–152, 1990.

72. G. A. Carpenter, S. Grossberg, and J. H. Reynolds, "ARTMAP: Supervised real-time learning and classification of nonstationary data by a self-organizing neural network," *Neural Networks*, vol. 4, pp. 565–588, 1991.

73. T. Kohonen, "Things you haven't heard about the self-organizing map," in *Proceedings of IEEE International Joint Conference on Neural Networks* (San Francisco, USA), pp. 1147–1156, 1993.

74. J. Moody and C. J. Darken, "Fast learning in networks of locally-tuned processing units," *Neural Computation*, vol. 1, pp. 281–294, 1989.

75. R. Hecht-Nielsen, "Counterpropagation networks," *Applied Optics*, vol. 26, pp. 4979–4984, 1987.

76. R. Hecht-Nielsen, "Applications of counterpropagation networks," *Neural Networks*, vol. 1, pp. 131–139, 1988.

77. J. Basak and S. K. Pal, "X-tron: An incremental connectionist model for category perception," *IEEE Transactions on Neural Networks*, vol. 6, pp. 1091–1108, 1995.

78. J. Basak, C. A. Murthy, and S. K. Pal, "Self-organizing network for mixed category perception," *Neurocomputing*, vol. 10, pp. 341–358, 1996.

79. J. Basak and S. K. Pal, "PsyCOP: A psychologically motivated connectionist system for object perception," *IEEE Transactions on Neural Networks*, vol. 6, pp. 1337–1354, 1995.

80. K. Fukushima, "Neocognitron: A hierarchical neural network capable of visual pattern recognition," *Neural Networks*, vol. 1, pp. 119–130, 1988.

81. K. Fukushima, "A neural network for visual pattern recognition," *IEEE Computer*, pp. 65–75, March 1988.

82. M. Okada and K. Fukushima, "Neocognitron learned by backpropagation," in *Proceedings of the 1990 International Conference on Fuzzy Logic and Neural Networks, Iizuka* (Japan), pp. 667–670, 1990.

83. A. Iwata, K. Hotta, H. Matsuo, N. Suzumura, S. Matsuda, and M. Yoshida, "A large scale neural network "CombNET" on a neural network accelerator Neuro-Turbo," in *Proceedings of the 1990 International Conference on Fuzzy Logic and Neural Networks, Iizuka* (Japan), pp. 329–333, 1990.

84. G. A. Carpenter, "Neural network models for pattern recognition and associative memory," *Neural Networks*, vol. 2, pp. 243–257, 1989.

85. R. P. Lippmann, "Pattern classification using neural networks," *IEEE Communications Magazine*, pp. 47–64, 1989.

86. B. Widrow and R. Winter, "Neural network for adaptive filtering and adaptive pattern recognition," *IEEE Computer*, pp. 25–39, March 1988.

87. S. K. Pal and J. Basak, "Visual pattern recognition–connectionist perspective," *Proceedings of National Academy of Sciences* (India), vol. LXVII, Section A, Part III, pp. 205–227, 1997.

88. S. I. Gallant, "Connectionist expert systems," *Communications of the Association for Computing Machinery*, vol. 31, pp. 152–169, 1988.

89. G. G. Towell and J. W. Shavlik, "Extracting refined rules from knowledge-based neural networks," *Machine Learning*, vol. 13, pp. 71–101, 1993.

90. S. Mitra and S. K. Pal, "Fuzzy multi-layer perceptron, inferencing and rule generation," *IEEE Transactions on Neural Networks*, vol. 6, pp. 51–63, 1995.

91. S. Mitra and S. K. Pal, "Fuzzy self organization, inferencing and rule generation," *IEEE Transactions on Systems, Man and Cybernetics, Part A: Systems and Humans*, vol. 26, pp. 608–620, 1996.

92. R. Andrews, J. Diederich, and A. B. Tickle, "A survey and critique of techniques for extracting rules from trained artificial neural networks," *Knowledge-Based Systems*, vol. 8, pp. 373–389, 1995.

93. S. Mitra, R. K. De, and S. K. Pal, "Knowledge-based fuzzy MLP for classification and rule generation," *IEEE Transactions on Neural Networks*, vol. 8, pp. 1338–1350, 1997.

94. A. B. Tickle, M. Golea, R. Hayward, and J. Diederich, "The truth is in there: Current issues in extracting rules from trained feedforward artificial neural networks," in *Proceedings of IEEE International Conference on Neural Networks* (Houston, USA), pp. 2530–2534, 1997.

95. S. Mitra, M. Banerjee, and S. K. Pal, "Rough knowledge-based network, fuzziness and classification," *Neural Computing and Applications*, vol. 7, pp. 17–25, 1998.

96. B. Kosko, *Neural Networks and Fuzzy Systems*. Englewood Cliffs, NJ: Prentice-Hall, 1991.

97. H. Takagi, "Fusion technology of fuzzy theory and neural network–survey and future directions," in *Proceedings of the 1990 International Conference on Fuzzy Logic and Neural Networks, Iizuka* (Japan), pp. 13–26, 1990.

98. B. Kosko, "Fuzzy systems as universal approximators," in *Proceedings of the First IEEE International Conference on Fuzzy Systems*, (San Diego), pp. 1153–1162, 1992.

99. J. J. Buckley and Y. Hayashi, "Numerical relationship between neural networks, continuous functions and fuzzy systems," *Fuzzy Sets and Systems*, vol. 60, no. 1, pp. 1–8, 1993.

100. J. J. Buckley, Y. Hayashi, and E. Czogala, "On the equivalence of neural nets and fuzzy expert systems," *Fuzzy Sets and Systems*, vol. 53, no. 2, pp. 129–134, 1993.

2

Fuzzy Logic and Neural Networks: Models, Integration, and Soft Computing

2.1 INTRODUCTION

In this chapter, first of all we describe some of the basic operations and tools of fuzzy set theory, and certain major ANN models, which are required in order to understand the remaining chapters of the book. The significance of these technologies to pattern recognition problem is also discussed. Different methodologies of integrating the theories, reported so far, are then explained in soft computing paradigm along with their merits and other hybridizations. More emphasis is given on those that are used mainly for classification and rule generation.

The preliminaries of fuzzy set theory, described here, include membership functions, basic operations, measures of fuzziness, followed by T-norms and T-conorms, and fuzzy implication operators. Evolution of fuzzy pattern recognition encompasses tasks like classification, feature selection and rule generation. The description of ANN models includes single-layer perceptron, multilayer perceptron, Kohonen network, radial basis function network, Hopfield network and adaptive resonance theory (ART), along with their distinguishing characteristics. The concept of knowledge-based networks, which initially incorporate some amount of domain knowledge among the connection weights, is also explained. This helps in speeding up the convergence, as compared to conventional ANNs, in the reduced search space. One may note that the theory of pattern recognition has a strong relationship with that of fuzzy sets and neural networks.

In neuro-fuzzy computing, one can integrate the concept of fuzzy sets at the input, output, and/or neuronal levels of an ANN. Similarly, an ANN can be used to represent and tune models and/or parameters of fuzzy systems. These hybrid models are found to incorporate both the generic and application-specific merits of neural networks as well as fuzzy set theory. This has resulted in the generation of more intelligent decision-making systems. These are described in detail along with different features, characteristics, and mathematical formulation.

Finally, the concept of soft computing is introduced in Section 2.7 through various examples. The relevance, characteristics, and merits of integrating different tools such as fuzzy sets, artificial neural networks, genetic algorithms, and rough sets in various forms are mentioned. Here all these tools act symbiotically, and not competitively, to enhance the application domain of each other.

2.2   FUZZY SETS

A fuzzy set A in a space of points $R = \{r\}$ is a class of events with a continuum of grades of membership and is characterized by a membership function $\mu_A(r)$ that associates with each element in R a real number in the interval $[0, 1]$ with the value of $\mu_A(r)$ at r representing the grade of membership of r in A. Formally, a fuzzy set A with its finite number of supports $r_1, r_2, \ldots, r_n$ is defined as a collection of ordered pairs

$$
\begin{aligned}
A &= \{(\mu_A(r_i), r_i), i = 1, 2, \ldots, n\} \\
&= \{(\tfrac{\mu_A(r_i)}{r_i}), i = 1, 2, \ldots, n\},
\end{aligned}
$$

where the support of A is an ordinary subset of R and is defined as

$$
S(A) = \{r | r \in R \text{ and } \mu_A(r) > 0\}.
$$

Here μ_i, the grade of membership of r_i in A, denotes the degree to which an event r_i may be a member of A or belong to A. Note that $\mu_i = 1$ indicates the strict containment of the event r_i in A. If, on the other hand, r_i does not belong to A, then $\mu_i = 0$.

If the support of a fuzzy set is only a single point $r_1 \in R$, then

$$
A = \frac{\mu_1}{r_1}
$$

is called a *fuzzy singleton*. Thus $A = (1/r_1)$, for $\mu_1 = 1$, would obviously denote a nonfuzzy singleton.

In terms of the constituent singletons the fuzzy set A with its finite number of supports $r_1, r_2, \ldots, r_n$ can also be expressed in union form as

$$\begin{aligned} A &= \frac{\mu_1}{r_1} + \frac{\mu_2}{r_2} + \cdots + \frac{\mu_n}{r_n} \\ &= \sum_i \frac{\mu_i}{r_i}, \ i = 1, 2, \ldots, n \\ &= \bigcup_i \frac{\mu_i}{r_i}, \ i = 1, 2, \ldots, n, \end{aligned} \qquad (2.1)$$

where the $+$ sign denotes the union.

Fuzzy logic is based on the theory of fuzzy sets and, unlike classical logic, aims at modeling the imprecise (or inexact) modes of reasoning and thought processes (with linguistic variables) that play an essential role in the remarkable human ability to make rational decisions in an environment of uncertainty and imprecision. This ability depends, in turn, on our ability to infer an approximate answer to a question based on a store of knowledge that is inexact, incomplete, or not totally reliable. In fuzzy logic everything, including truth, is a matter of degree [1]. Zadeh has developed a theory of approximate reasoning based on fuzzy set theory. By approximate reasoning we refer to a type of reasoning that is neither very exact nor very inexact. This theory aims at modeling the human reasoning and thinking process with linguistic variables [2] in order to handle both soft and hard data, as well as various types of uncertainty. Many aspects of the underlying concept have been incorporated in designing decision-making systems [3]–[7].

Because fuzzy sets are a generalization of the classical set theory, the embedding of conventional models into a larger setting endows fuzzy models with greater flexibility to capture various aspects of incompleteness or imperfection (*i.e.*, deficiencies) in whatever information and data are available about a real process. The flexibility of fuzzy set theory is associated with the elasticity property of the concept of its membership function. The grade of membership is a measure of the compatibility of an object with the concept represented by a fuzzy set. The higher the value of membership, the less will be the amount (or extent) to which the concept represented by a set needs to be stretched to fit an object. The meaning of a lexically imprecise proposition is represented as an elastic constraint on a variable, and the answer to a query is deduced through a propagation of elastic constraints [8].

Assignment of membership functions of a fuzzy subset is subjective in nature, and reflects the context in which the problem is viewed. It cannot be assigned arbitrarily. In many cases, it is convenient to express the membership function of a fuzzy subset in terms of standard S and π functions. Note that fuzzy membership function and probability density function are conceptually different. Probabilities convey information about relative frequencies of objects while fuzzy membership represents similarities of objects to imprecisely defined properties. It is to be noted that in this section we mention only certain aspects of fuzzy set theory such as membership functions, basic operations, measures of fuzziness, T-norm and T-conorm, and fuzzy implication operators, which are relevant to the subsequent chapters. Interested readers may refer to other publications [7], [9]–[16] for further information.

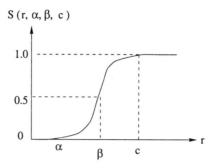

$S(r, \alpha, \beta, c)$

Fig. 2.1 Standard S function

2.2.1 Membership functions

It is frequently convenient to employ standardized functions with adjustable parameters, *e.g.*, the S and π functions, which are defined in the following equation (see also Fig. 2.1):

$$
\begin{aligned}
S(r; \, \alpha, \beta, c) &= \quad\quad 0 \quad\quad\quad\quad\text{for } r \leq \alpha \\
&= \quad 2(\tfrac{r-\alpha}{c-\alpha})^2 \quad\quad \text{for } \alpha \leq r \leq \beta \\
&= 1 - 2(\tfrac{r-c}{c-\alpha})^2 \quad \text{for } \beta \leq r \leq c \\
&= \quad\quad 1 \quad\quad\quad\quad \text{for } r \geq c.
\end{aligned}
\tag{2.2}
$$

$$
\begin{aligned}
\pi(r; \, c, \lambda) &= \quad S(r; c - \lambda, c - \tfrac{\lambda}{2}, c) \quad\quad \text{for } r \leq c \\
&= 1 - S(r; c, c + \tfrac{\lambda}{2}, c + \lambda) \quad \text{for } r \geq c.
\end{aligned}
\tag{2.3}
$$

In $S(r; \, \alpha, \beta, c)$, the parameter $\beta, \beta = (\alpha + c)/2$, is the *crossover point*, that is, the value of r at which S takes the value 0.5. In $\pi(r; c, \lambda)$, λ is the *bandwidth*, that is, the distance between the crossover points of π, while c is the central point at which π is unity.

Let us consider the linguistic variable age (x). Here the linguistic values *young* and *old* play the role of primary fuzzy sets which have a specified meaning, *e.g.*,

$$\mu_{young} = 1 - S(20, 30, 40), \tag{2.4}$$

$$\mu_{old} = S(50, 60, 70), \tag{2.5}$$

where the S and π functions are defined by eqns. (2.2) and (2.3), and μ_{young} and μ_{old} denote the membership functions of *young* and *old*, respectively.

In pattern recognition problems we often need to represent a class with fuzzy boundary in terms of a π function. A representation for such a π function, with range [0,1] and $r \in I\!R^n$, may be given as [17]

$$
\pi(r; c, \lambda) =
\begin{cases}
2\left(1 - \dfrac{\|r - c\|}{\lambda}\right)^2, & \text{for } \tfrac{\lambda}{2} \leq \|r - c\| \leq \lambda \\[2mm]
1 - 2\left(\dfrac{\|r - c\|}{\lambda}\right)^2, & \text{for } 0 \leq \|r - c\| \leq \tfrac{\lambda}{2} \\[2mm]
0, & \text{otherwise,}
\end{cases}
\tag{2.6}
$$

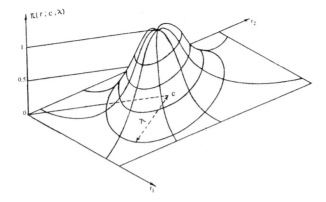

Fig. 2.2 π function when $r \in R^2$

where $\lambda > 0$ is the radius of the π function with c as the central point and $\|.\|$ denotes the Euclidean norm. This is shown in Fig. 2.2 for $r \in \mathbb{R}^2$. Note that when the pattern r lies at the central point c of a class, then $\|r - c\| = 0$ and its membership value is maximum, *i.e.*, $\pi(c; c, \lambda) = 1$. The membership value of a point decreases as its distance from the central point c, *i.e.*, $\|r - c\|$ increases. When $\|r - c\| = (\lambda/2)$, the membership value of r is 0.5 and this is called a *crossover* point.

2.2.2   Basic operations

Basic operations related to fuzzy subsets A and B of R having membership values $\mu_A(r)$ and $\mu_B(r)$, $r \in R$ respectively, are summarized here [15].

- A is equal to B $(A = B) \Rightarrow \mu_A(r) = \mu_B(r)$, for all $r \in R$.

- A is a complement of B $(A = \overline{B}) \Rightarrow \mu_A(r) = \mu_{\overline{B}}(r) = 1 - \mu_B(r)$ for all $r \in R$.

- A is contained in B $(A \subseteq B) \Rightarrow \mu_A(r) \leq \mu_B(r)$ for all $r \in R$.

- The union of A and B $(A \cup B) \Rightarrow \mu_{A \cup B}(r) = \vee(\mu_A(r), \mu_B(r))$ for all $r \in R$, where $\vee$ denotes maximum.

- The intersection of A and B $(A \cap B) \Rightarrow \mu_{A \cap B}(r) = \wedge(\mu_A(r), \mu_B(r))$ for all $r \in R$, where $\wedge$ denotes minimum.

- The *concentration* (*Con*) and *dilation* (*Dil*) operators [18] for a fuzzy set A

$$\mu_{Con(A)}(r) = (\mu_A(r))^2$$
$$\mu_{Dil(A)}(r) = (\mu_A(r))^{0.5}. \tag{2.7}$$

- Contrast intensification operator INT

$$\mu_{INT(A)}(r) = \begin{cases} 2\left[\mu_A(r)\right]^2 & \text{for } 0 \le \mu_A(r) \le 0.5 \\ 1 - 2\left[1 - \mu_A(r)\right]^2 & \text{otherwise.} \end{cases} \quad (2.8)$$

We also have the modifiers *not*, *very*, and *more or less*. We explain these with the help of the linguistic value *young* as follows:

$$\mu_{not\ young} = 1 - \mu_{young} \quad (2.9)$$

$$\mu_{very\ young} = \left(\mu_{young}\right)^2 \quad (2.10)$$

$$\mu_{not\ very\ young} = 1 - \left(\mu_{young}\right)^2 \quad (2.11)$$

$$\mu_{more\ or\ less\ young} = \left(\mu_{young}\right)^{0.5} \quad (2.12)$$

2.2.3 Measures of fuzziness

Let us now discuss some measures that give the degree of fuzziness in a fuzzy set A [13, 15]. The degree of fuzziness expresses the average amount of ambiguity in taking a decision as to whether an element belongs to the set. Such a measure (I, say) should have the following properties:

1. $I(A) = minimum$ iff $\mu_A(x_i) = 0$ *or* 1 $\forall i$.
2. $I(A) = maximum$ iff $\mu_A(x_i) = 0.5$ $\forall i$.
3. $I(A) \ge I(A^*)$,   where A^* is a *sharpened* version of A, defined as
   $$\mu_{A^*}(x_i) \ge \mu_A(x_i) \quad \text{if} \quad \mu_A(x_i) \ge 0.5$$
   $$\le \mu_A(x_i) \quad \text{if} \quad \mu_A(x_i) \le 0.5.$$
4. $I(A) = I(A^c)$,   where A^c is the *complement* set of A.

Several authors [9, 13], [19]–[21] have made attempts to define such measures. A few measures are described here.

2.2.3.1 Index of fuzziness The index of fuzziness of a fuzzy set A having n supporting points is defined as

$$\nu(A) = \frac{2}{n^k} d(A, \underline{A}), \quad (2.13)$$

where $d(A, \underline{A})$ denotes the distance between fuzzy set A and its nearest ordinary set $\underline{A}$. An ordinary set $\underline{A}$ nearest to the fuzzy set A is defined as

$$\mu_{\underline{A}}(x) = \begin{cases} 0 & \text{if} \quad \mu_A(x) \le 0.5 \\ 1 & \text{if} \quad \mu_A(x) \ge 0.5. \end{cases} \quad (2.14)$$

The value of k depends on the type of distance used. For example, $k = 1$ is used for generalized Hamming distance, whereas $k = 0.5$ for Euclidean distance. The corresponding indices of fuzziness are called *linear index of fuzziness* $\nu_l(A)$ and *quadratic index of fuzziness* $\nu_q(A)$. Thus we have

$$\nu_l(A) = \frac{2}{n} \sum_{i=1}^{n} |\mu_A(x_i) - \mu_{\underline{A}}(x_i)|$$

$$= \frac{2}{n} \sum_{i=1}^{n} [\min \{\mu_A(x_i), (1 - \mu_A(x_i))\}]. \tag{2.15}$$

Similarly, for Euclidean distance, we have

$$\nu_q(A) = \frac{2}{\sqrt{n}} \sqrt{[\sum_{i=1}^{n} \{\mu_A(x_i) - \mu_{\underline{A}}(x_i)\}^2]}. \tag{2.16}$$

2.2.3.2 Entropy   Entropy of a fuzzy set as defined by De Luca and Termini [19] is given by

$$H(A) = \frac{1}{n \ln(2)} \sum_{i=1}^{n} \{S_n(\mu_A(x_i))\}. \tag{2.17}$$

with

$$S_n(\mu_A(x_i)) = -\mu_A(x_i) \ln(\mu_A(x_i)) - \{1 - \mu_A(x_i)\} \ln\{1 - \mu_A(x_i)\}. \tag{2.18}$$

Another definition of entropy as given by Pal and Pal [21] is

$$H(A) = \frac{1}{n(\sqrt{e} - 1)} \sum_{i=1}^{n} \{S_n(\mu_A(x_i)) - 1\}. \tag{2.19}$$

with

$$S_n(\mu_A(x_i)) = \mu_A(x_i)e^{1-\mu_A(x_i)} + (1 - \mu_A(x_i))e^{\mu_A(x_i)}. \tag{2.20}$$

All these measures lie in $[0, 1]$ and satisfy properties 1 through 4.

It may be noted that a definition of *higher-order entropy* $[H^r(A) \geq 1]$ for a fuzzy set A (using both logarithmic and exponential gain functions) has also been reported [22], which takes into account the properties of collection of supports in the set. Equations (2.17)–(2.20) correspond to $r = 1$.

2.2.3.3 Index of nonfuzziness   Let us define another measure called "index of nonfuzziness" $\eta(A)$ as [23]

$$\eta(A) = \frac{1}{n} \sum_{i=1}^{n} |\mu_A(x_i) - \mu_{\overline{A}}(x_i)|, \tag{2.21}$$

where $\overline{A}$ is the complement of A. The index of nonfuzziness $(0 \leq \eta(A) \leq 1)$, as its name implies, measures the amount of nonfuzziness. Unlike $\nu_l(A)$, $\nu_q(A)$ and $H(A)$, its value decreases monotonically in $[0, 0.5]$ and monotonically increases in $[0.5, 1]$ with a minimum $(= 0)$ at $\mu = 0.5$.

2.2.4 T-norm and T-conorm

In Section 2.2.2 we have mentioned the basic operations of fuzzy sets. Here we deal with the *triangular norm and conorms* (T-operators), which are the generalized form of logical operations (connectives) such as OR (union) and AND (intersection). Let us express a and b over $[0, 1]$. Then we define AND (T-operation) as a T mapping function $T : [0,1] \times [0,1] \rightarrow [0,1]$ given by

$$y = [a \text{ AND } b] \triangleq [a \ T \ b] = T[a, b] \tag{2.22}$$

The generalized OR (t-conorm) is defined as an S mapping function $S : [0,1] \times [0,1] \rightarrow [0,1]$ given by

$$y = [a \text{ OR } b] \triangleq [aSb] = S[a, b] \tag{2.23}$$

Some important properties of the T operator [24] are
1. $T(a,b) = T(b,a)$, *commutativity*
2. $T(T(a,b),c) = T(a,T(b,c))$, *associativity*
3. $T(a,b) \geq T(c,d)$ if $a \geq c$ and $b \geq d$, *monotonicity*
4. $T(a,1) = a$, *boundary condition.*

Notable among this family of operators are

$$
\begin{aligned}
T^m(a,b) &= a \wedge b, \quad \min \\
T^p(a,b) &= a * b, \quad product \\
T^q(a,b) &= \max(0, x + y - 1), \quad quasilinear \\
T(a,b) &= a \text{ if } b = 1 \\
&= b \text{ if } a = 1 \\
&= 0 \text{ otherwise.}
\end{aligned}
$$

Yager [25] has introduced a whole parametrized family of these operators $T_p(x,y) = 1 - \min(1, ((1-x)^p + (1-y)^p)^{1/p})$, $p \geq 0$. For $p = \infty$ we recover the min operator. Other parametrized families have also been suggested [24].

A t-conorm differs from a t-norm only in property four - it has a different boundary condition. For t-conorms we require that $S(a,0) = a$.
Notable among these operators are

$$
\begin{aligned}
S^m(a,b) &= a \wedge b, \quad \max \\
S^p(a,b) &= a + b - ab, \quad probabilistic \ sum \\
S^q(a,b) &= \min(1, a + b), \quad quasilinear.
\end{aligned}
$$

Yager [25] has a parameterized family of t-conorm operators $S_p(a,b) = \min(1, (a^p + b^p)^{(1/p)})$ $p \geq 0$.
For $p = \infty$ we recover the max operator.
De Morgan's theorems can be stated as follows:

$$
\begin{aligned}
T(a,b) &= 1 - S(1-a, 1-b), \\
S(a,b) &= 1 - T(1-a, 1-b).
\end{aligned} \tag{2.24}
$$

Note that $T^p(a,b) \leq T^m(a,b) < S^m(a,b) \leq S^p(a,b)$ and (T^p, S^p), (T^m, S^m) are two special cases of the conjugate pair (T, S). It may be mentioned that these generalized operators are used by the fuzzy logical MLP in Section 3.4 for classification (Chapter 3), and Section 7.4 for inferencing and rule generation (Chapter 7). Fuzzy implication operators are also employed in the fuzzy logical MLP. These are defined in the next section.

2.2.5   Fuzzy implication operators

There exist many distinct meaningful ways of defining the containment of one fuzzy structure in another; these depend on the choice of a particular implication operator for the fuzzy power-set theory in hand. The choice of the semantic properties of a particular implication operator depends on some pragmatic consideration determined by the methodological questions of a particular application. Let us suppose that in the multivalued logic of the unit interval $I = [0,1]$, we have a fuzzy implication operator $\rightarrow$. Such an operation is a mapping from $I \times I$ into I, which agrees at the corners $(0,0)$, $(0,1)$, $(1,0)$, $(1,1)$ with the Boolean one. Here we mention a few fuzzy implication operators from the multivalued logic literature [26]. These are presented in order of increasing fuzziness.

For two variables X and Y, we have the *crisp* implication operators defined as *standard sharp*

$$X \rightarrow Y = \|X \subset Y\| = \begin{cases} 1 & \text{iff } X \neq 1 \text{ or } Y = 1 \\ 0 & \text{otherwise} \end{cases} \quad (2.25)$$

and *standard strict*

$$X \rightarrow Y = \|X \subset Y\| = \begin{cases} 1 & \text{iff } X \leq Y \\ 0 & \text{otherwise.} \end{cases} \quad (2.26)$$

These are observed to cause either *activity* or *disactivity* depending on the individual conditions, thereby drawing crisp conclusions from fuzzy premises. To alleviate this problem, one can introduce some interaction between the two variables using fuzzy concepts. A few fuzzy implication operators used to incorporate a degree of the amount of inclusion or containment [26, 27] are given below:

- Standard star
$$\|X \subset Y\| = \begin{cases} 1 & \text{iff } X \leq Y \\ Y & \text{otherwise} \end{cases} \quad (2.27)$$

- Gaines 43
$$\|X \subset Y\| = T^m \left(1, \frac{Y}{X}\right) \quad (2.28)$$

- Modified Gaines 43
$$\|X \subset Y\| = T^m \left(1, \frac{Y}{X}, \frac{1-X}{1-Y}\right) \quad (2.29)$$

- Lukasiewicz

$$\|X \subset Y\| = T^m(1, 1 - X + Y) \tag{2.30}$$

- Kleene–Dienes–Lukasiewicz

$$\|X \subset Y\| = 1 - X + XY \tag{2.31}$$

- Kleene–Dienes

$$\|X \subset Y\| = S^m(1 - X, Y) \tag{2.32}$$

- Early Zadeh

$$\|X \subset Y\| = S^m(T^m(X, Y), (1 - X)) \tag{2.33}$$

- Wilmott

$$\|X \subset Y\| = T^m(S^m((1 - X), Y), S^m(X, (1 - Y), T^m(Y, (1 - X)))), \tag{2.34}$$

where the S^m and T^m operators are as defined in Section 2.2.4.

It is to be noted that these operators introduce various degrees of mutual interaction between the two variables and hence their choice may be application-dependent. Let us consider the values of these implication operators on the 11-valued decile set [26]. The philosophical preconceptions behind the various operators clearly differ widely. A main division into types occurs between those down to and including *Lukasiewicz* and those after this, in that all of the former have ones all along the main diagonal, while none of the latter do. This reflects in the former type the desire to make the formula $X \to X$ into a *strong tautology*, versus the willingness in the latter type to allow it to be only a *moderate tautology*.

2.3   FUZZY MODELS FOR PATTERN RECOGNITION

From the very beginning of the development of fuzzy set theory, its application to pattern recognition played a very significant role. It is twofold: (1) a methodological one–this leads to treatment of fuzzy sets as a well-suited theory within which one can establish a plausible tool for modeling and mimicking the cognitive process of the human being, especially those concerning recognition aspects; and (2) secondly, fuzzy sets offer a lot of novel algorithms which are useful for the designing of feature analysis and classification procedures. Bezdek and Pal [16] have provided an excellent review on various approaches that helped in the evolution of fuzzy pattern recognition. One may also consult, in this context, the review article of Pedrycz [28]. Let us mention here some of the developments, in brief, that fall within the scope of the book.

Research on the application of fuzzy set theory to supervised pattern recognition was started in 1966 in the seminal note of Bellman *et al.* [29] where the two basic operations–abstraction and generalization–were proposed. Abstraction in fuzzy set theory means estimation of a membership function μ of a fuzzy class from the training samples. Having obtained the estimate, generalization is performed when this estimate is used to compute the values of μ for unknown objects not contained in the training set. Consideration of linguistic features and fuzzy relations in representing a class has also been suggested by Zadeh. Pal and Dutta Majumder [30] outline an early application of fuzzy sets for decision theoretic classification, where a pattern is considered as an array of linguistically phrased features denoting certain properties and where each of these features is a fuzzy set. The variation of the recognition score (for speech data) with the change of fuzziness in the linguistically phrased feature values has subsequently been investigated [15]. These classifiers have also been used for designing a self-supervised recognition system [31]. Nath *et al.* [32, 33] proposed a classification model applicable in the soft sciences (*e.g.*, medical diagnostics) where enough *a priori* knowledge about the classifier is available from the expert in linguistic form.

A fuzzy version of the well-known k *nearest neighbor* (k-NN) classifier has been provided by Keller *et al.* [34]. In the conventional approach [35]–[38], each of the labeled samples is given equal importance in deciding the class membership of an unknown pattern; this frequently causes problems in places where the labeled samples overlap. Keller *et al.* [34] tackled this problem by providing fuzzy label vectors for the samples as an indication of their class representativeness and this subsequently lead to a fuzzy classification rule. The fuzzy version of the k-NN rules seems to offer better performance (lower error rates) than crisp rules.

An adaptive system can be viewed as a learning machine, in which the system's decisions gradually approach the optimal decisions by acquiring the necessary information from the observed patterns. The approaches considered so far use a specified set of labeled data for the training of a classifier before it is used for classifying unknown patterns. Devi and Sarma [39] proposed an adaptive algorithm using a fuzzy approximation to the gradient descent technique for training a classifier sequentially. They suggested a method for eliminating or discarding doubtful or unreliable samples from the training procedure.

Although the task of feature selection plays an important role in designing a pattern recognition system, the research in this area using fuzzy set theory has not been significant. Bezdek and Castelaz [40] showed an application of the fuzzy c-means clustering algorithm to select an optimum feature subset from the available features to avoid appreciable loss of classifier performance with the reduced set of features. Pal and Chakraborty [41] explained an application of fuzziness measures (the index of fuzziness, entropy, and π-ness) of a set in selecting features without going through classification. This has then been extended to evaluate the importance of any subset of features to provide an average quantitative index of goodness [42].

Chang and Pavlidis [43] incorporated the concept of fuzzy decision trees in developing an efficient algorithm for making decisions in pattern recognition problems. Fuzzy tree automata are defined by Lee [44] for processing fuzzy tree representations of patterns using syntactic recognition. This shows how membership functions for structural patterns can be defined and how fuzzy language can be used for handling imprecision in structural pattern recognition.

There have been many attempts showing the application of fuzzy set theoretic approaches to real life recognition problems. Some of these can be found in the literature [15, 16, 45] for recognizing speech patterns that are biological in origin and indicating a considerable amount of fuzziness (vagueness). Pathak and Pal [46, 47] demonstrated an application of fuzzy and fractionally fuzzy grammars in syntactic recognition of ages of different bones from X-ray image patterns. They have shown that incorporation of the concept of fuzziness in defining sharp, fair, and gentle curves [48, 49] and the production rules used enable one to work with a smaller number of primitives and to use the same set of rules and nonterminals at each stage. Furthermore, these grammars need not be unambiguous, whereas nonambiguity is an absolutely necessary requirement for the nonfuzzy approach [46].

Automatic recognition of handwritten characters is another area where ambiguity occurs because of imprecision in writing rather than from randomness, and the fuzzy set theory has been used quite extensively both in feature extraction and in classification. Some details may be obtained in Refs. [15] and [16]. Rule based systems have also gained popularity in pattern recognition activities. By modeling the rules and facts in terms of fuzzy sets, it is possible to make interfaces using the concept of approximate reasoning. Such a system has been designed for automatic target recognition using 40 rules [50].

An extensive discussion on the application of fuzzy k-NN classifier for diagnosing gastric cancer has been provided [51]. Defining degrees of membership to correspond to the severity of *metastases*, the authors have formulated a fuzzy pattern recognition task with multiple class membership values. Another recent idea in pattern recognition is the partitioning of the initial feature space into regions and the application of different classification rules to them [52, 53]. A partition may be based on the geometric properties of the classes detected by a preliminary clustering method [52]. In the fuzzy classification rule described by Ishibuchi *et al.* [53], the partitioning is uniform, *i.e.*, the regions continue to be split until a sufficiently high certainty of the rule, generated by each region, is achieved. Ishibuchi *et al.* extended this work later [54] by using an idea of sequential partitioning of the feature space into fuzzy subspaces, until a predetermined stopping criterion is satisfied, and studied its application for solving various pattern classification problems.

A multivalued approach to supervised classification has been developed by Pal and Mandal [55] and Mandal *et al.* [56], based on approximate reasoning, where the system can accept imprecise input in linguistic form and provide output in multiple states. The feature space is decomposed by using linguistic property [55] and geometric structures [56] of training samples. The performance of the algorithms has been demonstrated on both the speech recognition problem and analysis of satellite imagery for detecting human-made objects [57]. The concept of multistate decision is found to be effective in connecting roadlike structures. The theoretical analysis of the methods including convergence property and relation with Bayes' decision regions has also been studied [58]. The concept of determining multiclass (fuzzy) boundary and shape of a pattern class from its sampled points (training samples) has been introduced in another study by Mandal *et al.* [59], in order to avoid committing oneself to a specific determination of boundary.

Besides the above-mentioned supervised classification methods, fuzzy set theory has been extensively used in clustering problems where the task is to provide class labels to input data (partitioning of feature space) under unsupervised mode based on certain criterion. A seminal contribution to cluster analysis was Ruspini's concept of a fuzzy partition [60]. A new direction in this line was initiated by Bezdek and Dunn in their work on fuzzy ISODATA and the fuzzy c-means algorithms [61, 62]. Another important branch called fuzzy image processing also grew up in parallel, based on the realization that many of the basic concepts in pattern analysis, *e.g.*, the concept of an edge or a corner, do not lend themselves to precise definition. Readers may consult other publications [11, 15, 16, 61], [63]–[71] for further details on these aspects.

The various approaches in fuzzy inferencing and rule generation include the approximate analogical reasoning based on similarity measures by Turksen and Zhong [72], the problem reduction method of Ishizuka *et al.* [73], modeling of physicians' decision processes by Esogbue and Elder [74] and inferencing in the framework of *inflammatory protein variations* by Sanchez and Bartolin [75] (using weighting). Wang and Mendel [76] developed a slightly different method for creating a fuzzy rule base, made up of a combination of rules generated from numerical examples and linguistic rules supplied by human experts. The input and output domain spaces are divided into a number of linguistic subspaces. Human intervention is sought to assign degrees to the rules, and conflicts are resolved by selecting those rules yielding the maximum of a computed measure corresponding to each linguistic subspace.

Rovatti and Guerrieri [77] have attempted to identify the correct rule structure of a fuzzy system when the target input–output behavior is sampled at random points. The assumption that a rule can either be included or excluded from the rule set is relaxed, and degrees of membership are exploited to achieve good approximation results. Defuzzification methodologies are then used to extract well-behaving crisp rule sets. Symbolic minimization is carried out to obtain a compact structure that captures the high-level characteristics of the target behavior. For other details, one may refer to standard literature [3, 5], [78]–[80].

2.4   ARTIFICIAL NEURAL NETWORKS

Artificial neural networks (ANNs) [81]–[98] attempt to replicate the *computational* power (lowlevel arithmetic processing ability) of biological neural networks and, thereby, hopefully endow machines with some of the (higher-level) *cognitive abilities* that biological organisms possess (due in part, perhaps, to their low-level computational prowess). These networks are reputed to possess the following basic characteristics.

- *Adaptivity*: the ability to adjust the connection strengths to new data or information

- *Speed*: due to massive parallelism

- *Robustness*: to missing, confusing, and/or noisy data

- *Ruggedness*: to failure of components

- *Optimality*: regarding the error rates in performance.

The various models are designated by the network topology, node characteristics, and the status updating rules. Network topology refers to the structure of interconnections among the various nodes (neurons) in terms of layers and/or feedback or feedforward links. Node characteristics mainly specify the operations it can perform, such as summing the weighted inputs incident on it and then amplifying or applying some aggregation operators on it. The updating rules may be for weights and/or states of the processing elements (neurons). Normally an objective function, representing the status of the network, is defined such that its set of minima correspond to the set of stable states of the network.

Tasks that neural networks can perform include pattern classification, clustering or categorization, function approximation, prediction or forecasting, optimization, retrieval by content, and control. ANNs can be viewed as weighted directed graphs in which artificial neurons are nodes and directed edges (with weights) are connections between neuron outputs and neuron inputs. On the basis of the connection pattern (architecture), ANNs can be grouped into two categories:

- *Feedforward* networks, in which graphs have no loops, *e.g.*, single-layer perceptron, multilayer perceptron, radial basis function networks, Kohonen network

- *Recurrent* (or *feedback*) networks, in which loops occur because of feedback connections, *e.g.*, Hopfield network, adaptive resonance theory (ART) models

Different connectivities yield different network behaviors. Generally speaking, feedforward networks are *static; i.e.*, they produce only one set of output values rather than a sequence of values from a given input. Feedforward networks are memory-less in the sense that their response to an input is independent of the previous network state. Recurrent or feedback networks, on the other hand, are *dynamic* systems. When a new input pattern is presented, the neuron outputs are computed. Because of the feedback paths, the inputs to each neuron are then modified, which leads the network to enter a new state.

ANNs store information among the synaptic connections. This scheme is different from programmed instruction sequences. Here a neuron is an elementary processor that performs primitive types of operations, like summing the weighted inputs coming to it and then amplifying or thresholding the sum. These networks can be trained by examples (as is often required in real life) and sometimes generalize well for unknown test cases. Performance is improved over time by iteratively updating the weights in the network. The worthiness of a network lies in its inferencing or generalization capabilities over such test sets. Connectionist learning procedures are suitable in domains with several graded features that collectively contribute to the solution of a problem. In the process of learning, a network may discover important underlying regularities in the task domain. The network architecture is selected depending on the objective of the problem to be tackled. Typically the models are based on parallel and distributed working principles, *i.e.*, all neurons work independently and in parallel.

The computational neuron model proposed by McCulloch and Pitts [99] is a simple binary threshold unit. The jth neuron computes the weighted sum of all its inputs x_i from other units and outputs a binary value, one or zero, depending on whether this weighted sum is greater than or equal to, or less than a threshold θ_j:

$$
\begin{aligned}
\text{Thus} \quad x_j\,(t+1) &= f(\textstyle\sum_i w_{ij}\,x_i(t) - \theta_j),\\
\text{where} \quad f(x) &= 1 \quad \text{if} \quad x \geq 0\\
&= 0 \quad \text{otherwise.}
\end{aligned}
$$

If the synaptic weight $w_{ij} > 0$, then it is called an *excitatory* connection; if $w_{ij} < 0$, it is viewed as an *inhibitory* connection. A simple generalization of McCulloch–Pitts neuron, by replacing the threshold function f with a more general nonlinear function, enhances the power of the networks built from such neurons. Even a synchronous assembly of McCulloch–Pitts neurons is capable, in principle, of universal computation for suitably chosen weights [82]. Such an assembly can perform any computation that an ordinary digital computer can. Neural networks are naturally parallel computing devices. Although the development of neural networks is inspired by models of brains, the purpose is not just to mimic biological neuron, but to use principles from nervous systems to solve complex problem in an efficient manner.

The adaptability of a neural network comes from its capability of learning from "environments." Broadly, there are three paradigms of learning: supervised, unsupervised (or self-organized), and reinforcement. Sometimes, reinforcement is viewed as a special case of supervised learning. Under each category there are many algorithms. In supervised learning (learning with a teacher), adaptation is done on the basis of direct comparison of the network output with known correct or desired answer. Unsupervised learning does not learn any specific input–output relation; rather, the network is tuned to the statistical regularities of the input data to form categories by optimizing, with respect to the free parameters of the network, some task-independent measure of quality of representation of the categories by the net. The reinforcement learning, on the other hand, attempts to learn the input–output mapping through trial and error with a view to maximizing a performance index called *reinforcement signal*. Here the system only knows whether the output is correct, but not what the correct output is.

Learning theory must address three fundamental and practical issues associated with learning from samples: capacity, sample complexity, and computational complexity. Capacity concerns how many patterns can be stored, and what functions and decision boundaries a network can form. Sample complexity determines the number of training patterns needed to train the network to guarantee a valid generalization. Too few patterns may cause "over-fitting," in which the network performs well on the training data set but poorly on independent test patterns drawn from the same distribution as the training patterns. *Computational complexity* refers to the time required for a learning algorithm to estimate a solution from training patterns. Many existing learning algorithms have high computational complexity.

Determination of the optimal size of a neural network is a problem of considerable importance, as this has a significant impact on the effectiveness of its performance. In general, it is desirable to have small networks. This is because increasing the number of hidden nodes or links may improve the approximation quality of an ANN at the expense of deteriorating its generalization capability (due to the resulting redundancy). An improperly chosen configuration may result in either overfitting of training patterns or non-convergence in learning. One way of improving the generalization behavior of an ANN is to reduce or *prune* its unimportant hidden nodes/links to some optimum size, after convergence. Moreover, smaller ANNs are faster when deployed. There exists various algorithms for pruning [100]–[106] ANNs. Another approach starts with a very small network, which is then gradually *grown* to the optimal size [107]–[110]. The performance of the network serves as a criterion for determining the termination of this procedure of adding nodes and links.

Let us now provide a detailed description of the single-layer perceptron, multilayer perceptron, Kohonen network, radial basis function network, Hopfield network and adaptive resonance theory (ART) in Sections 2.4.1–2.4.6.

2.4.1 Single-layer perceptron

The concept of *perceptron* [111, 112] was one of the most exciting developments during the early days of pattern recognition. The classical (single-layer) perceptron, given two classes of patterns, attempts to find a linear decision boundary separating the two classes.

A perceptron consists of a single neuron with adjustable weights, $w_j, j = 1, 2, \ldots, n$, and threshold θ. Given an input vector $x = [x_1, x_2, \ldots, x_n]^T$, the net input to the neuron is

$$v = \sum_{j=1}^{n} w_j x_j - \theta \qquad (2.35)$$

The output y of the perceptron is $+1$ if $v > 0$, and 0 otherwise. In a two-class classification problem, the perceptron assigns an input pattern to one class if $y = 1$, and to the other class if $y = 0$. The linear equation

$$\sum_{j=1}^{n} w_j x_j - \theta = 0$$

defines the decision boundary (a hyperplane in the n-dimensional input space) that halves the space. Rosenblatt [112] developed a learning procedure to determine the weights and threshold in a perceptron, given a set of training patterns. This algorithm is as follows:

1. Initialize the weights and threshold to small random numbers.

2. Present a pattern vector $[x_1, x_2, \ldots, x_n]^T$ and evaluate the output of the neuron.

3. Update the weights according to

$$w_j(t+1) = w_j(t) + \varepsilon(d - y)x_j, \qquad (2.36)$$

   where d is the desired output, t is the iteration number, and ε ($0.0 < \varepsilon < 1.0$) is the gain (step size).

Note that learning occurs only when the perceptron makes an error. Rosenblatt proved that when training patterns are drawn from two linearly separable classes, the perceptron learning procedure converges after a finite number of iterations. Many variations of the learning algorithm have been proposed in the literature [82]. Other activation functions that lead to different learning characteristics can also be used. However, a single-layer perceptron can only separate linearly separable patterns as long as a monotonic activation function is used.

If the pattern space is not linearly separable, the perceptron fails [113]. A single-layer perceptron is inadequate for situations with multiple classes and nonlinear separating boundaries. Hence the invention of the multilayer perceptron network.

2.4.2   Multilayer perceptron (MLP) using backpropagation of error

The multilayer perceptron (MLP) [83] consists of multiple layers of simple, two-state, sigmoid processing elements (nodes) or neurons that interact using weighted connections. After a lowermost input layer there are usually any number of intermediate or *hidden* layers, followed by an output layer at the top. There exist no interconnections within a layer, while all neurons in a layer are fully connected to neurons in adjacent layers. Weights measure the degree of correlation between the activity levels of neurons that they connect.

An external input vector is supplied to the network by clamping it at the nodes in the input layer. For conventional classification problems, during training, the appropriate output node is clamped to state 1 while the others are clamped to state 0. This is the desired output supplied by the *teacher*. The number of units in the output layer H corresponds to the number of output classes.

Consider the network given in Fig. 2.3. The total input x_j^{h+1} received by neuron j in layer $h+1$ is defined as

$$x_j^{h+1} = \sum_i y_i^h w_{ji}^h - \theta_j^{h+1}, \qquad (2.37)$$

where y_i^h is the state of the ith neuron in the preceding hth layer, w_{ji}^h is the weight of the connection from the ith neuron in layer h to the jth neuron in layer $h+1$ and θ_j^{h+1} is the threshold of the jth neuron in layer $h+1$. Threshold θ_j^{h+1} may be eliminated by giving the unit j in layer $h+1$ an extra input line with a fixed activity level of 1 and a weight of $-\theta_j^{h+1}$.

The output of a neuron in any layer other than the input layer ($h > 0$) is a monotonic nonlinear function of its total input, and is given as

$$y_j^h = \frac{1}{1 + e^{-x_j^h}}. \qquad (2.38)$$

For nodes in the input layer

$$y_j^0 = x_j^0, \qquad (2.39)$$

where x_j^0 is the jth component of the input vector clamped at the input layer. All neurons within a layer, other than the input layer, have their states set by eqns. (2.37)–(2.38) in parallel. Different layers have their states set sequentially in a *bottom–up* manner until the states of the neurons in the output layer H are determined. The learning procedure has to determine the internal parameters of the hidden units from its knowledge of the inputs and desired outputs. Hence learning consists of searching a very large parameter space and therefore is usually rather slow.

The least mean square (LMS) error in output vectors, for a given network weight vector $\boldsymbol{w}$, is defined as

$$E(\boldsymbol{w}) = \frac{1}{2} \sum_{j,c} (y_{j,c}^H(\boldsymbol{w}) - d_{j,c})^2, \qquad (2.40)$$

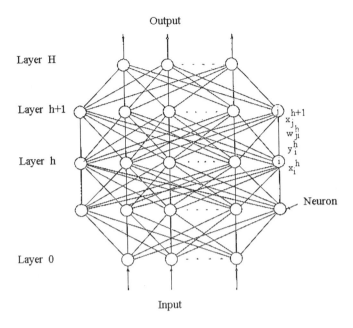

Fig. 2.3 MLP with three hidden layers

where $y_{j,c}^{H}(\boldsymbol{w})$ is the state obtained for output node j in layer H in input–output case c and $d_{j,c}$ is its desired state specified by the teacher. One method for minimization of $E(\boldsymbol{w})$ is to apply the method of gradient descent by starting with any set of weights and repeatedly updating each weight by an amount

$$\Delta w_{ji}^{h}(t) = -\varepsilon \frac{\partial E}{\partial w_{ji}} + \alpha \Delta w_{ji}^{h}(t-1), \tag{2.41}$$

where the positive constant ε controls the descent, $0 \le \alpha \le 1$ is the damping coefficient or momentum and t denotes the number of the iteration currently in progress. Generally ε and α are set at constant values, but there exist approaches that vary these parameters. Initially the connection weights w_{ji}^{h} between each pair of neurons i in layer h and j in layer $h+1$ are set to small random values lying in the range [-0.5,0.5]. One can adjust $\Delta w_{ji}^{h}(t)$ to ensure that $-0.1 \le \Delta w_{ji}^{h}(t) \le 0.1$ for each updating step, so that the possibility of *overshooting* of the weights may be minimized in the course of smoothly approaching a minimum error solution.

From eqns. (2.37)–(2.38) and (2.40), we have

$$\frac{\partial E}{\partial w_{ji}} = \frac{\partial E}{\partial y_j} \frac{dy_j}{dx_j} \frac{\partial x_j}{\partial w_{ji}} = \frac{\partial E}{\partial y_j} y_j^{h} \left(1 - y_j^{h}\right) y_i^{h-1} \tag{2.42}$$

For the output layer $(h = H)$, we substitute in eqn. (2.42)

$$\frac{\partial E}{\partial y_j} = y_j^H - d_j \qquad (2.43)$$

This assigns credit proportionately to those weights most responsible for the error, thus implementing gradient *steepest* descent in the weight space. The central idea is to first use a forward pass for each input–output case c, starting at the input neurons, to compute the activity levels of all the neurons in the network. Then a backward pass, starting at the output neurons, is used to compute the error derivative $(\partial E/\partial y_j)$ and backpropagate to enable weight updating until the input layer is reached. For the other layers, using eqn. (2.37), we substitute in eqn. (2.42)

$$\frac{\partial E}{\partial y_j} = \sum_k \frac{\partial E}{\partial y_k} \frac{dy_k}{dx_k} \frac{\partial x_k}{\partial y_j} = \sum_k \frac{\partial E}{\partial y_k} \frac{dy_k}{dx_k} w_{kj}^h, \qquad (2.44)$$

where units j and k lie in layers h and $h+1$, respectively.

Consider a multidimensional weight-space with an axis for each weight and one extra axis corresponding to the error measure. This weight space typically contains *ravines* with steep sides and a shallow gradient along the *ravine*. Acceleration methods used in eqn. (2.41) force the gradient to change the velocity of the current point in the weight space, help to hasten convergence, and rarely get stuck at poor local minima. The roles of ε and α in eqn. (2.41) have natural interpretations in terms of physical movement along this error surface, composed of *hills, valleys, ravines, ridges, plateaus,* and *saddle points,* in the weight space.

During training, each pattern of the training set is used in succession to clamp the input and output layers of the network. A sequence of forward and backward passes using eqns. (2.37)–(2.44) constitute a *cycle* and such a cycle through the entire training set is termed a *sweep*. After a number of sweeps through the training data, the error $E(w)$ in eqn. (2.40) may be minimized. At this stage the network is supposed to have discovered (learned) the relationship between the input and output vectors in the training samples.

In the testing phase the neural net is expected to be able to utilize the information encoded in its connection weights to assign the correct output labels for the test vectors that are now clamped only at the input layer. It should be noted that the optimal number of hidden layers and the number of units in each such layer are generally determined empirically, although growing, pruning and other optimization techniques are also in vogue.

Several other algorithms have been introduced to speed up the convergence of the MLP. These include quickpropagation (Quickprop) and resilient backpropagation (Rprop). *Quickprop* uses information about the curvature of the error surface to compute the weight change [108]. It assumes the error surface to be locally quadratic and attempts to jump in one step from the current position directly into the minimum of the quadratic. Rprop, on the other hand, uses the local topology of the error surface to make a more appropriate weight change [114]. This technique is efficient because the size of the weight step taken is no longer influenced by the size of the partial derivative. It is uniquely determined by the sequence of the signs of the derivatives, which provides a reliable hint about the topology of the local error function.

2.4.3 Kohonen network

The essential constituents of Kohonen neural network model are as follows [84], [115]–[118]:

- An array of neurons receiving coherent inputs and computing a simple output function

- A mechanism for comparing the neuronal outputs to select the neuron producing maximum output

- A local interaction between the selected neuron and its neighbors

- An adaptive mechanism that updates the interconnection weights

The self-organizing feature map (SOFM) is an unsupervised learning network [84], which transforms p-dimensional input patterns to a q-dimensional (usually $q = 1$ or 2) discrete map in a topologically ordered fashion. Input points that are close in p-dimension are also mapped closely on the q-dimensional lattice. Each lattice cell is represented by a neuron that has a p-dimensional adaptable weight vector associated with it. With every input the match with each weight vector is computed. Then the best matching weight vector and some of its topological neighbors are adjusted to match the input points a little better. Initially, the process starts with a large neighborhood; with passage of time (iteration), the neighborhood size is reduced gradually. At a given time instant, within the neighborhood, the weight vector associated with each neuron is not updated equally. The strength of interaction between the winner and a neighboring node is inversely related to the distance (on the lattice) between them.

Consider the self-organizing network given in Fig. 2.4. Let M input signals be simultaneously incident on each of an $N \times N$ array of neurons. The output of the ith neuron is defined as

$$
\eta_i(t) = \sigma \left[[\boldsymbol{m}_i(t)]^T \, \boldsymbol{x}(t) + \sum_{k \in S_i} w_{ki} \, \eta_k(t - \triangle t) \right], \tag{2.45}
$$

where $\boldsymbol{x}$ is the M-dimensional input vector incident on it along the connection weight vector $\boldsymbol{m}_i$, k belongs to the subset S_i of neurons having interconnections with the ith neuron, w_{ki} denotes the fixed feedback coupling between the kth and ith neurons, $\sigma[.]$ is a suitable sigmoidal output function, t denotes a discrete time index, and T stands for the transpose.

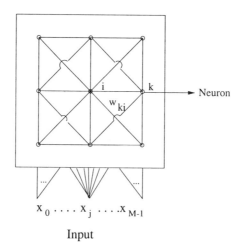

Fig. 2.4 Kohonen neural network

Initially the components of the m_i values are set to small random values lying in the range $[0, 0.5]$. If the best match between vectors m_i and x occurs at neuron c, then we have

$$\|x - m_c\| = \min_i \|x - m_i\|, \ \ i = 1, 2, \ldots, N^2, \tag{2.46}$$

where $\|.\|$ indicates the Euclidean norm.

The weight updating is given as [84, 116]

$$m_i(t+1) = \begin{cases} m_i(t) + \alpha(t)\,(x(t) - m_i(t)) & \text{for } i \in N_c \\ m_i(t) & \text{otherwise} \end{cases} \tag{2.47}$$

where $\alpha(t)$ is a positive constant that decays with time and N_c defines a topological neighborhood around the maximally responding neuron c, such that it also decreases with time. Note that $\alpha(t)$ is a particular case of the more general Gaussian term $h(x, t)$ [118]. Different parts of the network become selectively sensitized to different inputs in an ordered fashion so as to form a continuous map of the signal space. After a number of sweeps through the training data, with weight updating at each iteration obeying eqn. (2.47), the asymptotic values of m_i cause the output space to attain proper topological ordering. This is basically a variation of *unsupervised* learning. The self-organization using training patterns enables the ordering of the output neurons. These may then be calibrated with the class information by applying labeled training patterns at the input.

2.4.3.1 Learning vector quantization (LVQ) Vector quantization can be seen as a mapping from an n-dimensional Euclidean space into a finite set of prototypes. Based on this principle Kohonen proposed an unsupervised learning algorithm, which is a special case of SOFM and is known as LVQ [84]. In LVQ, only the weight vector associated with the winner node is updated with every data point by eqn. (2.47). The topological neighborhood is not updated here. Such a learning scheme, where all nodes compete to become the winner, is known as the *competitive learning scheme*. It is essentially a clustering network that does not care about preserving the topological order. Its main uses are for clustering and image data compression.

LVQ attempts to minimize an objective function that places all of its emphasis on the winning prototype for each data point. This is reasonable, but it ignores global information about the geometric structure of the data that is represented in the remaining losing prototypes. Thus, LVQ updating is a local strategy that ignores global relationship between the winner and the rest of the prototypes. For a better performance, the network should be allowed to influence the update of the winner, and perhaps be allowed to update some or all of the remaining prototypes also. This poses two questions: What would be the update neighborhood? What would be learning rate distribution over the neighbors? Note that here we are referring to the metrical neighbors, and not the topological neighbors.

Keeping in view these problems several new *soft competition* schemes, including fuzzy LVQ (FLVQ), generalized LVQ (GLVQ), fuzzy algorithms for LVQ (FALVQ), modified GLVQ (GLVQ-F), stochastic relaxation scheme (SRS), and Soft Competition Scheme (SCS) have been developed [119]–[123]. All these methods eliminate the need to define an update neighborhood by extending the update to all nodes and use learning rates that are functions of the distances of the prototypes to the data point. The salient features of the different soft versions of the LVQ are mentioned in Section 3.2.2 of Chapter 3, followed by a detailed description of the FLVQ (or fuzzy Kohonen clustering network).

There exists another family of LVQs, termed LVQ1 and LVQ2 [84]. These algorithms are conceptually different from the family of soft competition schemes just discussed. LVQ1 and LVQ2 are supervised learning schemes–essentially used as classifiers. The basic idea behind LVQ1 is as follows. If the winner prototype m_i has the same class label as that of the data point x, then bring m_i closer to x; otherwise, move m_i away from x. Nonwinner nodes are not updated. LVQ2, a modified form of LVQ1, is designed to make the learning scheme comply better with Bayes' decision-making philosophy. This algorithm considers both the winner and the runner-up (second winner).

2.4.4 Radial basis function network

A radial basis function (RBF) network [124, 125] consists of two layers as shown in Fig. 2.5. The connection weight vectors of the input and output layers are denoted as μ and w respectively. The basis (or kernel) functions in the hidden layer produce a localized response to the input stimulus. The output

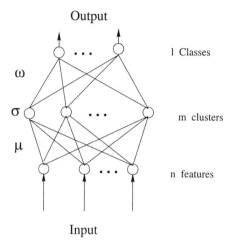

Fig. 2.5   Radial basis function network

nodes form a weighted linear combination of the basis functions computed by the hidden nodes.

The input and output nodes correspond to the input features and output classes, while the hidden nodes represent the number of clusters (specified by the user) that partition the input space. Let $x = (x_1, \ldots, x_i, \ldots, x_n) \in R^n$ and $y = (y_1, \ldots, y_i, \ldots, y_l) \in R^l$ be the input and output respectively and m be the number of hidden nodes.

The output u_j of the jth hidden node, using the *Gaussian kernel* function as a basis, is given by

$$u_j = \exp\left[-\frac{(x - \mu_j)^T (x - \mu_j)}{2\sigma_j^2}\right], \quad j = 1, 2, \ldots, m, \qquad (2.48)$$

where x is the input pattern, μ_j is its input weight vector (*i.e.*, the center of the Gaussian for node j), and σ_j^2 is the normalization parameter, such that $0 \leq u_j \leq 1$ (the closer the input is to the center of the Gaussian, the larger the response of the node).

The output y_j of the jth output node is

$$y_j = w_j^T u, \quad j = 1, 2, \ldots, l, \qquad (2.49)$$

where w_j is the weight vector for this node, and u is the vector of outputs from the hidden layer. The network performs a linear combination of the non linear basis functions of eqn. (2.48).

The problem is to minimize the error

$$E = \frac{1}{2} \sum_{p=1}^{N} \sum_{j=1}^{l} (y_j^p - d_j^p)^2, \qquad (2.50)$$

where d_j^p and y_j^p are desired and computed output at the jth node for the pth pattern, N is the size of the data set, and l is the number of output nodes. We shall omit the superscript p in the sequel, for ease of representation.

Learning in the hidden layer, typically, uses the c-means clustering algorithm [36]. Let the cluster centers, so determined, be denoted as μ_j, $j = 1, \ldots, m$. The normalization parameter σ_j represents a measure of the spread of data associated with each node.

Learning in the output layer is performed after the parameters of the basis functions have been determined. The weights are typically trained using the LMS algorithm given by

$$\triangle w_j = -\varepsilon(y_j - d_j)u, \qquad (2.51)$$

where ε is the learning rate.

2.4.5 Hopfield network

The idea behind the Hopfield network came from the analysis of some physical systems whose spontaneous behavior can be used as a general form of content-addressable memory. Suppose the status of such a system can be described by a set of coordinates. Thus, a point in the state space represents the instantaneous status of the system. The time evolution of such a system is merely a flow in the state space. If the flow pattern of the system is such that it moves toward a stable point in state space from anywhere in the neighborhood of the corresponding stable point, and the system has a reasonable number of stable points, then the system can be used as a content-addressable memory. The statistical mechanics of spin-glasses provides us with such a physical system. The Hopfield network is derived from this. It acts as a nonlinear associative memory that can retrieve a pattern stored in it in response to the presentation of an incomplete or noisy version of that pattern. It can also be used as a tool for optimization. The Boltzmann machine is a generalization of the Hopfield network, whose operation is based on a concept of statistical thermodynamics known as simulated annealing.

Let us consider a fully interconnected network for storing a set of p patterns x_i^μ, where $i = 1, 2, \ldots, N$ indicates the nodes and $\mu = 1, 2, \ldots, p$ denotes the patterns. When presented with a new pattern x_i', the network responds by producing whichever one of the stored patterns most closely resembles it. One usually takes the patterns to be made up of independent bits x_i which can each take on the values +1 and -1.

Starting from the initial configuration $S_i = x_i'$, one basically finds the set of connection weights w_{ij} such that the network reaches the state $S_i = x_i^{\mu_0}$, where $x_i^{\mu_0}$ has the smallest Hamming distance from x_i'. We use

$$S_i = \text{sgn}(\sum_j w_{ij} S_j). \qquad (2.52)$$

The connection weights are initialized as

$$w_{ij} = \frac{1}{N} \sum_{\mu=1}^{p} x_i^\mu x_j^\mu. \tag{2.53}$$

An associative memory model using the Hebb rule of eqn. (2.53) for all possible pairs ij, with binary units and asynchronous updating, is usually called a Hopfield model [126, 127].

The stability condition of a particular pattern x_i^v generalizes to

$$\text{sgn}(h_i^v) = x_i^v \quad \text{(for all } i), \tag{2.54}$$

where the net input h_i^v to unit i in pattern v is

$$h_i^v \equiv \sum_j w_{ij} x_j^v = \frac{1}{N} \sum_j \sum_\mu x_i^\mu x_j^\mu x_j^v. \tag{2.55}$$

Separating the sum on μ into the special term $\mu = v$ and all the rest, we have

$$h_i^v = x_i^v + \frac{1}{N} \sum_j \sum_{\mu \neq v} x_i^\mu x_j^\mu x_j^v \tag{2.56}$$

If the second term were zero, we could immediately conclude that pattern number v was stable according to eqn. (2.54). This is still true if the second term is small enough, *i.e.*, if its magnitude is smaller than 1 it cannot change the sign of h_i^v, and eqn. (2.54) will still be satisfied.

It turns out that the second term, which we call the *crosstalk* term, is less than 1 in many cases of interest if p (the number of patterns) is small enough. Then the stored patterns are all stable–if we start the system from one of them, it will stay there. Furthermore, a small fraction of bits different from a stored pattern will be overwhelmed in the sum $\sum_j w_{ij} S_j$ by the vast majority of correct bits. A configuration near (in Hamming distance) to x_i^v thus relaxes to x_i^v. This shows that the chosen patterns are truly *attractors* of the system. The system thus works as a content-addressable memory.

The energy function H of a Hopfield network is

$$H = -\frac{1}{2} \sum_{ij} w_{ij} S_i S_j. \tag{2.57}$$

The double sum is over all i and all j. The $i = j$ terms are of no consequence because $S_i^2 = 1$; they just contribute a constant to H, and in any case we could choose $w_{ii} = 0$. The energy function is a function of the configuration $\{S_i\}$ of the system, where $\{S_i\}$ means the set of all the S_i terms. We can thus imagine a hilly energy landscape.

The central property of an energy function is that *it always decreases (or remains constant) as the system evolves according to its dynamical rule.* Thus the attractors (memorized patterns) are at local minima of the energy surface. The dynamics can be thought of as similar to the motion of a particle on the energy surface under the influence of gravity and friction. From any starting point the particle (representing the whole state $\{S_i\}$ of the system) slides downhill until it comes to rest at one of these local minima–at one of the attractors. The basins of attraction correspond to the valleys around each minimum. Starting the system in a particular valley leads to the lowest point of that valley. The most general name for this energy function is *Lyapunov function*. For neural networks, in general, an energy function exists if the connection strengths are symmetric, *i.e.*, $w_{ij} = w_{ji}$.

For symmetric connections we can write eqn. (2.57) in the alternative form

$$H = C - \sum_{(ij)} w_{ij} S_i S_j, \qquad (2.58)$$

where (ij) means all the distant pairs ij, counting for example 12 as the same pair as 21. We exclude the ii terms from (ij); they give the constant C. It now is easy to show that the dynamical rule of eqn. (2.52) can only decrease the energy. Let S_i' be the new value of S_i given by eqn. (2.52) for some particular unit i,

$$S_i' = \text{sgn}(\sum_j w_{ij} S_j). \qquad (2.59)$$

Obviously if $S_i' = S_i$, the energy is unchanged. In the other case $S_i' = -S_i$ so, picking out the terms that involve S_i,

$$\begin{aligned} H' - H &= -\sum_{j \neq i} w_{ij} S_i' S_j + \sum_{j \neq i} w_{ij} S_i S_j \\ &= 2 S_i \sum_{j \neq i} w_{ij} S_j \\ &= 2 S_i \sum_j w_{ij} S_j - 2 w_{ii}. \end{aligned} \qquad (2.60)$$

Now the first term is negative from eqn. (2.59), and the second term is negative because the Hebb rule of eqn. (2.53) gives $w_{ii} = p/N$ for all i. Thus the energy decreases every time an S_i changes, as claimed.

2.4.6   Adaptive resonance theory (ART)

For a   competitive learning scheme, there is no guarantee that the different clusters formed will be stable unless the learning rate gradually approaches zero with iteration. When the learning rate is reduced to zero with iteration the network loses its plasticity. *Adaptive resonance theory* net [128] overcomes the stability-plasticity dilemma. In ART, with the progress of learning, new steady states are formed as the system discovers and learns prototypes that represent invariants of the set of all experienced patterns. This is known as the *plasticity* property of the network. Formation of the steady states is controlled to avoid possible sources of system instability. The ART system is plastic enough to learn significant new events, yet stable to irrelevant events.

In ART, a weight vector (prototype of a category) is adapted only when the input is sufficiently similar to the prototype; *i.e.*, when the input and a prototype resonate. When an input is not sufficiently similar to any prototype, a new category is formed using the input as the prototype with a previously uncommitted output unit. If there are no such uncommitted units left, then a novel input gives no response.

The meaning of *sufficiently similar* above is dependent on a *vigilance parameter* ρ, with $0 < \rho \leq 1$. If ρ is large the similarity condition becomes very stringent, so many finely divided categories are formed. On the other hand, a small ρ gives a coarse categorization. The vigilance level can be changed during learning; increasing it can prompt subdivision of existing categories. ART1 [129] is designed for binary 0/1 inputs, whereas ART2 [130] is for continuous-valued inputs. Carpenter *et al.* [131] have also developed a supervised binary version, called *adaptive resonance theory mapping* (ARTMAP), using a pair of ART1 modules. However, here we describe only ART1, which is the simplest among these.

It is easiest to present ART1 as an algorithm before describing the network implementation. Let us take input vectors $\mathbf{x}$ and stored prototype vectors $\mathbf{w_i}$, both with n binary 0/1 components. Here i indexes the output units, or categories, each of which can be *enabled* or *disabled*. We start with $\mathbf{w_i} = \mathbf{1}$ for all i, where $\mathbf{1}$ is the vector of all ones; this will represent an uncommitted state, not a category. Then the algorithm on presentation of a new input pattern $\mathbf{x}$ is as follows:

1. Enable all the output units.

2. Find the winner i^* among all the enabled output units (exit if there are none left). The winner is defined as the one for which $\overline{\mathbf{w}}_\mathbf{i} \cdot \mathbf{x}$ is largest, where $\overline{\mathbf{w}}_\mathbf{i}$ is a normalized version of $\mathbf{w_i}$. The normalization is given by

$$\overline{\mathbf{w}}_\mathbf{i} = \frac{\mathbf{w_i}}{\varepsilon + \sum_j w_{ji}}, \qquad (2.61)$$

where w_{ji} is the jth component of $\mathbf{w_i}$. The small number ε is included to break ties, selecting the longer of two $\mathbf{w_i}$ terms that both have all their bits in $\mathbf{x}$. Note that an uncommitted unit wins if there is no better choice.

3. Test whether the match between $\mathbf{x}$ and $\mathbf{w}_{\mathbf{i}^*}$ is good enough by computing the ratio

$$r = \frac{\mathbf{w}_{\mathbf{i}^*} \cdot \mathbf{x}}{\sum_j x_j} \qquad (2.62)$$

This is the fraction of bits in $\mathbf{x}$ that are also in $\mathbf{w}_{\mathbf{i}^*}$. If $r \geq \rho$, where ρ is the vigilance parameter, there is resonance; go to step 4. Otherwise if $r < \rho$, the prototype vector $\mathbf{w}_{\mathbf{i}^*}$ is rejected; disable unit i^* and go back to step 2.

4. Adjust the winning vector $\mathbf{w}_{i^*}$ by deleting any bits in it that are not also in $\mathbf{x}$. This is a logical AND operation, and is referred to as *masking* the input.

This algorithm can terminate in one of three ways. If we find a matching prototype vector, we adjust it (if necessary) in step 4 and output that category i^*. If we find no suitable prototype vector from among the previous categories, then one of the uncommitted vectors is selected and made equal to the input $\mathbf{x}$ in step 4; again we output the appropriate (new) category i^*. Finally, if there are no matches and no uncommitted vectors, we end up with all units disabled, and hence no output. The algorithm continues to have plasticity until all the output units are used up. It also has stability; a detailed analysis shows that all weight changes cease after a finite number of presentations of any fixed set of inputs. This comes essentially from the fact that the adaptation rule, step 4, can only remove bits from the prototype vector, never add any. Thus a given prototype vector can never cycle back to a previous value.

Note that the loop from step 3 back to step 2 constitutes a search through the prototype vectors, looking at the closest, next closest, and so on, by the maximum $\overline{\mathbf{w}}_i . \mathbf{x}$ criterion until one is found that satisfies the $r \geq \rho$ criterion. These criteria are different, so going further away by the first measure may actually bring us closer to the second. The first measure is concerned with the fraction of the bits in $\mathbf{w}_i$ that are also in $\mathbf{x}$, whereas r is the fraction of the bits in $\mathbf{x}$ that are also in $\mathbf{w}_i$. Of course this search is comparatively slow, but it occurs only before stability is reached for a given input set. After that each category is found on the first attempt and there is never a jump back from step 3.

Carpenter and Grossberg designed the ART1 network [129] using previously developed building blocks that were based on biologically reasonable assumptions. The selection of a winner, the input layer, the weight changes, and the enable/disable mechanism can all be described by realizable circuits governed by differential equations. There are at least three timescales involved: (1) the relaxation time of the winner-take-all circuit, (2) the cycling time of the search process, and (3) the rate of weight update. We describe a simpler version [82], taking the winner-take-all circuit for granted and simplifying certain other features. Figure 2.6 shows this reduced version. There are two layers, with units V_j in the input layer and O_i in the output layer fully connected in both directions. The forward weights $\overline{w}_{ij}$ are normalized copies of the backward weights w_{ji}, according to eqn. (2.61). Note that the w_{ji} are each 0 or 1, as are x_j, V_j, O_i, A, and R.

The output layer consists of winner-take-all units; only the unit with the largest net input $\sum_j \overline{w}_{ij} V_j$ among all enabled units has $O_i = 1$. If the "reset" signal R is turned on while a winner is active, that unit is disabled and removed from future competitions. All units can be reenabled by another

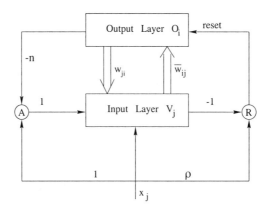

Fig. 2.6 ART network

signal that is not shown. The input units V_j are designed so that

$$V_j = \begin{cases} x_j & \text{if no output } O_i \text{ is on;} \\ x_j \wedge \sum_i w_{ji} O_i & \text{otherwise} \end{cases} \qquad (2.63)$$

where $\wedge$ means logical AND. For technical reasons, this is done using an auxiliary unit A, which is on ($A = 1$) if any input is on but no output is, and
off ($A = 0$) otherwise. A could be a 0/1 threshold unit with total input
$\sum_j x_j - n \sum_i O_i$ and threshold 0.5, as indicated by the connection weights
shown in the figure. The input units receive total input

$$h_j = x_j + \sum_i w_{ji} O_i + A \qquad (2.64)$$

and fire ($V_j = 1$) if this exceeds a threshold of 1.5. This is equivalent to
eqn. (2.63), and is referred to as the 2/3 rule; two out of its three inputs
x_j, $\sum_i w_{ji}O_i$, and A must be on for a unit V_j to fire. The disabling or
"reset" signal is generated when r from eqn. (2.62) is less than ρ. This can be
accomplished with a 0/1 threshold unit R that receives input $\rho \sum_j x_j - \sum_j V_j$
and has threshold 0, as shown by the connection weights in the figure.

Finally the backward weights are updated slowly according to

$$\frac{dw_{ji}}{dt} = \eta O_i(V_j - w_{ji}) \qquad (2.65)$$

so that the prototype vector $\mathbf{w_{i*j}}$ for the winner i^* becomes equal to the
masked input V_j after resonance has occurred. The forward weights have a
slightly more complicated learning rule that leads to a similar, but normalized,
result.

This network runs entirely autonomously, requiring no external sequencing
or control signals, and can cope stably with an infinite stream of input data.

It has fast access to well-known categories, automatic search for less-known categories, creation of new categories when necessary, and refusal to respond to unknown inputs when its capacity is exhausted. Moreover, its architecture is entirely parallel. In practice ART1 networks are somewhat tricky to adjust, and are very sensitive to noise in the input data. If random bits are sometimes missing from the input patterns, then the stored prototype vectors can be gradually degraded by the one-way masking form of the adaptation rule. ART1 networks are also rather inefficient in their storage requirements; we need one unit and $2N$ modifiable connections for each category, and many fixed connections for the A unit, R unit, and lateral inhibition. They also share the limitations of a grandmothering approach common to most competitive learning schemes. Some of these problems have been solved in the ART2 network.

2.5   NEURO-FUZZY COMPUTING

The need for integrating ANNs and fuzzy sets under the heading neuro-fuzzy computing has been explained in Section 1.6. Here we describe the various ways of integration, a mathematical formulation of a fuzzy neural network [132, 133], a neural implementation of possibility measure [134], and the equivalence of fuzzy systems and neural networks [135].

2.5.1   Various ways of integration

This section is devoted to describing the various approaches of neuro-fuzzy integration, keeping in mind the rich literature currently available in this field [16], [136]–[144]. Neuro-fuzzy hybridization is done broadly in two ways: a neural network equipped with the capability of handling fuzzy information [termed *fuzzy–neural network* (FNN)], and a fuzzy system augmented by neural networks to enhance some of its characteristics like flexibility, speed and adaptability [termed *neural–fuzzy system* (NFS)].

In an FNN either the input signals and/or connection weights and/or the outputs are fuzzy subsets or membership values to some fuzzy sets [145, 146]. Usually linguistic values such as *low, medium*, and *high*, or fuzzy numbers or intervals are used to model these. Neural networks with fuzzy neurons are also termed *FNN* as they are capable of processing fuzzy information.

A neural–fuzzy system (NFS), on the other hand, is designed to realize the process of fuzzy reasoning, where the connection weights of the network correspond to the parameters of fuzzy reasoning [147, 148]. Using the backpropagation-type learning algorithms, the NFS can identify fuzzy rules and learn membership functions of the fuzzy reasoning. Usually for an NFS, it is easy to establish a one-to-one correspondence between the network and the fuzzy system. In other words, the NFS architecture has distinct nodes for

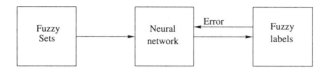

Fig. 2.7 Neural network implementing fuzzy classifier

antecedent clauses, conjunction operators, and consequent clauses. There can be, of course, another blackbox-type NFS where a multilayer network is used to determine the input–output relation represented by a fuzzy system. For such a system the network structure has no such relation to the architecture of the fuzzy reasoning system.

The state of the art for the different techniques of judiciously combining neuro-fuzzy concepts involves synthesis at various levels. In general, these methodologies can be broadly categorized as follows [149]. Figures 2.7–2.11 provide schematic diagrams of the five major categories of neuro-fuzzy integration methodologies. Note that categories 1, 3–5 relate to FNNs while category 2 refers to NFS.

1. Incorporating fuzziness into the neural net framework: fuzzifying the input data, assigning fuzzy labels to the training samples, possibly fuzzifying the learning procedure, and obtaining neural network outputs in terms of fuzzy sets [146], [150]–[163].

2. Designing neural networks guided by fuzzy logic formalism: designing neural networks to implement fuzzy logic and fuzzy decision making, and to realize membership functions representing fuzzy sets [119, 120, 147, 148], [164]–[170].

3. Changing the basic characteristics of the neurons: neurons are designed to perform various operations used in fuzzy set theory (like fuzzy union, intersection, aggregation) instead of the standard multiplication and addition operations [171]–[186].

4. Using measures of fuzziness as the error or instability of a network: the fuzziness or uncertainty measures of a fuzzy set are used to model the error or instability or energy function of the neural-network-based system [187]–[191].

5. Making the individual neurons fuzzy: the input and output of the neurons are fuzzy sets and the activity of the networks involving the fuzzy neurons is also a fuzzy process [145, 192, 193].

In the approaches under category 1, the integration can be viewed as incorporating the concept of fuzziness into a neural net framework for building *fuzzy neural network* classifiers. For example, the output of the neurons in the output layer, during both the training and testing phases, can be fuzzy

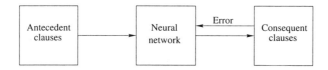

Fig. 2.8 Neural network implementing fuzzy logic

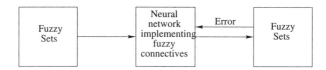

Fig. 2.9 Neural network implementing fuzzy connectives

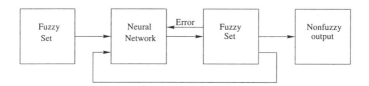

Fig. 2.10 Layered network implementing self-organization

label vectors. Besides, the input can be modeled as some fuzzy properties and the learning procedure can also be fuzzified. In this case the network itself functions as a fuzzy classifier. A good example is the work of Keller and Hunt [150].

Approaches under category 2 deal with neural networks that are used for a variety of computational tasks within the framework of a preexisting fuzzy model (*i.e.*, implementation of fuzzy logic formalism using neural networks). Huntsberger and Ajjimarangsee [164] and Bezdek *et al.* [165] have fuzzified the Kohonen network using a scheme that falls in this category.

Fusion made in category 3 replaces the integration/transformation operation at each node by the fuzzy aggregation operation (fuzzy union, intersection, *etc.*). Pedrycz [173, 174, 194] designed fuzzy layered neural net-based classifiers and Carpenter *et al.* [181, 182] developed fuzzy ART and fuzzy ARTMAP by using such logical operations.

The work of Ghosh *et al.* [187] falls under category 4, where various fuzziness measures are incorporated in a multi-layer network to make it perform (unsupervised) self-organizing task in image processing, in general, and object extraction in particular. A similar concept of using fuzziness measure as an objective function of a network is utilized [189]–[191] for feature selection and extraction under both supervised and unsupervised modes (described in detail in Chapter 6). Here a fuzzy feature evaluation index is minimized with a layered network, using gradient descent technique, such that the network pa-

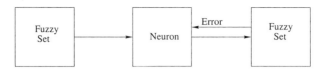

Fig. 2.11   Block diagram of a fuzzy neuron

rameters determine the importance of different input features or the extracted features.

The idea of making the individual neuron fuzzy falls under category 5, and was first promulgated in 1975 by Lee and Lee [145]. Some of the concepts of fuzzy set theory are employed to define a fuzzy neuron, which is a generalization of the classical neuron, and it allows both excitatory and inhibitory inputs. The activity of a fuzzy neuron is a fuzzy process. The input to such a neuron is a fuzzy set, and the outputs are equal to some positive numbers μ_js ($0 < \mu_j \leq 1$) if it is firing, and zero if it is quiet. μ_j denotes the degree to which the jth output is fired. Unlike conventional neurons, such a neuron has multiple outputs (set). In other words, it entertains graded input and output. The utility of neural networks with such fuzzy neurons has been demonstrated for synthesizing fuzzy automata. This concept, although introduced long back, has not been explored much as compared to others. ♣

Detailed review on various neuro-fuzzy approaches for classification, and inferencing and rule generation are provided in Sections 3.2 and 7.2 (of Chapters 3 and 7), respectively.

2.5.2   Mathematical formulation of a fuzzy neural network

Let us now provide a mathematical formulation of a layered fuzzy neural network [132, 133]. A neuron can be depicted as an information processing element which receives an n-dimensional input vector

$$\boldsymbol{X}(t) = [x_1(t), x_2(t), \ldots, x_n(t)] \in \mathcal{R}^n \qquad (2.66)$$

and yields a scalar neural output $y(t) \in \mathcal{R}^1$ at instant t (that can correspond to a pattern presentation in one epoch). The input vector, $\boldsymbol{X}(t) \in \mathcal{R}^n$, represents the signals being transmitted from the n neighboring neurons (including self-feedback signal) and/or the outputs (measurements) from the sensory neurons. Mathematically, the information processing ability of a neuron can be represented as a nonlinear mapping operation:

$$\boldsymbol{X}(t) \in \mathcal{R}^n \rightarrow y(t) \in \mathcal{R}^1. \qquad (2.67)$$

A confluence operation $\otimes$ essentially provides a measure of similarity between the neural input vector $\boldsymbol{X}(t)$ (new information) and the synaptic weight vector $\boldsymbol{W}(t)$ (accumulated knowledge base). Generally summation and product operations are used in this stage. A nonlinear activation function then performs a nonlinear mapping on the similarity measure through a nonlinear activation function $\psi[.]$. Hence

$$y(t) = \psi[\boldsymbol{W}(t) \otimes \boldsymbol{X}(t)]. \qquad (2.68)$$

A neural network can be viewed as a collection of such generic neurons connected to each other according to a specific topology. It, therefore, performs a mapping from the n-dimensional input space (input layer) to an l-dimensional output space (output layer) such that

$$\boldsymbol{X}(t) \in \mathcal{R}^n \to \boldsymbol{Y}(t) \in \mathcal{R}^l, \qquad (2.69)$$

where l refers to the number of output classes in the case of a classifier. The supervised learning uses a collection of N input–output training pairs $\{(\boldsymbol{X}(t), \boldsymbol{D}(t)), \ t = 1, \ldots, N\}$, where $\boldsymbol{X}(t) \in \mathcal{R}^n$ and $\boldsymbol{D}(t) \in \mathcal{R}^l$ are the input pattern and desired output, respectively. The objective is to optimize a cost function

$$E_N = \sum_{t=1}^{N} E_t = \sum_{t=1}^{N} d\left(\boldsymbol{Y}(t), \boldsymbol{D}(t)\right), \qquad (2.70)$$

where $d(.)$ is a distance in $\mathcal{R}^l$ and $\boldsymbol{Y}(t)$ is the computed output given by eqn. (2.69). A common choice, that simplifies the mathematical analysis, is that of considering the distance induced by an L_p norm ($1 \leq p \leq \infty$). The error-based gradient descent learning algorithm for weight updating is represented as

$$\boldsymbol{W}(t+1) = \boldsymbol{W}(t) + \varepsilon \triangle \boldsymbol{W}(t) \qquad (2.71)$$

for the N_w connection weights of the neural net, where ε is the learning rate.

A fuzzy neural network can incorporate fuzziness at the input–output level, in the connection weights, in the confluence operation or in the activation function. Let the fuzzy input and output vectors be represented as $\hat{\boldsymbol{X}}$ and $\hat{\boldsymbol{Y}}$, respectively, where these correspond to fuzzy numbers or intervals or the augmented space consisting of linguistic terms. Similarly, the connection weight vector may be represented as $\hat{\boldsymbol{W}}$. Arithmetic operations such as fuzzy addition and fuzzy multiplication can be used in the new confluence operation $\hat{\otimes}$. The nonlinear activation function $\hat{\psi}$ can incorporate fuzzy logic operations such as AND, OR and NOT. Hence the resultant mapping from the $\hat{n}$-dimensional input space to the $\hat{l}$-dimensional output space becomes

$$\hat{\boldsymbol{X}}(t) \in \mathcal{R}^{\hat{n}} \to \hat{\boldsymbol{Y}}(t) \in \mathcal{R}^{\hat{l}}, \qquad (2.72)$$

where a single fuzzy neuron implements the nonlinear operation

$$\hat{y}(t) = \hat{\psi}[\hat{\boldsymbol{W}}(t) \hat{\otimes} \hat{\boldsymbol{X}}(t)]. \qquad (2.73)$$

The training data $\{(\hat{\boldsymbol{X}}(t), \hat{\boldsymbol{D}}(t)), \hat{\boldsymbol{X}}(t) \in \mathcal{R}^{\hat{n}}, \hat{\boldsymbol{D}}(t) \in \mathcal{R}^{\hat{l}}, t = 1, \ldots, N\}$ are used to optimize the cost function

$$\hat{E}_N = \sum_{t=1}^{N} \hat{d}\left(\hat{\boldsymbol{Y}}(t), \hat{\boldsymbol{D}}(t)\right), \qquad (2.74)$$

where $\hat{d}(.)$ is a distance in $\mathcal{R}^{\hat{l}}$. The learning algorithm now becomes

$$\hat{W}(t+1) = \hat{W}(t) + \varepsilon \triangle \hat{W}(t) \tag{2.75}$$

for the $\hat{N}_w$ connection weights of the fuzzy neural net.

2.5.3   Neural implementation of possibility measure

Here we describe the neural implementation of the possibility measure and show its close relationship to the basic neural aggregation operation [134]. For any two fuzzy subsets of the set X, F, and G, one has possibility

$$Poss\,[F|G] = \max_x [H(x)], \tag{2.76}$$

where $H = F \cap G$. The operation of intersection of fuzzy sets can be implemented by using any t-norm operator T. Thus using the product t-norm,

$$H(x) = F(x) * G(x).$$

Using this definition for intersection,

$$Poss\,[F|G] = \max_x [F(x) * G(x)]. \tag{2.77}$$

As stated previously, the *max* operator is an example of a t-conorm operator. In the most general setting one can use any other t-conorm operator in the definition of possibility. One useful class of t-conorm operators is the parameterized family of operators, introduced by Yager [25]:

$$S_p(a, b) = \min(1, (a^p + b^p)^{1/p}) \ \ p \geq 0.$$

The associativity of these operators easily allows one to extend this aggregation to any number of elements,

$$S_p(a_1, a_2, \cdots, a_n) = \min(1, (\sum a_i^p)^{1/p}) \ \ p \geq 0. \tag{2.78}$$

Using this choice of t-conorm, we get

$$Poss\,[F|G] = \min[1, \sum_i (H(x_i)^p)^{1/p}], \tag{2.79}$$

where $H(x_i) = F(x_i) * G(x_i)$. One case of the Yager family, worthy of note is $p = 1$; here

$$Poss\,[F|G] = \min[1, \sum_i (F(x_i) * G(x_i))]. \tag{2.80}$$

This implementation for t-conorm is called the *quasilinear* t-conorm. This formulation for the possibility measure of F given G easily can be seen to correspond to a typical artificial neuron.

We recall the standard (typical or default) neuron as having weights (or strength of connection) w, input firing levels a, evaluation (or activation) function f, and output firing level y. The functioning of this standard neuron is such that $y = f(net)$, where net $= \sum_i w_i a_i$.

To make the correspondence between the possibility function $poss[F/G]$, and this neuron, one proceeds as follows. Associate with each element in X an input line. Thus, if n is the cardinality of the base set X, one has n input lines. Associate $G(x_i)$ with the weight w_i and $F(x_i)$ with the input firing level a_i. Using this association

$$net = \sum_i F(x_i)G(x_i).$$

Associate the output firing level y with the possibility measure, such that

$$y = Poss\,[F|G] = f(\text{net}). \qquad (2.81)$$

Because

$$Poss\,[F|G] = \min(1, net) = f(\text{net}), \qquad (2.82)$$

the activation function is as follows:

$f(net) = 0 \quad net < 0$
$f(net) = net \quad 0 \le net < 1$
$f(net) = 1 \quad net \ge 1.$

Thus, the possibility measure can be expressed as a neuron where the weights are the membership of one of the sets and the input the membership of the other. In addition, further generality can be had by replacing net with any function net_p, where $net_p = (\sum_i (H(x_i))^p)^{1/p}$.

2.5.4   Fuzzy and neural systems: universal approximators and equivalence

The motivation for approximating fuzzy systems by neural networks [7], [195]–[197] lies in the inherent capability of neural networks to perform massive parallel processing of information. This is important in fuzzy systems that are required to process large numbers of fuzzy inference rules in real time. When the neural network representing a given fuzzy system is implemented in hardware, all relevant fuzzy inference rules are processed in parallel. This results in high computational efficiency, which is crucial in many applications. Furthermore, the neural network representation is capable of introducing adaptivity or learning into the system. This can be utilized for modifying fuzzy inference rules of the system on the basis of experience. On the other hand, one can translate the knowledge embedded in the neural network into a more cognitively acceptable language in terms of fuzzy rules. This leads to an understandable interpretation of neural nets, resulting in rule generation.

An important connection between fuzzy rule-based systems and neural networks, which has been recognized and investigated since the early 1990s, is that they are both universal approximators of continuous functions of a rather general class [198, 199]. The term "universal approximation" has the following precise mathematical meaning.

Let X be a compact subset of $\mathcal{R}^n$ (*i.e.*, a subset of $\mathcal{R}^n$ that is closed and bounded), and let $C(X; n, l)$ denote the set of all continuous functions f of the form $f : X \to \mathcal{R}^l$. Then a universal approximator, A, is a set of functions g of the form $g : X \to \mathcal{R}^l$ that satisfies the following:

> For any given function $f \in C(X; n, l)$ and any real number $\varepsilon > 0$, there exists a function $g \in A$ such that $\mid f(\mathbf{x}) - g(\mathbf{x}) \mid < \varepsilon$ for all $\mathbf{x} \in X$. While A is usually a subset of $C(X; n, l)$, the two sets may also be disjoint.

The latter case takes place when functions in A are not continuous.

The following is a summary of the main results regarding computational equivalence between continuous functions, neural networks, and rule-based fuzzy systems:

1. Feedforward neural networks with n inputs l outputs ($n \geq 1, l \geq 1$), one hidden layer, and a continuous activation function (*e.g.*, the sigmoid function) in each neuron are universal approximators. Comparable neural networks with more than one hidden layer are universal approximators as well.

2. Fuzzy systems based on multiconditional approximate reasoning can approximate feedforward neural networks with n inputs, l outputs, one or more hidden layers, and a continuous activation function in each neuron, provided the range of the input variable is discretized into n values and the range of the output variable is discretized into l values.

3. It follows from items 1 and 2 that fuzzy systems of the type described in 2 are also universal approximators. Fuzzy input–output controllers, that is, fuzzy rule-based systems using multiconditional approximate reasoning and a defuzzification of obtained conclusions, are also universal approximators.

Hayashi and Buckley [135] proved that (1) any rule-based fuzzy system may be approximated by a neural net; and (2) any neural net (feedforward, multilayered) may be approximated by a rule-based fuzzy system. This kind of equivalence between fuzzy rule-based systems and neural networks is also studied in [196, 200, 201].

2.6   KNOWLEDGE-BASED NETWORKS

Generally ANNs consider a fixed topology of neurons connected by links in a predefined manner. These connection weights are usually initialized by small random values. Knowledge-based networks (KBNs) [202, 203] constitute a special class of ANNs that consider crude domain knowledge to generate the initial network architecture, which is later refined in the presence of training data. Recently, there have been some attempts in improving the efficiency of neural computation by using knowledge-based nets. This helps in reducing the searching space and time while the network traces the optimal solution. Such a model has the capability of outperforming a standard MLP as well as other related algorithms including symbolic and numerical ones [202, 203].

A major development in knowledge-based neural networks is the integration of symbolic expert rule-based knowledge into neural networks. First, data attributes or variables are assigned to input units (nodes), target concepts, or final hypotheses are assigned to output units, and intermediate concepts or hypotheses are assigned to hidden units. Then, initial domain rules determine how the attributes and concepts link and how the links are weighted.

Each rule has an antecedent (premise) consisting of one or more conditions as well as a single consequent in the form of "*If* α_1 and $\alpha_2, \ldots$, *then* β," where α_i is a condition and β is a conclusion or action. The conjunction of α_is constitutes the rule's premise. In the network configuration, the premise is assigned a hidden unit, each condition corresponds to an assigned attribute or concept node, and the consequent corresponds to an assigned concept node. Each condition node is connected to the premise node, which, in turn, is connected to the consequent node. Under such construction, the rule strength corresponds to the weight associated with the connection from the premise node to the consequent node. Note that a hidden unit is introduced to explicitly represent the conjunction of one or more conditions in a rule's premise. Such a hidden unit is called a *conjunction unit*. In addition to knowledge-based connections, we may add some hypothetical nodes and connections to increase the learning capacity of the network. After the network topology is determined, weights are initialized properly according to given knowledge. Depending on the type of activation function chosen, a different weight initialization scheme is taken.

2.6.1 Generalization capability

In the case of knowledge-based networks [204, 205], some weights are initially fixed by crude domain knowledge. In conventional multilayer perceptrons, on the other hand, all weights are typically freely adjustable during learning. It is formally shown [204] that such knowledge-based networks require relatively small sample sizes for correct generalization.

Suppose that there are n sample points in d dimensions belonging to two categories. Each point is labeled either ω_1 or ω_2. A hyperplane separating the points labeled ω_1 from the points labeled ω_2 is called a *linear dichotomy*.

Given a set of instances S, a concept hypothesis h in H can partition the set into two groups. The instances in one group satisfy the hypothesis h and those in the other group do not. The partition is called the *dichotomy induced by h*. H can be a class of $\{0, 1\}$-valued functions F in which a dichotomy induced by f is a partition of S into two disjoint subsets S^+ and S^- such that $f(\mathbf{x}) = 1$ for $\mathbf{x} \in S^+$ and $f(\mathbf{x}) = 0$ for $\mathbf{x} \in S^-$. The maximum number of dichotomies induced by hypotheses in H on any set of m instances is defined as the *growth function* of H with respect to m, denoted by $G_H(m)$ here. The Vapnik–Chervonenkis (VC)dim [206] of H is the largest m such that the corresponding growth function is equal to 2^m. That is, H can induce all possible dichotomies of m instances drawn from the instance space if and only if the VCdim of H is m. Thus, the VCdim of H measures the capacity of H. It turns out that the VCdim of a single perceptron with a d-dimensional input is $d + 1$ [92].

The *generalization error* of the network is defined as the difference between the generalization on the training data (which forms an estimate of the true generalization) and the generalization on the actual problem. Since the network tends to fit the training data, the generalization with respect to it will be overly optimistic. However, in many cases, the generalization error can be bounded (a worst-case analysis), and this bound can be made arbitrarily small by increasing the number of training instances. Vapnik and Chervonenkis [206] show that a useful bound can be established when the number of training instances exceeds the VCdim (defined earlier). Assume the hard-limiting activation function. The VCdim of a one-hidden-layer perceptron, with full connectivity between the layers, is in the range [92]

$$2 \left\lfloor \frac{N_h}{2} \right\rfloor d \leq \text{VCdim} \leq 2N_w \log(eN_n), \qquad (2.83)$$

where $\lfloor . \rfloor$ is the *floor* operation that returns the largest integer less than its argument, N_h is the number of hidden units, N_w is the total number of weights in the network, N_n is the total number of nodes in the network, e is the base of the natural logarithm, and d is the number of input units. The upper bound holds no matter what the number of layers and the connectivity are. As a rule of thumb, the number of weights can give a rough estimate of the VCdim. A knowledge-based network can have a smaller VCdim than a conventional multilayer perceptron with the same number of connection weights since some weights in the former can be fixed by prior knowledge. The result suggests that a knowledge-based network requires a smaller number of training instances for valid generalization than a conventional multilayer perceptron.

However, in the absence of knowledge, one has to resort to a purely data driven mode of learning as in the simple connectionist models. When the initial knowledge fails to explain many instances, additional hidden units and connections need to be added (often empirically). In the case of knowledge-based networks, the initial encoded knowledge may be refined with experience by performing learning in the data environment. Node growing and link pruning are made in order to generate the optimal network architecture. The resulting networks generally involve less redundancy in their topology.

2.6.2 Fuzzy knowledge-based networks

The merits of neuro-fuzzy computation can also help in designing more efficient (intelligent) knowledge-based networks. Let us describe here mathematically a fuzzy knowledge-based network. Consider a knowledge-based net in
line with eqns. (2.66)–(2.71). It implements a mapping

$$\boldsymbol{X}'(t) \in \mathcal{R}^{n'} \rightarrow \boldsymbol{Y}(t) \in \mathcal{R}^{l} \tag{2.84}$$

from the n'-dimensional input space to the l-dimensional output space, where
$n' \leq n$ and

$$y(t) = \psi[\boldsymbol{W}'(t) \otimes \boldsymbol{X}'(t)]. \tag{2.85}$$

The training data $\{(\boldsymbol{X}'(t), \boldsymbol{D}(t)), \boldsymbol{X}'(t) \in \mathcal{R}^{n'}, \boldsymbol{D}(t) \in \mathcal{R}^{l}, t = 1, \ldots, N\}$ are
used to optimize the cost function E_N of eqn. (2.70). The learning algorithm
becomes

$$\boldsymbol{W}'(t+1) = \boldsymbol{W}'(t) + \varepsilon \triangle \boldsymbol{W}'(t) \tag{2.86}$$

for the N'_w connection weights, where $N'_w \leq N_w$ of eqn. (2.71) and ε is the
learning rate.

On incorporating the concept of fuzzy sets, analogous to the idea of eqns.
(2.72)–(2.75), the mapping from the $\hat{n}'$-dimensional input space to the $\hat{l}$-
dimensional output space can be represented as

$$\hat{\boldsymbol{X}}'(t) \in \mathcal{R}^{\hat{n}'} \rightarrow \hat{\boldsymbol{Y}}(t) \in \mathcal{R}^{\hat{l}}, \tag{2.87}$$

where $\hat{n}' \leq \hat{n}$ and

$$\hat{y}(t) = \hat{\psi}[\hat{\boldsymbol{W}}'(t) \hat{\otimes} \hat{\boldsymbol{X}}'(t)]. \tag{2.88}$$

The training data $\{(\hat{\boldsymbol{X}}'(t), \hat{\boldsymbol{D}}(t)), \hat{\boldsymbol{X}}'(t) \in \mathcal{R}^{\hat{n}'}, \hat{\boldsymbol{D}}(t) \in \mathcal{R}^{\hat{l}}, t = 1, \ldots, N\}$ are
used to optimize the cost function $\hat{E}_N$ of eqn. (2.74). The learning algorithm
becomes

$$\hat{\boldsymbol{W}}'(t+1) = \hat{\boldsymbol{W}}'(t) + \varepsilon \triangle \hat{\boldsymbol{W}}'(t) \tag{2.89}$$

for the $\hat{N}_w'$ connection weights such that $\hat{N}_w' \leq \hat{N}_w$ of eqn. (2.75). Review
of various models of knowledge-based and fuzzy knowledge-based networks,
used for classification and rule generation, are provided in Section 8.2.   ♣

One of the major problems in connectionist/neuro-fuzzy design is the choice
of the optimal network structure. This has an important bearing on any performance evaluation. Moreover, the models are generally very data-dependent,
and the appropriate network size also depends on the available training data.
Various methodologies developed for selecting the optimal network structure
include growing and pruning of nodes and links, employing genetic search, and
embedding initial knowledge in the network topology. The last approach–
embedding initial knowledge–is usually followed in the case of knowledge-
based networks. Two such models will be described in Chapters 8 and 9 in
detail.

Before leaving this chapter, let us explain the significance of neuro-fuzzy approach in soft computing paradigm. Here we describe what soft computing is, the relevance of various soft computing tools (fuzzy sets, neural networks, genetic algorithms, *etc.*) and their different hybridizations.

2.7   SOFT COMPUTING

A computer can complete a job more efficiently than a human being when the job involves substantial amount of routine computation; like inversion of a matrix of large dimension. On the other hand, if the task requires perceptual power or cognitive capability of human beings, the VonNeumann machine is far behind human beings. For example, human beings can recognize shapes of different sizes and orientations, even in an occluded environment, more efficiently than a computer.

A VonNeumann machine is good for well structured problems. Typically, human brains are better for solving real world ill-defined, imprecisely formulated problems requiring huge computations. To overcome the limitations of traditional computing paradigm, scientists have been searching for new computational approaches that can be used to model, at least partially, the human thinking process and the functioning of brains, and can be used to solve real world problems efficiently. As a result in the recent past several novel modes of computation have emerged, some of which are collectively known as *soft computing* [207]–[210].

In traditional hard computing, the prime desiderata are precision, certainty, and rigor. By contrast, in soft computing the principal notion is that precision and certainty carry a cost; and that computation, reasoning, and decision making should exploit (wherever possible) the tolerance for imprecision, uncertainty, approximate reasoning, and partial truth for obtaining low cost solutions. This leads to the remarkable human ability of understanding distorted speech, deciphering sloppy handwriting, comprehending the nuances of natural language, summarizing text, recognizing and classifying images, driving a vehicle in dense traffic, and, more generally, making rational decisions in an environment of uncertainty and imprecision.

Information processing in a biological system is a complex phenomenon, which enables us to survive by accomplishing tasks such as recognition of surroundings, making prediction, planning, and acting accordingly. Human type information processing involves both logical and intuitive information processing. Conventional computer systems are good for the former but their capability for the latter is far behind that of human beings. As a first step to accomplish humanlike intuitive information processing, a computer system should be flexible enough to support the following three characteristics: *openness, robustness* and *real time* processing. Openness of a system is its ability to adapt or extend itself on its own to cope with changes encountered in the real world. Robustness of a system means its stability and tolerance when confronted with distorted, incomplete, or imprecise information. The real-time characteristic implies the ability of the system to react within a reasonable time in response to an event.

Information processing systems with all these three characteristics are, sometimes, known as *real world computing* (RWC) systems. An RWC system should, therefore, be capable of distributed representation of information, massively parallel processing, learning, and self-organization in order to achieve flexibility in information processing. Thus, soft computing can be viewed as the key ingredient of RWC systems.

2.7.1   Relevance

The traditional hard computing paradigm is seldom suitable for many real life problems. Let us illustrate it with an example. Suppose that X is driving a car and X watches a "red light" (traffic signal). X has to stop. So X has to decide when to press the brake and how strongly. In a "precise framework," the steps followed by X may be to find the distance of the car from the "light," and then, depending on the current speed of the car, press the brake. To realize this, the car should be provided with a laser-gun-type arrangement so that the distance can be obtained. X should also know a set of rules of the form

"*If the car is at a distance of d ft and moving at a speed of s ft/s then press the brake with p poundal for t seconds right now.*"

This is a precise rule governed by the laws of physics. Hence, if the brake is applied according to such rules, the car will stop where X wants it to. Theoretically, such concepts are fine, but practically they are useless because of the following reasons:

- The addition of a laser gun to a car increases its cost.

- The number of precise rules required will be too great to realize in a practical system.

- For the sake of argument, even if we assume that we know the rules to be followed, application of the brakes following the rule will be a very difficult task.

Precise solutions are not always feasible. In fact, we do not need a precise solution to such a problem. The exact position where the car stops is not important, but it should stop before the "red light" and should not hit any other car standing ahead of it. Hence an approximate idea about the distance of the car and the speed of the car should be enough. Under this situation X can control the car using rules of the form "If the car is moving *very fast* and the 'red light' is *close*, then press the brake *pretty hard*".

Note that the rule has three vague clauses "very fast," "close" and "pretty hard." These make the rule an imprecise one, and it will generate an approximate solution to the problem. The solution is less expensive and fast

(real-time) also. This is one facet of what soft computing paradigm for emu-
lating the humanlike decision making (also, a real world computing system)
attempts to achieve. Thus, to achieve higher machine IQ, the system should
have the capability of modeling vagueness and making approximate decisions
on that basis. Fuzzy sets are good for handling this aspect of soft computing.
In fact, this distinguished characteristic of fuzzy sets led to the emergence of
soft computing.

Another example is the problem of parking a car [211]. Generally, a car can
be parked rather easily because the final position of the car is not specified
exactly. If it were specified to within, say, a fraction of a millimeter and a
few seconds of arc, it would take hours or days of maneuvering and precise
measurements of distance and angular position to solve the problem. What
this simple example points to is the fact that, in general, high precision carries
a high cost, and in many situations high precision is not necessary. The
challenge, then, is to exploit the tolerance for imprecision by devising methods
of computation that lead to *an acceptable solution at low cost*. This, in essence,
is the guiding principle of soft computing.

Let us now make the driving problem a bit more complex. Suppose that X
is driving on a very crowded road and has to reach the destination D. From
the present coordinate of X, there are a couple of alternative paths to reach
D. Depending on the traffic conditions X should try to pick up an optimal
path. Note that the traffic conditions (traffic flows in either direction, number
of traffic signals that will appear on a path, raining or clear *etc.*) change with
time, and hence what X thinks as the optimal path now may not remain
optimal after some time. Consequently, X has to dynamically (adaptively)
change his/her route. Human beings make approximate decisions for such
problems on the basis of their experience (learning from previous driving
experiences). If we want an information or intelligent system to achieve this
capability, it should have the ability to learn from experience and examples.
Artificial neural networks are adaptive systems, and can deal with this aspect
of the problem.

Any artificial network that can be used for handling the problem just mentioned, must be fed with relevant information. In other words, the ANN
system has to be trained with adequate number of examples. The popular
gradient descent (say, backpropagation)-type learning algorithms are usually
very slow in learning and may get stuck at some local minimum. *Genetic
algorithms* (GAs), in such situations, may be very effectively used for learning. If the number of free parameters of the network is large, GAs may also
become slow, but for GA-based learning the chance of getting stuck to a local
minimum would be low. Consequently, we can expect a better generalization
ability of the network.

In conclusion, *soft computing is a consortium of methodologies that works
synergetically and provides in one form or another flexible information processing capability for handling real life ambiguous situations. Its aim is to
exploit the tolerance for imprecision, uncertainty, approximate reasoning, and*

partial truth in order to achieve tractability, robustness, and low-cost solutions. The guiding principle is to devise methods of computation that lead to an acceptable solution at low cost by seeking for an approximate solution to an imprecisely/precisely formulated problem. Its major components, at this juncture, are fuzzy logic (FL), neural computing (NC), and probabilistic reasoning (PR), with PR subsuming belief networks, genetic algorithms (GA), and chaotic systems. FL is concerned mainly with providing algorithms for dealing with imprecision and approximate reasoning. NC provides the machinery for learning and curve fitting. PR, on the other hand, deals with probabilistic uncertainty, propagation of belief, and searching and optimization.

2.7.2   Different hybridizations

Let us now discuss the different hybridizations of FL, ANN, and GAs in soft computing framework. One may note that the literature in the field of neuro-fuzzy computing (as evident from this book) is considerably rich; the other hybrid paradigms, such as integration of GAs with FL and ANN, are comparatively less explored. Before mentioning them, we describe the relevance of GAs to pattern recognition.

The methods developed for pattern recognition and image processing are usually problem-dependent. Moreover, many tasks involved in the process of analyzing or identifying a pattern need appropriate parameter selection and efficient search in complex spaces in order to obtain optimal solutions. This not only makes the process computationally intensive, but also leads to a possibility of losing the exact solution.

Genetic algorithms are randomized search and optimization techniques guided by the principles of evolution and natural genetics. They are efficient, adaptive, and robust search processes, producing near-optimal solutions and having a large amount of implicit parallelism. Therefore, the application of genetic algorithms for solving certain problems of pattern recognition (which need optimization of computation requirements, and robust, fast, and close approximate solution) appears to be appropriate and natural [212]. Some applications of GAs in the areas of classification, feature selection, segmentation, image enhancement, and primitive extraction are available in the literature [212]–[221]. Since GAs have been used in Chapter 5, their basic principles and characteristic features are described in Appendix A for the convenience of readers. Some of the attempts on its hybridization with FL and ANNs are mentioned below.

2.7.2.1   Genetic–Fuzzy integration   Fusion of fuzzy systems and genetic algorithms can be done for tuning of the former [222]–[224]. For example, this can be for membership function selection and tuning [225]–[227]. Such a fusion of the two technologies, does not enhance the power of the fuzzy system, but makes it easy to get an optimal design of the same. In this context we mention that the merits of integrating FL with GAs to improve the capability of the latter has not yet been established.

2.7.2.2 Genetic–Neural integration While integrating neural networks with genetic and evolutionary algorithms, the two components may interact in many ways [228]–[231]. For example, GAs can be used to select the cloning templates of a cellular neural network [232]; again it can help to avoid the tedious backpropagation algorithm for an MLP, thereby overcoming some limitations of neural networks [233]. The optimal topology of a neural network can also be evolved using GAs [234]–[241]. Such an integrated approach may be termed *genetic–neural*. As it stands, the use of ANN for improving the performance of GAs is not yet explored.

2.7.2.3 Neuro-Fuzzy–Genetic integration Finally, we can have approaches that exploit the benefits of all three soft-computation tools. Such systems may be termed neuro-fuzzy–genetic (NFG) [188], [242]–[247]. For example, a fuzzy reasoning system may be implemented using a multilayer network, where the free parameters of the system may be learned using GAs. Similarly, the parameters of an FNN may also be learned using GAs. An application of NFG approach to object extraction is described in detail in Chapter 5 (Section 5.3).

The theory of *rough sets* [248, 249] has recently emerged as another major mathematical tool for managing uncertainty that arises from granularity in the domain of discourse, *i.e.*, from the indiscernibility between objects in a set. Hybridizations, exploiting the characteristics of rough sets, include the *rough–fuzzy* [250]–[252] and *rough–neuro-fuzzy* [253, 254] approaches. The primary role of rough sets here is in managing uncertainty and extracting domain knowledge. One such integration (along with some preliminaries of rough sets) will be elaborated on in Chapter 9.

Over the last few decades, information technology has passed through a revolution. The growth of information technology in terms of computing power ranges from conventional computing (whose kernel is data processing) to RWC systems (whose kernel is flexible information processing) via fifth-generation computing (whose kernel is knowledge information processing). Thus, as it stands, *these hybrid paradigms will not only continue to remain in the forefront research area for the coming decades but also play a key role in the development of future technology, including sixth-generation computing systems.*

REFERENCES

1. L. A. Zadeh, "The role of fuzzy logic in the management of uncertainty in expert systems," *Fuzzy Sets and Systems*, vol. 11, pp. 199–227, 1983.

2. L. A. Zadeh, "The concept of a linguistic variable and its application to approximate reasoning: Part 1, 2, and 3," *Information Sciences*, vol. 8, 8, 9, pp. 199–249, 301–357, 43–80, 1975.

3. H. -J. Zimmermann, *Fuzzy Sets, Decision Making and Expert Systems.* Boston, MA: Kluwer Academic Publishers, 1987.

4. M. M. Gupta, A. Kandel, W. Bandler, and J. B. Kiszka, eds., *Approximate Reasoning in Expert Systems.* Amsterdam: North Holland, 1985.

5. A. Kandel, ed., *Fuzzy Expert Systems.* Boca Raton, FL: CRC Press, 1991.

6. H. -J. Zimmermann, *Fuzzy Set Theory and its Applications.* Boston, MA: Kluwer, 1991.

7. G. J. Klir and B. Yuan, *Fuzzy Sets and Fuzzy Logic: Theory and Applications.* Englewood Cliffs, NJ: Prentice-Hall, 1995.

8. L. A. Zadeh, "Fuzzy logic," *Computer*, vol. 21, pp. 83–92, 1988.

9. A. Kaufmann, *Introduction to the Theory of Fuzzy Subsets–Fundamental Theoretical Elements*, vol. 1. New York: Academic Press, 1975.

10. D. Dubois and H. Prade, *Fuzzy Sets and Systems: Theory and Applications.* Boston: Academic Press, 1980.

11. J. C. Bezdek, *Pattern Recognition with Fuzzy Objective Function Algorithms.* New York: Plenum Press, 1981.

12. A. Kandel, *Fuzzy Techniques in Pattern Recognition.* New York: Wiley-Interscience, 1982.

13. A. Kandel, *Fuzzy Mathematical Techniques with Applications.* Reading, MA: Addison-Wesley, 1986.

14. A. Kaufmann and M. Gupta, *Introduction to Fuzzy Mathematics.* New York: Van Nostrand Reinhold, 1985.

15. S. K. Pal and D. Dutta Majumder, *Fuzzy Mathematical Approach to Pattern Recognition.* New York: Wiley (Halsted Press), 1986.

16. J. C. Bezdek and S. K. Pal, eds., *Fuzzy Models for Pattern Recognition: Methods that Search for Structures in Data.* New York: IEEE Press, 1992.

17. S. K. Pal and P. K. Pramanik, "Fuzzy measures in determining seed points in clustering," *Pattern Recognition Letters*, vol. 4, pp. 159–164, 1986.

18. L. A. Zadeh, "Outline of a new approach to the analysis of complex systems and decision processes," *IEEE Transactions on Systems, Man, and Cybernetics*, vol. 3, pp. 28–44, 1973.

19. A. De Luca and S. Termini, "A definition of a non probabilistic entropy in the setting of fuzzy set theory," *Information and Control*, vol. 20, pp. 301–312, 1972.

20. B. Kosko, "Fuzzy entropy and conditioning," *Information Sciences*, vol. 40, pp. 165–174, 1986.

21. N. R. Pal and S. K. Pal, "Entropy: A new definition and its applications," *IEEE Transactions on Systems, Man, and Cybernetics*, vol. 21, pp. 1260–1270, 1991.

22. N. R. Pal and S. K. Pal, "Higher order fuzzy entropy and hybrid entropy of a set," *Information Sciences*, vol. 61, pp. 211–231, 1992.

23. S. K. Pal, "A measure of edge ambiguity using fuzzy sets," *Pattern Recognition Letters*, vol. 4, pp. 51–56, 1986.

24. D. Dubois and H. Prade, "A review of fuzzy sets aggregation connectives," *Information Sciences*, vol. 36, pp. 85–121, 1985.

25. R. R. Yager, "On a general class of fuzzy connectives," *Fuzzy Sets and Systems*, vol. 4, pp. 235–242, 1980.

26. W. Bandler and L. J. Kohout, "Semantics of implication operators and fuzzy relational products," in *Fuzzy Reasoning and Its Applications*, E. H. Mamdani and B. R. Gaines, eds., New York: Academic Press, 1981.

27. I. B. Turksen, "Four methods of approximate reasoning with interval-valued fuzzy sets," *International Journal of Approximate Reasoning*, vol. 3, pp. 121–142, 1989.

28. W. Pedrycz, "Fuzzy sets in pattern recognition: Methodology and methods," *Pattern Recognition*, vol. 23, pp. 121–146, 1990.

29. R. Bellman, R. Kalaba, and L. A. Zadeh, "Abstraction and pattern classification," *Journal of Mathematical Analysis Applications*, vol. 13, pp. 1–7, 1966.

30. S. K. Pal and D. Dutta Majumder, "Fuzzy sets and decision making approaches in vowel and speaker recognition," *IEEE Transactions on Systems, Man, and Cybernetics*, vol. 7, pp. 625–629, 1977.

31. A. Pathak and S. K. Pal, "On the convergence of a self-supervised vowel recognition system," *Pattern Recognition*, vol. 20, pp. 237–244, 1987.

32. A. K. Nath and T. T. Lee, "On the design of a classifier with linguistic variables as input," *Fuzzy Sets and Systems*, vol. 11, pp. 265–286, 1983.

33. A. K. Nath, S. W. Liu, and T. T. Lee, "On some properties of linguistic classifier," *Fuzzy Sets and Systems*, vol. 17, pp. 297–311, 1985.

34. J. M. Keller, M. R. Gray, and J. A. Givens, "A fuzzy k nearest neighbor algorithm," *IEEE Transactions on Systems, Man, and Cybernetics*, vol. 15, pp. 580–585, 1985.

35. R. O. Duda and P. E. Hart, *Pattern Classification and Scene Analysis*. New York: Wiley, 1973.

36. J. T. Tou and R. C. Gonzalez, *Pattern Recognition Principles*. London: Addison-Wesley, 1974.

37. P. A. Devijver and J. Kittler, eds., *Pattern Recognition Theory and Applications*. Berlin: Springer-Verlag, 1987.

38. K. Fukunaga, *Introduction to Statistical Pattern Recognition*. New York: Academic Press, 1972.

39. B. B. Devi and V. V. S. Sarma, "A fuzzy approximation scheme for sequential learning in pattern recognition," *IEEE Transactions on Systems, Man, and Cybernetics*, vol. 16, pp. 668–679, 1986.

40. J. C. Bezdek and P. F. Castelaz, "Prototype classification and feature selection with fuzzy sets," *IEEE Transactions on Systems, Man, and Cybernetics*, vol. 7, pp. 87–92, 1977.

41. S. K. Pal and B. Chakraborty, "Fuzzy set theoretic measure for automatic feature evaluation," *IEEE Transactions on Systems, Man, and Cybernetics*, vol. 16, pp. 754–760, 1986.

42. S. K. Pal, "Fuzzy set theoretic measures for automatic feature evaluation: II," *Information Sciences*, vol. 64, pp. 165–179, 1992.

43. R. L. P. Chang and T. Pavlidis, "Fuzzy decision tree algorithms," *IEEE Transactions on Systems, Man, and Cybernetics*, vol. 7, pp. 28–35, 1977.

44. E. T. Lee, "Fuzzy tree automata and syntactic pattern recognition," *IEEE Transactions on Pattern Analysis and Machine Intelligence*, vol. 4, pp. 445–449, 1982.

45. R. De Mori and P. Laface, "Use of fuzzy algorithms for phonetic and phonemic labeling of continuous speech," *IEEE Transactions on Pattern Analysis and Machine Intelligence*, vol. 2, pp. 136–148, 1980.

46. A. Pathak and S. K. Pal, "Fuzzy grammars in syntactic recognition of skeletal from x-rays," *IEEE Transactions on Systems, Man, and Cybernetics*, vol. 16, pp. 657–667, 1984.

47. A. Pathak, S. K. Pal, and R. A. King, "Syntactic recognition of skeletal maturity," *Pattern Recognition Letters*, vol. 2, pp. 193–197, 1984.

48. S. K. Pal and R. A. King, "On edge detection of X-ray images using fuzzy sets," *IEEE Transactions on Pattern Analysis and Machine Intelligence*, vol. 5, pp. 69–77, 1983.

49. S. K. Pal, R. A. King, and A. A. Hashim, "Image description and primitive extraction using fuzzy sets," *IEEE Transactions on Systems, Man, and Cybernetics*, vol. 13, pp. 94–100, 1983.

50. A. Nafarieh and J. Keller, "A fuzzy logic rule-based automatic target recognition," *International Journal of General Systems*, vol. 6, pp. 295–312, 1991.

51. H. F. Wang, C. W. Wu, C. H. Ho, and M. J. Hsieh, "Diagnosis of gastric cancer by fuzzy pattern recognition," *Journal of Systems Engineering*, vol. 2, pp. 151–163, 1993.

52. K. Hirota and W. Pedrycz, "Geometric-logical pattern classification," in *Proceedings of 2nd International Conference on Fuzzy Logic and Neural Networks, Iizuka* (Japan), pp. 675–678, 1992.

53. H. Ishibuchi, K. Nozaki, and H. Tanaka, "Distributed representation of fuzzy rules and its application to pattern classification," *Fuzzy Sets and Systems*, vol. 52, pp. 21–32, 1992.

54. H. Ishibuchi, K. Nozaki, and H. Tanaka, "Efficient fuzzy partition of pattern space for classification problems," *Fuzzy Sets and Systems*, vol. 59, pp. 295–304, 1993.

55. S. K. Pal and D. P. Mandal, "Linguistic recognition system based on approximate reasoning," *Information Sciences*, vol. 61, pp. 135–161, 1992.

56. D. P. Mandal, C. A. Murthy, and S. K. Pal, "Formulation of a multi-valued recognition system," *IEEE Transactions on Systems, Man, and Cybernetics*, vol. 22, pp. 607–620, 1992.

57. D. P. Mandal, C. A. Murthy, and S. K. Pal, "Analysis of IRS imagery for detecting man-made objects with a multivalued recognition system," *IEEE Transactions on Systems, Man, and Cybernetics, Part A*, vol. 26, pp. 241–247, 1996.

58. D. P. Mandal, C. A. Murthy, and S. K. Pal, "Theoretical performance of a multivalued recognition system," *IEEE Transactions on Systems, Man, and Cybernetics*, vol. 24, pp. 1001–1021, 1994.

59. D. P. Mandal, C. A. Murthy, and S. K. Pal, "Determining the shape of a pattern class from sampled points in R^2," *International Journal of General Systems*, vol. 20, pp. 307–339, 1992.

60. E. H. Ruspini, "A new approach to clustering," *Information and Control*, vol. 15, pp. 22–32, 1969.

61. J. C. Bezdek, "A physical interpretation of fuzzy ISODATA," *IEEE Transactions on Systems, Man, and Cybernetics*, vol. 6, pp. 387–389, 1976.

62. J. C. Dunn, "A fuzzy relative of the ISODATA process and its use in detecting compact well-separated clusters," *Journal of Cybernetics*, vol. 3, pp. 32–57, 1973.

63. S. K. Pal, "Uncertainty management in space station autonomous research: Pattern recognition perspective," *Information Sciences*, vol. 72, pp. 1–63, 1993.

64. S. K. Pal, *Fuzzy Set Theory on Gray Tone Image Processing*. Ph.D. thesis, Imperial College, University of London, UK, 1982.

65. M. Roubens, "Pattern classification problems and fuzzy sets," *Fuzzy Sets and Systems*, vol. 1, pp. 239–253, 1978.

66. I. Gath and A. B. Geva, "Unsupervised optimal fuzzy clustering," *IEEE Transactions on Pattern Analysis and Machine Intelligence*, vol. 11, pp. 773–781, 1989.

67. S. K. Pal and S. Mitra, "Fuzzy dynamic clustering algorithm," *Pattern Recognition Letters*, vol. 11, pp. 525–535, 1990.

68. S. K. Pal, *Fuzzy Set Theoretic Tools for Image Analysis*, vol. 88 of *Advances in Electronics and Electron Physics*, pp. 247–296. Academic Press, 1994.

69. E. Backer and A. K. Jain, "A clustering performance measure based on fuzzy set decomposition," *IEEE Transactions on Pattern Analysis and Machine Intelligence*, vol. 3, pp. 66–75, 1981.

70. R. N. Dave and K. Bhaswan, "Adaptive fuzzy c-shells clustering and detection of ellipses," *IEEE Transactions on Neural Networks*, vol. 3, pp. 643–662, 1992.

71. R. Krishnapuram, O. Nasraoui, and H. Frigui, "The fuzzy c spherical shells algorithm: A new approach," *IEEE Transactions on Neural Networks*, vol. 3, pp. 663–671, 1992.

72. I. B. Turksen and Z. Zhong, "An approximate analogical reasoning schema based on similarity measures and interval-valued fuzzy sets," *Fuzzy Sets and Systems*, vol. 34, pp. 323–346, 1990.

73. M. Ishizuka, K. S. Fu, and J. T. P. Yao, "Inference procedures under uncertainty for the problem-reduction method," *Information Sciences*, vol. 28, pp. 179–206, 1982.

74. A. O. Esogbue and R. C. Elder, "Fuzzy sets and the modelling of physician decision processes, Part I: The initial interview–information gathering session," *Fuzzy Sets and Systems*, vol. 2, pp. 279–291, 1979.

75. E. Sanchez and R. Bartolin, "Fuzzy inference and medical diagnosis, a case study," *Biomedical Fuzzy Systems Bulletin*, vol. 1, pp. 4–21, 1990.

76. L. X. Wang and J. M. Mendel, "Generating fuzzy rules by learning from examples," *IEEE Transactions on Systems, Man, and Cybernetics*, vol. 22, pp. 1414–1427, 1992.

77. R. Rovatti and R. Guerrieri, "Fuzzy sets of rules for system identification," *IEEE Transactions on Fuzzy Systems*, vol. 4, pp. 89–102, 1996.

78. S. Abe and M. S. Lan, "Fuzzy rules extraction directly from numerical data for function approximation," *IEEE Transactions on Systems, Man, and Cybernetics*, vol. 25, pp. 119–129, 1995.

79. J. A. Dicherson and B. Kosko, "Fuzzy function approximation with ellipsoidal rules," *IEEE Transactions on Systems, Man, and Cybernetics, Part B*, vol. 26, pp. 542–560, 1996.

80. T. Hong and C. Lee, "Induction of fuzzy rules and membership functions from training examples," *Fuzzy Sets and Systems*, vol. 84, pp. 33–37, 1996.

81. S. Haykin, *Neural Networks: A Comprehensive Foundation*. New York: Macmillan, 1994.

82. J. Hertz, A. Krogh, and R. G. Palmer, *Introduction to the Theory of Neural Computation*. Reading, MA: Addison-Wesley, 1994.

83. D. E. Rumelhart and J. L. McClelland, eds., *Parallel Distributed Processing: Explorations in the Microstructures of Cognition*, vol. 1. Cambridge, MA: MIT Press, 1986.

84. T. Kohonen, *Self-Organization and Associative Memory*. Berlin: Springer-Verlag, 1989.

85. S. Grossberg, ed., *Neural Networks and Natural Intelligence*. Cambridge, MA: MIT Press, 1988.

86. P. D. Wassermann, *Neural Computing: Theory and Practice*. New York: Van Nostrand Reinhold, 1990.

87. R. Rosenfeld and J. Anderson, eds., *Neuro Computing*. Cambridge, MA: MIT, 1988.

88. R. P. Lippmann, "An introduction to computing with neural nets," *IEEE Acoustics, Speech and Signal Processing Magazine*, vol. 4, pp. 4–22, 1987.

89. J. Dayhoff, *Neural Network Architectures: An Introduction.* New York: Van Nostrand Reinhold, 1990.

90. P. Simpson, *Artificial Neural Systems: Foundations, Paradigms, Applications and Implementations.* Elmsford, NY: Pergamon Press, 1990.

91. J. M. Zurada, *Introduction to Artificial Neural Systems.* Boston, MA: PWS, 1992.

92. D. R. Hush and B. G. Horne, "Progress in supervised neural networks," *IEEE Signal Processing Magazine,* pp. 8–39, January 1993.

93. A. K. Jain and J. Mao, "Artificial neural networks: A tutorial," *IEEE Computer,* pp. 31–44, March 1996.

94. S. K. Pal and P. K. Srimani, eds., *Special Issue on Neural Networks: Theory and Applications, IEEE Computer,* vol. 29, no. 3. 1996.

95. S. K. Pal, ed., *Special Issue on Neural Networks, Journal of the Institute of Electronics and Telecommunications Engineers,* vol. 42, nos. 4, 5. 1996.

96. J. A. Freeman and D. M. Skupura, *Neural Networks Algorithms, Applications and Programming Techniques.* New York: Addison-Wesley, 1991.

97. J. A. Anderson and E. Rosenfeld, eds., *Neurocomputing Foundations of Research.* Cambridge, MA: MIT, 1988.

98. G. E. Hinton, "Connectionist learning procedures," *Artificial Intelligence,* vol. 40, pp. 185–234, 1989.

99. W. S. McCulloch and W. Pitts, "A logical calculus of the idea immanent in nervous activity," *Bulletin of Mathematical Biophysics,* vol. 5, pp. 115–133, 1943.

100. R. Reed, "Pruning algorithms - a survey," *IEEE Transactions on Neural Network,* vol. 4, no. 5, pp. 740–747, 1993.

101. J. Sietsma and R. Dow, "Creating artificial neural networks that generalize," *Neural Networks,* vol. 4, pp. 67–79, 1991.

102. M. Hagiwara, "A simple and effective method for removal of hidden units and weights," *Neurocomputing,* vol. 6, pp. 207–218, 1994.

103. E. D. Karnin, "A simple procedure for pruning back-propagation trained neural networks," *IEEE Transactions on Neural Networks,* vol. 1, pp. 239–242, 1990.

104. C. C. Teng and B. W. Wah, "Automated learning for reducing the configuration of a feedforward neural network," *IEEE Transactions on Neural Networks,* vol. 7, pp. 1072–1085, 1996.

105. M. Ishikawa, "Structural learning with forgetting," *Neural Networks*, vol. 9, pp. 509–521, 1996.

106. S. Yasui, "Convergence suppression and divergence facilitation: Minimum and joint use of hidden units by multiple outputs," *Neural Networks*, vol. 10, pp. 353–367, 1997.

107. S. G. Romaniuk and L. O. Hall, "Divide and conquer neural networks," *Neural Networks*, vol. 6, pp. 1105–1116, 1993.

108. S. E. Fahlman and C. Lebiere, "The cascade-correlation learning architecture," in *Advances in Neural Information Processing Systems*, D. S. Touretzky, ed., pp. 524–532. Los Altos, CA: Morgan-Kaufmann, 1990.

109. Y. Hirose, K. Yamashita, and S. Hijiya, "Back-propagation algorithm which varies the number of hidden units," *Neural Networks*, vol. 4, pp. 61–66, 1991.

110. N. B. Karayiannis, "ALADIN: Algorithms for learning and architecture determination," *IEEE Transactions on Circuits and Systems*, vol. 41, pp. 752–759, 1994.

111. F. Rosenblatt, "The perceptron: A probabilistic model for information storage and organization in the brain," *Psychological Review*, vol. 65, pp. 386–408, 1958.

112. F. Rosenblatt, *Principles of Neurodynamics, Perceptrons and the Theory of Brain Mechanisms*. Washington DC: Spartan Books, 1961.

113. M. Minsky and S. Papert, *Perceptrons: An Introduction to Computational Geometry*. Cambridge, MA: MIT Press, 1969.

114. A. Joshi, N. Ramakrishnan, E. N. Houstis, and J. R. Rice, "On neurobiological, neuro-fuzzy, machine learning, and statistical pattern recognition techniques," *IEEE Transactions on Neural Networks*, vol. 8, pp. 18–31, 1997.

115. T. Kohonen, "An introduction to neural computing," *Neural Networks*, vol. 1, pp. 3–16, 1988.

116. T. Kohonen, "The neural phonetic typewriter," *IEEE Computer*, vol. 21, pp. 11–22, 1988.

117. T. Kohonen, "Analysis of a simple self-organizing process," *Biological Cybernetics*, vol. 44, pp. 135–140, 1982.

118. H. Ritter and K. Schulten, "On the stationary state of Kohonen's self-organizing sensory mapping," *Biological Cybernetics*, vol. 54, pp. 99–106, 1986.

119. E. Tsao, J. C. Bezdek, and N. R. Pal, "Fuzzy Kohonen clustering networks," *Pattern Recognition*, vol. 27, pp. 757–764, 1992.

120. N. R. Pal, J. C. Bezdek, and E. Tsao, "Generalized clustering networks and Kohonen's self-organizing scheme," *IEEE Transactions on Neural Networks*, vol. 4, pp. 549–558, 1993.

121. N. B. Karayiannis and P. I. Pai, "Fuzzy algorithms for learning vector quantization," *IEEE Transactions on Neural Networks*, vol. 7, pp. 1196–1211, 1996.

122. N. B. Karayiannis, J. C. Bezdek, N. R. Pal, R. J. Hathaway, and P. I. Pai, "Repairs to GLVQ: A new family of competitive learning schemes," *IEEE Transactions on Neural Networks*, vol. 7, pp. 1062–1071, 1996.

123. E. Yair, K. Zeger, and A. Gersho, "Competitive learning and soft competition for vector quantizer design," *IEEE Transactions on Signal Processing*, vol. 40, pp. 294–309, 1992.

124. J. Moody and C. J. Darken, "Fast learning in networks of locally-tuned processing units," *Neural Computation*, vol. 1, pp. 281–294, 1989.

125. D. R. Hush, B. Horne, and J. M. Salas, "Error surfaces for multilayer perceptrons," *IEEE Transactions on Systems, Man, and Cybernetics*, vol. 22, pp. 1152–1161, 1993.

126. J. J. Hopfield, "Neural network and physical systems with emergent collective computational abilities," *Proceedings of National Academy of Sciences, USA*, vol. 79, pp. 2554–2558, 1982.

127. J. J. Hopfield, "Neurons with graded response have collective computational property like those of two-state neurons," *Proceedings of National Academy of Sciences, USA*, vol. 81, pp. 3088–3092, 1984.

128. G. A. Carpenter and S. Grossberg, "The ART of adaptive pattern recognition by a self organizing neural network," *IEEE Computer*, pp. 77–88, March 1988.

129. G. A. Carpenter and S. Grossberg, "A massively parallel architecture for a self-organising neural pattern recognition machine," *Computer Vision, Graphics and Image Processing*, vol. 37, pp. 54–115, 1987.

130. G. A. Carpenter and S. Grossberg, "ART2: Self-organization of stable category recognition codes for analog input patterns," *Applied Optics*, vol. 26, pp. 4919–4930, 1987.

131. G. A. Carpenter, S. Grossberg, and J. H. Reynolds, "ARTMAP: Supervised real-time learning and classification of nonstationary data by a

self-organizing neural network," *Neural Networks*, vol. 4, pp. 565–588, 1991.

132. S. Mitra and S. K. Pal, "Neuro-fuzzy expert systems: Relevance, features and methodologies," *Journal of the Institute of Electronics and Telecommunications Engineers*, vol. 42, pp. 335–347, 1996.

133. S. K. Pal and.S. Mitra, "Expert systems in soft computing paradigm," in *Fuzzy Logic and Expert System Applications*, C. T. Leondes, ed., vol. 6 of *Neural Network Systems Techniques and Applications*, pp. 211–241. San Diego: Academic Press, 1998.

134. R. R. Yager, "Modeling and formulating fuzzy knowledge bases using neural networks," *Neural Networks*, vol. 7, pp. 1273–1283, 1994.

135. Y. Hayashi and J. J. Buckley, "Approximations between fuzzy expert systems and neural networks," *International Journal of Approximate Reasoning*, vol. 10, pp. 63–73, 1994.

136. J. C. Bezdek, "On the relationship between neural networks, pattern recognition and intelligence," *International Journal of Approximate Reasoning*, vol. 6, pp. 85–107, 1992.

137. *Proc. of IEEE International Conference on Fuzzy Systems (FUZZ-IEEE)* (USA), September 1996.

138. Y. H. Pao, *Adaptive Pattern Recognition and Neural Networks*. Reading, MA: Addison-Wesley, 1989.

139. M. M. Gupta and D. H. Rao, "On the principles of fuzzy neural networks," *Fuzzy Sets and Systems*, vol. 61, pp. 1–18, 1994.

140. J. J. Buckley and Y. Hayashi, "Fuzzy neural networks: A survey," *Fuzzy Sets and Systems*, vol. 66, pp. 1–13, 1994.

141. C. T. Lin and C. S. George Lee, *Neural Fuzzy Systems–A Neuro-Fuzzy Synergism to Intelligent Systems*. Englewood Cliffs, NJ: Prentice-Hall, 1996.

142. B. Kosko, *Neural Networks and Fuzzy Systems*. New Jersey: Prentice Hall, 1991.

143. N. Kasabov, *Foundations of Neural Networks, Fuzzy Systems and Knowledge Engineering*. Cambridge, MA: MIT Press, 1996.

144. S. Mitra, *Neuro-Fuzzy Models for Classification and Rule Generation*. PhD thesis, Indian Statistical Institute, Calcutta, India, 1995.

145. S. C. Lee and E. T. Lee, "Fuzzy neural networks," *Mathematical Biosciences*, vol. 23, pp. 151–177, 1975.

146. S. K. Pal and S. Mitra, "Multi-layer perceptron, fuzzy sets and classification," *IEEE Transactions on Neural Networks*, vol. 3, pp. 683–697, 1992.

147. J. M. Keller and H. Tahani, "Implementation of conjunctive and disjunctive fuzzy logic rules with neural networks," *International Journal of Approximate Reasoning*, vol. 6, pp. 221–240, 1992.

148. J. M. Keller, R. R. Yager, and H. Tahani, "Neural network implementation of fuzzy logic," *Fuzzy Sets and Systems*, vol. 45, pp. 1–12, 1992.

149. S. K. Pal and A. Ghosh, "Neuro-fuzzy computing for image processing and pattern recognition," *International Journal of Systems Science*, vol. 27, pp. 1179–1193, 1996.

150. J. K. Keller and D. J. Hunt, "Incorporating fuzzy membership functions into the perceptron algorithm," *IEEE Transactions on Pattern Analysis and Machine Intelligence*, vol. 7, pp. 693–699, 1985.

151. B. R. Kammerer, "Incorporating uncertainty in neural networks," *International Journal of Pattern Recognition and Artificial Intelligence*, vol. 6, pp. 179–192, 1992.

152. S. Mitra and S. K. Pal, "Self-organizing neural network as a fuzzy classifier," *IEEE Transactions on Systems, Man and Cybernetics*, vol. 24, no. 3, pp. 385–399, 1994.

153. S. Mitra and S. K. Pal, "Fuzzy multi-layer perceptron, inferencing and rule generation," *IEEE Transactions on Neural Networks*, vol. 6, pp. 51–63, 1995.

154. S. Mitra and S. K. Pal, "Fuzzy self organization, inferencing and rule generation," *IEEE Transactions on Systems, Man and Cybernetics, Part A: Systems and Humans*, vol. 26, pp. 608–620, 1996.

155. S. Mitra, "Fuzzy MLP based expert system for medical diagnosis," *Fuzzy Sets and Systems*, vol. 65, pp. 285–296, 1994.

156. S. K. Pal and S. Mitra, "Noisy fingerprint classification using multilayer perceptron with fuzzy geometrical and textural features," *Fuzzy Sets and Systems*, vol. 80, pp. 121–132, 1996.

157. X. Zhi-xing, X. Han-zhong, and N. Xing-bao, "Application of fuzzy neural network to ECG diagnosis," in *Proceedings of IEEE International Conference on Neural Networks*, (Houston, USA), pp. 62–66, 1997.

158. J. N. K. Liu and K. Y. Sin, "Fuzzy neural networks for machine maintenance in mass transit railway systems," *IEEE Transactions on Neural Networks*, vol. 8, pp. 932–941, 1997.

159. J. Chang, G. Han, J. M. Valverde, N. C. Griswold, J. F. Duque-Carrillo, and E. Sanchez-Sinencio, "Cork quality classification system using a unified image processing and fuzzy neural network methodology," *IEEE Transactions on Neural Networks*, vol. 8, pp. 964–974, 1997.

160. A. Senthil Kumar, S. K. Basu, and K. L. Majumdar, "Robust classification of multispectral data using multiple neural networks and fuzzy integral," *IEEE Transactions on Geoscience and Remote Sensing*, vol. 35, pp. 787–790, 1997.

161. C. K. Chak, G. Feng, and M. Palaniswami, "A fuzzy neural network based on hierarchical space partitioning," in *Proceedings of IEEE International Conference on Neural Networks* (Houston, USA), pp. 414–419, 1997.

162. A. Fadzil M. H. and L. C. Choon, "Face recognition system based on neural networks and fuzzy logic," in *Proceedings of IEEE International Conference on Neural Networks* (Houston, USA), pp. 1638–1643, 1997.

163. G. Purushothaman and N. B. Karayiannis, "Quantum neural networks (QNN's): Inherently fuzzy feedforward neural networks," *IEEE Transactions on Neural Networks*, pp. 679–693, 1997.

164. T. L. Huntsberger and P. Ajjimarangsee, "Parallel self-organizing feature maps for unsupervised pattern recognition," *International Journal of General Systems*, vol. 16, pp. 357–372, 1990.

165. J. C. Bezdek, E. C. Tsao, and N. R. Pal, "Fuzzy Kohonen clustering networks," in *Proceedings of 1st IEEE International Conference on Fuzzy Systems* (San Diego, USA), pp. 1035–1043, 1992.

166. H. Takagi and I. Hayashi, "Artificial neural network driven fuzzy reasoning," *International Journal of Approximate Reasoning*, vol. 5, pp. 191–212, 1991.

167. H. Takagi, N. Suzuki, T. Koda, and Y. Kojima, "Neural networks designed on approximate reasoning architecture and their applications," *IEEE Transactions on Neural Networks*, vol. 3, pp. 752–760, 1992.

168. H. Ishibuchi, H. Tanaka, and H. Okada, "Interpolation of fuzzy if-then rules by neural networks," *International Journal of Approximate Reasoning*, vol. 10, pp. 3–27, 1994.

169. S. C. Newton, S. Pemmaraju, and S. Mitra, "Adaptive fuzzy leader clustering of complex data sets in pattern recognition," *IEEE Transactions on Neural Networks*, vol. 3, pp. 794–800, 1992.

170. J. Nie, "Constructing fuzzy model by self-organizing counterpropagation network," *IEEE Transactions on Systems, Man, and Cybernetics*, vol. 25, pp. 963–970, 1995.

171. R. Krishnapuram and J. Lee, "Fuzzy-set-based hierarchical networks for information fusion in computer vision," *Neural Networks*, vol. 5, pp. 335–350, 1992.

172. J. M. Keller, R. Krishnapuram, and F. C. -H. Rhee, "Evidence aggregation networks for fuzzy logic inference," *IEEE Transactions on Neural Networks*, vol. 3, pp. 761–769, 1992.

173. W. Pedrycz, "Neurocomputations in relational systems," *IEEE Transactions on Pattern Analysis and Machine Intelligence*, vol. 13, pp. 289–297, 1991.

174. W. Pedrycz, "Fuzzy neural networks with reference neurons as pattern classifiers," *IEEE Transactions on Neural Networks*, vol. 3, pp. 770–775, 1992.

175. W. Pedrycz, "Fuzzy neural networks and neurocomputations," *Fuzzy Sets and Systems*, vol. 56, no. 1, pp. 1–28, 1993.

176. J. M. Keller, Y. Hayashi, and Z. Chen, "Interpretation of nodes in networks for fuzzy logic," in *Proceedings of 2nd IEEE International Conference on Fuzzy Systems* (San Francisco, USA), pp. 1203–1207, 1993.

177. S. Mitra and S. K. Pal, "Logical operation based fuzzy MLP for classification and rule generation," *Neural Networks*, vol. 7, pp. 353–373, 1994.

178. Y. Hayashi, J. J. Buckley, and E. Czogala, "Fuzzy neural network with fuzzy signals and weights," *International Journal of Intelligent Systems*, vol. 8, no. 4, pp. 527–537, 1993.

179. P. K. Simpson, "Fuzzy min-max neural networks: 1.Classification," *IEEE Transactions on Neural Networks*, vol. 3, pp. 776–786, 1992.

180. P. K. Simpson, "Min-max neural networks: 2.Clustering," *IEEE Transactions on Fuzzy Systems*, vol. 1, pp. 32–45, 1993.

181. G. A. Carpenter, S. Grossberg, and D. B. Rosen, "Fuzzy ART: Fast stable learning and categorization of analog patterns by an adaptive resonance system," *Neural Networks*, vol. 4, pp. 759–771, 1991.

182. G. A. Carpenter, S. Grossberg, N. Markuzon, J. H. Reynolds, and D. B. Rosen, "Fuzzy ARTMAP: a neural network architecture for incremental supervised learning of analog multidimensional maps," *IEEE Transactions on Neural Networks*, vol. 3, pp. 698–713, 1992.

183. A. Baraldi and F. Parmiggiani, "Fuzzy combination of Kohonen's and ART neural network models to detect statistical regularities in a random sequence of multi-valued input patterns," in *Proceedings of IEEE International Conference on Neural Networks* (Houston, USA), pp. 281–286, 1997.

184. M. Figueiredo and F. Gomide, "A neural fuzzy approach for fuzzy system design," in *Proceedings of IEEE International Conference on Neural Networks* (Houston, USA), pp. 420–425, 1997.

185. R. Dogaru, A. T. Murgan, and L. O. Chua, "Do we really need multiplier-based synapses for neuro-fuzzy classifiers?," in *Proceedings of IEEE International Conference on Neural Networks* (Houston, USA), pp. 995–999, 1997.

186. W. Pedrycz and M. H. Smith, "Fuzzy inference networks: An introduction," in *Proceedings of IEEE International Conference on Neural Networks* (Houston, USA), pp. 2342–2346, 1997.

187. A. Ghosh, N. R. Pal, and S. K. Pal, "Self-organization for object extraction using multilayer neural network and fuzziness measures," *IEEE Transactions on Fuzzy Systems*, vol. 1, pp. 54–68, 1993.

188. S. K. Pal and D. Bhandari, "Genetic algorithms with fuzzy fitness function for object extraction using cellular neural networks," *Fuzzy Sets and Systems*, vol. 65, pp. 129–139, 1994.

189. S. K. Pal, J. Basak, and R. K. De, "Fuzzy feature evaluation index and connectionist realization," *Information Sciences*, vol. 105, pp. 173–188, 1998.

190. J. Basak, R. K. De, and S. K. Pal, "Fuzzy feature evaluation index and connectionist realization–II: Theoretical analysis," *Information Sciences*, vol. 111, pp. 1–17, 1998.

191. J. Basak, R. K. De, and S. K. Pal, "Unsupervised feature selection using neuro-fuzzy approach," *Pattern Recognition Letters*, vol. 19, pp. 997–1006, 1998.

192. S. C. Lee and E. T. Lee, "Fuzzy sets and neural networks," *Journal of Cybernetics*, vol. 4, no. 2, pp. 83–103, 1974.

193. T. Yamakawa, E. Uchino, T. Miki, and H. Kusanagi, "A neo fuzzy neuron and its application to system identification and prediction of the system behaviour," in *Proceedings of 2nd International Conference on Fuzzy Logic and Neural Networks, Iizuka* (Japan), pp. 477–483, 1992.

194. W. Pedrycz, "A referential scheme of fuzzy decision making and its neural network structure," *IEEE Transactions on Systems, Man, and Cybernetics*, vol. 21, pp. 1593–1604, 1991.

195. J. J. Buckley and Y. Hayashi, "Numerical relationship between neural networks, continuous functions and fuzzy systems," *Fuzzy Sets and Systems*, vol. 60, no. 1, pp. 1–8, 1993.

196. J. J. Buckley, Y. Hayashi, and E. Czogala, "On the equivalence of neural nets and fuzzy expert systems," *Fuzzy Sets and Systems*, vol. 53, no. 2, pp. 129–134, 1993.

197. J. J. Buckley and Y. Hayashi, "Neural nets can be universal approximators for fuzzy functions," in *Proceedings of IEEE International Conference on Neural Networks* (Houston, USA), pp. 2347–2350, 1997.

198. K. Hornik, M. Stinchcombe, and H. White, "Multilayer feedforward networks are universal approximators," *Neural Networks*, vol. 2, pp. 359–366, 1989.

199. B. Kosko, "Fuzzy systems as universal approximators," *IEEE Transactions on Computers*, vol. 43, pp. 1324–1333, 1994.

200. J. S. R. Jang and C. T. Sun, "Functional equivalence between radial basis function networks and fuzzy inference systems," *IEEE Transactions on Neural Networks*, vol. 4, pp. 156–158, 1992.

201. J. M. Benitez, J. L. Castro, and I. Requena, "Are artificial neural networks black boxes?," *IEEE Transactions on Neural Networks*, vol. 8, pp. 1156–1164, 1997.

202. L. M. Fu, "Knowledge-based connectionism for revising domain theories," *IEEE Transactions on Systems, Man, and Cybernetics*, vol. 23, pp. 173–182, 1993.

203. G. G. Towell and J. W. Shavlik, "Knowledge-based artificial neural networks," *Artificial Intelligence*, vol. 70, pp. 119–165, 1994.

204. L. M. Fu, "Learning capacity and sample complexity on expert networks," *IEEE Transactions on Neural Networks*, vol. 7, pp. 1517–1520, 1996.

205. R. C. Lacher, S. I. Hruska, and D. C. Kuncicky, "Back-propagation learning in expert networks," *IEEE Transactions on Neural Networks*, vol. 3, pp. 62–72, 1992.

206. V. N. Vapnik and A. Y. Chervonenkis, "On the uniform convergence of relative frequencies of events to their probabilities," *Theory Probability Applications*, vol. 16, pp. 264–280, 1971.

207. *Proc. of Third Workshop on Rough Sets and Soft Computing (RSSC'94)*, (San Jose, USA), November 1994.

208. *Proceedings of the Fourth International Conference on Soft Computing (IIZUKA96), Iizuka, Fukuoka* (Japan), October 1996.

209. S. K. Pal and N. R. Pal, "Soft computing: Goals, tools and feasibility," *Journal of the Institute of Electronics and Telecommunications Engineers*, vol. 42, pp. 195–204, 1996.

210. J. S. R. Jang, C. T. Sun, and E. Mizutani, *Neuro-Fuzzy and Soft Computing*. Englewood Cliffs, NJ: Prentice-Hall, 1997.

211. L. A. Zadeh, "Fuzzy logic, neural networks, and soft computing," *Communications of the ACM*, vol. 37, pp. 77–84, 1994.

212. S. K. Pal and P. P. Wang, eds., *Genetic Algorithms for Pattern Recognition*. Boca Raton, FL: CRC Press, 1996.

213. E. S. Gelsema, ed., *Special Issue on Genetic Algorithms, Pattern Recognition Letters*, vol. 16, no. 8. 1995.

214. B. P. Buckles and F. E. Petry, eds., *Genetic Algorithms*. Los Alamitos, CA: IEEE Computer Society Press, 1994.

215. C. A. Murthy and N. Chowdhury, "In search of optimal clusters using genetic algorithms," *Pattern Recognition Letters*, vol. 17, pp. 825–832, 1996.

216. R. Srikanth, R. George, N. Warsi, D. Prabhu, F. E. Petry, and B. P. Buckles, "A variable-length genetic algorithm for clustering and classification," *Pattern Recognition Letters*, vol. 16, pp. 789–800, 1995.

217. F. Z. Brill, D. E. Brown, and W. N. Martin, "Fast genetic selection of features for neural network classifiers," *IEEE Transactions on Neural Networks*, vol. 3, pp. 324–328, 1992.

218. S. Bandyopadhyay, C. A. Murthy, and S. K. Pal, "Pattern classification using genetic algorithms," *Pattern Recognition Letters*, vol. 16, pp. 801–808, 1995.

219. S. Bandyopadhyay and S. K. Pal, "Pattern classification with genetic algorithms: Incorporation of chromosome differentiation," *Pattern Recognition Letters*, vol. 18, pp. 119–131, 1997.

220. S. K. Pal, S. Bandyopadhyay, and C. A. Murthy, "Genetic algorithms for generation of class boundaries," *IEEE Transactions on Systems, Man, and Cybernetics, Part B*, vol. 25, pp. 816–828, 1998.

221. S. Bandyopadhyay, S. K. Pal, and U. Maulik, "Incorporating chromosome differentiation in genetic algorithms," *Information Sciences*, vol. 104, pp. 293–319, 1998.

222. W. Pedrycz, ed., *Fuzzy Evolutionary Computation*. Boston: Kluwer Academic, 1997.

223. H. Ishibuchi, K. Nozaki, N. Yamamoto, and H. Tanaka, "Selecting fuzzy If-Then rules for classification problems using genetic algorithms," *IEEE Transactions on Fuzzy Systems*, vol. 3, pp. 260–270, 1995.

224. K. S. Leung, Y. Leung, L. So, and K. F. Yam, "Rule learning in expert systems using genetic algorithm: 1, Concepts; 2, Empirical studies," in *Proceedings of 2nd International Conference on Fuzzy Logic and Neural Networks, Iizuka* (Japan), pp. 201–208, 1992.

225. A. Homaifar and E. McCormick, "Simultaneous design of membership functions and rule sets for fuzzy controllers using genetic algorithms," *IEEE Transactions on Fuzzy Systems*, vol. 3, pp. 129–139, 1995.

226. H. Shehadeh and R. N. Lea, "A genetic algorithms approach for altering the membership functions in fuzzy logic controllers," in *Proceedings of the North American Fuzzy Logic Processing Society (NAFIPS '92)* (Mexico), pp. 515–523, 1992.

227. S. Mitra, S. K. Pal, and S. Banerjee, "Tuning of class membership using genetic algorithms," in *Proceedings of EUFIT* (Aachen, Germany), pp. 1420–1424, August, 1995.

228. X. Yao, "A review of evolutionary artificial neural networks," *International Journal of Intelligent Systems*, vol. 8, pp. 539–567, 1993.

229. D. B. Fogel, L. J. Fogel, and V. W. Porto, "Evolving neural networks," *Biological Cybernetics*, vol. 63, pp. 487–493, 1990.

230. J. D. Schaffer, R. A. Caruana, and L. J. Eshelman, "Using genetic search to exploit the emergent behavior of neural networks," *Physica D*, vol. 42, pp. 244–248, 1990.

231. S. Saha and J. P. Christensen, "Genetic design of sparse feedforward neural networks," *Information Sciences*, vol. 79, pp. 191–200, 1994.

232. S. K. Pal, D. Bhandari, P. Harish, and M. K. Kundu, "Cellular neural networks, genetic algorithms and object extraction," *Far East Journal of Mathematical Sciences*, vol. 1, pp. 139–155, 1993.

233. H. Muhlenbein, "Limitations of multi-layer perceptron networks–step towards genetic neural networks," *Parallel Computing*, vol. 14, pp. 249–260, 1990.

234. S. Bornholdt and D. Graudenz, "General asymmetric neural networks and structure design by genetic algorithms," *Neural Networks*, vol. 5, pp. 327–334, 1992.

235. S. K. Sin and R. J. P. de Figueiredo, "An evolution-oriented learning algorithm for the optimal interpolative net," *IEEE Transactions on Neural Networks*, vol. 3, pp. 315–323, 1992.

236. D. Whitley, T. Starkweather, and C. Bogart, "Genetic algorithms and neural networks: Optimizing connections and connectivity," *Parallel Computing*, vol. 14, pp. 347–361, 1990.

237. V. Maniezzo, "Genetic evolution of the topology and weight distribution of neural networks," *IEEE Transactions on Neural Networks*, vol. 5, pp. 39–53, 1994.

238. B. A. Whitehead and T. D. Choate, "Cooperative-Competitive genetic evolution of radial basis function centers and widths for time series prediction," *IEEE Transactions on Neural Networks*, vol. 7, pp. 869–880, 1996.

239. P. J. Angeline, G. M. Saunders, and J. B. Pollack, "An evolutionary algorithm that constructs recurrent neural networks," *IEEE Transactions on Neural Networks*, vol. 5, pp. 54–65, 1994.

240. S. K. Pal and D. Bhandari, "Selection of optimum set of weights in a layered network using genetic algorithms," *Information Sciences*, vol. 80, pp. 213–234, 1994.

241. S. K. Pal, S. De, and A. Ghosh, "Designing Hopfield type networks using genetic algorithms and its comparison with simulated annealing," *International Journal of Pattern Recognition and Artificial Intelligence*, vol. 11, pp. 447–461, 1997.

242. W. A. Farag, V. H. Quintana, and G. Lambert-Torres, "Neuro-fuzzy modeling of complex systems using genetic algorithms," in *Proceedings of IEEE International Conference on Neural Networks* (Houston, USA), pp. 444–449, 1997.

243. T. Furuhashi, S. Matsushita, H. Tsutsui, and Y. Uchikawa, "Knowledge extraction from hierarchical fuzzy model obtained by fuzzy neural networks and genetic algorithm," in *Proceedings of IEEE International Conference on Neural Networks* (Houston, USA), pp. 2374–2379, 1997.

244. H. Ishibuchi, M. Nii, and T. Murata, "Linguistic rule extraction from neural networks and genetic-algorithm-based rule selection," in *Proceedings of IEEE International Conference on Neural Networks* (Houston, USA), pp. 2390–2395, 1997.

245. R. J. Machado and A. F. da Rocha, "Evolutive fuzzy neural networks," in *Proceedings of 1st IEEE International Conference on Fuzzy Systems* (San Diego, USA), pp. 493–500, 1992.

246. E. Sanchez, "Genetic algorithms, neural networks and fuzzy logic systems," in *Proceedings of 2nd International Conference on Fuzzy Logic and Neural Networks, Iizuka* (Japan), pp. 17–19, 1992.

247. Y. -Q. Zhang and A. Kandel, *Compensatory Genetic Fuzzy Neural Networks and their Applications*. Singapore: World Scientific, 1998.

248. Z. Pawlak, *Rough Sets, Theoretical Aspects of Reasoning about Data.* Dordrecht: Kluwer Academic, 1991.

249. R. Slowiński, ed., *Intelligent Decision Support, Handbook of Applications and Advances of the Rough Sets Theory.* Dordrecht: Kluwer Academic, 1992.

250. M. Banerjee and S. K. Pal, "Roughness of a fuzzy set," *Information Sciences (Informatics & Computer Science)*, vol. 93, pp. 235–246, 1996.

251. M. Sarkar and B. Yegnanarayana, "Rough-fuzzy set theoretic approach to evaluate the importance of input features in classification," in *Proceedings of IEEE International Conference on Neural Networks* (Houston, USA), pp. 1590–1595, 1997.

252. S. K. Pal and A. Skowron, eds., *Rough-Fuzzy Hybridization: New Trends in Decision Making.* Singapore: Springer Verlag, 1999.

253. S. Mitra, M. Banerjee, and S. K. Pal, "Rough knowledge-based network, fuzziness and classification," *Neural Computing and Applications*, vol. 7, pp. 17–25, 1998.

254. M. Banerjee, S. Mitra, and S. K. Pal, "Rough fuzzy MLP: Knowledge encoding and classification," *IEEE Transactions on Neural Networks*, vol. 9, pp. 1203–1216, 1998.

3

Pattern Classification

3.1 INTRODUCTION

Pattern recognition and pattern classification are cognitive tasks that humans perform more efficiently than machines. Such tasks are intrinsically better suited to methodologies that work in a manner more similar to the way humans think or act. This is quite unlike schemes involving precise mathematical formulation. Theories of ANNs, fuzzy sets and neuro-fuzzy computing have shown great promise in these areas by providing a more natural setting for obtaining approximate solutions of real life ambiguous problems. One may note that pattern recognition has had a seminal influence on the development of all these theories.

In the previous chapter (Section 2.5), we have described different categories of fuzzy–neural integration. This chapter discusses some of the neuro-fuzzy techniques and methodologies in a unified fashion along with their salient features. Here the uncertainty handling capacity of fuzzy sets is mainly combined with the ability of ANNs in generating highly nonlinear decision boundaries. After describing various models for classification and clustering, we provide the experimental results and comparative performance, in detail, for three fuzzy–neural networks (FNNs).

These FNNs are fuzzy multilayer perceptron (MLP) [1], fuzzy logical MLP [2], and fuzzy Kohonen network [3] that incorporate concepts from fuzzy sets at various stages. Unlike conventional systems, these models are capable of handling input available in quantitative and/or linguistic form and in providing output decision in terms of class membership values. The components of the input vector consist of membership values to the overlapping partitions of linguistic properties *low, medium,* and *high* corresponding to each input feature. This provides scope for incorporating linguistic information in both the training and testing phases of the said models and increases their robustness in tackling imprecise or uncertain input specifications. An n-dimensional feature space is decomposed into 3^n overlapping sub-regions corresponding to the three primary properties [4]. This enables the models to utilize more local information of the feature space and is found to be suitable in handling overlapping regions.

During training of the fuzzy MLP [1] and fuzzy logical MLP [2], the backpropagated error has inherently more weight in case of nodes with higher membership values. The contribution of ambiguous or uncertain vectors to the weight correction is automatically reduced. The utility of this approach to model output values may be further appreciated by considering a point lying in a region of overlapping classes in the feature space. In such cases its membership in each of these classes may be nearly equal. Then there is no reason why one should follow the *crisp* approach of classifying this pattern as belonging to the class corresponding to that output neuron with a slightly higher activation, and thereby neglect the smaller yet significant response obtained for the other overlapping class(es).

The fuzzy logical MLP [2, 5, 6] of Section 3.4 incorporates fuzziness additionally at the neuronal level. The backpropagation algorithm is appropriately modified to model the logical operators AND and OR used in place of the conventional weighted sum and sigmoidal function. Various fuzzy implication operators are used to introduce different amounts of interaction during error backpropagation. The relational structures, realized by max–min or min–max and *product–probabilistic sum* operators, introduced into the fuzzy model help in classifying patterns that exhibit a logical structure.

The fuzzy Kohonen network [3] of Section 3.5 functions as a classifier. This serves as an extension to Kohonen's model [7] that is normally used for clustering. A separate testing phase is added to evaluate the performance of the classifier in recognizing a separate set of test patterns, in terms of class membership values. First a set of training data is used by the network to initially self-organize the connection weights and finally *calibrate* the output space. After a number of sweeps through the training set the output space becomes appropriately ordered. An index of disorder is computed to evaluate a measure of this ordering. Calibration refers to the labeling of the neurons, relative to the training pattern classes. A *fuzzy* partitioning of the output space is generated to produce an appropriate topological ordering with fuzzy data. During training, the input vector also includes some contextual information regarding the finite output membership of the pattern to one or more class(es). This technique produces a more efficient modeling in cases where the feature space has overlapping or ill-defined clusters by introducing partial supervision. However, during self-organization, this part of the input vector is assigned a lower weight to allow the linguistic and/or quantitative input properties to dominate.

Results demonstrating the effectiveness of these models both on real life speech recognition problem, where the classes have ill-defined fuzzy boundaries, and synthetic data are provided. Comparison is made with the standard Bayes' classifier, k nearest neighbor (k-NN) classifier and the nonfuzzy versions of the neural networks, and the performance of the fuzzy versions is found to be better. Effects of fuzzification at the input as well as the output of the networks are investigated. The contribution of the *a priori* probabilities of the pattern classes in the error derivative of the backpropagation procedure for weight updating is also demonstrated.

3.2 NEURO-FUZZY MODELS

Here we describe the relevant existing literature on pattern classification, both supervised and unsupervised, sequentially grouped under the various categories of integration mentioned in Section 2.5.1 of Chapter 2. Some of the well-known methods are emphasized.

3.2.1 Incorporating fuzziness in neural net framework

Under this category, Keller and Hunt [8] were the first to suggest a way of incorporating the concept of fuzzy sets in the single layer perceptron for pattern recognition applications. Kwon *et al.* [9] incorporated interval-valued fuzzy sets in a multilayer perceptron. In this section we describe in detail these two models, before mentioning a couple of other methods falling under this category.

3.2.1.1 Method by Keller and Hunt This method [8] fuzzifies the labeled target data for training the perceptron, described in Section 2.4.1 of Chapter 2. Assignment of membership functions to the label vectors is found to provide a good stopping criterion for linearly nonseparable classes (cases where the classical perceptron usually oscillates). In order to modify the perceptron algorithm so that vectors of high uncertainty (membership values close to 0.5) have less influence on the results, it is necessary to modify the weight vector correction step [eqn. (2.36)] that is performed when a vector is misclassified by the current weight vector. In the crisp perceptron, the correction step is $w_j(t+1) = w_j(t) + \varepsilon(d-y)x_j$. In order to incorporate the membership function values, this step is modified to

$$w_j(t+1) = w_j(t) + |\mu_1 - \mu_2|^{m'}\varepsilon(d-y)x_j, \qquad (3.1)$$

where m' is a constant (fuzzifier) and μ_i refers to the membership of the pattern vector in class i. Here the properties $\sum_{i=1}^{l} \mu_i = 1$ and $\mu_i \in [0,1]$ hold. This modification has two main advantages:

- It retains the property of finding a separate hyperplane in a finite number of iterations in the linearly separable case.

- Since $|\mu_1 - \mu_2|^{m'} = 1$ when $\mu_1, \mu_2 \in \{0, 1\}$, the fuzzy perceptron reduces to the crisp perceptron when the membership function values are crisp.

Note that in the totally ambiguous case, when $\mu_1 = \mu_2 = 0.5$, the resulting correction term will be zero since $|\mu_1 - \mu_2| = 0$. The value of m' that is chosen to obtain good results, depends on the method of assigning fuzzy memberships to the sample sets.   ♣

Pal and Mitra [1] incorporated fuzzy concepts at the input and output levels of a multilayer perceptron. The input was encoded by linguistic terms *low, medium,* and *high,* and the output was represented in terms of class membership values. Similar concepts were used by them to develop a fuzzy Kohonen net [3] for classification. (These models are described in detail in Sections 3.3 and 3.5, respectively). Pal and Mitra [10] have also used fuzzy geometric and textural features at the input of an MLP for handling geometrical ambiguity in fingerprint classification. (This is described in detail in Section 4.4 of Chapter 4.)

3.2.1.2 Method by Kwon et al.

Kwon *et al.* [9] have developed another approach for designing a fuzzy MLP with the help of interval-valued fuzzy sets. The input, output and connection weights vectors of the MLP (described in Section 2.4.2 of Chapter 2) are taken to be intervals in this model. Interval arithmetic is applied at each step. The salient features are described here. Let the input vector be denoted as

$\boldsymbol{X}_p^0 = (X_{p1}^0, X_{p2}^0, ...X_{pi}^0, ..., X_{pn}^0)$, where $X_{pi}^0 = [x_{pi}^{0L}, x_{pi}^{0U}], i = 1, ..., n$.

Let the target (desired) output vector be

$\boldsymbol{D}_p = (D_{p1}, D_{p2}, ...D_{pj}, ..., D_{pl})$, where $D_{pj} = [d_{pj}^L, d_{pj}^U], j = 1, ..., l$,

and L, U indicate the lower and upper bounds, respectively of the interval under consideration.

Therefore, the operations at the input $(h = 0)$ and hidden and output layers $(h > 0)$ are denoted respectively as

$$Y_{pi}^h = X_{pi}^h, i = 1, ..., n$$

and

$$Y_{pk}^h = f(X_{pk}^h), k = 1, ..., m^h, \tag{3.2}$$

where

$$X_{pk}^h = \sum_{i=1}^{m_{h-1}} Y_{pi}^{h-1} W_{ki}^{h-1} + \Theta_k^h, k = 1, ..., m^h$$

and m^h indicates the number of hidden nodes in layer h.

The node function is the conventional sigmoid given as $f(x) = 1/[1 + exp(-x)]$. Note that W_{ki}^h, Θ_k^h are intervals. Basic concepts from interval arithmetic such as

$$A + B = [a^L, a^U] + [b^L, b^U] = [a^L + b^L, a^U + b^U] \qquad (3.3)$$

and

$$
\begin{aligned}
A.B &= [a^L, a^U].[b^L, b^U] \\
&= [\min\{a^L b^L, a^L b^U, a^U b^L, a^U b^U\}, \max\{a^L b^L, a^L b^U, a^U b^L, a^U b^U\}]
\end{aligned}
$$
$$(3.4)$$

are applied on the different relations.

The error at the output layer is computed as

$$E_p = \sum_{j=1}^{l} E_{pj} = \sum_{j=1}^{l} (e_{pj}^L + e_{pj}^U), \qquad (3.5)$$

where $e_{pj}^L = (y_{pj}^{HL} - d_{pj}^L)^2/2$, $e_{pj}^U = (y_{pj}^{HU} - d_{pj}^U)^2/2$, and H indicates the output layer.

The backpropagation learning rule is as follows:

$$\triangle w_{ji}^{hL}(t+1) = -\varepsilon \frac{\partial E_p}{\partial w_{ji}^{hL}} + \alpha \triangle w_{ji}^{hL}(t)$$

$$\triangle w_{ji}^{hU}(t+1) = -\varepsilon \frac{\partial E_p}{\partial w_{ji}^{hU}} + \alpha \triangle w_{ji}^{hU}(t), \qquad (3.6)$$

where ε is the learning rate and α is the momentum coefficient.

Some of the characteristic features of interval arithmetic are valid for this interval MLP. For example, for any pair of interval input vectors $\boldsymbol{X}_p^h$ and $\boldsymbol{X}_q^h$ at layer h the following relation holds:

$$X_{pi}^h \subseteq X_{qi}^h, \quad i = 1, 2, \dots, m^h \Rightarrow Y_{pk}^h \subseteq Y_{qk}^h, \quad k = 1, 2, \dots, m^h, \qquad (3.7)$$

where Y_{pk}^h and Y_{qk}^h are the interval outputs from the kth output unit corresponding to the interval input vectors $\boldsymbol{X}_p^h$ and $\boldsymbol{X}_q^h$, respectively. Note that this approach is different from the interval-based method of Hayashi et al. [11] (described under category 3 in Section 3.2.3.3). ♣

A method was also suggested by Kammerer [12] to incorporate known uncertainty of the data in the computational process of neural networks. A measure of certainty is used on each input element in order to modulate the element's contribution to the whole input activity. Some improvements on the classification accuracy have been demonstrated on optical character recognition problems. The technique basically shows an effect of fuzzifying input on the classification accuracy.

Besides the strict embedding of the theory of fuzzy sets and ANNs, as described in the aforesaid models, there are many attempts for pattern classification where these individual tools are used in isolation at different stages of the decision-making process. The recent work of Senthil Kumar *et al.* [13] is of this kind, where the concept of fuzzy integrals (FI) is used for combining the outputs of an ensemble of MLPs for multispectral data classification. As a result, the collective decision of all the networks is less likely to be erroneous than that of any individual network (which may get stuck in local minima). The FI is further employed for integrating original data with its smoothed version. Similarly, for multisource integration the evidence at the classifier level for a set of networks is first combined to obtain a partial evaluation of the class at each source level. Each source also has a different degree of importance in the recognition of each class, which is the percentage accuracy of the classification results with the test data.

The algorithm is validated on three spectral bands B2 (0.52–0.58 μm), B3 (0.62–0.68 μm), and B4 (0.77–0.86 μm) of the IRS-1A multispectral data with ground spatial resolution of 72 m over a scene in the northeastern part of India. From the full scene data (2400 × 2048) pixels, some major classes are identified visually and windows extracted. The window data are then divided into two halves to form the training and test sets.

3.2.2 Designing neural net by fuzzy logic formalism

This category includes designing neural networks to implement fuzzy logic and fuzzy decision making, and to realize membership functions representing fuzzy sets. Here neural networks are used for a variety of computational tasks within the framework of a preexisting fuzzy model (*i.e.*, implementation of fuzzy logic formalism using neural networks). Here we mention the salient features of the various soft versions of the Kohonen's learning vector quantization (LVQ) (Section 2.4.3 of Chapter 2). These include the fuzzy LVQ (FLVQ) [14], generalized LVQ (GLVQ) [15], fuzzy algorithms for LVQ (FALVQ) [16, 17], modified GLVQ (GLVQ-F) [18], and soft competition scheme (SCS) [19]. All these methods incorporate some soft competition scheme in their learning and extend the update neighborhood to all nodes in the network.

SCS is a sequential, deterministic method with learning rates that are partially based on posterior probabilities. In GLVQ, the LVQ objective function is modified so that the winner and nonwinner get different importance, but all of them are updated [15]. A loss function measuring the locally weighted error of the input vector with respect to the winning prototype is minimized. However, the GLVQ can behave erratically for certain scaling of the input data [18]. The GLVQ-F algorithms are designed to alleviate this problem. FLVQ [14] is a batch algorithm whose learning rate is derived from fuzzy memberships. It is a hybridization of the fuzzy *c*-means (FCM) [20] clustering algorithm and the LVQ. Here the update neighborhood is implicitly defined through the use of FCM membership function in the update equations. This algorithm is now described in detail.

Huntsberger and Ajjimarangsee [21] were the first to modify Kohonen network for generating a fuzzy self-organizing feature map by replacing the learning rate of eqn. (2.47) (Chapter 2) with the fuzzy membership value as follows [21]:

$$\mathbf{m}_i(t+1) = \mathbf{m}_i(t) + u_{ki}N_i(t)(\mathbf{x}_k - \mathbf{m}_i(t)), \qquad (3.8)$$

where $\mathbf{m}_i$ is the centroid of the ith cluster, u_{ki} is the fuzzy membership value of the input pattern $\mathbf{x}_k$ in the ith cluster, and $N_i(t)$ is the size of neighborhood. The fuzzy membership value of the input pattern in a cluster depends on the inverse of squared distance between the input pattern and a cluster centroid:

$$u_{ij} = \left(\sum_{k=1}^{c} \left(\frac{d_{ij}}{d_{ik}} \right) \right)^{-1}, \qquad (3.9)$$

where c is the number of clusters and $d_{ij} = (\mathbf{x}_i - \mathbf{m}_j)^T(\mathbf{x}_i - \mathbf{m}_j)$. The algorithm is forced to terminate by just reducing the size of the neighborhood $N_i(t)$ in eqn. (3.8) to zero. Such a modification does not guarantee convergence of the weights.

Bezdek *et al.* fuzzified Kohonen network (KCN), by integrating the fuzzy c-means (FCM) model into its learning rule [14, 22] and generated the FLVQ (or FKCN). They combined the fuzzy membership value and parallel learning of the FCM model with the structure of the Kohonen network. In the conventional Kohonen network, the learning rates and the size of the neighborhoods are heuristically decreased for the convergence of weights. But in the fuzzy Kohonen network (FLVQ), these are controlled by decreasing the value of the weight exponent (fuzzifier) from a certain positive constant larger than one to one. This algorithm guarantees convergence of the weights by minimizing the objective function as in the FCM model. The method requires parallel learning that necessitates storing of the information about input patterns. After the whole set of input patterns is presented, all cluster centroids are updated, requiring a large memory capacity. But it circumvents the problem of the result being dependent on the order of the input data in sequential learning.

The decrease of the fuzzifier, with time, is defined as

$$m_t' = m_0' + \frac{t(m_f' - m_0')}{t_{\max}}, \qquad (3.10)$$

where m_0', m_f' are the initial and final values (respectively) of the fuzzifier ($7 > m_0' > m_f' > 1.1$) and $t_{\max}$ is the iteration limit. The fuzzified learning rate is defined as

$$\alpha_{ik}(t) = (u_{ik}(t))^{m_t'}, \qquad 1 \le i \le c, \qquad (3.11)$$

where $u_{ik}(t)$ is the fuzzy membership value of the input pattern $\mathbf{x}_k$ with respect to the ith cluster at iteration t. When m_t' approaches one, $u_{ik}(t)$ can be zero or one as in the hard c-means (HCM) model. In this limit, the learning rule of the FLVQ becomes the competitive learning rule, with the learning rate in the winning cluster being one and the learning rates in other clusters being zero. The summary of this algorithm is as follows:

1. Fix the number of clusters c. Select $\varepsilon > 0$.

2. Select $t_{\max}$ & $m'_0 > 1$. Initialize cluster centers, $\mathbf{m}_1(0), \mathbf{m}_2(0), \ldots, \mathbf{m}_c(0)$.

3. For $t = 1, 2, \ldots, t_{\max}$.

    a. For $k = 1, 2, \ldots, N$ (the number of input patterns),

        i. Calculate the learning rates from eqns. (3.10)–(3.11), where

$$u_{ik}(t) = \left[\sum_{j=1}^{c} \left(\frac{\|\mathbf{x}_k - \mathbf{m}_i(t-1)\|}{\|\mathbf{x}_k - \mathbf{m}_j(t-1)\|} \right)^{2/m'_t - 1} \right]^{-1}, \quad \text{for } 1 \le i \le c.$$

$$(3.12)$$

        ii. If $k = N$ stop; otherwise, next k.

    b. Update all weights:

$$\mathbf{m}_i(t) = \mathbf{m}_i(t-1) + \frac{\left[\sum_{k=1}^{N} \alpha_{ik}(t)(\mathbf{x}_k - \mathbf{m}_i(t-1)) \right]}{\sum_{k=1}^{N} \alpha_{ik}(t)}. \quad (3.13)$$

    c. Compute

$$E(t) = \|\mathbf{m}(t) - \mathbf{m}(t-1)\|^2. \quad (3.14)$$

    d. If $E(t) \le \varepsilon$ stop; otherwise, next t.

Another neural network architecture that can be used for fuzzy clustering and classification was suggested by Newton et al. [23]. The system uses a control structure similar to that found in adaptive resonance theory (ART) [24]; and employs a learning strategy, similar to that of the fuzzy c-means algorithm, to update the centroid position of the clusters. Functionally the architecture is similar to the leader clustering algorithm.

3.2.3   Changing basic characteristics of neurons

As mentioned under category 3 in Section 2.5.1 of Chapter 2, here the neurons are designed to perform various operations used in fuzzy set theory (like fuzzy union, intersection, aggregation) instead of doing the standard multiplication and addition operations (Fig. 2.9). In this section we elaborate on fuzzy ART [25] based on ART (described in Section 2.4.6 of Chapter 2), fuzzy min–max network [26, 27], and a model by Hayashi et al. [11], besides mentioning a few more models falling under this category.

3.2.3.1 Fuzzy ART   The fuzzy ART [25], designed by Carpenter et al., can cluster analog data because of the replacement of the logical AND operator in ART1 by fuzzy min operator and other modifications. Each category is represented by a hyperbox determined by on-cell/off-cell responses that are similar to min–max points of Simpson's model [26, 27]. This hyperbox can grow only because the weights can only decrease. But the hyperbox can grow only within the bound determined by the vigilance parameter. If the value of the vigilance parameter is low, the size of hyperboxes is large and vice versa. The similarity measure used for vigilance criterion is fuzzy Hamming distance from the edges of the hyperbox. The algorithm is as follows:

1. Initialization:

   a. Weight vector $\mathbf{w}_j \equiv (w_{j1}, ..., w_{jn})$, where initially $w_{ji} = 1$, $1 \le i \le n$ and $1 \le j \le l$.

   b. Choice parameter $\varepsilon > 0$.

   c. Learning rate parameter $\beta \in [0, 1]$.

   d. Vigilance parameter $\rho \in [0, 1]$.

2. Apply new input vector. $\mathbf{x} \equiv (x_1, ...x_n)$, where $x_i \in [0, 1]$.

3. Compute choice function T_j for each input $\mathbf{x}$ and category j:

$$T_j(\mathbf{x}) = \frac{|\mathbf{x} \wedge \mathbf{w}_j|}{\varepsilon + |\mathbf{w}_j|}, \tag{3.15}$$

   where $|\mathbf{a}| = \sum_i |a_i|$ and the fuzzy AND operator $\wedge$ is defined by $(x \wedge y)_i \equiv \min(x_i, y_i)$.

4. Select maximal (best) category J.

$$T_J = \max\{T_j\} \quad \text{for} \quad j = 1, ..., l. \tag{3.16}$$

   (If a tie occurs among T_j terms choose the category with smallest j index.)

5. Compute match function. Is $\frac{|\mathbf{x} \wedge \mathbf{w}_j|}{|\mathbf{x}|} \ge \rho$?

   a. Yes (resonance occurs, learning ensues). Go to step 7.

   b. No (memory search ensues). Go to step 6.

6. Disable best matching category J.

   a. $T_J = -1$ (prevents selection of category J during subsequent search operations).

   b. Go to step 4.

7. Adapt weight vector $\mathbf{w}_J$.

   a. Learning rule:

$$\mathbf{w}_J^{new} = \beta(\mathbf{x} \wedge \mathbf{w}_J^{old}) + (1 - \beta)\mathbf{w}_J^{old} \tag{3.17}$$

   b. Go to step 2.

A high vigilance value leads to narrow generalization with many clusters representing few input patterns. Conversely, a low vigilance value leads to wide generalization with few clusters representing many, perhaps even dissimilar patterns. In a resonance state the weights for the category's prototype may be adjusted by the input pattern $\mathbf{x}$ to incorporate new information, hence the term adaptive resonance. If the input pattern $\mathbf{x}$ fails to match an established category it becomes the model for a new cluster, therefore learning and establishing a new category. This process is repeated for all N input patterns. The number of clusters is dependent on the distance metric and the threshold parameter. Carpenter *et al.* have also developed fuzzy ARTMAP [28], which is a generalization of the supervised binary ARTMAP [29].

3.2.3.2 Fuzzy min–max neural network   A fuzzy min–max classifier [26] and a clustering network [27] that utilize min–max hyperboxes as fuzzy sets (which are aggregated into fuzzy set classes) were introduced by Simpson. The classifier network has a three layered architecture consisting of the input, hidden, and output layers. Each hidden layer neuron represents a hyperbox fuzzy set having two types of connections from the input layer representing the min and max points of the inputs. Learning is a single-pass procedure. It proceeds by placing and adjusting the hyperboxes in pattern space. Initially, the system starts with an empty set of hyperboxes. As each pattern is *taught* to the network, either an existing hyperbox (of the same class) is expanded to include the pattern or a new hyperbox is created to represent it. The latter case arises when one does not have an already existing hyperbox of the same class, or when such a hyperbox exists but cannot expand any further beyond a limit θ set on such expansions. The model is capable of finding reasonable decision boundaries in overlapping classes and for learning highly nonlinear relations. The summary of this algorithm is as follows:

1. Select the threshold of hyperbox $\theta, 0 \leq \theta \leq 1$, and the sensitivity parameter γ, $0 \leq \gamma \leq 1$. Initialize all the min points $(\mathbf{v}_j)$ and the max points $(\mathbf{w}_j)$; $\mathbf{v}_j = (1, ..., 1)$, $\mathbf{w}_j = (0, ..., 0)$.

2. Apply the n-dimensional input pattern $\mathbf{x}$.

3. If there is no committed neuron, assign the input pattern $\mathbf{x}$ as the first category: $\mathbf{v}_j = \mathbf{w}_j = \mathbf{x}$, and go to step 2; otherwise, go to step 4.

4. Calculate the hyperbox membership value

$$b_j(\mathbf{x}, \mathbf{v}_j, \mathbf{w}_j) = \frac{1}{n} \sum_{i=1}^{n} [1 - f(x_i - w_{ij}, \gamma) - f(v_{ij} - x_i, \gamma)], \qquad (3.18)$$

where

$$f(z, \gamma) = \begin{cases} 1, & \text{if } z\gamma > 1, \\ z\gamma, & \text{if } 0 \leq z\gamma \leq 1, \\ 0, & \text{if } z\gamma < 0 \end{cases} \qquad (3.19)$$

for all committed neurons j.

5. Select a winner

$$b_J(\mathbf{x}, \mathbf{v}_J, \mathbf{w}_J) = \max \{b_j (\mathbf{x}, \mathbf{v}_j, \mathbf{w}_j)\}, \qquad (3.20)$$

where j consists of the output neurons which are not temporarily reset.

6. Vigilance test. If

$$\sum_{i=1}^{n} [\max(w_{ij}, x_i) - \min(v_{ij}, x_i)] \leq \theta, \qquad (3.21)$$

go to step 8; otherwise, go to step 7.

7. Reset temporarily the winning neuron. If all committed neurons are reset, activate the first uncommitted neuron, form a new category, and go to step 8; otherwise, go to step 5.

8. Update weights of the winning neuron:

$$\begin{aligned} v_{iJ}^{new} &= \min(v_{iJ}^{old}, x_i), & \forall \, i = 1, ..., n, \\ w_{iJ}^{new} &= \max(w_{iJ}^{old}, x_i), & \forall \, i = 1, ..., n. \end{aligned} \qquad (3.22)$$

9. Overlap test. Determine whether the recent expansion caused any overlap between hyperboxes.

10. Contraction. If there are any overlapping hyperboxes, contract them to eliminate the overlap.

11. Enable reset neurons and go to step 2.

The fuzzy min–max neural network clusters analog data, and does not assume the initial number of clusters. It updates this number in the same manner as in ART1. To find a winner, it does not use the maximum dot product between the input pattern but uses the hyperbox membership function. The category in which the input pattern has the highest degree of membership, becomes a winner. Two parameters are used to tune the performance of this fuzzy–neural network. One is the threshold of hyperbox θ, $0 \leq \theta \leq 1$, that is similar to the vigilance parameter in ART1 and controls the maximum size of the hyperbox. The other is the sensitivity parameter γ, that controls the fuzziness of the cluster membership and regulates how fast the hyperbox membership value decreases when the input pattern is located outside the hyperbox. The larger the value of γ, the more crisp is the value of the hyperbox membership.

3.2.3.3 Model by Hayashi et al. The fuzzy neural network model proposed by Hayashi *et al.* [11] also falls under this category. It is obtained by directly fuzzifying the classical feedforward neural network with one or more layers. All real numbers that characterize a classical neural network become fuzzy numbers in its fuzzified counterpart. These are numbers that characterize inputs to the network, outputs of neurons at hidden layers and the output layer, and weights at all layers. Consider, for example, all numbers relevant to a particular output neuron, ON_k, of a single-layer feedforward neural network. If ON_k is a fuzzy neuron, then the inputs $X_{k0}, X_{k1}, \ldots, X_{kn}$, the weights $W_0, W_1, \ldots, W_n$, and the output Y_k of this neuron are all *fuzzy numbers*.

The output of each neuron is defined as

$$Y_k = f(\sum_{j=0}^{n} W_j X_{kj}), \tag{3.23}$$

where f is a sigmoid function. Since symbols W_j and X_{kj} in (3.23) designate fuzzy numbers, the sum

$$A_k = \sum_{j=0}^{n} W_j X_{kj} \tag{3.24}$$

needs to be calculated by fuzzy arithmetic. The output of the neuron,

$$Y_k = f(A_k), \tag{3.25}$$

is then determined by using the extension principle.

Error function E_p, employed in the backpropagation learning algorithm in a fuzzy neural network with l outputs, for each training sample p, is

$$E_p = \frac{1}{2} \sum_{k=1}^{l} (D_k^p - Y_k^p)^2, \tag{3.26}$$

where D_k^p is the desired output and Y_k^p is the actual output of neuron ON_k for training sample p. Here, again, fuzzy arithmetic is used to calculate E_p. Otherwise, E_p would become exactly the same as its counterpart for classical neural networks.

The stopping criterion for fuzzy neural networks must also be properly fuzzified. Assume that $D_k^p = Y_k^p$ for all k, which represents a perfect match of the actual outputs with the target outputs. Then, assuming that the support of D_k^p (and Y_k^p) is the interval $[d_{k_1}^p, d_{k_2}^p]$, the support of E_p is included in the interval $[-\lambda, \lambda]$, where

$$\lambda = \frac{1}{2} \sum_{k=1}^{l} (d_{k_2}^p - d_{k_1}^p)^2. \tag{3.27}$$

Choosing some number $\varepsilon > 0$ as an acceptable deviation from the value of E_p when $D_k^p = Y_k^p$ for all k, it is reasonable to stop the learning algorithm whenever E_p is included in the interval $[-\lambda - \varepsilon, \lambda + \varepsilon]$.

Finally, we need to fuzzify the backpropagation learning algorithm. One way, proposed by Hayashi et al. [11], is to replace the real numbers in the standard formulas with their fuzzy counterparts and apply fuzzy arithmetic to them. Note that this algorithm is different from that of Kwon *et al.* [9], as mentioned in Section 3.2.1. Kwon *et al.* use a real-valued cost function in eqn. (3.5) that is minimized by the conventional backpropagation algorithm. Hayashi *et al.*, on the other hand, fuzzify the backpropagation learning algorithm based on a fuzzy-valued cost function defined by fuzzy numbers [eqn. (3.27)], in addition to using fuzzy signals and weights represented by triangular fuzzy numbers. ♣

Now let us mention the salient features of some other neuro-fuzzy models that can also be grouped under this category. Pedrycz [30] used logical operators max and min, with *crisp* implication operator and a performance index, for designing two-layered neural nets capable of handling multiclass problems. Application of the model for solving a system of relational equations is demonstrated. The concept of reference neurons at the hidden layer, corresponding to the number of clusters, was introduced [31, 32] to design pattern classifiers. The input to the network consists of the logical combinations of the input variables, and the *Lukasiewicz* implication operator is used. Watanabe *et al.* [33] also used min–max operations but with two kinds of weight vector and a different scheme of backpropagation for a three-layered network.

Another related work in this category is that reported by Krishnapuram and Lee [34]. They used fuzzy aggregation connectives with compensatory behavior (lying in the range between the two extremes, *viz.*, min and max) as the activation functions of the neurons. A modified version of backpropagation is used to determine the proper type of the aggregation at each node and its parameters, given an approximate dependency structure of the network. Various union, intersection, generalized mean, and multiplicative hybrid operators (which are used in fuzzy sets literature to aggregate imprecise information in order to arrive at a decision in uncertain environments) are implemented by the layered networks. The model of Zimmermann and Zysno [35] is used in the hybrid (compensatory) operator. An iterative algorithm to determine the type of aggregation function and its parameters at each node in the network is also provided, thereby making the network more flexible. The approach provides a tool for modeling and managing uncertainty in the process of combination of evidence from complementary and supplementary knowledge sources. The technique also provides a mechanism for selecting powerful features and discarding irrelevant features via the detection of redundancy.

To achieve faster convergence the additive hybrid operator was studied, under the above-mentioned framework, by Keller *et al.* [36] as an alternative connective in such networks. Hirota and Pedrycz [37] designed a three-layer network topology consisting of two types of generic OR and AND neuron. The logical connectives use standard triangular norms for their realization, whereas their compensatory character is achieved by developing some structural relationships between the layers of the network.

Mitra and Pal [2] developed a fuzzy logical MLP by incorporating fuzzy set theoretic concepts at the input, neuronal and output levels. Various fuzzy implication operators were introduced to model different amounts of fuzziness during the backpropagation of error. This algorithm is described in detail in Section 3.4.

3.2.4   Measures of fuzziness as error of network

Integration under this category includes the use of fuzziness or uncertainty measures of a fuzzy set to model the error or instability or energy function of a neural-network-based system. In this context, Ghosh *et al.* [38] developed a self-organized multilayer perceptron for object extraction. The network architecture is basically a feedforward one, with a feedback path. In each layer every neuron corresponds to an image pixel. Each neuron is connected to the corresponding neuron in the previous layer and its neighbors. The status of neurons in the output layer is described as a fuzzy set representing object regions. A fuzziness measure (*e.g.*, index of fuzziness and entropy [39]) of this set is used to quantify system error (instability of the network) and is backpropagated to correct weights. After the weights have been adjusted, the output of the neurons in the output layer is fed back to the corresponding neurons in the input layer. The second pass is then continued with this as input. The iteration (updating of weights) is continued until the network stabilizes–the error value (measure of fuzziness)–becomes negligible. This integration has made a layered network (which is normally used as a supervised classifier) capable of acting as an unsupervised one, in addition to providing robust noise-insensitive segmentation algorithm.

On the basis of a similar concept, Pal and Bhandari [40] developed an object extraction algorithm for noisy images using a cellular neural network. A detailed description of these algorithms is provided in Chapter 5.   ♣

So far we have described various neuro-fuzzy models for classification under supervised and unsupervised modes. In the following sections, we examine some of them in more detail by mentioning their characteristic features, merits, and also demonstrating their effectiveness on synthetic as well as real life data. A comparative study with various related algorithms is also provided. In this regard, we consider a fuzzy MLP [1], a fuzzy logical MLP [2], and a fuzzy Kohonen network [3] in Sections 3.3–3.5. The fuzzy MLP and fuzzy Kohonen network belong to category 1 while the fuzzy logical MLP falls under category 3 of the neuro-fuzzy integration methodologies (Section 2.5.1).

3.3   FUZZY MLP

The fuzzy MLP model of Pal and Mitra [1, 41] incorporates fuzziness at the input and output levels of the MLP (Fig. 2.3, Chapter 2), and is capable

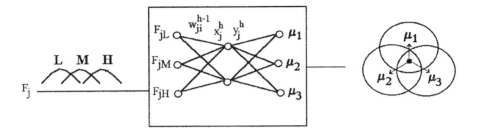

Fig. 3.1 Block diagram of classification phase of fuzzy MLP

of handling exact (numerical) and/or inexact (linguistic) forms of input data. Any input feature value is described in terms of some combination of membership values in the linguistic property sets *low* (L), *medium* (M), and *high* (H). Class membership values (μ) of patterns are represented at the output layer of the fuzzy MLP. During training, the weights are updated by backpropagating errors with respect to these membership values such that the contribution of uncertain vectors is automatically reduced. A schematic diagram depicting the whole procedure is provided in Fig. 3.1. The various phases of the algorithm are described below.

3.3.1 Pattern representation in linguistic form

In conventional statistical designs, the input patterns are quantitatively exact to within the resolution of the sensors used to collect them. However, real processes may also possess imprecise or incomplete input features. The impreciseness (or ambiguity) at the input may arise from various reasons. For example, instrumental error or noise corruption in the experiment for computing a feature, or the high expense incurred in extracting its precise or exact value, may lead (as mentioned in Section 1.4) to such uncertainties. In these cases it may become convenient to use linguistic variables and hedges [39] such as *low, medium, high, very,* and *more or less* to augment or even replace numerical input feature information.

As mentioned in Section 2.2.1 of Chapter 2, a fuzzy set with membership function $\pi(\boldsymbol{r}; \boldsymbol{c}, \lambda)$ represents a set of points clustered around $\boldsymbol{c}$ [eqn. (2.6)]. In the fuzzy MLP, the π function (in the one-dimensional form) is used to assign membership values for the input features. Each input feature F_j (in quantitative and/or linguistic form) can be expressed in terms of membership values to each of the three linguistic properties *low, medium,* and *high.* Therefore an n-dimensional pattern $\boldsymbol{F}_i = [F_{i1}, F_{i2}, \ldots, F_{in}]$ may be represented as a $3n$-dimensional vector [1]

$$
\begin{aligned}
\boldsymbol{F}_i &= \left[\mu_{\text{low}(F_{i1})}(\boldsymbol{F}_i), \mu_{\text{medium}(F_{i1})}(\boldsymbol{F}_i), \mu_{\text{high}(F_{i1})}(\boldsymbol{F}_i), \ldots, \mu_{\text{high}(F_{in})}(\boldsymbol{F}_i)\right] \\
&= \left[x_1^0, \ldots, x_{3n}^0\right],
\end{aligned}
$$

(3.28)

where $x_1^0, \ldots, x_{3n}^0$ refer to the neuronal inputs at the input layer of the MLP (eqn. (2.39) of Chapter 2). Figure 3.2 shows the overlapping structure of the three π functions, representing *low, medium,* and *high* for a particular input feature F_j.

When the input feature F_j is linguistic, its membership values for the π sets *low, medium,* and *high* are quantified as [42]

$$
Low \equiv \left\{ \frac{0.95}{L}, \frac{\pi\left(F_j\left(\frac{0.95}{L}\right); c_{\text{medium}}, \lambda_{\text{medium}}\right)}{M}, \frac{\pi\left(F_j\left(\frac{0.95}{L}\right); c_{\text{high}}, \lambda_{\text{high}}\right)}{H} \right\},
$$

$$
Medium \equiv \left\{ \frac{\pi\left(F_j\left(\frac{0.95}{M}\right); c_{\text{low}}, \lambda_{\text{low}}\right)}{L}, \frac{0.95}{M}, \frac{\pi\left(F_j\left(\frac{0.95}{M}\right); c_{\text{high}}, \lambda_{\text{high}}\right)}{H} \right\},
$$

$$
High \equiv \left\{ \frac{\pi\left(F_j\left(\frac{0.95}{H}\right); c_{\text{low}}, \lambda_{\text{low}}\right)}{L}, \frac{\pi\left(F_j\left(\frac{0.95}{H}\right); c_{\text{medium}}, \lambda_{\text{medium}}\right)}{M}, \frac{0.95}{H} \right\},
$$

(3.29)

where $c_{\text{low}}, \lambda_{\text{low}}, c_{\text{medium}}, \lambda_{\text{medium}}, c_{\text{high}}, \lambda_{\text{high}}$ refer to the centers and radii of the three linguistic properties, and $F_j(0.95/L)$, $F_j(0.95/M)$, $F_j(0.95/H)$ refer to the corresponding feature values F_j at which the three linguistic properties attain membership values of 0.95. (Note that the membership value is heuristically considered here to be 0.95 instead of unity when F_j is identified as *low, medium,* or *high.* Since the concept is fuzzy, the notion of strict containment, *i.e.,* unity membership value, is avoided.)

When F_j is numerical, the π fuzzy set of eqn. (2.6) with appropriate c and λ is used. Hence, in trying to express an input $\boldsymbol{F}_i$ with linguistic properties one effectively divides the dynamic range of each feature into three overlapping partitions, as in Fig. 3.2. The centers and radii of the π functions along each feature axis are determined automatically from the distribution of the training patterns. It should be noted in this context that triangular functions, having properties of eqn. (2.6), can also be used in generating the input features of the network.

The processing at the input layer is summarized in the block diagram in Fig. 3.3. Depending on the numerical or linguistic nature of the input feature F_j, eqn. (2.6) or eqn. (3.29) is used to convert F_j to its three-dimensional form given by eqn. (3.28).

3.3.1.1 Choice of parameters of π functions for numerical features

Let m_j be the mean of the pattern points along the jth axis. Then m_{j_l} and m_{j_h} are defined as the mean (along the jth axis) of the pattern points having co-ordinate values in the range $[F_{j_{\min}}, m_j)$ and $(m_j, F_{j_{\max}}]$ respectively, where $F_{j_{\max}}$ and $F_{j_{\min}}$ denote the upper and lower bounds of the dynamic range of feature F_j (for the training set) considering numerical values only. For the three linguistic property sets, the centers and the corresponding radii are

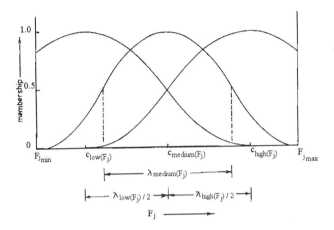

Fig. 3.2   Overlapping structure of π functions

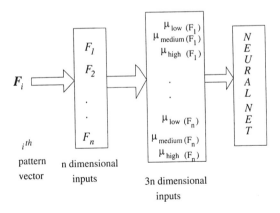

Fig. 3.3   Block diagram of input phase of fuzzy MLP

defined as [42]

$$c_{\text{medium}(F_j)} = m_j$$
$$c_{\text{low}(F_j)} = m_{j_l} \qquad (3.30)$$
$$c_{\text{high}(F_j)} = m_{j_h}$$

and

$$\lambda_{\text{low}(F_j)} = 2\left(c_{\text{medium}(F_j)} - c_{\text{low}(F_j)}\right)$$
$$\lambda_{\text{high}(F_j)} = 2\left(c_{\text{high}(F_j)} - c_{\text{medium}(F_j)}\right)$$
$$\lambda_{\text{medium}(F_j)} = fno *$$
$$\frac{\lambda_{\text{low}(F_j)} * \left(F_{j\max} - c_{\text{medium}(F_j)}\right) + \lambda_{\text{high}(F_j)} * \left(c_{\text{medium}(F_j)} - F_{j\min}\right)}{F_{j\max} - F_{j\min}}$$

$$(3.31)$$

respectively, where fno is a multiplicative parameter controlling the extent of the overlapping. Here we take into account the distribution of the pattern points along each feature axis, while choosing the corresponding centers and radii of the linguistic properties. Besides, the amount of overlap between the three linguistic properties can be different along the different axes, depending on the pattern set.

This combination of choices for the λs and cs automatically ensures that each quantitative input feature value r_j along the jth axis for pattern $\boldsymbol{F}_i$ is assigned membership value combinations in the corresponding three-dimensional linguistic space of eqn. (3.28) in such a way that at least one of $\mu_{\text{low}(F_{ij})}(\boldsymbol{F}_i)$, $\mu_{\text{medium}(F_{ij})}(\boldsymbol{F}_i)$ or $\mu_{\text{high}(F_{ij})}(\boldsymbol{F}_i)$ is greater than 0.5 in the interval $[c_{\text{low}} - (\lambda_{\text{low}}/2), c_{\text{high}} + (\lambda_{\text{high}}/2)]$. Note that this range corresponds to that region of the feature axis that contains the majority of the pattern points and thereby represents the relevant region of the feature space *sans* outliers. This is because the centers and radii of the three π functions, used to represent the input to the neural network, are chosen automatically from the distribution of the training patterns. It also enables one to minimize the effect of those regions of the feature space that are empty. This allows a pattern $\boldsymbol{F}_i$ to have strong membership to at least one of the properties *low, medium,* or *high*.

3.3.2 Class memberships as output vectors

During training, the output nodes of a conventional MLP take on *crisp* two-state values. During testing, a *winner-take-all* mechanism causes the test pattern to be classified as belonging to that class corresponding to the output node with the highest activation.

In real life problems, the data are generally ill-defined with overlapping or fuzzy class boundaries. Each pattern used in training may possess non-zero belongingness to more than one class. To model such data the desired membership values, lying in the range [0,1], are clamped at the output nodes during training. Then the network backpropagates the error(s) with respect to these desired membership value(s) at the output(s). When a separate set of test patterns is presented at the input layer, the output nodes automatically generate the class membership values of the patterns to the corresponding classes. This procedure of assigning *fuzzy* output membership values, instead of the more conventional binary output values, enables the fuzzy MLP to more efficiently classify fuzzy data having overlapping class boundaries.

3.3.2.1 *Class membership function*

Consider an l-class problem domain such that there are l nodes in the output layer. Let the n-dimensional vectors $\boldsymbol{m}_k$ and $\boldsymbol{v}_k$ denote the mean and standard deviation, respectively, of the numerical training data for the kth class. The weighted distance of the training pattern $\boldsymbol{F}_i$ from the kth class is defined as

$$z_{ik} = \sqrt{\sum_{j=1}^{n} \left[\frac{F_{ij} - m_{kj}}{v_{kj}} \right]^2} \quad \text{for } k = 1, \ldots, l, \qquad (3.32)$$

where F_{ij} is the value of the jth component of the ith pattern point and C_k is the kth class. The weight $(1/v_{kj})$ is used to take care of the variance of the classes so that a feature with higher variance has less weight (significance) in characterizing a class. Note that when all the feature values of a class are the same, then the standard deviation will be zero. In that case, one considers $v_{kj} = 1$ such that the weighting coefficient becomes one. This is obvious because any feature occurring with identical magnitudes in all members of a training set is certainly an *important* feature of the set and hence its contribution to the membership function should not be reduced [39].

The membership [39] of the ith pattern to class C_k is defined as

$$\mu_k(\boldsymbol{F}_i) = \frac{1}{1 + \left(\frac{z_{ik}}{f_d} \right)^{f_e}}, \qquad (3.33)$$

where z_{ik} is the weighted distance from eqn. (3.32) and the positive constants f_d and f_e are the denominational and exponential fuzzy generators controlling the amount of fuzziness in this class-membership set (*i.e.*, in the distance set). Obviously $\mu_k(\boldsymbol{F}_i)$ lies in the interval [0,1]. Here eqn. (3.33) is such that the higher the distance of a pattern from a class, the lower is its membership value to that class. It is to be noted that when the distance is zero, the membership value is one (maximum) and when the distance is infinite, the membership value is zero (minimum).

As the training data have fuzzy class separation, a pattern point $\boldsymbol{F}_i$ may correspond to one or more classes in the input feature space. So a pattern point belonging to two classes (say, C_{k_1} and C_{k_2}) corresponds to two *hard* labels in the training data, with $\boldsymbol{F}_i$ tagged to classes C_{k_1} and C_{k_2}, respectively. In other words, there are two or more occurrences of point $\boldsymbol{F}_i$ in the training set such that sometimes it is tagged to class C_{k_1} and sometimes to class C_{k_2}.

In this case F_i is used in computing m_{k_1}, m_{k_2}, v_{k_1}, and v_{k_2} for both C_{k_1} and C_{k_2}. Here the l-dimensional vector z_i has only two nonzero components: z_{ik_1} and z_{ik_2}. However in the *hard* case F_i corresponds to only one *hard* label in the training data, say, C_{k_1}, such that F_i is used in computing m_{k_1} and v_{k_1} only. Note that z_i has l nonzero components in the *fuzziest* case and only one non-zero component in the hard case. In the *fuzziest* case, one can use the fuzzy modifier INT of eqn. (2.8) (Chapter 2) to enhance contrast in class membership. This is needed to increase the contrast within class membership values, *i.e.*, to decrease the ambiguity in making a decision.

When the training input is linguistic, z_{ik} is given as [1]

$$z_{ik} = \sqrt{\sum_{j=1}^{n} \left[\sum_{p=1}^{3} \frac{1}{3} \left(\mu_p(F_{ij}) - \mu_p(m_{kj}) \right)^2 \right]} \text{ for } k = 1, \dots, l. \quad (3.34)$$

Here $\mu_1(F_{ij})$, $\mu_2(F_{ij})$, $\mu_3(F_{ij})$ correspond to the membership values given by eqn. (3.29). $\mu_p(m_{kj})$ corresponds to the $3n$-dimensional representation by eqns. (3.28), (3.30), and (3.31) of the class mean m_k computed using the numerical input values.

3.3.2.2 Desired output

For the ith input pattern, the desired output of the jth output node is defined as

$$d_j = \begin{cases} \mu_{INT(j)}(F_i) & \text{in the } \textit{fuzziest} \text{ case} \\ \mu_j(F_i) & \text{otherwise,} \end{cases} \quad (3.35)$$

where $0 \le d_j \le 1$ for all j. The l output neurons are clamped with the fuzzy output membership values of eqn. (3.35) during training and the error back-propagated for appropriate weight updating by eqn. (2.41) (as described for the MLP in Chapter 2).

During testing the output of the jth output neuron y_j^H, for the test pattern F_t, indicates the inferred membership value of the pattern F_t to the jth class. So the output is generated as a measure of finite belongingness to each class. This is unlike the conventional *crisp* concept of either belonging or not belonging to a class.

3.3.3 Weight updating

For a pattern point lying in a region of overlapping in the feature space, there may be more than one output node with (say) $d_j > 0.5$ indicating appreciable belongingness to more than one pattern class. In the conventional MLP, for such a case, only that node with a slightly higher activation is clamped to state 1 while the others are clamped to state 0. This may result in oscillations on the decision surface separating the pattern classes while training the network, because nearly identical patterns may be clamped to different classes. In such a case, terminating the algorithm at an arbitrary point may or may not yield a *good* weight vector. The pattern vectors that cause the classes to overlap are probably responsible for the oscillatory behavior of the algorithm because these *ambiguous* vectors, although relatively less characteristic of their classes, are given full weight in one class while backpropagating the corresponding errors.

The fuzzy MLP overcomes this problem by assigning the class membership values (desired) to the corresponding output nodes. Thus, for an incorrect output decision, the error to be backpropagated has more weight in case of nodes with higher membership values and hence can induce larger corrections in favor of that class for input data that demands such an adjustment. This is desirable, as points that have a larger belongingness to a particular pattern class and possess less ambiguity should influence positively the positioning of the decision surface separating the pattern classes. Analogously pattern vectors having lower output membership values (closer to 0) that imply a degree of *not belonging* to a class, involve less ambiguity and have a significant impact during weight updating. The contribution of ambiguous or uncertain vectors (*i.e.*, those with output membership close to 0.5) to the weight correction in favor of any particular class is automatically reduced. As the actual output vectors are modified to approximate the corresponding *ambiguous* desired output vectors, it helps to prevent oscillations on the decision surface in such cases and thus enables the model to function efficiently in environments with fuzzy class separation.

The conventional MLP uses a fixed learning rate ε [43]. However, it has been pointed out [44] that there is an *optimal step size region* (*osr*) with the interval $[\varepsilon_{opt} - \delta_l, \varepsilon_{opt} + \delta_r]$ for every problem. For all ε lying in this region, the learning converges reasonably fast and remains stable. One does not know *a priori* where the *osr* is located for a particular problem. The width of the *osr* scales with the absolute value of ε_{opt} [44]. The network size and training set seem to influence the *osr*. To overcome this problem, a technique for heuristically decreasing the learning rate ε is designed.

Classification performance of the network is measured with the mean square error (*mse*) and the cross-entropy (*ce*), which are defined as

$$mse = \left[\sum_{\mathbf{F} \in \, trainset} \sum_{j=1}^{l} \left(d_j - y_j^H \right)^2 \right] / \left(l * |trainset| \right) \tag{3.36}$$

and

$$ce = \frac{\left[\sum_{\mathbf{F} \in \, trainset} \sum_{j=1}^{l} \left\{ -d_j \ln y_j^H - (1 - d_j) \ln(1 - y_j^H) \right\} \right]}{(\ln 2 * l * |trainset|)}. \tag{3.37}$$

Here |*trainset*| refers to the number of input pattern vectors in the training set, and d_j corresponds to the jth desired output component. The closer y_j^H is able to approach d_j, the lower is the value of *ce*. Note that both *mse* and *ce* decrease as y_j^H approaches d_j for all j.

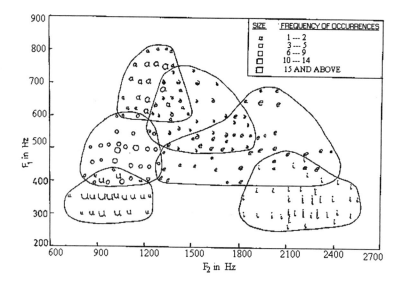

Fig. 3.4   Vowel diagram in F_1–F_2 plane

Let the various values of ε be $\varepsilon_0 = 2, \varepsilon_1 = 1, \ldots, \varepsilon_q = 0.001$ such that ε_i indicates the $(i+1)$th value of ε, taking values from a set $\{2, 1, 0.5, 0.3, 0.1, 0.05, 0.01, 0.005, 0.001\}$. Let $\alpha_0 = 0.9$ and $\alpha_1 = \alpha_2 = \ldots = \alpha_q = 0.5$. Note that α close to zero is avoided because small values of α are unable to prevent unwanted oscillations. Then [1]

$$i = \begin{cases} i+1 & \text{if } mse(nt - kn) - mse(nt) < \delta \\ & \text{or } ce(nt - kn) - ce(nt) < \delta \\ i & \text{otherwise,} \end{cases} \qquad (3.38)$$

where $i = 0$ initially, $|\varepsilon| = q + 1$ and $0 < \delta \leq 10^{-2}$ [1]. Here $mse(nt)$ and $ce(nt)$ denote the mean square error by eqn. (3.36) and cross entropy by eqn. (3.37) respectively at the end of the ntth sweep through the training set; kn is a positive integer such that mse and ce are sampled at intervals of kn sweeps. The process is terminated when $i > q$ and $\varepsilon_q = 0.001$. At this stage the network is said to have converged to a *good* minimum error solution if $90 \leq b \leq 100$, where b is the *best match*. The corresponding value of nt indicates the maximal number of sweeps required in the process. It is to be mentioned that $\Delta mse_j < \Delta mse_i$ and $\Delta ce_j < \Delta ce_i$, when $\varepsilon_j < \varepsilon_i$.

3.3.4   Results

Here we present some results demonstrating the effectiveness of the algorithm on a set of 871 Indian Telugu vowel sounds [45], and three sets of artifi-cially generated patterns involving intractable regions. As a comparison, the

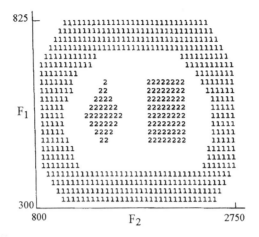

Fig. 3.5 Pattern set *A*

performance of the standard Bayes classifier, the *k* nearest neighbor (*k*-NN) algorithm (having the capability of generating piecewise linear boundaries for the aforesaid three linearly nonseparable pattern sets), and the conventional MLP has been provided on these data sets wherever applicable.

The vowel sounds, collected by trained personnel, were uttered by three male speakers in the age group of 30–35 years, in a *consonant–vowel–consonant* context. The details of the method are available in Refs. [39] and [45]. The data set has three features–F_1, F_2 and F_3–corresponding respectively to the first, second, and third vowel formant frequencies obtained through spectrum analysis of speech data (http://www.isical.ac.in/~sushmita/patterns). The dimension of the input vector in eqn. (3.28) for the fuzzy MLP becomes 9. Note that the boundaries of the classes in the given data set are seen to be ill-defined (fuzzy). Figure 3.4 shows a two-dimensional (2D) projection of the three-dimensional (3D) feature space of the six vowel classes (∂, a, i, u, e, o) in the F_1–F_2 plane, for ease of depiction.

Three sets (*A,B,C*) of artificially generated linearly nonseparable pattern classes involving nonconvex decision regions, are shown in Figs. 3.5–3.7 (http://www.isical.ac.in/~sushmita/patterns). Each of these pattern sets consists of 880 sample points. The input vector is six-dimensional in this case. Note that the region of *no pattern points* has been modeled as the class *none* (*no class*). Moreover, the output vector in this case is nonfuzzy with components $d_j = \{0, 1\}$.

Usually, *fno* = 1 was chosen in eqn. (3.31) to model the general case. This is varied to alter the amount of overlapping between the π functions in order to study the effect of fuzzification at the input (see Table 3.6). Two

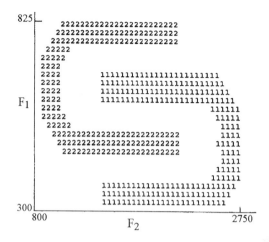

Fig. 3.6 Pattern set B

measures of *percent* correct classification have been used for the training set. The output, after a number of updating, is considered a *perfect match (perf)* if the value of each output neuron y_j^H is within a margin of 0.1 of the desired membership value d_j. This is a *stricter* criterion than the *best match*, where one tests whether the jth neuron output y_j^H (for a particular training pattern) has the highest (or maximum) activation when the jth component d_j of the desired output vector also has the highest value, provided $y_j^H > 0.5$.

3.3.4.1 Vowel data   Figure 3.8 is drawn to illustrate the (crisp) output partitioning capability of the fuzzy MLP with three hidden layers using α-*cuts*. An α-cut of a fuzzy set A is defined as $A_{\alpha'} = \{r | \mu_A(r) \geq \alpha'\}, 1 \geq \alpha' > 0$. The network consists of $m = 10$ nodes in each hidden layer and is trained using $perc = 50\%$ of the samples. Results shown here correspond to $f_d = 5$, $f_e = 1$ [eqn. (3.33)], and $kn = 10$, $\delta = 0.0001$ [eqn. (3.38)]. A pattern with output membership value $y_j^H > \alpha'(= 0.5)$ is plotted as a member of class j. The $l = 6$ vowel classes are labeled by their corresponding class numbers. Figure 3.8(*a*) depicts the resultant output map (class boundaries) over the entire pattern set (both training and testing data) in the two-dimensional formant frequency space showing the fuzzy overlapping, as expected. In Fig. 3.8(*b*), the training samples for each class are superimposed on the generated partitions to demonstrate their generalization capability and impact on the classification performance of the model. Note that the topological ordering of the vowel classes with respect to each other and the amount of overlapping between them bear much similarity to the actual partitioning illustrated in Fig. 3.4. This shows that the fuzzy MLP helps to satisfactorily preserve the structure of ambiguous (fuzzy) classes.

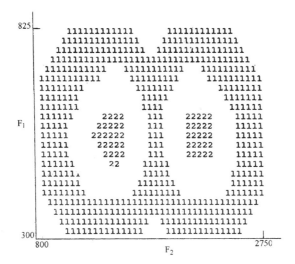

Fig. 3.7   Pattern set C

Figure 3.9 illustrates the variation of the best match b and perfect match p performance (denoted by solid curves) and the mean square error mse (plotted using a dotted curve) with the number of sweeps over the training set. A five-layered network with $perc = 50\%$ and $m = 10$ nodes in each hidden layer is used. The solid points along the curves mark the sweep number at which the learning rate ε_i is changed to ε_{i+1} by eqn. (3.38). It is observed that initially high ε and α are necessary to cause fast weight updating in roughly the right direction without getting stuck at undesirable local minima. As the weight vectors approach a "correct" orientation, improvement in b, p, and mse becomes slower, as indicated by the flatter nature of the curves for lower ε (for higher iterations and/or sweeps). The need to model finer intermediate output values requires ε to be gradually decreased.

The necessity of modeling a number of intermediate output values in the range [0,1] seems to cause the weight space to have ravines with a corresponding error surface of great complexity, so that there exist a large number of local minima. One typically starts a long way from the minimum error solution, and spends a lot of time oscillating across ravines in the weight space before numerical convergence is attained. A larger ε is initially necessary to cause weight updating along the gradient to occur fast in roughly the right direction without getting stuck at poor local minima. The momentum term with α helps maintain movement along a stable direction, and hence should be high in the early stages to prevent the weights from accidentally attaining large values because of the initially high gradient that may often be in incorrect directions. After several sweeps (varying from 20 to 300, say), when the weight vectors have settled somewhat, ε appears to be too large for the $\triangle w_{ji}^h$

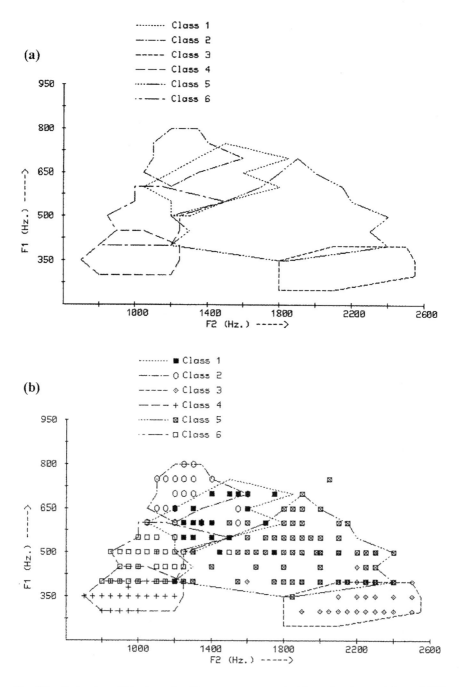

Fig. 3.8 Output partitioning of pattern space generated by a five-layered fuzzy MLP for *vowel* data: (*a*) class boundaries, with (*b*) superimposition of training samples

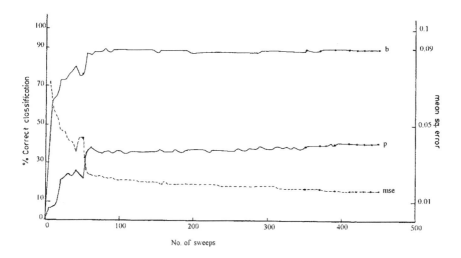

Fig. 3.9 Variation of perfect match (%), best match (%), and mean square error with number of sweeps through the training set for *vowel* data, as learning rate is decreased in discrete steps from 2 to 0.001, for the fuzzy MLP

values to change by the small amount now required to attain the necessary minimum along the more shallow gradient encountered here. The model may oscillate between local minima, as the weights tend to *overshoot* the minimum error solution; at this point ε needs to be decreased. At this time it is preferable to decrease α to speed progress along the most effective direction. This allows more weight to the gradient (now with lower ε) to model finer intermediate output values while also maintaining some damping (via α) to prevent oscillations. It has been observed that one may choose initially $0.6 < \alpha < 1.0$, $1.0 < \varepsilon < 2.5$, and finally $0.2 < \alpha < 0.6$, $0.0001 < \varepsilon \leq 0.1$ for good results.

Table 3.1 compares the average percent correct recognition score t (on the test set using the *best match* criterion, both classwise and overall) of the five-layered fuzzy MLP to that of a conventional MLP, its hard version and the standard Bayes' classifier (described in Section 1.3.3, Chapter 1). The training and test sets each constitute 50% of the pattern data. A comparison of the overall performance, on the training set, between the various neural net model variations is also provided. For this, both the *best match* b and *perfect match* p criteria are used. Here the Bayes classifier for multivariate normal patterns has been used with the *a priori* probabilities $p_i = (|C_i|/N)$, where $|C_i|$ indicates the number of patterns in the ith class and N is the total number of pattern points. The covariance matrices are different for each pattern class. The choice of normal densities for the vowel data has been found to be justified [46]. The MLP and its variations all use three hidden layers with m hidden nodes in each such layer. The first two MLP versions in Table 3.1 use *crisp* binary representation at the output. However in columns

Table 3.1 Comparison of percent correct recognition scores, between Bayes' classifier and various versions of MLP, on *vowel* data

	Bayes' class-ifier	MLP models					
		(a) Conventional		(b) Hard ling. input		(c) Fuzzy version	
		$m = 10$	$m = 20$	$m = 10$	$m = 20$	$m = 10$	$m = 20$
∂	41.6	55.5	44.4	24.4	34.1	51.2	55.5
a	91.1	86.6	88.8	64.4	60.0	84.4	80.0
i	93.0	81.4	81.4	88.8	90.9	81.9	91.5
u	94.7	88.1	90.7	76.2	55.7	86.8	86.6
e	71.1	92.3	86.5	69.7	65.6	92.4	85.9
o	71.1	86.6	85.5	85.9	91.4	89.5	81.3
Net t	79.2	84.6	82.8	72.5	70.2	84.2	83.6
Perf p	–	49.6	43.6	35.3	6.3	55.6	58.1
Best b	–	86.0	87.6	77.7	71.5	92.2	92.2

(a) the actual input features in the n-dimensional feature space are normalized to the range [0,1] and this is termed the *conventional* model. In columns (b) $3n$ linguistic input features with *crisp* values are used such that corresponding to a pattern $\boldsymbol{F}_i$, along the jth axis, the highest of $\mu_{\text{low}(F_{ij})}(\boldsymbol{F}_i)$, $\mu_{\text{medium}(F_{ij})}(\boldsymbol{F}_i)$ and $\mu_{\text{high}(F_{ij})}(\boldsymbol{F}_i)$ of eqn. (3.28) is clamped to 1 while the remaining two are kept clamped at 0. This is referred to as the MLP model with hard linguistic input features. In columns (c) the fuzzy MLP is used.

Although model (a) is found to generate somewhat high recognition scores (%) using *best match*, the outputs in most such *winning* cases were observed to be less than 0.5. This is perhaps an aftereffect of the *crisp* output labeling used for the training data. Hence the output partitioning of the feature space using α-cut value $\alpha' = 0.5$ fails to generate the boundaries for classes ∂ and o (using $m = 20$) and for class o (using $m = 10$). Besides, the other class boundaries are also observed to be not very appropriate. This behavior of models (a) and (b) correspond to the poorer recognition score (%) on the training set using the *perfect match* criterion p. Model (b) is found to have the worst efficiency. It is found to be able to generate all the output partitions, even though distorted in several cases. The *crisp* output labeling in models (a) and (b) is perhaps therefore responsible for the resultant hindrance to *proper* convergence, leading to *poor* output partitioning. However, the fuzzy MLP is found to provide a very satisfactory overall performance. Note also that although models (a) and (c) yield somewhat comparable performance on the test set, the fuzzy MLP [model (c)] has additional advantage of handling linguistic and imprecise/missing inputs.

It is to be noted that a good statistical (Bayes) classifier requires a lot of sequential computation and a large number of reference vectors, while, on the other hand, a neural network is massively parallel and can generalize

Table 3.2 Performance of fuzzy MLP and k-NN classifier on pattern set A

Model	Fuzzy MLP						k-NN classifier			
Layers	3		4		5					
$k =$							1		3	
Perc	10	50	10	50	10	50	10	50	10	50
Nodes m	17	17	19	19	10	10				
Best b (%)	100.	98.7	100.	98.	97.7	95.9				
Perf p (%)	34.5	3.4	81.6	53.6	77.	24.2				
1 (%)	89.3	95.2	93.2	95.6	91.5	98.6	89.6	93.5	88.4	96.1
2 (%)	75.	93.9	71.6	91.8	62.5	93.8	62.5	79.6	58.0	73.4
None (%)	84.5	86.4	82.4	90.7	86.2	82.	72.9	81.5	67.7	86.4
Net t (%)	86.0	91.8	86.9	93.4	86.4	92.	80.5	87.5	77.4	90.0

appreciably well. Incorporation of fuzzy concepts in the neural net further enhances its capability in handling the impreciseness in input patterns and the uncertainty arising from overlapping/ill-defined regions.

Note that only three linguistic terms *low, medium,* and *high* have been used in the input stage of the model. Incorporation of the fuzzy hedges such as *more or less, very* or *nearly* as additional properties might enhance performance of the model, due to the resulting more detailed input description, but then the cost of nodes and interconnections would also increase.

Table 3.3 Performance of fuzzy MLP and k-NN classifier on pattern set B

Model	Fuzzy MLP						k-NN classifier			
Layers	3		4		5					
$k =$							1		3	
Perc	10	50	10	50	10	50	10	50	10	50
Nodes m	11	11	14	14	10	10				
Best b (%)	100.	86.6	100.	99.3	98.9	94.6				
Perf p (%)	62.1	12.1	65.5	69.1	70.1	44.				
1 (%)	78.6	93.7	88.5	96.4	83.1	91.9	74.6	83.0	63.7	83.9
2 (%)	84.	68.	77.7	91.7	74.8	64.9	72.0	83.5	50.3	86.6
None (%)	84.9	84.9	83.9	88.3	86.1	84.	79.4	84.9	71.0	86.6
Net t (%)	83.1	83.4	83.7	91.1	82.8	81.8	76.5	84.1	64.6	85.9

3.3.4.2 Synthetic data (A, B, C) Tables 3.2–3.4 demonstrate the performance of the fuzzy MLP with three and more layers (having m nodes in each hid-

Table 3.4   Performance of fuzzy MLP and k-NN classifier on pattern set C

Model	Fuzzy MLP						k-NN classifier			
Layers	3		4		5					
$k =$							1		3	
Perc	10	50	10	50	10	50	10	50	10	50
Nodes m	13	13	12	12	10	10				
Best b (%)	100.	67.9	100.	97.3	95.4	90.9				
Perf p (%)	32.2	0.	73.6	37.6	67.8	41.5				
1 (%)	83.9	100.	79.7	95.7	80.3	98.4	88.5	89.6	89.1	94.2
2 (%)	84.8	0.	28.2	84.6	28.2	76.9	63.0	88.5	50.0	88.5
None (%)	59.5	0.	62.7	87.1	81.7	69.6	67.7	81.9	57.3	87.7
Net t (%)	75.4	58.9	70.7	92.	77.8	87.	79.7	86.8	75.7	91.6

den layer) trained in the *batch mode* using *perc* = 10 and 50%. The *perfect match p*, *best match b*, and *mean square error* correspond to the training set, while the individual classwise scores for classes 1, 2, and *none*, the *overall score t* and mse_t refer to the test set. Results of the k nearest neighbor (k-NN) classifier (described in Section 1.3.3, Chapter 1), with $k = 1$ and 3, are also included in the said tables. The k-NN classifier is reputed to be able to generate piecewise linear decision boundaries and, thereby, is quite efficient in handling concave and linearly nonseparable pattern classes. Therefore, a comparison of the performance of the fuzzy MLP with that of the k-NN classifier on handling the complex decision regions of the aforesaid three synthetic pattern sets is justified.

Figure 3.10 demonstrates the results of using three-layered conventional MLP (model O') with fixed learning rates $\varepsilon = 2$ (f), 1 (c), 0.5 (d), 0.3 (e), 0.1 (g) and the fuzzy MLP (model O) (b) with $m = 17$ nodes on pattern set A. It is seen that model O (b) had the best overall behavior, although (c), (d), (e) also exhibit satisfactory performance. However, a four-layered version of model O (a) with $m = 19$ converges to a lower final value of mse over a fewer number of sweeps through the training set. But simultaneously this also entails a larger number of weight updates. Note that as reported by Tollenaere [44], the choice of the appropriate value of ε is very problem-dependent. Here lies the utility of choosing adaptive algorithms for varying the learning rate.

Effect of *a priori* class information on backpropagation   It may be noted from Figs. 3.5 and 3.7 that the *a priori* probability of class 2 for pattern sets A and C is very low as compared to that of the other two classes. Therefore the contribution of class 2 pattern vectors toward weight correction of the MLP (positioning of the decision surface) is much smaller relative to that of the other cases. This makes the nonfuzzy model O', with its n-dimensional input space, unable to recognize test patterns from class 2 in case

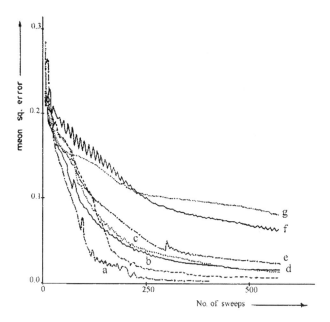

Fig. 3.10 Variation of mean square error with number of sweeps over pattern set A using models O' and O

of pattern sets A and C. This effect of low *a priori* probabilities has also been experimentally studied by Barnard and Botha [47].

An appropriate basis for studying this issue is provided by the theory of Bayes' classifiers. Consider a two-class problem with *a priori* probabilities p_1 and p_2, and class-conditional probability densities $P_1(x)$ and $P_2(x)$, respectively. Then minimal error is obtained by classifying a sample x_p into class 1, if $P_1(x_p) > [P_2(x_p)p_2/p_1]$, and into class 2, otherwise. One immediate implication of this formulation is that it is indeed possible for optimal decision boundaries to completely exclude a class if its *a priori* probability is too low, even if that is not exactly zero.

In order to take into account this fact an error correction term is introduced in eqn. (2.43) of the backpropagation algorithm, such that [48]

$$\frac{\partial E}{\partial y_j} = \left(y_j^H - d_j\right) * l\,(1 - p_j) \quad \text{for } h = H, \tag{3.39}$$

where $p_j = (|C_j|/N)$ is the *a priori* probability of class C_j, $|C_j|$ denotes the number of samples in class C_j and l indicates the number of pattern classes. The correction term ensures that the lower the value of p_j, the higher is its contribution in positioning the decision surface.

Table 3.5 demonstrates the effect of eqn. (3.39) on the backpropagation procedure of the MLP, in improving the performance of the model in case of pattern sets A and C. Note that this modification is effective in case of pattern classes having widely varying *a priori* probabilities. The use of the multiplicative factor serves to counteract the insignificant contribution (to weight correction and, hence, to the positioning of the decision surface) of a pattern class having very few samples.

Table 3.5 Contribution of *a priori* probability on output performance of MLP

Pattern set	A				C			
Nodes m	17				13			
Model	O'	O'_p	O	O_p	O'	O'_p	O	O_p
Best b (%)	73.6	72.5	100.	100.	77.1	86.2	100.	100.
Perfect p (%)	3.5	0.0	34.5	1.2	8.1	5.8	32.2	41.4
Mse	.096	.094	.006	.008	.104	.06	.008	.006
T 1 (%)	97.8	95.9	89.3	87.4	87.1	89.1	83.9	80.9
e 2 (%)	0.0	45.4	75.0	73.8	0.0	40.9	84.8	76.0
s *None* (%)	72.1	57.0	84.5	88.3	51.6	59.8	59.5	69.9
t Overall t (%)	77.5	76.0	86.0	86.2	69.6	73.0	75.4	76.8

Models O'_p and O_p refer respectively to the variations of the three-layered models O' (nonfuzzy) and O (fuzzy) using the contribution of the *a priori* probabilities. Each network uses m hidden nodes with $perc = 10\%$ training samples chosen from each pattern class. Note that the recognition score of class 2 patterns improves radically for both pattern sets A and C in case of model O'_p. The performance on the whole is superior for both the models O'_p and O_p (relative to models O' and O respectively), particularly for pattern set C (involving more complicated decision regions).

In this connection, it is worth mentioning that Qi *et al.* [49] have also proposed a technique for modeling multicenter pattern classes, having grossly unequal pattern points, by computing output membership around cluster centroids with a factor accounting for the number of data in each cluster. However all such information, like the number of vectors (samples) in each cluster, the number of clusters in each class, and the centroid vector, need to be obtained on *a posteriori* basis.

Effect of fuzzification at input   The input feature information is given in the $3n$-dimensional space of eqn. (3.28) in terms of the linguistic property sets *low*, *medium*, and *high*. The π functions representing these properties are defined by the radius λ and center c values given by eqns. (3.30)-(3.31).

Varying $\lambda_{\mathrm{medium}}$, while keeping λ_{low} and λ_{high} of eqn. (3.31) fixed, one can alter the overlapping among the three π functions. As fno is decreased, the radius $\lambda_{\mathrm{medium}}$ decreases around c_{medium} such that ultimately there is insignificant overlapping between the π functions *medium* and *low* or *medium* and *high*. This implies that certain regions along the feature axis F_j go under-

Table 3.6 Effect of varying fuzziness at input for the three-layered fuzzy MLP

$fno =$	0.6	0.7	0.8	0.9	1.0	1.1	1.2	1.3	1.4	1.5
Best b (%)	94.3	98.9	100.	100.	100.	100.	100.	100.	100.	100.
Perf p (%)	21.9	0.0	54.1	18.4	34.5	36.8	17.3	46.0	21.9	19.6
Mse	.039	.019	.006	.008	.006	.006	.007	.005	.008	.012
1 (%)	85.0	90.5	90.8	88.4	89.3	86.7	87.9	86.0	78.9	86.4
2 (%)	75.0	69.3	60.2	67.0	75.0	73.8	57.9	64.7	57.9	54.5
None (%)	69.7	75.9	89.0	86.6	84.5	91.0	83.8	81.7	78.3	69.4
Net *t* (%)	78.3	82.8	86.7	85.3	86.0	86.8	83.1	82.1	76.4	76.6

represented such that $\mu_{\text{low}(F_{ij})}(\mathbf{F}_i)$, $\mu_{\text{medium}(F_{ij})}(\mathbf{F}_i)$ and $\mu_{\text{high}(F_{ij})}(\mathbf{F}_i)$ attain small values. Note that the particular choice of the values of the λs and cs by eqns. (3.30)-(3.31) ensure that for any pattern point $\mathbf{F}_i$ along the jth axis, at least one of $\mu_{\text{low}(F_{ij})}(\mathbf{F}_i)$, $\mu_{\text{medium}(F_{ij})}(\mathbf{F}_i)$ and $\mu_{\text{high}(F_{ij})}(\mathbf{F}_i)$ should be greater than 0.5. On the other hand, as fno is increased the radius λ_{medium} increases around c_{medium} such that the amount of overlapping between the π functions increases.

Table 3.6 demonstrates the performance of the fuzzy MLP with different values of fno on pattern set A. One hidden layer having 17 nodes with $perc = 10\%$ is used to keep uniformity with the results of Table 3.2, where this network configuration yielded a good recognition score. It is observed that the network generates good performance for $0.7 < fno < 1.2$. Very large or very small amounts of overlapping among the linguistic properties of the input feature are found to be undesirable.   ♣

The fuzzy MLP has been used for an industrial application by Chang *et al.* [50] for developing a cork stopper quality classification system. The method involves morphological filtering for feature extraction, followed by classification using the fuzzy MLP. A fully functioning prototype of the system has been built and successfully tested. The human experts in the cork stopper industry rated this classification approach as excellent [50].

3.4   FUZZY LOGICAL MLP

Let us now describe the fuzzy logical MLP [2, 5] used for pattern classification. The model consists of logical neurons employing conjugate pairs of *t-norms* T and *t-conorms* S (described in Section 2.2.4 of Chapter 2) in place of the *weighted sum* and *sigmoid* functions of the conventional MLP. Its input and output vector representations are analogous to those of the fuzzy MLP of Section 3.3. The *backpropagation* algorithm is modified to incorporate the logical operations in the error derivative term.

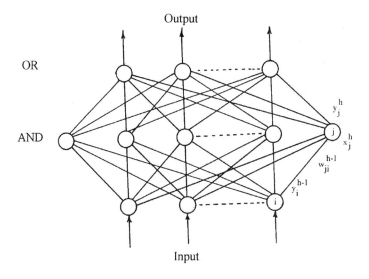

Fig. 3.11   Three-layered logical MLP

3.4.1   The model

Two special cases of the conjugate pair of *t-norm* T and *t-conorm* S, *viz.*, *min–max* and *product probabilistic sum* operators are considered to represent the AND and OR nodes at the hidden and output layers, respectively. The AND nodes in the hidden layer use $T(a, b) = a \wedge b$ while the OR nodes in the output layer use $S(a, b) = a \vee b$.

Let us consider the three-layered model as shown in Fig. 3.11 with $H = 2$, such that there are n_1 and n_2 neurons in the layers $h = 0$ and 1, respectively. The output y_j^1 of the jth neuron in the first layer is defined as

$$y_j^1 = T \left[S \left(y_1^0, w_{j1}^0 \right), \ldots, S \left(y_{n_1}^0, w_{jn_1}^0 \right) \right]. \tag{3.40}$$

Here the input vector is in the $3n$-dimensional space of eqn. (3.28), y_i^0 is the output of neuron i in the input layer, w_{ji}^0 denotes the corresponding connection weight, and $i = 1, \ldots, n_1$. The T operation is performed over all n_1 S operation outputs corresponding to the neurons in the input layer.

Analogously, the output y_k^2 in the second layer is given as

$$y_k^2 = S \left[T \left(y_1^1, w_{k1}^1 \right), \ldots, T \left(y_{n_2}^1, w_{kn_2}^1 \right) \right], \tag{3.41}$$

where y_j^1 (for $j = 1, \ldots, n_2$) is given by eqn. (3.40) and the S operation is performed over all n_2 T-operation outputs corresponding to the neurons in the first layer.

Note that for the *probabilistic sum* operator S^p, the output is computed iteratively as

$$y_k^2 = S_{n-1}^p$$

such that

$$S_{j+1}^p = a_{j+2} + S_j^p - a_{j+2}S_j^p \tag{3.42}$$

for $j = 1, 2, \ldots, n - 2$, where

$$S_1^p = a_1 + a_2 - a_1 a_2$$
$$a_j = y_j^1 w_{kj}^1. \tag{3.43}$$

It is to be mentioned that the pair T^p and S^p (defined in Section 2.2.4) are interactive and their results depend on the values of both the arguments. However the lattice operations T^m and S^m are completely noninteractive. Hence various implication operators of eqns. (2.26) and (2.30)–(2.33), as described in Chapter 2, are used to introduce different amounts of interaction during backpropagation of errors with the T^m and S^m operations.

3.4.2 Backpropagation algorithm based on logical operations

Use of logical operators in place of conventional *weighted sum* and *sigmoid* functions of the MLP necessitates modification of the derivatives involved in the traditional backpropagation scheme. The LMS error E given by eqn. (2.40) (in Chapter 2) is minimized by the gradient descent technique of eqn. (2.41), with the restriction that $0 \le w_{ji}^h \le 1$ for $0 < h \le 2$. This is done by first truncating each weight update $\Delta w_{ji}^h(t)$ so that $0 \le |\Delta w_{ji}^h(t)| \le 0.1$ and then truncating the corresponding w_{ji}^h values. The error derivative $(\partial E/\partial w_{ji})$ is computed as [2]

$$\frac{\partial E}{\partial w_{ji}} = \frac{\partial E}{\partial y_j} \frac{\partial y_j^h}{\partial w_{ji}}. \tag{3.44}$$

For the output layer $(h = H)$ substitute

$$\frac{\partial E}{\partial y_j} = y_j^H - d_j. \tag{3.45}$$

In the case of hidden layer

$$\frac{\partial E}{\partial y_j} = \sum_k \frac{\partial E}{\partial y_k} \frac{\partial y_k^{h+1}}{\partial y_j} = \sum_k (y_k^H - d_k) \frac{\partial y_k^{h+1}}{\partial y_j}, \tag{3.46}$$

where neurons j and k lie in layers h and $h + 1$ respectively.

In order to evaluate the derivative $(\partial y_j^h/\partial w_{ji})$ of eqn. (3.44), for $h > 0$, define

$$sm^h = T\left[S\left(y_1^{h-1}, w_{j1}^{h-1} \right), \ldots, S\left(y_{i-1}^{h-1}, w_{j(i-1)}^{h-1} \right), S\left(y_{i+1}^{h-1}, w_{j(i+1)}^{h-1} \right), \ldots, S\left(y_{n_1}^{h-1}, w_{jn_1}^{h-1} \right) \right]$$

if $h = 1$; and, otherwise

$$sm^h = S\left[T\left(y_1^{h-1}, w_{j1}^{h-1} \right), \ldots, T\left(y_{i-1}^{h-1}, w_{j(i-1)}^{h-1} \right), T\left(y_{i+1}^{h-1}, w_{j(i+1)}^{h-1} \right), \ldots, T\left(y_{n_2}^{h-1}, w_{jn_2}^{h-1} \right) \right], \tag{3.47}$$

where the $T(S)$ operation at layer h is performed over all $l = 1, \ldots, i-1, i+1, \ldots, n_1(n_2)$ $S(T)$ operation outputs from the neurons in the preceding layer $h-1$, provided $l \neq i$, for $h = 1(2)$ respectively; also let

$$sm_i^h = \begin{cases} S\left(y_i^{h-1}, w_{ji}^{h-1}\right) & \text{if } h = 1 \\ T\left(y_i^{h-1}, w_{ji}^{h-1}\right) & \text{otherwise.} \end{cases} \tag{3.48}$$

Using eqns. (3.40)–(3.41) and (3.47)–(3.48), one may write

$$\frac{\partial y_j^h}{\partial w_{ji}} = \begin{cases} \frac{\partial}{\partial w_{ji}} \left[T\left(sm^h, sm_i^h\right)\right] & \text{if } h = 1 \\ \frac{\partial}{\partial w_{ji}} \left[S\left(sm^h, sm_i^h\right)\right] & \text{otherwise,} \end{cases} \tag{3.49}$$

where the *t-norm* T and *t-conorm* S are given either as T^m or T^p in order to model the logical operators AND and OR.

3.4.2.1 The max and min operators Using any of the implication operators from eqns. (2.26), (2.30), (2.31)–(2.33) and eqns. (3.47)-(3.48) in eqn. (3.49), the derivative $(\partial y_j^h / \partial w_{ji})$ for the conjugate pair (T^m, S^m) is computed as [2]

$$\frac{\partial y_j^h}{\partial w_{ji}} = \begin{cases} \|w_{ji}^{h-1} \subset y_i^{h-1}\| * \|sm^h \subset sm_i^h\| & \text{if } h = 2 \\ \|y_i^{h-1} \subset w_{ji}^{h-1}\| * \|sm_i^h \subset sm^h\| & \text{otherwise,} \end{cases} \tag{3.50}$$

where $h > 0$. Similarly, the sensitivity measure $(\partial y_k^h / \partial y_j)$ from the hth layer by eqn. (3.46), for $h = 2$, is evaluated as

$$\frac{\partial y_k^h}{\partial y_j} = \|y_k^{h-1} \subset w_{jk}^{h-1}\| * \|sm^h \subset sm_k^h\|, \tag{3.51}$$

where sm^h and sm_k^h are given by eqns. (3.47)–(3.48) with k substituted for i.

3.4.2.2 The product and probabilistic sum operators For the conjugate pair (T^p, S^p), using eqns. (3.42)–(3.43) and (3.47)–(3.49), we have

$$\frac{\partial y_j^h}{\partial w_{ji}} = \begin{cases} (1 - sm^h)y_i^{h-1} & \text{if } h = 2 \\ sm^h(1 - y_i^{h-1}) & \text{otherwise.} \end{cases} \tag{3.52}$$

Analogously, the sensitivity measure is computed as

$$\frac{\partial y_k^h}{\partial y_j} = (1 - sm^h)w_{jk}^{h-1}. \tag{3.53}$$

Substituting the values of $(\partial y_j^h / \partial w_{ji})$ and $(\partial y_k^h / \partial y_j)$ from eqns. (3.50)–(3.51) or eqns. (3.52)–(3.53), as the case may be, into eqns. (3.44) and (3.46) enables one to evaluate the error derivative $(\partial E / \partial w_{ji})$ of eqn. (2.41) and thereby update the connection weights during training.

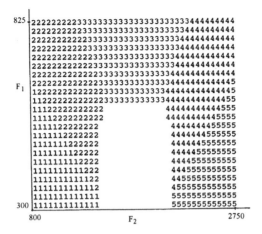

Fig. 3.12   Pattern set D

3.4.3   Results

Here we present some results demonstrating the effectiveness of fuzzy logical MLP on the vowel data (Fig. 3.4) and on two sets of artificially generated patterns D,E (Figs. 3.12 and 3.13). Unless stated otherwise, the experimental conditions are generally the same as described in Section 3.3.4. Each of the two sets (D,E) consists of 880 pattern points in the feature space F_1–F_2. Note that these patterns are considerably simpler than the linearly nonseparable pattern sets A, B, and C of Figs. 3.5–3.7. Pattern set D consists of six classes while the set E is made up of two classes. Like pattern sets A, B, C, the output vector $d_j = \{0,1\}$, *i.e.*, nonfuzzy here.

Since the logical model, based on AND and OR operations, has been developed using a single hidden layer, the implementation reported here refers to three-layered models only. Note that H, L, KDL, KD, and EZ refer to the *crisp, Lukasiewicz, Kleene–Dienes–Lukasiewicz, Kleene–Dienes* and *early Zadeh* operators of eqns. (2.26), (2.30), and (2.31)–(2.33), respectively for the conjugate pair (T^m, S^m). The model P, on the other hand, refers to the logical operators (T^p, S^p). The performance of the fuzzy MLP (with no logical operators) is given under *fuzzy (O)* while the conventional MLP (with inputs in the range [0,1] and *crisp* output decision) is denoted as *nonfuzzy (O′)*.

3.4.3.1   Vowel data   Table 3.7 compares the performance of the fuzzy logical MLP (models P and KDL) and the fuzzy MLP (model O) on the vowel data. To maintain parity between the models, a fuzzy MLP with one hidden layer is chosen. The results in Table 3.7 correspond to $m = 20$ and 22, and $perc = 10\%$. Model O gives good overall performance. Since the other models

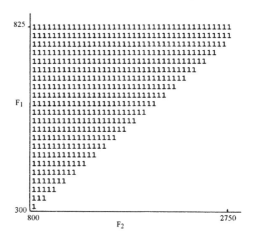

Fig. 3.13   Pattern set E

e.g., H, L, KD, EZ, and O' provided very poor results, their details are not
included here.

Table 3.7   Performance of models KDL, P, and O on *vowel* data

Model		Logical				Fuzzy	
used		P		KDL		O	
Hidden nodes m		20	22	20	22	20	22
Perfect p (%)		3.6	8.3	0.0	0.0	22.4	0.0
Best b (%)		74.2	74.2	20.0	0.0	91.8	87.1
Mse		.036	.031	.077	.084	.011	.027
T	∂ (%)	31.2	24.6	9.3	1.5	44.6	69.8
e	a (%)	76.5	93.8	97.5	96.3	65.4	72.8
s	i (%)	90.2	92.2	96.7	98.7	79.2	81.8
t	u (%)	80.0	93.5	85.9	100.	88.3	85.9
s	e (%)	75.1	62.3	15.8	0.0	75.0	75.0
e	o (%)	86.5	77.9	3.0	0.0	85.7	87.2
t	Overall t (%)	77.8	77.1	48.8	47.3	76.8	80.1

Effect of fuzzification at input and output   Table 3.8 demonstrates
the effect on the performance of the network using a *fully fuzzified* output
representation with $perc = 10\%$. In this case the jth desired output d_j,
as expressed by eqn. (3.35), consists of l nonzero components for an l-class
problem domain. This is unlike the scheme of model O of Table 3.7, which
involves one or more nonzero components corresponding to the training set
samples. Note that the desired fuzzy output vector d of eqn. (3.35) now

becomes dependent on the class means and hence on the training set selected. Therefore, a higher value of the *perfect match p* is more indicative of good performance as compared to the maximum-activation-related *best match b* which is more dependent on the choice of the training patterns. This fully fuzzified output representation is used in Tables 3.8–3.10.

It is observed from Table 3.8 that model KDL fares poorer as compared to model P. This is because of the fact that the max and min operations of KDL cause the different *input-connection weight* combinations to be less interactive, with only the maximum or minimum term(s) controlling the neuronal activation(s). The *product* and *probabilistic sum* operators, which are more *cooperative*, yield better results. For the same reason, if one replaces the logical operator by the original sigmoidal function, the results (shown as model O) improve. The use of logical operators seem to cause deterioration in the classification efficiency of the neural model, perhaps because of the inherent loss of some information. It may also be noted that the generalization ability on the test set for the fully fuzzified version seems to be better in the case of models O and P. The *perfect match* is also found to be significantly higher for the fully fuzzified case of model O.

Table 3.8 Performance of the fully fuzzified logical models on *vowel* data

Model	P			KDL			O		
$m =$	19	20	21	19	20	21	19	20	21
$Perf\,p$ (%)	28.3	34.2	25.9	2.4	1.2	1.2	82.4	70.6	67.1
$Best\,b$ (%)	84.7	78.9	75.3	28.3	18.9	28.3	78.9	82.4	84.7
Mse	.006	.007	.008	.032	.039	.034	.001	.002	.002
T ∂ (%)	66.1	76.8	32.3	46.3	100.	67.6	82.7	85.3	95.1
e a (%)	91.5	46.5	98.8	0.0	0.0	0.0	97.9	99.0	77.4
s i (%)	98.1	100.	89.9	83.5	99.2	55.9	100.	100.	98.4
t u (%)	99.2	65.9	92.1	87.9	69.1	45.4	88.2	99.4	95.9
s e (%)	81.0	85.3	89.9	60.3	40.9	74.2	95.3	92.1	91.9
e o (%)	92.0	91.3	99.3	10.3	0.0	48.9	92.8	100.	95.2
t t (%)	88.1	84.1	90.5	50.1	48.7	52.4	93.7	96.5	92.8

The effect of fuzzification at the input and output using model P (having fully fuzzified output representation), with $perc = 10\%$ and $m = 20$ hidden nodes, is provided in Tables 3.9 and 3.10. The amount of overlapping between the linguistic properties *low, medium,* and *high* has been varied by changing fno in eqn. (3.31). It may be seen from Table 3.9 that, in general, there is no pronounced change in the output performance with variation in input overlapping. However, it is observed that very large amount of overlapping among the linguistic properties of the input feature lead to poorer recognition scores. It is also evident that very small overlapping (for low values of the multiplicative factor fno) sometimes results in poor performance. Note that in Tables 3.8 and 3.9, $f_d = 2$ and $f_e = 2$ for computing the output class membership values by eqn. (3.33), while $fno = 1$ in Tables 3.8 and 3.10.

Table 3.9   Effect of fuzzification at input, with model P, on *vowel* data

$fno =$		0.5	0.6	0.7	0.8	0.9	1.0	1.1	1.2	1.3
Perfect p (%)		10.6	15.3	18.9	22.4	30.6	34.2	34.2	22.4	25.9
Best b (%)		71.8	71.8	75.3	80.0	77.7	78.9	77.7	74.2	75.3
Mse		.011	.011	.009	.009	.008	.007	.008	.01	.009
T	∂ (%)	84.2	74.7	78.9	82.1	73.6	76.8	76.8	77.9	76.8
e	a (%)	34.8	39.5	37.2	55.8	46.5	46.5	55.8	16.2	16.2
s	i (%)	94.2	94.2	98.5	99.2	99.2	100.	100.	98.5	97.8
t	u (%)	69.1	69.1	65.9	65.9	65.9	65.9	82.9	82.9	84.0
s	e (%)	82.4	84.4	91.7	87.3	87.3	85.3	87.3	86.8	87.8
e	o (%)	89.9	86.1	91.3	92.3	91.3	91.3	91.3	90.9	90.9
t	Net t (%)	82.5	81.1	85.2	85.8	84.1	84.1	87.1	84.6	84.7

Table 3.10 demonstrates the variation in performance of model P with different amounts of fuzziness at the output. Here f_d and f_e of eqn. (3.33) are varied. Note that higher values of f_e and lower values of f_d help in enhancing the contrast among the output membership values and generally lead to a higher recognition score. However, excessively high contrast (very low f_d) results in poor performance. Model P of Table 3.10 (with fully fuzzified

Table 3.10   Effect of fuzzification at output, with model P, on *vowel* data

$f_d =$	2			3		4		5		
$f_e =$	1	2	4	2	4	2	4	1	2	4
Perf p (%)	34.2	34.2	25.9	29.5	27.1	55.3	40.0	43.6	60.0	50.6
Best b (%)	69.5	78.9	80.0	83.6	84.7	85.9	70.6	71.8	71.8	61.2
Mse	.006	.007	.014	.008	.01	.005	.007	.004	.004	.006
∂ (%)	66.3	76.8	78.9	77.9	82.1	82.1	67.3	87.3	72.6	54.7
a (%)	51.1	46.5	51.1	0.0	37.2	2.3	72.1	0.0	53.4	65.1
i (%)	99.2	100.	100.	97.1	90.7	93.5	85.0	94.2	97.1	88.5
u (%)	48.9	65.9	82.9	53.2	63.8	52.1	24.4	0.0	1.0	0.0
e (%)	87.3	85.3	84.4	90.7	93.6	93.6	95.6	88.7	92.6	99.5
o (%)	77.0	91.3	90.4	91.3	89.4	93.3	94.7	92.8	93.3	76.5
Net t (%)	77.6	84.1	86.1	81.0	83.9	82.1	80.2	75.2	78.1	72.2

output representation) has good overall performance for $f_d = 2$ with $f_e = 2$ and 4, and $f_d = 3$ with $f_e = 4$ (that correspond to high contrast). It is revealed under investigation that this choice of parameter values enables the membership function curves of the various pattern classes to represent the dynamic range of the given pattern points more suitably. The classwise recognition score in most other cases of f_d–f_e combinations is seen to be rather poor, especially in the cases of classes a and u.

Table 3.11   Performance of models P, O, and O' on pattern set D

Model	Logical P				Fuzzy O	Nonfuzzy O'
Hidden nodes m	10	11	12	13	12	12
Perfect p (%)	1.2	0.0	2.4	7.0	65.2	0.0
Best b (%)	80.3	83.8	88.4	87.2	100.0	98.9
Mse	.046	.042	.039	.038	.004	.017
T 1 (%)	72.3	84.0	85.1	76.6	76.6	95.7
e 2 (%)	91.0	81.4	81.4	84.6	89.1	94.2
s 3 (%)	81.5	84.2	83.5	86.9	96.5	86.3
t 4 (%)	83.8	81.9	83.2	83.2	92.9	80.0
s 5 (%)	83.1	83.1	81.0	83.1	86.3	100.0
e 6 (%)	85.8	84.4	91.9	87.8	91.2	91.2
t Overall (%)	83.7	83.1	84.5	84.2	89.8	90.3

3.4.3.2   *Synthetic data (D,E)*   It is observed from Table 3.11 that the conjugate pair (T^p, S^p) (model P) is capable of modeling the nonlinear decision surface of pattern set D. However the fuzzy MLP O yields an overall better performance for the same number of nodes in the hidden layer. This is especially evident from the high values of *perfect match p* and low values of *mse*. The *nonfuzzy* model O' also provides good recognition scores. Table 3.12 shows that the simple two-class pattern set E can be handled by the neural net models O, O', P, KDL, L, H, KD, and EZ in decreasing orders of performance.

The more interactive logical model P gives the best overall performance on the artificially generated pattern sets as compared to the logical models using the conjugate pair (T^m, S^m). Note that pattern set D cannot be suitably modeled by the latter. However as the decision surface becomes simpler in pattern set E, the less interactive conjugate pair (T^m, S^m) is also able to model the pattern classes using the different implication operators (involving various degrees of interaction among the arguments during error propagation). The fuzzy MLP O (with the more general sigmoidal neurons) is found to yield a slightly superior performance, usually on the training sets. The nonfuzzy MLP O' generally gives a lower value of p and higher value of *mse*, as compared to model O. Otherwise the performance of O' is comparable and sometimes superior to model O. This is perhaps because the given pattern sets can be suitably modeled in the n-dimensional feature space of model O'

and do not require the larger amount of local information available in the 3^n fuzzy subregions generated in the input space of model O.

Table 3.12   Performance of models L, H, KD, EZ, KDL, P, O, and O' on pattern set E

	Logical								O	O'
	(T^m, S^m)						(T^p, S^p)			
	KDL		L	H	KD	EZ	P			
Model	*Min max*	*Min min*	*Min max*				*Prod sum*	*Sum sum*		
Perf (%)	46.6	25.0	46.6	46.6	13.7	0.0	47.8	42.1	70.5	8.0
Best (%)	88.7	88.7	86.4	86.4	76.2	59.1	86.4	89.8	100.	100.
Mse	.081	.096	.08	.082	.091	.146	.062	.077	.011	.014
1 (%)	73.3	73.3	73.3	73.3	73.3	99.5	92.8	84.7	96.5	98.3
2 (%)	78.6	78.6	78.6	78.6	78.6	56.4	84.4	85.8	96.9	100.
Net (%)	75.6	75.7	75.6	75.6	75.6	79.8	88.9	85.2	96.6	99.1

The *Sum-Sum* version for model P in Table 3.12 refers to the case where both layers 1 and 2 use the OR neurons. The *Min–Min* version for model KDL in Table 3.12 refers to the case involving only AND neurons in both the layers. The other logical models use AND neurons in layer 1 followed by OR neurons in layer 2. This AND–OR combination of logical neurons is found to result in a better classificatory performance, compared to the AND–AND architecture. Note that the AND–OR and OR–AND combination of neurons are equivalent in Boolean logic, resulting in expressions in *sum-of-products* and *product-of-sums* forms, respectively.   ♣

During classification the fuzzy MLP has, therefore, been found to perform better than the different fuzzy logical models. Among the logical models used, the *product–probabilistic sum* operators have resulted in higher recognition scores as compared to the *max–min* operators. In this connection, it may be noted that the use of AND and OR neurons in place of the *weighted sum* and *sigmoid* functions of the conventional MLP is expected to decrease the amount of computations required. The hardware implementation of logical neurons might also be easier.

3.5   FUZZY KOHONEN NETWORK FOR CLASSIFICATION

Given the burgeoning interest in fuzzy self-organizing maps [21, 22, 51], it is worth highlighting the major contribution of the fuzzy Kohonen model described by Mitra and Pal [3]. Basically, the Kohonen clustering network is used here as a symbol map. There are phenomena that are inherently fuzzy but are associated with physical manifestations that can be characterized quite precisely by physical measurements. Clustering or classifying solely on the basis of these physical measurements is not useful, however, because meaningful clusters can be constructed only with the assistance of additional factors that cannot be elucidated directly from these physical measurements. Human language, probably at all levels but especially in the area of phonology, is perhaps the best example of such a phenomenon. Thus, while a listener recognizes a phoneme from physical cues alone, exactly which phoneme class a particular conflation of physical features is assigned to by a listener depends on factors that are not inherent in these physical features (*e.g.*, the formant values used here), but that depend on physically extraneous factors such as (in particular but not limited to) the language that the listener assumes is being spoken. There are also, for many reasons, variations among speakers such as are evident in the vowel data used here (Fig. 3.4). Thus, assignment of speech sounds to phonemes yields clusters that are fuzzy at the very least in the sense that different listeners may disagree on what they believe themselves to be hearing and that different speakers may produce different physical manifestations of the same phoneme. The essential properties of phoneme clusters, therefore, must be elucidated by appeal to essentially psycholinguistic experimentation of one kind or another. Now, how can one build a self-organizing network that can perform this same classification? Simply by doing exactly what has been done, which is to replace the arbitrary encoding of the abstract portion of the data vectors with fuzzy class memberships. Note that this violates Ritter and Kohonen's *no information about similarities between the items* condition [52] (p. 247) but it does not matter, because a kind of orthogonality is maintained by the fact that x_a (attribute part) and x_s (symbol part) of the data vectors here are characterized by different *levels* of description (phonetic and phonemic). The value of this approach is manifested in calibration (clustering, labeling) and in classification, since the organized network yields a good fuzzy clustering of the neurons after calibration and functions as an effective fuzzy classifier. Thus, where there is reason to believe that the elements of x_s and x_a relate to each other not so much as purely arbitrary and purely physical (or at least arbitrary, in some sense) but rather as two levels of abstraction, and where there is reason to believe that at least one of the levels (the *higher* one) is fuzzy, the fuzzification of x_s is justifiable and yields excellent results. Attempts at crisp calibration and/or the use of purely arbitrary class labels [as in the pure Ritter–Kohonen approach, where the labels (the semantic concepts) are not connected to each other except through the data vectors they label] in such cases will prove to be fruitless. Note that this does indeed amount to a kind of partial supervision as suggested earlier [3], but it is an extremely interesting kind of partial supervision in that it arises from reasonable assumptions about the nature of human language itself (*i.e.*, its multilingual properties) and not directly from expert intervention (*i.e.*, the learning is guided not by intelligence but by intuition)!

Let us now explain this network [3] which incorporates fuzziness at the input and output levels of the conventional Kohonen network of Fig. 2.4,

Chapter 2. While the traditional Kohonen model was used for clustering purposes, one may note that this fuzzy version has been extended to function as a classifier.

3.5.1 Incorporating class information in input vector

In the traditional (unsupervised) Kohonen network [7, 53], the input vector consists of quantitative information only regarding the patterns. Generally the training patterns, used during self-organization, are also used later for calibrating the output space. This refers to a *hard* labeling of each output neuron by the pattern class corresponding to a training pattern for which it elicits the maximum response.

The input to the fuzzy Kohonen network [3], on the other hand, consists of two portions. The first part encodes the linguistic properties *low, medium,* and *high* (as discussed in Section 3.3.1 with reference to the fuzzy MLP). The second part deals with some contextual information [52] regarding the fuzzy class membership of each pattern.

Since in many real life problems, a pattern may possess finite belongingness to more than one class, such cases are modeled by incorporating some contextual information regarding class membership as part of the input vector. This involves some sort of partial supervision in addition to the associated higher input space dimensionality. However during self-organization this part of the input vector is assigned a lower weight so that the linguistic properties dominate in determining the ordering of the output space. During calibration the contextual class membership information part of the input vector [in *crisp* form as in eqn. (3.56)] is used only for determining the *hard* labeling of the output space. A separate fuzzy partitioning, that allows scope for producing overlapping clusters, is also introduced.

During testing, only the feature information of the patterns is used. The calibrated partition of the neuron eliciting the maximum response for a test pattern is inferred to be its recognized class. The value of the inferred class membership of the test pattern is dependent on the membership of the responding neuron (during calibration) to the appropriate partition.

3.5.1.1 Self-organization As mentioned before, let the pattern $F_i = [x]$, which is a concatenation of the linguistic properties in eqn. (3.28) and the contextual information regarding class membership, be expressed as [3]

$$x = [x', x'']^T = [x', 0]^T \cup [0, x'']^T, \qquad (3.54)$$

where x' contains the linguistic information in the $3n$-dimensional space of eqn. (3.28) and x'' covers the class membership information in an l-dimensional space for an l-class problem domain. So the input vector x lies in an $(3n+l)$-dimensional space. Both x' and x'' are expressed as membership values. The representation of x' has already been discussed in Section 3.3.1 with reference to the fuzzy MLP.

For the ith pattern, x'' is defined as

$$x'' = \begin{cases} s * \left[\mu_{INT(1)}(F_i), \ldots, \mu_{INT(l)}(F_i) \right]^T & \text{in the } fuzziest \text{ case} \\ s * \left[\mu_1(F_i), \ldots, \mu_l(F_i) \right]^T & \text{otherwise,} \end{cases} \qquad (3.55)$$

using eqns. (3.32)–(3.33), where $0 < s \leq 1$ is the scaling factor. This enables a training pattern with membership (say) 0.9 to class C_{k_1} be mapped perhaps to a neuron that is not the same as that to which another training pattern with membership (say) 0.5 to class C_{k_1} or (say) 0.5 to class C_{k_2} is mapped. However, to ensure that the norm of the linguistic part x' predominates over that of the class membership part x'' in eqn. (3.54) during self-organization, one should choose $s < 0.5$.

3.5.1.2 Calibration During calibration of the output space the input vector chosen is $x = [0, x'']$, where x'' is given by eqn. (3.55) such that

$$\mu_q(F_i) = \begin{cases} 1 & \text{if } q = k \\ 0 & \text{otherwise,} \end{cases} \qquad (3.56)$$

for $k \in \{1, \ldots, l\}$ and $s = 1$. The N^2 neuron outputs η_i are calibrated with respect to the l classes. Here the class information of the training patterns is given full weight while the input feature information is suppressed. The resulting *hard* (labeled) partitioning of the output space may be used to qualitatively assess the topological ordering of the pattern classes with respect to the input feature space. A *fuzzy* partitioning of the output space is made by labeling the output neurons with the fuzzy membership values of their output responses. This concept is explained in detail in the next section.

Let us consider the following situation. A pattern having class memberships of (say) 0.52 to class C_{k_1} and 0.48 to class C_{k_2} may be mapped to a neuron i (eliciting maximum response) that is calibrated as belonging to the *hard* partition of class C_{k_1}. However, in the case of *fuzzy* partitioning, this neuron i is calibrated as belonging to both the classes C_{k_1} and C_{k_2}, *albeit* with different membership values.

3.5.2 The algorithm

Consider an $(3n + l)$-dimensional input space with the input vector $x = [x', x'']^T$ of eqn. (3.54) being incident simultaneously on the $N \times N$ array of neurons.

• Concept of r neighborhood. Each neuron $\nu(ii, jj)$ has a topological r neighborhood $N_r(ii, jj)$, as depicted in Fig. 3.14, where ii, jj denote the row and column numbers, respectively, of the neuron. We have

$$N_r(ii, jj) = \{\nu(u, v) | \max \{|u - ii|, |v - jj|\} = r\}, 1 \leq u, v \leq N, \qquad (3.57)$$

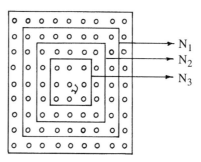

Fig. 3.14   Topological r neighborhoods N_r

where $r = 0, 1, \ldots, 3$. The neighborhood slowly decreases in size over time from $r = 3$ to $r = 1$. Note that the indices ii and jj will be omitted in future reference to avoid clutter.

• Output of a neuron.   The output of the ith neuron of a Kohonen network is computed using eqn. (2.45) of Chapter 2, with the subset S_i of neurons being defined as its r neighborhood N_r. The transformation chosen is

$$\sigma(q) = \left\{ \begin{array}{ll} 0 & \text{if } q < 0, \\ q & \text{otherwise,} \end{array} \right. \tag{3.58}$$

such that $\sigma(q) \geq 0$. Also

$$w_{ki} = \left\{ \begin{array}{ll} b & \text{for } r = 1, \\ -\frac{b}{2} & \text{for } r = 2, \\ 0 & \text{otherwise.} \end{array} \right. \tag{3.59}$$

Here b is the mutual interaction weight such that the lateral coupling w_{ki} has the form of a *Mexican hat (sombrero)*.

3.5.2.1   Weight updating
Let the best match between vectors m_i and x, selected using eqn. (2.46) (as described for the Kohonen network in Chapter 2), occur at neuron c. From eqn. (2.47), the weight updating expression may be stated as

$$m_i(t+1) = \left\{ \begin{array}{ll} m_i(t) + h_{ci} * (x(t) - m_i(t)) & \text{for } i \in N_r, \ r = 0, 1, \ldots, 3 \\ m_i(t) & \text{otherwise,} \end{array} \right. \tag{3.60}$$

where N_r defines an r neighborhood by eqn. (3.57) around neuron c, such that $|h_{ci}|$ is the largest when $i = c$ and gradually decreases to zero with increasing distance from c. Here the gain factor h_{ci} is defined as

$$h_{ci} = \frac{(1 - r * f) * \alpha}{\left[1 + \left(\frac{nt}{cdenom} \right)^2 \right]}, \tag{3.61}$$

where nt is the number of training sweeps currently made, $cdenom$ is a positive constant suitably chosen and $0 < f, \alpha < 1$. The decay of $|h_{ci}|$ with time is controlled by nt. The slowly decreasing radius of the *bell-shaped* function h_{ci} and the corresponding change in $|h_{ci}|$ are controlled by parameters r and f.

3.5.2.2 Index of disorder

An index of disorder D is defined to provide a measure of this ordering. Let msd denote the mean square distance between the input vector and the weight vectors in the r neighborhood of neuron c. Then [3]

$$msd = \frac{1}{|trainset|} \sum_{\boldsymbol{x} \in trainset} \left[\sum_{r=0}^{3} \left\{ \left(\frac{1}{|N_r|} \sum_{i \in N_r} \|\boldsymbol{x} - \boldsymbol{m}_i\|^2 \right) * (1 - r * f) \right\} \right],$$
$$(3.62)$$

where $|trainset|$ refers to the number of input pattern vectors in the training set. This definition ensures that neurons nearer c (smaller r) contribute more towards msd than those farther away. Also

$$f = \begin{cases} \frac{1}{4}, & 0 \le r \le 3 & \text{for } ncnt = 1, \\ \frac{1}{3}, & 0 \le r \le 2 & \text{for } ncnt = 2, \\ \frac{1}{2}, & 0 \le r \le 1 & \text{otherwise.} \end{cases} \qquad (3.63)$$

Here $|N_r|$ denotes the number of neurons in the r neighborhood of neuron c, such that $|N_1| \le 8$, $|N_2| \le 16$ and $|N_3| \le 24$ depending on the position of c in the two-dimensional array. Note that N_0 implies the neuron c itself.

The expression for the index of disorder is given as

$$D = msd(nt - kn) - msd(nt), \qquad (3.64)$$

where $msd(nt)$ denotes the mean square distance by eqn. (3.62) at the end of the ntth sweep through the training set and kn is a suitable positive integer such that D is sampled at intervals of kn sweeps. Initially $ncnt$ is set to 1. Then

$$ncnt = \begin{cases} ncnt + 1 & \text{if } D < \delta, \\ ncnt & \text{otherwise,} \end{cases} \qquad (3.65)$$

where $0 < \delta \le 0.001$. The process is terminated when $ncnt > 3$, so that in eqn. (3.63) one always obtains $r \ge 1$. For good self-organization, the value of msd and therefore D should gradually decrease. Note that r and f of eqns. (3.60)–(3.61), which control $|h_{ci}|$, obey eqn. (3.63). The parameter $ncnt$ of eqn. (3.65), depending on D of eqn. (3.64), controls r and f of eqn. (3.63).

3.5.2.3 Partitioning during calibration

During calibration the input vector $\boldsymbol{x} = [0, \boldsymbol{x}'']$ of eqn. (3.54) is applied to the neural network. Let the $[(i1)_k]$th neuron generate the highest output η_{f_k} for class C_k. Then a membership value for the output of neuron i when calibrated for class C_k can be defined as

$$\mu_k(\eta_i) = \frac{\eta_{i_k}}{\eta_{f_k}} \text{ for } i = 1, \ldots, N^2, \text{ and } k = 1, \ldots, l, \qquad (3.66)$$

such that $0 \leq \mu_k(\eta_i) \leq 1$ and $\mu_k(\eta_i) = 1$ for $i = (i1)_k$.

Each neuron i may be marked by the output class C_k, among all l classes, that elicits the maximal response η_{i_k}. This generates a hard partitioning of the output space that is used in Ritter and Kohonen's model [52].

On the other hand, each neuron i has a finite belonging or output membership $\mu_k(\eta_i)$ to class C_k by eqn. (3.66). The *crisp* boundaries may therefore be generated for the fuzzy partitioning of the output space by considering for each of the l classes the α-cut set $\{i | \mu_k(\eta_i) > \alpha'\}$, $0 < \alpha' \leq 1$, where α' is a suitably chosen value. In the cases where the data are fuzzy and overlapping classes exist, the hard partitioning contains apparent disorder and/or discontinuity. It has been observed that the incorporation of the fuzzy membership concept alleviates this problem.

3.5.2.4 Testing phase

During this phase the input test vector $\boldsymbol{x} = [\boldsymbol{x}', 0]^T$, consisting of only the linguistic information in the $3n$-dimensional space defined by eqn. (3.28), is applied to the network. Let the $(p1)$th and $(p2)$th neurons generate the highest and second highest outputs η_{f_p} and η_{s_p} respectively, for test pattern $\boldsymbol{p}$. Besides, let $\mu_{k_1}(\eta_{f_{pm}})$ and $\mu_{k_2}(\eta_{s_{pm}})$ be the highest and second highest output membership values generated, during testing, with respect to classes C_{k_1} and C_{k_2}, respectively. Note that $k_1 = k_2$ for both choices for pattern points not lying in regions of overlapping classes, and there is no ambiguity of decision in such cases. Define

$$\mu_{k_1}(\eta_{f_{pm}}) = \mu_{k1'}(\eta_{p1}),$$
$$\mu_{k_2}(\eta_{s_{pm}}) = \frac{1}{\eta_{f_p}} \mu_{k2'}(\eta_{p2}) * \eta_{s_p}, \qquad (3.67)$$

and $k_1 = k1'$, $k_2 = k2'$, if $\mu_{k1'}(\eta_{p1}) \geq \frac{1}{\eta_{f_p}} \mu_{k2'}(\eta_{p2}) * \eta_{s_p}$. Otherwise,

$$\mu_{k_1}(\eta_{f_{pm}}) = \frac{1}{\eta_{f_p}} \mu_{k2'}(\eta_{p2}) * \eta_{s_p},$$
$$\mu_{k_2}(\eta_{s_{pm}}) = \mu_{k1'}(\eta_{p1}), \qquad (3.68)$$

such that $k_1 = k2'$ and $k_2 = k1'$. Here $k1'$ and $k2'$ refer to the output classes (hard partitions) $C_{k1'}$ and $C_{k2'}$ that elicited maximal strength responses at the $(p1)$th and $(p2)$th neurons, respectively, during calibration. On the other hand, C_{k_1} and C_{k_2} are dependent both on the actual output responses during testing and the membership values evaluated during calibration with respect to classes $C_{k1'}$ and $C_{k2'}$. The membership values on the right hand side of eqns. (3.67)–(3.68) are defined as

$$\mu_{k1'}(\eta_{p1}) = \frac{\eta_{(p1)_{k1'}}}{\eta_{f_{k1'}}} \qquad (3.69)$$

from eqn. (3.66), where $\eta_{f_{k1'}}$ and $\eta_{(p1)_{k1'}}$ are obtained during calibration for class $C_{k1'}$. Hence pattern $\boldsymbol{p}$ may be classified as belonging to class C_{k_1} with membership μ_{k_1} $\left(\eta_{f_{pm}}\right)$ lying in the interval $[0,1]$, using the first choice and to class C_{k_2} with membership μ_{k_2} $\left(\eta_{s_{pm}}\right)$ using the second choice. One may note that classes C_{k_1} and C_{k_2} are determined from classes $C_{k1'}$ and $C_{k2'}$ by eqns. (3.67)–(3.68).

3.5.3 Results

An experiment for testing the performance of the model for various sizes of two-dimensional arrays of neurons, using the vowel data (Fig. 3.4) and the three sets of linearly nonseparable synthetic data (Figs. 3.5–3.7), has been reported [3]. Some of the results corresponding to $s = 0.2$ in eqn. (3.55), $b = 0.02$ in eqn. (3.59), $\alpha = 0.9$ in eqn. (3.61) and $\delta = 0.0001$ in eqn. (3.65) are provided here.

3.5.3.1 Vowel data Figure 3.15 shows the output map generated for an 10×10 array of neurons with $perc = 15\%$ and $cdenom = 100$ [eqn. (3.61)]. In Fig. 3.15, part (a) corresponds to the hard partitioning obtained by mapping each neuron to the vowel class to which it is most sensitive. The class number k (1 for ∂, 2 for a, 3 for i, 4 for u, 5 for e, 6 for o) marks the neuron eliciting the maximum response η_{f_k} for that class C_k, while the neighboring dot indicates the neuron generating the second highest response. Parts (b)–(d) of the same figure indicate the boundaries for the fuzzy partitioning of the output space by eqn. (3.66) for the three pairs (drawn for the convenience of understanding) of the six classes using $\alpha' = 0.1$. Observe that the topological ordering of the vowel classes in the two-dimensional output space (considering fuzzy partitioning) bears much similarity, including the amount of overlapping, to the original Fig. 3.4 in the two-dimensional feature space.

The hard partitioning illustrates one discontinuous mapping for class 3. However, the incorporation of fuzzy partitioning alleviates this problem and there is overlapping between classes 1,2; 1,5; 2,5; 2,6; 3,5; 4,5; 4,6; and 5,6. This compares favorably with the overlapping observed in the feature space of Fig. 3.4. Note that, unlike in Fig. 3.4, the classes 3 and 4 are seen to be adjacent in part (a) here. This is because there exist no pattern points between these two classes in the input feature space, and in this sense they may be termed *adjacent*. To alleviate this problem, one may model the region of the feature space with *no patterns* as a separate class. This may result in mapping the actual ordering between the classes, along with their interclass spaces, on to the neuronal array.

Table 3.13 compares the recognition score (on test set) of a 10×10 fuzzy Kohonen network (with $perc = 10\%$ and $cdenom = 20$) to that of the Bayes classifier [54, 55] and the standard fully supervised fuzzy approach [45]. The overall performance of the fuzzy Kohonen network is found to be quite satisfactory.

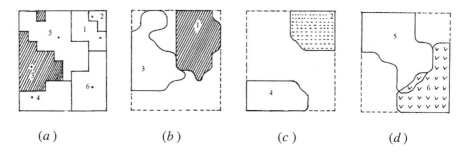

Fig. 3.15 Fuzzy Kohonen model: (*a*) hard and (*b*)–(*d*) fuzzy partitioning for *vowel* data

Table 3.13 Comparative study of the recognition scores of Bayes classifier, standard fuzzy classifier, and fuzzy Kohonen network on *vowel* data

Class	Bayes' classifier	Standard fuzzy classifier	Fuzzy Kohonen net
∂ (%)	44.6	51.4	23.0
a (%)	83.9	81.7	97.5
i (%)	81.9	78.0	74.8
u (%)	88.9	67.6	73.5
e (%)	82.8	77.7	88.7
o (%)	77.7	78.8	92.6
Net (%)	79.6	73.4	79.6

Table 3.14 Recognition scores of fuzzy Kohonen network with *cdenom* = 60 and *perc* = 10% on *vowel* data

Class	First choice	Second choice	Net score
∂ (%)	53.8	7.7	61.5
a (%)	76.5	21.0	97.5
i (%)	79.3	3.9	83.2
u (%)	66.9	13.2	80.1
e (%)	64.7	23.0	87.7
o (%)	90.1	1.9	92.0
Overall (%)	73.5	11.2	84.7

The correct classification rate for a 10×10 network considering both the first and second choices by eqns. (3.67) and (3.68) is illustrated in Table 3.14. Generally the confusion in recognizing a test pattern, considering the first choice, arises only as a result of misclassification as one of the neighboring classes constituting a vowel triangle. This is in agreement with those observed in [39, 45]. Further details on the confusion matrix have been reported by Mitra and Pal [3].

Table 3.15 Recognition scores of the fuzzy and conventional Kohonen network, for various training set sizes, on *vowel* data

Model	Conventional Kohonen net					Fuzzy Kohonen net				
Perc	10	20	30	40	50	10	20	30	40	50
∂ (%)	43.0	44.8	39.2	77.2	80.5	47.7	43.1	43.1	61.3	47.2
a (%)	96.3	65.2	90.4	40.7	0.0	74.0	59.7	47.6	0.0	37.7
i (%)	31.6	26.8	53.7	36.5	34.8	74.8	78.9	57.0	78.8	62.8
u (%)	27.9	44.6	0.0	39.5	31.5	63.9	72.7	49.0	39.5	48.6
e (%)	59.3	83.7	76.5	79.2	77.8	70.0	74.1	91.0	88.0	98.0
o (%)	56.8	79.8	57.9	47.2	92.2	94.4	62.5	95.2	95.3	93.3
Net (%)	50.3	59.8	53.2	53.2	56.5	73.5	68.3	69.4	68.0	71.1

Table 3.15 illustrates a comparison in performance on test set (using first choice) of the fuzzy Kohonen network with the conventional Kohonen network (using fuzzy linguistic feature information x' of eqns. (3.28) and (3.54) only at the input) for various sizes of training data set *perc* (using 10×10 array with *cdenom* = 100). This is to demonstrate the necessity of incorporating the contextual class membership information x'' at the input for modeling fuzzy data. It is observed that the fuzzy Kohonen network has a superior recognition score compared to its more conventional counterpart. An increase in the size of the training set (abundance of attribute data) for the vectors under analysis has no appreciable impact on the performance of the conventional model. On the other hand, the incorporation of the contextual class membership information, with $s > 0$, seems to boost the classification efficiency of the fuzzy model (with identical parameter values).

3.5.3.2 Synthetic data (A, B, C) Tables 3.16–3.18 are used to compare the performance of the fuzzy Kohonen network and its nonfuzzy version for the three pattern sets A, B, and C respectively. The fuzzy Kohonen network is found to result in better performance in all the three cases, considering individual class-wise behavior. However, considering Tables 3.2–3.4 for these data, the *k*-NN classifier performs better than the conventional MLP, and both the fuzzy and conventional Kohonen nets, while the fully supervised fuzzy MLP fares the best.

Table 3.16 Recognition scores of fuzzy Kohonen network and its nonfuzzy version on pattern set *A*

Model	Fuzzy						Nonfuzzy	
Size	14 × 14		16 × 16		18 × 18		14 × 14	
Perc	50	10	50	10	50	10	50	10
1 (%)	77.4	33.3	65.6	55.8	56.5	55.3	96.9	93.2
2 (%)	67.3	60.2	69.3	68.2	63.3	87.5	0.0	0.0
None (%)	55.5	68.3	53.7	52.2	49.4	57.7	4.3	98.6
Overall (%)	68.3	49.2	61.2	55.9	54.6	59.8	52.1	49.2

Table 3.17 Recognition scores of fuzzy Kohonen network and its nonfuzzy version on pattern set *B*

Model	Fuzzy						Nonfuzzy	
Size	14 × 14		16 × 16		18 × 18		16 × 16	
Perc	50	10	50	10	50	10	50	10
1 (%)	63.4	58.7	83.0	64.1	51.7	54.2	10.7	0.0
2 (%)	50.5	30.8	55.6	30.2	40.2	42.3	6.1	0.0
None (%)	50.4	78.1	55.6	63.5	56.0	62.4	94.4	100.
Overall (%)	53.7	62.8	62.6	56.4	51.5	55.9	53.7	52.6

Table 3.18 Recognition scores of fuzzy Kohonen network and its nonfuzzy version on pattern set *C*

Model	Fuzzy						Nonfuzzy	
Size	14 × 14		16 × 16		18 × 18		16 × 16	
Perc	50	10	50	10	50	10	50	10
1 (%)	77.3	50.6	82.7	51.7	72.7	26.1	53.4	2.8
2 (%)	53.8	58.7	19.2	84.7	65.3	32.6	0.0	0.0
None (%)	44.5	51.6	55.4	35.8	53.5	73.1	72.9	96.4
Overall (%)	64.4	51.5	69.4	48.0	65.5	43.0	57.1	35.6

In addition, Table 3.19 compares of the classification performance of a 14×14 fuzzy Kohonen net, trained on pattern set A using $perc = 50\%$ of the samples, for different values of the scale factor s of eqn. (3.55). Here $s = 0.2$ is found to yield the best results. Details on this are available in [3].

Table 3.19   Effect of varying s, with fuzzy Kohonen network, on pattern set A

	Scale factor s				
Class	0.1	0.2	0.3	0.5	1.0
1 (%)	70.0	77.4	66.0	39.1	40.0
2 (%)	69.3	67.3	73.4	73.4	93.8
None (%)	58.0	55.5	62.3	51.2	44.4
Overall (%)	65.5	68.3	65.5	47.4	47.6

Figure 3.16 illustrates, as an example, the output maps generated for the pattern set A, using 50% of the samples from each class during self-organization. Parts (a) and (b) of Fig. 3.16 show the fuzzy partitioning for classes 1 and 2 separately, while part (c) gives the hard partitioning of the output space (considering all classes).

Table 3.20   Effect of varying fuzziness at input, with fuzzy Kohonen network

$fno =$	0.6	0.7	0.8	0.9	1.0	1.1	1.2	1.3
1 (%)	67.8	70.0	67.8	80.8	77.4	60.0	58.7	43.9
2 (%)	55.1	53.0	59.1	77.5	67.3	63.2	81.6	91.8
None (%)	45.6	42.6	53.7	53.7	55.5	58.0	53.7	58.0
Overall t (%)	58.2	58.0	61.6	70.5	68.3	59.6	59.4	54.4

Effect of fuzzification at input   Table 3.20 demonstrates the performance of the fuzzy Kohonen network with different values of fno on pattern set A. It is observed that the network with $0.8 < fno < 1.2$ gives good results.   ♣

Note that the fuzzy Kohonen network employs partial supervision incorporating contextual class information in the input vector. Unlike the conventional Kohonen model, which is basically used for clustering, the network here functioned as a classifier. In other words, the model [3] that is described in Section 3.5 shows how the Kohonen network, which is usually used for clustering (unsupervised classification), can also act as a classifier (in partially supervised mode).

Since the fuzzy Kohonen network acts as a partially supervised classifier, it provides relatively poor performance as compared to the fully supervised fuzzy MLP. This is evident from the results of vowel recognition (Table 3.1 for

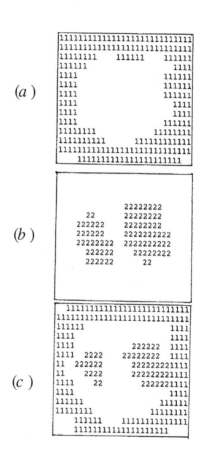

Fig. 3.16 Output map generated by 14 × 14 fuzzy Kohonen network for pattern set A: (a)–(b) fuzzy and (c) hard partitioning

fuzzy MLP and Table 3.13 for fuzzy Kohonen network) and classification of synthetic data (A, B, C) (Tables 3.2–3.4 for fuzzy MLP and Tables 3.16–3.18 for fuzzy Kohonen network).

The classification performance of the fuzzy logical MLP is found to be poorer than that of the other models. For this reason, its effectiveness is demonstrated here on pattern sets D and E, which are simpler than pattern sets A, B, and C.

REFERENCES

1. S. K. Pal and S. Mitra, "Multi-layer perceptron, fuzzy sets and classification," *IEEE Transactions on Neural Networks*, vol. 3, pp. 683–697, 1992.

2. S. Mitra and S. K. Pal, "Logical operation based fuzzy MLP for classification and rule generation," *Neural Networks*, vol. 7, pp. 353–373, 1994.

3. S. Mitra and S. K. Pal, "Self-organizing neural network as a fuzzy classifier," *IEEE Transactions on Systems, Man and Cybernetics*, vol. 24, no. 3, pp. 385–399, 1994.

4. S. K. Pal and D. P. Mandal, "Linguistic recognition system based on approximate reasoning," *Information Sciences*, vol. 61, pp. 135–161, 1992.

5. S. Mitra and S. K. Pal, "Fusion of fuzzy sets and layered neural networks at the input, output and neuronal levels," *Indian Journal of Pure and Applied Mathematics*, vol. 24, pp. 121–133, 1994.

6. S. Mitra and S. K. Pal, "Neuro-fuzzy expert systems: Overview with a case study," in *Fuzzy Reasoning in Information, Decision and Control Systems*, S. G. Tzafestas and A. N. Venetsanopoulos, eds., pp. 121–143, Boston/Dordrecht: Kluwer Academic Publishers, 1994.

7. T. Kohonen, *Self-Organization and Associative Memory*. Berlin: Springer-Verlag, 1989.

8. J. K. Keller and D. J. Hunt, "Incorporating fuzzy membership functions into the perceptron algorithm," *IEEE Transactions on Pattern Analysis and Machine Intelligence*, vol. 7, pp. 693–699, 1985.

9. K. Kwon, H. Ishibuchi, and H. Tanaka, "Neural networks with interval weights for nonlinear mapping of interval vectors," *IEICE Transactions on Information and Systems*, vol. E77-D, pp. 409–417, 1994.

10. S. K. Pal and S. Mitra, "Noisy fingerprint classification using multilayer perceptron with fuzzy geometrical and textural features," *Fuzzy Sets and Systems*, vol. 80, pp. 121–132, 1996.

11. Y. Hayashi, J. J. Buckley, and E. Czogala, "Fuzzy neural network with fuzzy signals and weights," *International Journal of Intelligent Systems*, vol. 8, no. 4, pp. 527–537, 1993.

12. B. R. Kammerer, "Incorporating uncertainty in neural networks," *International Journal of Pattern Recognition and Artificial Intelligence*, vol. 6, pp. 179–192, 1992.

13. A. Senthil Kumar, S. K. Basu, and K. L. Majumdar, "Robust classification of multispectral data using multiple neural networks and fuzzy integral," *IEEE Transactions on Geoscience and Remote Sensing*, vol. 35, pp. 787–790, 1997.

14. E. Tsao, J. C. Bezdek, and N. R. Pal, "Fuzzy Kohonen clustering networks," *Pattern Recognition*, vol. 27, pp. 757–764, 1992.

15. N. R. Pal, J. C. Bezdek, and E. Tsao, "Generalized clustering networks and Kohonen's self-organizing scheme," *IEEE Transactions on Neural Networks*, vol. 4, pp. 549–558, 1993.

16. N. B. Karayiannis and P. I. Pai, "Fuzzy algorithms for learning vector quantization," *IEEE Transactions on Neural Networks*, vol. 7, pp. 1196–1211, 1996.

17. N. B. Karayiannis, "A methodology for constructing fuzzy algorithms for learning vector quantization," *IEEE Transactions on Neural Networks*, vol. 8, pp. 505–518, 1997.

18. N. B. Karayiannis, J. C. Bezdek, N. R. Pal, R. J. Hathaway, and P. I. Pai, "Repairs to GLVQ: A new family of competitive learning schemes," *IEEE Transactions on Neural Networks*, vol. 7, pp. 1062–1071, 1996.

19. E. Yair, K. Zeger, and A. Gersho, "Competitive learning and soft competition for vector quantizer design," *IEEE Transactions on Signal Processing*, vol. 40, pp. 294–309, 1992.

20. J. C. Bezdek, *Pattern Recognition with Fuzzy Objective Function Algorithms*. New York: Plenum Press, 1981.

21. T. L. Huntsberger and P. Ajjimarangsee, "Parallel self-organizing feature maps for unsupervised pattern recognition," *International Journal of General Systems*, vol. 16, pp. 357–372, 1990.

22. J. C. Bezdek, E. C. Tsao, and N. R. Pal, "Fuzzy Kohonen clustering networks," in *Proceedings of 1st IEEE International Conference on Fuzzy Systems* (San Diego, USA), pp. 1035–1043, 1992.

23. S. C. Newton, S. Pemmaraju, and S. Mitra, "Adaptive fuzzy leader clustering of complex data sets in pattern recognition," *IEEE Transactions on Neural Networks*, vol. 3, pp. 794–800, 1992.

24. S. Grossberg, ed., *Neural Networks and Natural Intelligence.* Cambridge, MA: MIT Press, 1988.

25. G. A. Carpenter, S. Grossberg, and D. B. Rosen, "Fuzzy ART: fast stable learning and categorization of analog patterns by an adaptive resonance system," *Neural Networks*, vol. 4, pp. 759–771, 1991.

26. P. K. Simpson, "Fuzzy min-max neural networks: 1. Classification," *IEEE Transactions on Neural Networks*, vol. 3, pp. 776–786, 1992.

27. P. K. Simpson, "Min-max neural networks: 2. Clustering," *IEEE Transactions on Fuzzy Systems*, vol. 1, pp. 32–45, 1993.

28. G. A. Carpenter, S. Grossberg, N. Markuzon, J. H. Reynolds, and D. B. Rosen, "Fuzzy ARTMAP: A neural network architecture for incremental supervised learning of analog multidimensional maps," *IEEE Transactions on Neural Networks*, vol. 3, pp. 698–713, 1992.

29. G. A. Carpenter, S. Grossberg, and J. H. Reynolds, "ARTMAP: Supervised real-time learning and classification of nonstationary data by a self-organizing neural network," *Neural Networks*, vol. 4, pp. 565–588, 1991.

30. W. Pedrycz, "Neurocomputations in relational systems," *IEEE Transactions on Pattern Analysis and Machine Intelligence*, vol. 13, pp. 289–297, 1991.

31. W. Pedrycz, "Fuzzy neural networks with reference neurons as pattern classifiers," *IEEE Transactions on Neural Networks*, vol. 3, pp. 770–775, 1992.

32. W. Pedrycz, "A referential scheme of fuzzy decision making and its neural network structure," *IEEE Transactions on Systems, Man, and Cybernetics*, vol. 21, pp. 1593–1604, 1991.

33. T. Watanabe, M. Matsumoto, and T. Hasegawa, "A layered neural network model using logic neurons," in *Proceedings of the 1990 International Conference on Fuzzy Logic and Neural Networks, Iizuka* (Japan), pp. 675–678, 1990.

34. R. Krishnapuram and J. Lee, "Fuzzy-set-based hierarchical networks for information fusion in computer vision," *Neural Networks*, vol. 5, pp. 335–350, 1992.

35. H. -J. Zimmermann and P. Zysno, "Decisions and evaluations by hierarchical aggregation of information," *Fuzzy Sets and Systems*, vol. 10, pp. 243–260, 1983.

36. J. M. Keller, Y. Hayashi, and Z. Chen, "Interpretation of nodes in networks for fuzzy logic," in *Proceedings of 2nd IEEE International Conference on Fuzzy Systems* (San Francisco, USA), pp. 1203–1207, 1993.

37. K. Hirota and W. Pedrycz, "Or/And neuron in modeling fuzzy set connectives," *IEEE Transactions on Fuzzy Systems*, vol. 2, pp. 151–161, 1994.

38. A. Ghosh, N. R. Pal, and S. K. Pal, "Self-organization for object extraction using multilayer neural network and fuzziness measures," *IEEE Transactions on Fuzzy Systems*, vol. 1, pp. 54–68, 1993.

39. S. K. Pal and D. Dutta Majumder, *Fuzzy Mathematical Approach to Pattern Recognition*. New York: Wiley (Halsted Press), 1986.

40. S. K. Pal and D. Bhandari, "Genetic algorithms with fuzzy fitness function for object extraction using cellular neural networks," *Fuzzy Sets and Systems*, vol. 65, pp. 129–139, 1994.

41. S. Mitra and S. K. Pal, "Layered neural net as a fuzzy classifier," in *Proceedings of the 4th International Conference of AI and Expert Systems, Hawaii* (USA), pp. 128–137, 1991.

42. S. Mitra, "Fuzzy MLP based expert system for medical diagnosis," *Fuzzy Sets and Systems*, vol. 65, pp. 285–296, 1994.

43. D. E. Rumelhart and J. L. McClelland, eds., *Parallel Distributed Processing: Explorations in the Microstructures of Cognition*, vol. 1. Cambridge, MA: MIT Press, 1986.

44. T. Tollenaere, "Super SAB: fast adaptive backpropagation with good scaling properties," *Neural Networks*, vol. 3, pp. 561–573, 1990.

45. S. K. Pal and D. Dutta Majumder, "Fuzzy sets and decision making approaches in vowel and speaker recognition," *IEEE Transactions on Systems, Man, and Cybernetics*, vol. 7, pp. 625–629, 1977.

46. S. K. Pal, *Studies on the Application of Fuzzy Set-Theoretic Approach in Some Problems of Pattern Recognition and Man-Machine Communication by Voice*. Ph.D. thesis, University of Calcutta, Calcutta, India, 1978.

47. E. Barnard and E. C. Botha, "Back-propagation uses prior information efficiently," *IEEE Transactions on Neural Networks*, vol. 4, pp. 794–802, 1993.

48. S. K. Pal and S. Mitra, "Fuzzy versions of Kohonen's net and MLP-based classification: Performance evaluation for certain nonconvex decision regions," *Information Sciences*, vol. 76, pp. 297–337, 1994.

49. Y. Qi, B. R. Hunt, and N. Bi, "The use of fuzzy membership in network training for isolated word recognition," in *Proceedings of IEEE International Joint Conference on Neural Networks* (San Francisco, USA), pp. 1823–1828, 1993.

50. J. Chang, G. Han, J. M. Valverde, N. C. Griswold, J. F. Duque-Carrillo, and E. Sanchez-Sinencio, "Cork quality classification system using a unified image processing and fuzzy neural network methodology," *IEEE Transactions on Neural Networks*, vol. 8, pp. 964–974, 1997.

51. W. Pedrycz and H. C. Card, "Linguistic interpretation of self-organizing maps," in *Proceedings of 1st IEEE International Conference on Fuzzy Systems*, (San Diego, USA), pp. 371–378, 1992.

52. H. Ritter and T. Kohonen, "Self-organizing semantic maps," *Biological Cybernetics*, vol. 61, pp. 241–254, 1989.

53. T. Kohonen, "An introduction to neural computing," *Neural Networks*, vol. 1, pp. 3–16, 1988.

54. R. O. Duda and P. E. Hart, *Pattern Classification and Scene Analysis*. New York: Wiley, 1973.

55. J. T. Tou and R. C. Gonzalez, *Pattern Recognition Principles*. London: Addison-Wesley, 1974.

4

Other Applications of Fuzzy MLP

4.1 INTRODUCTION

In the previous chapter we have described various neuro-fuzzy methods for pattern classification. These include, among others, development of fuzzy MLP [1], fuzzy logical MLP [2], and fuzzy Kohonen network [3], and demonstrating their significance in classifying various artificially generated data sets and recognizing vowel sounds. Superiority of the fuzzy MLP, as compared to other models, has been established. In this chapter we demonstrate the effectiveness of the said network to other application domains: medical diagnosis and fingerprint classification. A concept of selective partitioning is also explained in this regard.

Automated fingerprint classification constitutes a complex problem in the pattern recognition domain. Conventional approaches to fingerprint classification and recognition involve various tasks such as noise cleaning and enhancement of the images, thinning of ridges, feature extraction, and then matching. As the regions are not always well defined (particularly because of the presence of noise, cut marks, blurs, excess ink, or loss of information), any hard decision made at an operation would have an impact on the higher-level tasks; thereby introducing or enhancing the uncertainty in the final decision. Moreover, as the size of the database increases, the overall recognition task may become computationally more intensive.

Similarly medical data, or rather more specifically, the results of biochemical tests involve imprecision, noise, and individual difference. Often one cannot clearly distinguish the difference between normal and pathological values.

Biochemical test results cannot be precisely evaluated by crisp sets. Sometimes the patient can also be simultaneously diagnosed as suffering in different degrees from multiple diseases. Incorporation of fuzziness at the input and output levels of the neural network under consideration appears to be a good solution to such problems.

An effective handling of certain medical diagnosis problems involving hepatobiliary disorders [4], and kala-azar [5] is demonstrated. Here we deal with the classification part only. (The inferencing and rule generation capabilities of the fuzzy MLP for these data have been described in Section 7.3.5 of Chapter 7.) This is followed by describing a way of selective partitioning of the input feature space in two stages [6]–[8] with the fuzzy MLP. The performance of the model at the end of the first stage is used as a criterion for guiding the selection of the appropriate partition to be further subdivided at the second stage. A comparative study is provided with relevant models, to demonstrate the superiority of this algorithm.

Finally, the classification of noisy fingerprint images, using fuzzy geometrical and textural features [9, 10] (instead of the linguistic features of the fuzzy MLP), is described. The output is provided in terms of five fingerprint categories: *whorl, left loop, right loop, twin loop,* and *plain arch.* Simulation includes random perturbation of pixel gray values, and cut marks and loss of information in certain regions, to model damaged or distorted patterns.

4.2   APPLICATION TO THE MEDICAL DOMAIN

Here we consider the problem of diagnosing *hepatobiliary disorders* [4], and *kala-azar* [5], using the fuzzy MLP. A comparative study is made with that of the fuzzy-neural model of Hayashi [11]–[13] in the case of hepatobiliary disorders data (which is subsequently referred to as *hepato* data).

4.2.1   Hepatobiliary disorders

The data *hepato* (http://www.isical.ac.in/~sushmita/patterns) consists of 536 patient cases of various hepatobiliary disorders [12]. The nine input features are the results of different biochemical tests: glutamic oxalacetic transaminate (GOT; Karmen unit), glutamic pyruvic transaminase (GPT; Karmen unit), lactate dehydrase (LDH; iu/liter), gamma glutamyl transpeptidase (GGT; mu/ml), blood urea nitrogen (BUN; mg/dl), mean corpuscular volume of red blood cell (MCV; fl), mean corpuscular hemoglobin (MCH; pg), total bilirubin ($TBil$; mg/dl), and creatinine ($CRTNN$; mg/dl). The 10th feature corresponds to the sex of the patient and is represented in binary mode as (1,0) or (0,1). The hepatobiliary disorders alcoholic liver damage (ALD), primary hepatoma (PH), liver cirrhosis (LC), and cholelithiasis (C), constitute the four output classes.

Table 4.1 Upper and lower bounds, and mean of *hepato* data

Feature	Unit	$F_{j_{\min}}$	m_j	$F_{j_{\max}}$
GOT	Karmen unit	8.0	113.0	4356.0
GPT	Karmen unit	3.0	54.5	1124.0
LDH	iu/liter	179.0	476.3	6327.0
GGT	mu/ml	4.0	144.1	3075.0
BUN	mg/dl	3.3	17.2	91.0
MCV	fl	66.7	96.1	160.5
MCH	pg	20.3	32.1	52.5
TBil	mg/dl	0.1	3.2	37.0
CRTNN	mg/dl	0.4	1.1	4.3

Note that these data have appreciably skewed distributions along most of the feature axes. The upper and lower bounds $F_{j_{\max}}$, $F_{j_{\min}}$ and the mean m_j along the jth axis for each of the nine features are indicated in Table 4.1. This sort of data distribution is suitably handled by the choice of parameters given in eqns. (3.30)–(3.31) for the linguistic π sets.

Table 4.2 Comparison of percent correct recognition scores on *hepato* data

Model	Hayashi's model, choice: Best	Hayashi's model, choice: 2nd best	Fuzzy MLP, choice: best	Fuzzy MLP, choice: 2nd best
Best match b	94.6	–	100.0	–
2nd best match b_2	–	100.0	–	100.0
Perfect match p	–	–	97.4	–
ALD	54.5	69.7	65.7	88.6
PH	66.6	82.3	87.0	90.7
LC	40.0	71.4	65.7	89.4
C	59.1	81.8	80.5	86.1
Best net score t	56.4	–	76.0	–
2nd best score t_2	–	77.3	–	88.9

Tables 4.2 and 4.3 provide some of the results [4] corresponding to $f_d = 5$, $f_e = 1$ in eqn. (3.33) and $fno = 1$ in eqn. (3.31) of Chapter 3. The factors b_2 and t_2 correspond to the performance of the fuzzy MLP when one also considers the second best choice for the training and test sets, respectively.

Table 4.2 compares the classificatory performance of the fuzzy MLP (using three hidden layers having 40 nodes each) with that of Hayashi's method [11, 12]. Both models have used 70% of the pattern set as training data. Note that the classwise recognition score, *using best choice, of fuzzy MLP* is comparable to the scores, *including the second best choice, of Hayashi's model.*

Moreover, in the case of Hayashi's model the various cutoff levels for receptor responses of each feature were set manually after consultation with domain experts. Generally 50,000 iterations were required for convergence. In the case of fuzzy MLP, the choice of parameters for the linguistic features along each feature axis is automated, depending on the pattern set distribution. Besides, convergence is also achieved generally within 500 sweeps. The use of linear discriminant analysis on the same data has been reported by Hayashi *et al.*, but the results were rather poor [11, 12].

Table 4.3 Performance on *hepato* data, using different network configurations

Layers	3			4			5		
Perc	10	50	70	10	50	70	10	50	70
Nodes	20	30	10	15	15	20	15	25	40
b (%)	98.1	94.8	79.0	100.	96.6	93.8	100.	99.2	100.
b_2 (%)	98.1	98.9	88.7	100.	98.5	98.1	100.	99.2	100.
p (%)	56.9	23.9	9.2	98.1	26.9	54.7	96.1	90.3	97.4
Mse	.006	.017	.056	.001	.012	.014	.001	.001	.001
Sweeps	350	280	200	180	370	470	210	430	400
ALD (%)	31.4	53.4	42.8	62.8	56.9	62.8	44.7	60.3	65.7
PH (%)	44.7	65.2	81.4	59.6	77.5	68.5	55.2	80.9	87.0
LC (%)	56.2	58.1	55.2	33.0	56.4	68.4	46.4	59.7	65.7
C (%)	80.3	79.7	83.3	65.4	89.8	83.3	68.2	84.7	80.5
t (%)	52.3	64.2	67.4	55.4	70.9	70.5	53.8	72.4	76.0
t_2 (%)	71.3	83.2	80.9	72.1	83.2	82.2	75.2	84.3	88.9

Table 4.3 provides a study of the effect on the recognition score (%) using different numbers of hidden layers, nodes, and training set size *perc*. The number of hidden nodes in each case corresponds to the network configuration (found experimentally) providing the best results with the given combination of number of layers and training set size. It is observed that better results are obtained in cases representing large training set coupled with large network configuration (in terms of hidden layers and nodes). Small training sets usually result in poor generalization capabilities on the test set.

4.2.2 Kala-azar

Here we provide some results [5] of performance of the fuzzy MLP on *kala-azar* (http://www.isical.ac.in/~sushmita/patterns) [14], a tropical disease, using a set of 68 patient cases. The input features are the symptoms while the output indicates the presence or absence of the disease. The symptoms are the measurements of *blood urea* (mg%), *serum creatinine* (mg%), *urinary creatinine* (mg%), and *creatinine clearance* (ml/min) indicated respectively as F_1, F_2, F_3, and F_4. These are represented in the linguistic form of eqn. (3.28).

Table 4.4 Output performance on *kala-azar* data

Layers $H + 1$	3		4
Nodes m	10	5	10
Perfect p (%)	93.4	90.0	100.0
Best b (%)	100.0	100.0	100.0
Net t (%)	86.8	81.5	86.8
Mse	0.002	0.004	0.001

The classification performance for various sizes of the network is depicted in Table 4.4, when it is trained using 30 (20 diseased and 10 control/normal) cases. The test set consists of 38 samples constituting the responses of the above-mentioned 20 diseased patients (over the next 20 days) to the ongoing treatment [14]. Some of these patients were cured while the conditions of a few others worsened, sometimes ultimately culminating in death. The instances of patients cured constitute the output class *normal/cured* while the remaining cases have been clubbed under the output class *diseased*.   ♣

An application of the MLP for classifying *electroencephalography (EEG)* results as *normal* or *depressed* has been recently reported by Mitra *et al.* [15]. Here 30 input features, corresponding to the percentage of fast Fourier transform (FFT) of EEG at each integer frequency from 1 to 30 Hz, were used. Note that this could be extended to the linguistic input space of the fuzzy MLP. However, that would entail a large increase in input dimensionality. Some results on the rules generated from this data are provided in Section 7.3.5.3 of Chapter 7.

4.3   SELECTIVE PARTITIONING OF FEATURE SPACE

The concept of partitioning of the feature space into regions and the application of different classification rules to them [16]–[19] is a well-established strategy in pattern recognition. This strategy bears an analogy with the diagnostic process in medicine. A physician who does not feel competent to resolve a special case may summon a consultation team of professionals in that particular field.

Every rule-based classifier performs partitioning through antecedent clauses and assigns a classification rule to each region through the implication. A partition may be based on the geometric properties of the classes detected by a preliminary clustering [16]. In the fuzzy classification rule [17, 20] the partitioning is uniform; specifically, the regions continue to be split until a sufficiently high certainty of the rule, generated by each region, is achieved.

Takagi *et al.* [21] have reported the development of a neural network architecture based on the structure of the fuzzy inference rules involved. The identification error is analyzed to improve the performance of the structured network. For this, the appropriate region of the feature space is further clustered and the corresponding *Then* parts accordingly added.

Here we demonstrate the enhanced classification performance of the fuzzy MLP [6] by incorporating a selective partitioning of the input space. The method has two phases. In the first phase, the performance index of the classifier (fuzzy MLP) is used to guide the selection of a partition that needs to be subdivided in the second phase. The generation of the overlapping π functions (in terms of centers and radii), corresponding to each second-level partition along the different feature axes, is automatically determined using the training data. Note that the process is restricted to two levels only, as each level of partitioning has an associated overhead due to the increase in number of neurons at the input layer and connection weights of the fuzzy MLP. This also helps in avoiding the problem of overlearning; thereby reducing the possibility of poor generalization of the network. Unlike that due to Takagi *et al.* [21], this scheme corresponds to augmentation of the IF parts of the relevant rules for the required pattern classification problem.

The ability of the model to achieve higher classification accuracy is demonstrated on two sets of synthetic data and the medical data *hepato*. In order to signify the inclusion of the scheme of selective partitioning, the output performance of the system is compared with that of the fuzzy MLP. Comparison is also provided with the conventional MLP, linear discriminant analysis and the k nearest neighbor algorithm.

4.3.1 Algorithm

In the process of selective partitioning of a feature space, one may note that the distribution of patterns plays an important role. Besides, some regions of the input space may require finer partitioning than others. Let us describe here a method [6] in which the fuzzy MLP is used to determine an effective selective partitioning using linguistic π functions.

An n-dimensional pattern space is initially divided into 3^n overlapping partitions of different sizes, depending on the centers and radii of the linguistic π functions determined automatically from the training set distribution using eqns. (3.28) and (3.30)–(3.31) (Chapter 3). The upper and lower bounds for partition x, corresponding to linguistic property p, along axis j are defined as $c_{xp_j} + (\lambda_{xp_j}/2)$ and $c_{xp_j} - (\lambda_{xp_j}/2)$ respectively. Here c_{xp_j} and λ_{xp_j} refer to the center and radius of the π function defining the linguistic property p for partition x along the jth axis. Next the classification performance of the fuzzy MLP corresponding to the recognition score, with respect to each of these partitions, is evaluated. The fuzzy subspace producing the largest number of misclassification is selected for further subdivision into 3^n overlapping regions defined by the π functions of eqns. (3.30)–(3.31). This is designated as the *doubtful* region, while the remaining part of the feature space is termed the *more certain* region. In this manner one can generate a total of $h.3^n - h + 1$ subspaces at the end of the hth stage. It is observed from the results that this selective partitioning scheme serves to enhance the performance of the model to a considerable and satisfactory extent.

Let the xth subspace be selected for further division at the end of the first stage. The appropriate linguistic properties p_j corresponding to this subspace x are determined along each feature axis j. Let m_{xp_j} be the mean of the pattern points in this subspace along the jth axis. Equation (3.30) is used for subdividing this axis into three partitions as

$$
\begin{aligned}
c_{xp_{\text{medium}(F_j)}} &= m_{xp_j} \\
c_{xp_{\text{low}(F_j)}} &= m_{xp_{j_l}} \\
c_{xp_{\text{high}(F_j)}} &= m_{xp_{j_h}},
\end{aligned}
\tag{4.1}
$$

where $m_{xp_{j_l}}$ and $m_{xp_{j_h}}$ are the means of all the pattern points that lie in the range $\left[c_{xp_j} - (\lambda_{xp_j}/2), m_{xp_j} \right)$ and $\left(m_{xp_j}, c_{xp_j} + (\lambda_{xp_j}/2) \right]$ respectively of partition x (for linguistic property p). The corresponding radii along the three new linguistic property sets, along this axis, are defined analogously to eqn. (3.31) (Chapter 3). The new enhanced set of input features is now considered as the input of the fuzzy MLP, which is again trained on the given pattern set.

4.3.2 Results

At first, we provide some of the results [6] when the aforesaid system is implemented on two different two-dimensional artificially generated data (*viz.*, *random* and *cluster*), having two equiprobable classes with the same discrimination boundary (http://www.isical.ac.in/~sushmita/patterns). *Random* uses a pseudouniform distribution, while *cluster* contains three pseudo-Gaussian clusters. These are illustrated in Figs. 4.1 and 4.2, respectively, with dots and triangles indicating the two classes. The decision boundary in the F_1–F_2 plane for these data sets is given as

$$ f = -0.25 \sin \left(7\pi F_1^3 \right) + F_2 - 0.5. $$

The generated membership functions along feature axes F_1 and F_2, both at the end of the first and second stages (*i.e.*, before and after splitting), are depicted in Figs. 4.3 and 4.4 for the *random* and the *cluster* data sets respectively. Note that the linguistic π sets *low*, *medium*, and *high* defined by eqns. (2.6), (3.29)–(3.31) and (4.1) are used in the process. The subspace (*high, medium*), corresponding to (F_1, F_2), is partitioned in both cases.

Table 4.5 provides some sample results comparing the recognition scores, using the fuzzy MLP both at the end of the first and second stages; the crisp and fuzzy k nearest neighbor algorithms; the conventional MLP; and

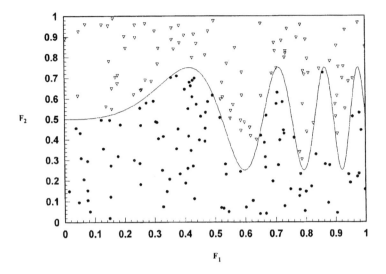

Fig. 4.1 Pattern set *random*

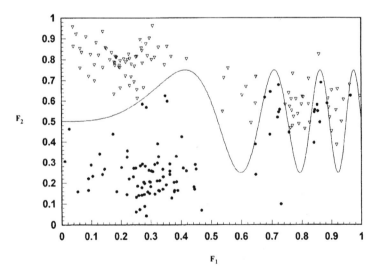

Fig. 4.2 Pattern set *cluster*

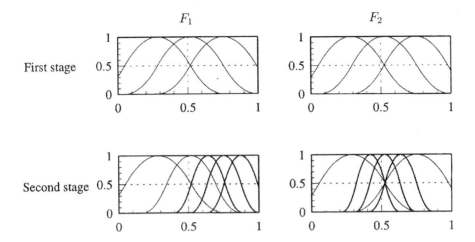

Fig. 4.3 Generated membership functions for *random* data

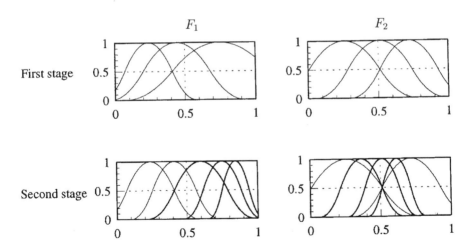

Fig. 4.4 Generated membership functions for *cluster* data

the linear discriminant analysis technique. These results correspond to a network with one hidden layer for the *random* data and two hidden layers for the *cluster* data, with 13 nodes in each such layer. For both data sets, the algorithm selected the subspace *high, medium* (corresponding to the first and second feature axes) for the second-level partitioning. This corresponds to the regions [0.518,0.99] and [0.294,0.756] along the two feature axes, respectively. It can be verified from both Figs. 4.1 and 4.2 that this area refers to the most complicated decision region in the feature space with respect to the two pattern classes. It is observed that the selective partitioning at the second level provides appreciably better results on the *cluster* data with respect to the other algorithms. This is perhaps because this pattern set has some inherent structure embedded in it, as compared to the randomness involved in the *random* data set. However, the generalization capability of the fuzzy MLP on the separate test set is enhanced after the second-level partitioning in both cases. On the whole, the fuzzy MLP performed better than the *k* nearest neighbor, linear discriminant analysis and the conventional MLP for both the data sets.

Table 4.5 Comparative study of percent correct recognition scores on *random* and *cluster* data

Data set	Model	k nearest neighbor				Linear discrm analys	Conv MLP	Fuzzy MLP Stage =	
		Crisp, k =		Fuzzy, k =					
		1	3	1	3			1	2
Random	Train b	93.5	90.5	93.5	92.5	83.0	90.0	99.5	98.5
	Test t	92.8	93.0	92.8	92.9	85.4	88.2	92.8	93.2
Cluster	Train b	92.0	92.0	92.0	93.0	89.0	91.0	92.5	100.0
	Test t	91.7	91.2	91.7	91.7	87.2	86.0	86.7	94.5

Table 4.6 Comparative study of recognition scores on *hepato* data

Model	k nearest neighbor				Linear discrim. analysis	Fuzzy MLP Stage =	
	Crisp		Fuzzy				
	k = 1	k = 3	k = 1	k = 3		1	2
Best b (%)	71.7	70.9	71.7	74.1	67.0	97.8	100.0
T ALD (%)	83.9	61.3	83.9	67.7	57.6	48.5	60.0
e PH (%)	77.2	68.4	77.2	71.9	64.7	70.3	75.9
s LC (%)	68.4	55.3	68.4	68.4	65.7	68.4	73.7
t C (%)	82.9	85.7	82.9	88.6	63.6	80.5	94.4
Net t (%)	77.6	67.7	77.6	73.9	63.2	67.5	76.1

Let us provide some sample results [6] in Table 4.6, for the data *hepato*, when the fuzzy MLP used 20 hidden nodes in each of the three layers. Note that the conventional MLP provided very poor results–56.2% overall recognition score during training–and the results are therefore omitted from the table.

Table 4.7 Performance of fuzzy MLP on *random* data, before and after partitioning

Layers	3						4			
Nodes	11		12		13		10		11	
Stage	1	2	1	2	1	2	1	2	1	2
b (%)	99.0	99.5	93.5	99.5	99.5	98.5	99.0	98.0	93.0	99.5
p (%)	74.0	69.0	56.5	81.5	58.5	63.0	95.5	94.5	86.5	90.0
Sweeps	940	320	310	290	980	420	860	350	420	480
Class1(%)	93.7	93.3	92.3	93.2	92.8	94.4	94.0	94.7	95.1	91.8
Class2(%)	89.9	90.6	89.6	91.1	92.8	91.5	89.1	90.6	88.4	93.5
t (%)	92.1	92.2	91.2	92.3	92.8	93.2	92.0	93.0	92.3	92.5

The point to be emphasized here is the selection strategy. The first stage partition provided by the fuzzy MLP can be further processed by other classification techniques. Some encouraging results have been obtained by applying the *k*-NN rules separately to the *certain* and *doubtful* regions after detection in the first stage by the fuzzy MLP [7]. It seems natural that a properly trained scheme based on this strategy would outperform a single *k*-NN rule applied on the whole sample.

Table 4.8 Performance of fuzzy MLP on *cluster* data, before and after partitioning

Layers	3						4			
Nodes	16		17		18		12		13	
Stage	1	2	1	2	1	2	1	2	1	2
b (%)	91.5	99.5	93.0	100.	91.5	99.5	91.5	99.5	92.5	100.
p (%)	65.0	89.0	70.0	85.0	43.5	89.0	72.0	93.5	76.0	93.0
Sweeps	350	630	460	920	370	480	350	920	570	760
Class1(%)	76.0	89.0	76.2	89.8	76.2	93.1	74.2	88.8	78.1	94.5
Class2(%)	97.0	93.9	96.1	94.3	96.7	94.7	97.4	93.7	95.5	94.5
t (%)	86.3	91.4	86.0	92.0	86.3	93.9	85.6	91.2	86.7	94.5

Tables 4.7–4.9 demonstrate the effect on the recognition score (%) with the *random, cluster,* and *hepato* data respectively, using different numbers of hidden layers and nodes. Table 4.8 indicates better results for the *cluster* data

set in all cases, after the second stage of partitioning, as compared to the case of the *random* data set of Table 4.7. This is perhaps because of the absence of any inherent class structure in the pattern space of the *random* data of Fig. 4.1, relative to the *cluster* data of Fig. 4.2.

Table 4.9   Performance of fuzzy MLP on *hepato* data, before and after partitioning

Layers	3				4		5			
Nodes	20				15		20			
Perc	10		50		50		50		70	
Stage	1	2	1	2	1	2	1	2	1	2
$b(\%)$	98.0	100.	88.4	94.8	96.6	97.4	100.	98.9	97.8	100.
$b_2(\%)$	98.0	100.	94.0	97.0	98.5	99.6	100.	99.6	99.4	100.
$p(\%)$	56.9	98.0	27.3	56.4	26.9	74.6	41.8	84.7	68.9	86.1
Sweeps	350	200	410	270	370	270	360	340	480	250
ALD	31.4	44.8	37.9	58.6	56.9	53.4	56.9	60.3	48.5	60.0
PH	44.7	55.3	59.5	73.0	77.5	77.5	74.1	79.8	70.3	75.9
LC	56.2	51.8	59.6	69.4	56.4	72.6	48.4	61.3	68.4	73.7
C	80.3	74.8	71.2	55.9	89.8	76.3	74.5	79.7	80.5	94.4
$t(\%)$	52.3	56.5	57.4	65.3	70.9	70.9	64.5	71.3	67.5	76.1
$t_2(\%)$	71.3	79.2	79.1	85.1	83.2	85.1	80.2	84.7	79.7	85.9

It is observed from Table 4.9 that generally better results are obtained for the data *hepato*, with fewer training cycles, after incorporating the selective partitioning technique. This is valid for different training sets *perc*. Usually cases representing large training set size coupled with large network configuration (in terms of hidden layers and nodes) provided better results. Small training set sizes resulted in poor generalization capabilities on the test set.

Table 4.10   Effect of f_d, f_e, fno on percent correct recognition scores, for *hepato* data

f_d	3.0	4.0	5.0						6.0	7.0
f_e	1.0	1.0	0.25	0.5				1.0	2.0	1.0	1.0
fno	1.0	1.0	1.0	0.9	1.0	1.1	1.2	1.0	1.0	1.0	1.0
b	98.6	98.6	100.	97.8	99.4	97.8	99.2	97.3	85.5	95.1	95.9
b_2	99.7	99.2	100.	98.6	99.4	98.9	99.7	97.3	94.6	98.1	97.5
p	88.5	79.4	96.0	77.5	89.3	82.9	87.2	56.3	8.6	64.9	61.7
t	73.0	71.1	72.4	73.0	74.2	73.0	74.2	72.4	71.1	75.4	73.6
t_2	85.2	89.5	90.1	87.7	86.5	90.1	90.1	89.5	86.5	85.8	85.8

Some results demonstrating the effect of f_d and f_e [eqn. (3.33)], and fno [eqn. (3.31)] on the classification performance of a four-layered fuzzy MLP with 25 nodes in each hidden layer and $perc = 70\%$, for the data *hepato*, are provided in Table 4.10. Note that f_d and f_e control the amount of fuzziness in the output membership, whereas fno controls the extent of overlap among the linguistic π sets at the input.

4.4 FINGERPRINT CLASSIFICATION

In this section we describe another application of neuro-fuzzy integration under category 1 (Section 2.5.1, Chapter 2) where the MLP uses fuzzy geometric and textural features at the input, unlike the linguistic features of the fuzzy MLP. As the n-dimensional space is very large in this case, the extension to the $3n$-dimensional space of the fuzzy MLP has not been attempted here. However, the model could easily be extended to incorporate this.

In pattern recognition and image analysis we often want to measure geometric properties of regions in an image that are not crisply defined. Many of the standard geometric properties of and relationship among regions are generalized to fuzzy subsets. Fuzzy geometric measures [22]–[25] have been found to reflect the spatial (geometrical) ambiguity of an image. They seem to be useful in computing image properties and providing soft decision for image description and analysis by not allowing one to commit hard decisions.

Texture is one of the important characteristics used in identifying objects or regions of interest in an image [26]–[28]. It is often described as a set of statistical measures of the spatial distribution of gray levels in an image. The method based on second-order statistical features, obtained from the gray level cooccurrence matrix [26], assumes that the texture information in an image is contained in the overall or "average" spatial relationships that the gray tones have with one another. This scheme has been found to provide a powerful input feature representation for various recognition problems.

As mentioned in Section 4.1, automated fingerprint classification constitutes a complex problem in the pattern recognition domain. Fingerprints are often distorted because of the presence of noise, cut marks, blurs, excess ink, or loss of information. In such cases, the conventional tasks involving hard decisions frequently become unsuitable by introducing/enhancing uncertainty in the various stages of the decision. Moreover, the enormity of the database results in an increase of the computational complexity of the problem.

A connectionist approach, with the input features being directly computed from the raw fingerprints without doing low-level operations, may therefore be considered [9, 10] as a solution for efficiently tackling such huge sets of complicated data and in handling uncertainties in the decision-making process. Note that other connectionist approaches, using low-level operations for preprocessing the fingerprint images, include the work reported in Ref. [29] (using extracted feature ridge pattern as input and different subnetworks for each fingerprint category), in Ref. [30] (using moment invariants for fingerprint matching), and in Ref. [31] (employing hierarchical classification of enhanced images).

Here we present some results demonstrating the capability of an MLP for classifying fingerprints in the aforesaid framework, where fuzzy geometrical features, and textural and directional features of the fingerprint images are considered as input [9, 10]. The generalization capability of the MLP in identifying noisy, incomplete, blurred, distorted, and cut marked fingerprints, particularly when it is trained only with unambiguous (correct) samples is also demonstrated. The output is expressed in terms of the various fingerprint categories: whorl, left loop, right loop, twin loop, and plain arch.

4.4.1   Feature extraction

4.4.1.1   Fuzzy geometric features   A fuzzy subset of a set S is a mapping μ from S into $[0, 1]$. For any $p \in S$, $\mu(p)$ is known as the degree of membership of p in μ. A crisp (ordinary or nonfuzzy) subset of S can be regarded as a special case of a fuzzy subset in which the mapping μ is into $\{0, 1\}$. Some of the fuzzy geometric properties of μ, relevant to the present work, are described below [22, 24, 25]. Let $\mu(I)$ denote a fuzzy representation of an $N_x \times N_y$ gray level image I, *i.e.*, a mapping μ from $I \in \{1, \ldots, N_g\}$ into $[0, 1]$ representing a fuzzy subset of I, where N_g is the maximum gray value. For convenience, we shall use μ only to denote $\mu(I)$ in this section.

Area   The area of a fuzzy subset μ is defined as

$$a(\mu) = \int \mu, \tag{4.2}$$

where the integration is taken over a region outside which $\mu = 0$. For μ being piece-wise constant (in case of digital image) the area is

$$a(\mu) = \sum \mu, \tag{4.3}$$

the summation being considered over a region outside which $\mu = 0$. The area is therefore the weighted sum of the regions on which μ is constant, weighted by these values.

Perimeter   If μ is piecewise constant, the perimeter of μ is defined as

$$p(\mu) = \sum_{i,j,k} |\mu(i) - \mu(j)| \times |A(i, j, k)|. \tag{4.4}$$

This is just the weighted sum of the lengths of the arcs $A(i, j, k)$ along which the regions having μ values $\mu(i)$ and $\mu(j)$ meet, weighted by the absolute difference of these values. In case of an image, if we consider the pixels as the piecewise constant regions and the common arc length for adjacent pixels as unity, then the perimeter of an image is defined by

$$p(\mu) = \sum_{i,j} |\mu(i) - \mu(j)|, \tag{4.5}$$

where $\mu(i)$ and $\mu(j)$ are the membership values of two adjacent pixels.

Compactness The compactness $(Comp)$ of a fuzzy set μ having area $a(\mu)$ and perimeter $p(\mu)$ is defined as

$$Comp(\mu) = \frac{a(\mu)}{p^2(\mu)}. \tag{4.6}$$

Physically, compactness means the fraction of maximum area (that can be encircled by the perimeter) actually occupied by the fuzzy region/concept represented by μ.

Height and width The height $h(\mu)$ and width $w(\mu)$ of a fuzzy set μ are defined as

$$h(\mu) = \int \max_x \{\mu(x,y)\} dy \tag{4.7}$$

and

$$w(\mu) = \int \max_y \{\mu(x,y)\} dx, \tag{4.8}$$

where the integration is taken over a region outside which $\mu(x,y) = 0$. For a digital picture the definitions take the form

$$h(\mu) = \sum_y \max_x \{\mu(x,y)\} \tag{4.9}$$

and

$$w(\mu) = \sum_x \max_y \{\mu(x,y)\}. \tag{4.10}$$

So, height (width) of a digital picture is the sum of the maximum membership values of each row (column).

Length The length of a fuzzy set μ is defined as

$$l(\mu) = \max_x \{\int \mu(x,y) dy\}, \tag{4.11}$$

where the integration is taken over the region outside which $\mu(x,y) = 0$. In case of a digital picture the expression takes the form

$$l(\mu) = \max_x \{\sum_y \mu(x,y)\}. \tag{4.12}$$

Breadth The breadth of a fuzzy set μ is defined as

$$b(\mu) = \max_y \{\int \mu(x,y) dx\}, \tag{4.13}$$

where the integration is taken over the region outside which $\mu(x,y) = 0$. For a digital image

$$b(\mu) = \max_y \{\sum_x \mu(x,y)\}. \tag{4.14}$$

The length (breadth) of an image fuzzy subset gives its longest expansion in the y direction (x direction). If μ is crisp, $\mu(x, y) = 0$ or 1; then length (breadth) is the maximum number of pixels in a column (row).

Index of area coverage ($IOAC$) The index of area coverage of a fuzzy set is defined as

$$IOAC(\mu) = \frac{a(\mu)}{l(\mu) \times b(\mu)}. \tag{4.15}$$

$IOAC$ of a fuzzy image subset represents the fraction (which may be improper also) of the maximum area (that can be covered by the length and breadth of the image) actually occupied by the image.

4.4.1.2 Textural and directional features

The textural features are computed from a set of angular nearest neighbor gray-tone spatially dependent matrices [26]. The contextual texture information is specified by the matrix of relative frequencies P_{ij} with which two neighboring resolution cells, having gray levels i and j and separated by a distance δ, occur in the image.

The unnormalized frequencies are defined by the elements $P(i, j, \delta; \theta)$ of a set of cooccurrence matrices, where θ is 0°, 45°, 90° and 135° for horizontal, right-diagonal, vertical, and left-diagonal neighbor pairs, respectively. For nearest neighbor pairs, we have $\delta = 1$. Then the number of neighboring resolution cell pairs R is given by

$$R = \begin{cases} 2N_y(N_x - 1) & \text{for } \theta = 0^\circ \\ 2N_x(N_y - 1) & \text{for } \theta = 90^\circ \\ 2(N_x - 1)(N_y - 1) & \text{otherwise.} \end{cases} \tag{4.16}$$

Angular second moment The angular second moment (A) gives a measure of the homogeneity of the texture and is defined as

$$A = \sum_{i=1}^{N_g} \sum_{j=1}^{N_g} \left(\frac{P(i, j)}{R} \right)^2. \tag{4.17}$$

Note that R, from eqn. (4.16), is used as the normalizing constant.

Homogeneity The measure Hm also provides an indication of the amount of homogeneity [32] in the texture. It is expressed as

$$Hm = \sum_{n=0}^{N_g-1} \frac{1}{1 + n^2} \left\{ \sum_{|i-j|=n} \frac{P(i, j)}{R} \right\}. \tag{4.18}$$

Note that the notation θ was omitted in eqns. (4.17)–(4.18) to avoid clutter. Each measure may be calculated four times, corresponding to each of the four directional cooccurrence matrices. The average values A_I and Hm_I provide a nondirectional (rotation-invariant) texture representation, and are defined as

$$A_I = \frac{1}{4}(A_0 + A_{45} + A_{90} + A_{135})$$

$$Hm_I = \frac{1}{4}(Hm_0 + Hm_{45} + Hm_{90} + Hm_{135}). \tag{4.19}$$

Next, let us consider the $N_x \times N_y$ image to be traversed along the right diagonal, vertically (across the middle), along the left diagonal and horizontally (along the middle and also the lower region), such that each of the five directional traversals encompasses a band of w pixels.

Frequency   Frequency is defined as the number of times one encounters humps or local maxima (valleys or local minima) among the gray tone values in the course of the traversal. An average value is computed along each direction, considering the group of w pixels. Here

$$F = \frac{1}{w}\sum_w (\text{No. of local maxima or minima}). \tag{4.20}$$

Difference   Difference is evaluated as the square of the *difference* in the gray-level values, between successive pixels, along the direction of traversal. This is defined as

$$D = \frac{1}{w}\sum_w \sum_p (G_p - G_{p+1})^2, \tag{4.21}$$

where p and $p+1$ refer to consecutive pixels along the chosen direction.

Directional height   This is computed as the normalized sum of the maximum gray tone value (among the band of w pixels) along the direction of traversal. It is expressed as

$$T = \frac{1}{N_g}\sum_p \max_w \{G_p\}, \tag{4.22}$$

where the summation over p refers to the set of pixels along the direction of traversal.

Directional contrast   Directional contrast (for vertical traversal with orientation θ) is computed as

$$K_\theta = \frac{1}{2w}\sum_{n=0}^{N_g-1} n^2 \left\{ \sum_{|i-j|=n} \frac{P'_\theta(i,j)}{N_y - 1} \right\}, \tag{4.23}$$

where $P'(i,j)$ refers to the relative frequency with which two nearest neighbor cells, having gray levels i and j, occur along the vertical band of w pixels in the image. Here, the normalizing constant is $2w(N_y - 1)$.

4.4.2   Fingerprint categories

Fingerprint images essentially consist of ridges and valleys. The ridges run somewhat parallely and slowly over the fingers. The ridge structure and the skin texture provide the uniqueness to the fingerprint, and this remains unchanged during one's lifetime. A fingerprint consists of three regions: core area, marginal area, and base area. The ridges from these three areas meet at a triangular formation called the *delta region*. The centroid of this region is identified as the *delta point*.

Depending on the ridge flow on the core area and the number of delta points, fingerprints can be broadly classified (according to Henry) [33] as

- *Plain arch*: Ridges enter from the left side, rise in the middle and leave on the right side.

- *Tented arch*: Same as in plain arch, but the amount of rise in the middle is more here.

- *Loop*: This is the most common type. Ridges enter from one side, proceed toward the center and then turn to leave from the same side. There are two categories: left loop and right loop, depending on the direction of the loop formed.

- *Whorl*: Ridge flow in the core area is circular, and two delta points are defined.

- *Twin loop*: The core area consists of ridges from two distinct loop patterns.

- *Accidental*: This type consists of those patterns that cannot be classified under any of the categories listed above.

The results that will be presented here deal only with the following five common classes: whorl, left loop, right loop, twin loop, and plain arch. Figure 4.5 shows some typical images of these categories.

4.4.3   Noisy pattern generation

In practice, one gets fingerprints that are noisy. Noise may be of different types. There may be one or more cut mark(s) in the fingerprint, some portion of the fingerprint image may be missing because of an improperly taken impression, or noise may be distributed throughout the image. To model such situations, noisy fingerprint data are generated using the following techniques [10].

4.4.3.1   Random distribution of noise   Here a predefined percentage of pixels is randomly selected and then random noise injected in the corresponding gray values. Let the magnitude of noise so added be represented by $X = x$,

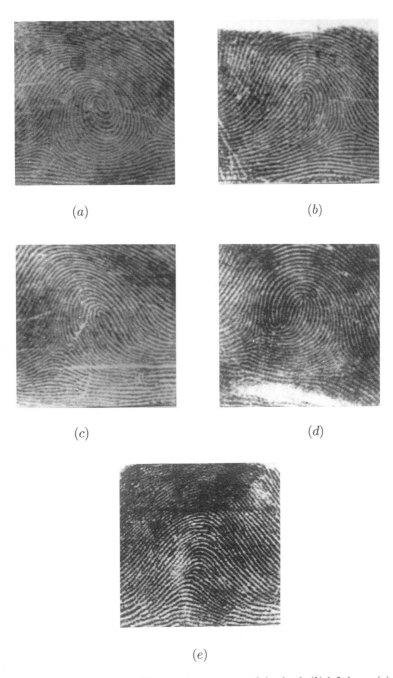

Fig. 4.5   Different categories of fingerprint patterns: (*a*) whorl; (*b*) left loop; (*c*) right loop; (*d*) twin loop; (*e*) plain arch

where X is normally distributed *i.e.*, $X \sim N(m, \sigma)$, m is the mean and the σ is the standard deviation of the normal distribution. Thus, if a pixel p with gray value G_p is selected randomly, its new gray value becomes

$$G_p = G_p + x, \qquad (4.24)$$

such that $0 < G_p \leq N_g$.

4.4.3.2 Cut mark   Any two points in the fingerprint image are randomly selected, and the pixels lying on a line of width b_w joining these two points are set to the highest gray value, N_g. In other words,

$$G_p = N_g \qquad (4.25)$$

for all pixels p lying along the generated line (of width b_w), to simulate a cut mark on the fingerprint image. The cut marks are generated in two different orientations (along the left and right diagonals through the image), such that they are 90° apart. These are termed as the *forward* and *reverse* directions respectively for all later references.

4.4.3.3 Missing information   To model the occurrence of loss of information in a certain portion of a fingerprint image, a portion of the image is selected randomly. Setting all the pixels within this portion to the highest (N_g) or lowest (1) gray value simulates the loss of information in that region. So one has $G_p = N_g(1)$ for all pixels p lying within the randomly selected portion of the image. Note that setting $G_p = N_g$ models the case of insufficient inking of the fingerprint in the said region, whereas setting $G_p = 1$ simulates the condition of excess inking or blotches.

4.4.3.4 Other noisy versions   Several seed points are randomly selected and boxes of size $b_s \times b_s$ generated around these points. Then the gray values of the pixels within these regions are replaced by the average of all pixels within the respective boxes.

4.4.4   Results

Figure 4.6 illustrates some example images representing the various types of noisy patterns used. Sample results corresponding to a normal distribution, with mean 2 and standard deviation 10 for inserting noise in 10% of the pixels, are provided here. In the case of cut marks a band of width $b_w = 5$ in eqn. (4.25), and for the averaging of gray values boxes of length $b_s = 21$ were used.

4.4.4.1 Using fuzzy geometric features   The whole fingerprint image was divided into 16 blocks, each of size 64×64. The eight (basic) fuzzy geometric features of eqns. (4.2)–(4.15) were computed for each such subimage, and a

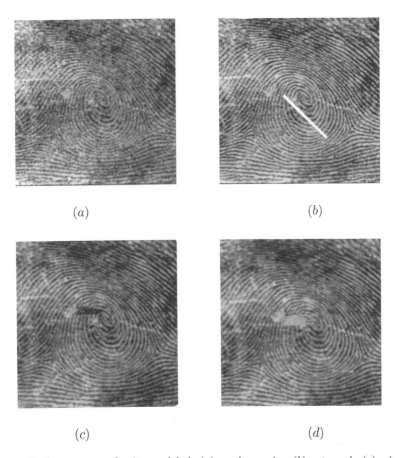

Fig. 4.6   Different types of noise modeled: (a) random noise; (b) cut mark; (c) missing information (black); (d) missing information (white)

total of 128 features generated as input to the network. A total of around 1000 sweeps were required to reduce the error sufficiently during training. The effect of reducing the rather large number of input features was also investigated using five (out of the eight) basic features: *perimeter, compactness, width, breadth,* and *IOAC*. These were calculated for each subimage, generating a total of 80 input features. Results on the noisy and distorted data using a three-layered network with 25 hidden nodes, producing 100% classification accuracy for the training set, are provided in Table 4.11.

Table 4.11 Percent correct recognition scores of noisy fingerprint data, with different fuzzy geometric features

Noise type	Random noise		Cut mark		Information loss				Averaging gray values	
					Black		White			
Features	128	80	128	80	128	80	128	80	128	80
Whorl	60.	60.	100.	100.	100.	100.	60.	60.	100.	100.
L.Loop	100.	100.	100.	100.	100.	100.	100.	100.	100.	100.
R.Loop	100.	100.	100.	100.	100.	100.	100.	100.	100.	100.
T.Loop	100.	100.	100.	85.7	100.	85.7	71.4	42.9	100.	100.
P.Arch	71.4	57.2	100.	100.	100.	100.	57.1	66.7	100.	100.
Net t	81.3	75.	100.	96.9	100.	96.9	68.8	65.6	100.	100.

In order to demonstrate the effect of computing all the eight fuzzy geometrical features of eqns. (4.2)–(4.15) globally, on the whole image, without dividing it into blocks, one may refer to Table 4.12. Here a network with eight input nodes (and seven hidden nodes), producing 96.8% classification accuracy on the training set, was considered.

It is observed from Tables 4.11 and 4.12 that the performance is very sensitive to the presence of random noise. The performance is found to be best in the case of patterns where the gray values had been averaged over small regions. As expected, the performance deteriorates (on the whole) with a reduction in the number of input features. Recently, the effectiveness of the aforesaid fuzzy geometric features has also been investigated for identifying distorted overlapping prints [34].

4.4.4.2 *Using textural and directional input features* A total of 27 textural and directional features were generated from the whole image using eqns. (4.17)–(4.23). Sample results corresponding to a width of $w = 5$ in eqns. (4.20)–(4.23), using a three-layered MLP with 15 hidden nodes, are provided in Table 4.13. The training and test sets are the same as used in case of the fuzzy geometric features described earlier. Each input feature was computed along the four directions,–vertical, horizontal, right diagonal, and left diagonal–in order to capture the directional properties of the image pattern. (Note that this technique is different from the division into blocks as described for the

Table 4.12   Recognition scores of noisy fingerprint data, with eight fuzzy geometric features

Noise type	Random noise	Cut mark		Information loss		Averaging gray values
		Forward	Reverse	Black	White	
Whorl	40.0	60.0	60.0	60.0	40.0	100.0
L. Loop (%)	0.0	66.7	66.7	66.7	66.7	66.7
R. Loop (%)	33.3	100.0	100.0	66.7	66.7	100.0
T. Loop (%)	100.0	71.4	71.4	57.1	100.0	100.0
P. Arch (%)	28.6	100.0	100.0	100.0	64.3	100.0
Overall t (%)	43.8	84.4	84.4	78.1	71.9	96.9

fuzzy geometric features.)   The performance for the textural and directional features is found to be poorer (Table 4.13) than that obtained with the fuzzy geometric features (Tables 4.11 and 4.12). Once again, the network generated the worst results in the case of random noise and best results (comparable to that of Tables 4.11 and 4.12) in the case of the averaging of gray values.

Table 4.13   Recognition scores of noisy fingerprint data, with textural and directional features

Noise type	Random noise	Cut mark		Information loss		Averaging gray values
		Forward	Reverse	Black	White	
Whorl (%)	20.0	60.0	100.0	20.0	20.0	100.0
L. Loop (%)	100.0	100.0	100.0	66.7	33.3	100.0
R. Loop (%)	0.0	66.7	0.0	100.0	100.0	100.0
T. Loop (%)	0.0	71.4	28.6	40.0	40.0	85.7
P. Arch (%)	57.2	100.0	90.3	100.0	100.0	100.0
Overall t (%)	37.5	84.4	71.9	68.8	65.6	96.9

The fact that the *cut marks* or *loss of information* could be better classified by the neural network brings out an interesting point for further investigation. Perhaps the 10% random noise, which visually damaged the pattern very little, caused some major changes in the feature values computed (both in cases of fuzzy geometric, and textural and directional features). It should also be noted that the 10% locations of a 256×256 image consist of many more pixels than a cut mark of size (say) 21×5 or a region of information loss of size (say) 21×21. This probably accounts for the better performance in the latter case even though the distortion may have been in a sensitive region of the image that is relevant for the classification.

REFERENCES

1. S. K. Pal and S. Mitra, "Multi-layer perceptron, fuzzy sets and classification," *IEEE Transactions on Neural Networks*, vol. 3, pp. 683–697, 1992.

2. S. Mitra and S. K. Pal, "Logical operation based fuzzy MLP for classification and rule generation," *Neural Networks*, vol. 7, pp. 353–373, 1994.

3. S. Mitra and S. K. Pal, "Self-organizing neural network as a fuzzy classifier," *IEEE Transactions on Systems, Man and Cybernetics*, vol. 24, no. 3, pp. 385–399, 1994.

4. S. Mitra, "Fuzzy MLP based expert system for medical diagnosis," *Fuzzy Sets and Systems*, vol. 65, pp. 285–296, 1994.

5. S. Mitra and S. K. Pal, "Fuzzy multi-layer perceptron, inferencing and rule generation," *IEEE Transactions on Neural Networks*, vol. 6, pp. 51–63, 1995.

6. S. Mitra and L. I. Kuncheva, "Improving classification performance using fuzzy mlp and two-level selective partitioning of the feature space," *Fuzzy Sets and Systems*, vol. 70, pp. 1–13, 1995.

7. L. I. Kuncheva and S. Mitra, "A two-level classification scheme trained by a fuzzy neural network," in *Proceedings of 12th International Conference on Pattern Recognition* (Jerusalem, Israel), pp. 467–469, October 1994.

8. S. Mitra and L. I. Kuncheva, "Change-glasses pattern classification with a fuzzy neural network," in *Proceedings of 1st Workshop on Fuzzy Based Expert Systems* (Sofia, Bulgaria), pp. 29–32, October 1994.

9. S. Mitra, S. K. Pal, and M. K. Kundu, "Fingerprint classification using fuzzy multilayer perceptron," *Neural Computing and Applications*, vol. 2, pp. 227–233, 1994.

10. S. K. Pal and S. Mitra, "Noisy fingerprint classification using multilayer perceptron with fuzzy geometrical and textural features," *Fuzzy Sets and Systems*, vol. 80, pp. 121–132, 1996.

11. K. Yoshida, Y. Hayashi, A. Imura, and N. Shimada, "Fuzzy neural expert system for diagnosing hepatobiliary disorders," in *Proceedings of the 1990 International Conference on Fuzzy Logic and Neural Networks, Iizuka* (Japan), pp. 539–543, 1990.

12. Y. Hayashi, "A neural expert system with automated extraction of fuzzy if-then rules and its application to medical diagnosis," in *Advances in Neural Information Processing Systems*, R. P. Lippmann, J. E. Moody,

and D. S. Touretzky, eds., pp. 578–584. Los Altos: Morgan Kaufmann, 1991.

13. Y. Hayashi, "Neural expert system using fuzzy teaching input and its application to medical diagnosis," *Information Sciences Applications*, vol. 1, pp. 47–58, 1994.

14. D. K. Biswas, *Study of Kala-azar with Special Reference to Renal Function*. Master's thesis, School of Tropical Medicine, University of Calcutta, Calcutta, India, 1989.

15. S. Mitra, S. N. Sarbadhikari, and S. K. Pal, "An MLP-based model for identifying qEEG in depression," *International Journal of Biomedical Computing*, vol. 43, pp. 179–187, 1996.

16. K. Hirota and W. Pedrycz, "Geometric-logical pattern classification," in *Proceedings of 2nd International Conference on Fuzzy Logic and Neural Networks, Iizuka* (Japan), pp. 675–678, 1992.

17. H. Ishibuchi, K. Nozaki, and H. Tanaka, "Distributed representation of fuzzy rules and its application to pattern classification," *Fuzzy Sets and Systems*, vol. 52, pp. 21–32, 1992.

18. L. I. Kuncheva, "'Change-glasses' approach in pattern recognition," *Pattern Recognition Letters*, vol. 14, pp. 619–623, 1993.

19. L. A. Rastrigin and R. H. Erenstein, *Method of Collective Recognition* (in Russian). Moscow: Energoizdat, 1981.

20. H. Ishibuchi, K. Nozaki, and H. Tanaka, "Efficient fuzzy partition of pattern space for classification problems," *Fuzzy Sets and Systems*, vol. 59, pp. 295–304, 1993.

21. H. Takagi, N. Suzuki, T. Koda, and Y. Kojima, "Neural networks designed on approximate reasoning architecture and their applications," *IEEE Transactions on Neural Networks*, vol. 3, pp. 752–760, 1992.

22. A. Rosenfeld, "Fuzzy geometry of image subsets," *Pattern Recognition Letters*, vol. 2, pp. 311–317, 1984.

23. A. Rosenfeld, "Fuzzy geometry: an overview," in *Proceedings of 1st IEEE International Conference on Fuzzy Systems* (San Diego, USA), pp. 113–117, 1992.

24. S. K. Pal and A. Ghosh, "Fuzzy geometry in image analysis," *Fuzzy Sets and Systems*, vol. 48, pp. 23–40, 1992.

25. S. K. Pal and A. Ghosh, "Index of area coverage of fuzzy image subsets and object extraction," *Pattern Recognition Letters*, vol. 11, pp. 831–841, 1990.

26. R. M. Haralick, K. Shanmugam, and I. Dinstein, "Textural features for image classification," *IEEE Transactions on Systems, Man, and Cybernetics*, vol. 3, pp. 610–621, 1973.

27. J. S. Weszka, C. R. Dyer, and A. Rosenfeld, "A comparative study of texture measures for terrain classification," *IEEE Transactions on Systems, Man, and Cybernetics*, vol. 6, pp. 269–285, 1976.

28. H. Tamura, S. Mori, and T. Yamawaki, "Textural features corresponding to visual perception," *IEEE Transactions on Systems, Man, and Cybernetics*, vol. 8, pp. 460–473, 1978.

29. M. Kamijo, "Classifying fingerprint images using neural network: Deriving the classification state," in *Proceedings of IEEE International Joint Conference on Neural Networks* (San Francisco, USA), pp. 1932–1937, 1993.

30. S. C. Newton, S. Pemmaraju, and S. Mitra, "Adaptive fuzzy leader clustering of complex data sets in pattern recognition," *IEEE Transactions on Neural Networks*, vol. 3, pp. 794–800, 1992.

31. A. M. Ozbayoglu and C. H. Dagli, "Unsupervised hierarchical fingerprint matching," in *Proceedings of IEEE International Conference on Neural Networks* (Houston, USA), pp. 1439–1442, 1997.

32. R. Krishnapuram and J. Lee, "Fuzzy-set-based hierarchical networks for information fusion in computer vision," *Neural Networks*, vol. 5, pp. 335–350, 1992.

33. C. E. Chapel, *Fingerprinting: A Manual of Identification*. Coward McCunn, 1941.

34. S. K. Pal and S. N. Sarbadhikari, "Classification of distorted overlapping fingerprints with fuzzy geometrical features," *International Journal of Knowledge-based Intelligent Engineering Systems*, vol. 1, pp. 120–137, 1997.

5

Self-Organization, Pixel Classification, and Object Extraction

5.1 INTRODUCTION

In Chapters 3 and 4 we mainly dealt with supervised neuro-fuzzy models for pattern classification, and explained some of the application-specific merits. This chapter, on the other hand, focuses on certain unsupervised (self-organizing) neuro-fuzzy systems in this regard. Here we consider the problem of pixel classification for object extraction. Object extraction involves segmenting an image into two region types: object region and background region. Two neuro-fuzzy models–a self-organizing MLP [1] and a cellular neural network incorporating genetic algorithms with fuzziness measures [2]–are described for this purpose.

Image segmentation and object extraction play a key role in image analysis and computer vision. Most of the existing techniques, both classical [3, 4] and fuzzy set theoretic [5], are sequential in nature and the segmented output cannot be obtained in real-time. On the other hand, there are some relaxation type algorithms [4] for which parallel implementations are possible, but robustness of these algorithms usually depends on some prior knowledge about the image (which may be difficult to obtain). Good reviews on image segmentation methods are available in Refs. [6] and [7].

A few approaches to object extraction using neural networks can be found in Refs. [8]–[12]. In addition to these, several authors [13]–[15] have used the MLP for image segmentation and texture discrimination. Blanz and Gish [13] used a three-layered perceptron trained with a set of similar images for pixel classification. On the other hand, Babaguchi *et al.* [14] used a similar concept for histogram thresholding. It is to be noted that all these perceptron-based techniques require a set of images for learning, which may not always be available in real life situations. For example, the conventional *MLP* requires several input patterns from different classes for learning and acts as a multidimensional pattern discriminator (supervised classifier). If the types of image to be processed are of similar nature (*i.e.*, have some common characteristics), then one can train the network with a set of images and use the trained net on future images. However, if the images do not share some common features and a set of images with known targets (may be synthetic images) is not available, this network, as such, may not be used for image segmentation or classification.

In Section 5.2 we describe a self-organizing MLP of Ghosh *et al.* [1] with fuzziness measures for object extraction from noisy images. Here the neuro-fuzzy integration demonstrates a way of using the MLP (which is usually operated in the supervised mode) as an unsupervised classifier. In other words, the ability of MLP for generating a nonlinear boundary is exploited with the help of fuzziness measures for extracting object regions from noisy image data, thereby providing an application specific merit of neuro-fuzzy computation.

A cellular neural network (CNN) is an unsupervised neural network proposed by Chua and Yang [16]. It is made of a massive aggregate of analog circuit components called *cells*. Any cell in a cellular neural network is connected only to its neighboring cells and interacts only with those cells. Key features of this network are asynchronous processing, continuous-time dynamics, and local interaction between the cells (processing elements). Cells not directly connected together affect each other as a result of propagation effects. The continuous-time feature of a CNN imparts it real-time signal processing capability, while the local interconnections make it amenable to very large scale integrated circuit implementation. Its application lies in image processing problems: edge detection, noise removal, and horizontal and vertical line detection [16].

Setting up a CNN needs a proper selection of circuit parameters of cells. The set of circuit parameters, collectively called the *cloning template*, determines the dynamics of the network and its application domain. In Section 5.3 we describe a methodology [2] of using fuzziness measures and genetic algorithms (Section 2.7.2 and Appendix A) for automatically determining the cloning templates of a CNN used for object extraction. (The methodology can be extended to other image processing tasks.)

5.2   SELF-ORGANIZING MULTILAYER NEURAL NETWORK WITH FUZZINESS MEASURES

A *self-organizing multilayer neural network* architecture suitable for image processing [1] is described in this section. The architecture is feedforward with backpropagation of errors; but unlike the conventional *MLP* it does not require any supervised learning. The learning technique employed is *self-supervised*, thereby attaining self-organizing capability. Each neuron is connected to the corresponding neuron in the previous layer and its neighbors. Another structural difference from the conventional MLP is that there exists a feedback path from the output to the input layer. The output status of neurons in the output layer is described as a fuzzy set. A fuzziness measure of this fuzzy set is used as a measure of error in the system (instability of the network).

Different mathematical models for calculating the error of the system have been described. A comparative study on the rate of learning for these models is also done. Given a single input, the system automatically finds the structure in the input data by self-supervision and/or self-organization. The final output comes in two types only, one with output status *zero* and the other with output status *one*. An application of the network is demonstrated for object extraction from noisy environment.

5.2.1   Description and operation of the network

It has already been mentioned that an *MLP*, per se, cannot be used for image segmentation or object extraction when only one input image is available. In such cases there will not be enough scope of learning (*supervised*). For this type of problems it is appropriate if one can apply some sort of *self-supervised* learning technique. Besides, for an $N_x \times N_y$ image if one connects each neuron with every other one, the connectivity becomes drastically high. On the basis of this realization, Ghosh *et al.* [1] have described a new self-organizing multilayer neural network model whose basic principles are similar to the *MLP* (of Section 2.4.2), but differ structurally and functionally to a great extent. The superscript h, indicating the layer, will be omitted in the sequel for clarity of understanding.

Before describing the architecture of the network, one has to define the dth-order neighbor N_{ij}^d of any element (i,j) of an $N_x \times N_y$ lattice (L) as

$$N_{ij}^d = \{(i,j) \in L\},$$

such that

- $(i,j) \notin N_{ij}^d$

- If $(k,l) \in N_{ij}^d$,   then $(i,j) \in N_{kl}^d$.

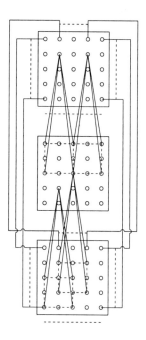

Fig. 5.1 Schematic representation of self-organizing multilayer neural network

Different-ordered neighborhood systems can be defined considering different sets of neighboring pixels of (i, j). $N^1 = \{N_{ij}^1\}$ can be obtained by taking the four nearest neighbor pixels. Similarly, $N^2 = \{N_{ij}^2\}$ consists of the eight pixels neighboring (i, j) and so on [1].

5.2.1.1 Architecture In Fig. 5.1 we depict the three-layered version of the network architecture. In each and every layer there are $N_x \times N_y$ neurons (for an $N_x \times N_y$ image). Each neuron corresponds to a single pixel. Besides the input and output layers, there can be a number of hidden layers (more than zero). Neurons in the same layer do not have any connections among themselves. Each neuron in a layer is connected to the corresponding neuron in the previous layer and to its neighbors (over N^d); thus each neuron in layer $i(i > 1)$ will have $|N^d| + 1$ (where $|N^d|$ is the number of pixels in N^d) links to the $(i - 1)$th layer. For N^1, a neuron has 5-links, whereas for N^2, 9-links will be associated with every neuron. However, for boundary nodes (pixels) number of links may be less than $|N^d| + 1$. Every neuron in the output layer is also connected to the corresponding neuron in the input layer. It may be noted that this architecture differs from the standard *MLP* in two major points:

- The distribution of links

- The feedback connection from the output layer to the input layer.

5.2.1.2 Initialization The input to a neuron in the input layer is given as a real number in $[0, 1]$ which is proportional to the gray value of the corresponding pixel. Since the objective is to eliminate noise and extract spatially compact regions, all initial weights are set to one (1). No external bias is imposed on the weights. Random initialization (of weights) may act as a pseudonoise, and the compactness of the extracted regions may be lost. As all the weights are set to unity, the total input (initially) to any node lies in $[0, \; n_l]$ (where n_l is the number of links a neuron has); hence the most unbiased choice for the threshold value θ [for the input–output transfer function, eqns. (2.37)–(2.38)] would be $n_l/2$ (the middlemost value of the total input range).

5.2.1.3 Operation The input value (x_j^h) of the jth neuron in the hth layer [except the input layer] is calculated using eqn. (2.37). The transfer function of eqns. (2.37)–(2.38) is then applied to get the output status of the neurons in this layer. These outputs are fed as input to the next layer. Starting from the input layer, the input pattern is passed on to the output layer this way, and the corresponding output states are calculated. The output value of each neuron lies in $[0, 1]$.

Here the intention is to extract spatially compact regions through the process of self-organization, using only one noise corrupted realization of a scene. The organization of the network, under ideal conditions when the image is not noisy, makes the output status of most of the neurons in the output layer to be either 0 or 1. But due to the effect of noise the output status of the neurons in the output layer usually lies in $[0,1]$, and thus the status value represents the degree of brightness (darkness) of the corresponding pixel in the image. Therefore, the output status in the output layer may be viewed to represent a fuzzy set, "bright (dark) pixels." The number of supports of this fuzzy set is equal to the number of neurons in the output layer. The measure of *fuzziness* of this set, on the global level, may be considered the *error* or *instability of the whole system* as this reflects the deviation from the desired state of the network (considering properties 1–4 of Section 2.2.3). Thus when one does not have any *a priori* target output value, one can take the fuzziness value as a measure of system error and backpropagate it to adjust the weights (mathematical expressions given later) so that the system error reduces with passage of time, and in the limiting case becomes zero. The error measure E can also be taken as a suitable function of a fuzziness measure:

$$E \;=\; g(I'), \qquad\qquad (5.1)$$

where I' is a *measure of fuzziness* [eqns. (2.15)–(2.17), (2.19)] of the fuzzy set.

After the weights have been adjusted properly, the output of the neurons in the output layer is fed back to the corresponding neurons in the input layer. The second pass has this as input. The iteration (updating of weights) is continued as in the previous case until the network stabilizes: *i.e.*, the error value (measure of fuzziness) becomes negligible. When the network stabilizes the output status of the neurons in the output layer becomes either 0 or 1. Neurons with output value 0 constitute one group and those having output value 1 constitute the other group. It may be mentioned here that the scene can have any number of compact regions.

Note that the system actually does some sort of *self-supervised* learning, thereby *self-organizing* and finding out the structure in the input data. Thus for problems like clustering, where there is no concept of *a priori* teaching, such systems will be of utmost importance. In self-supervised learning the system learns to respond to "interesting" patterns in the input. In general, such a scheme should be able to form the basis for the development of feature detectors and should reveal statistically salient features of the input population. Unlike the other learning methods, there is no *a priori* set of categories into which the patterns are to be classified. Here, the system develops its own feature-based representation of the input stimuli that captures the most salient features of the population of the input pattern. In this context it can be mentioned that this type of learning resembles biological learning to a great extent.

5.2.2 Weight correction for different error (fuzziness) measures

The mathematical derivations for weight updating rules using backpropagation with different fuzziness measures [eqns. (2.15)–(2.17) and (2.19)] are as follows. These are given only for correcting the weights of the links connected to the output layer. For other layers similar expressions as in eqn. (2.44) (for the MLP) are applicable.

5.2.2.1 Weight correction for linear index of fuzziness   Let us consider

$$
\begin{aligned}
E &= g(\nu_l) \\
&= \nu_l,
\end{aligned}
\tag{5.2}
$$

where the linear index of fuzziness [eqn. (2.15)] is expressed as

$$
\nu_l = \frac{2}{n} \sum_{j=1}^{n} \{\min(y_j, 1 - y_j)\},
\tag{5.3}
$$

n being the number of supports (number of neurons in the output layer). Here

$$
-\frac{\partial E}{\partial y_j} = \left\{
\begin{array}{ll}
-\frac{2}{n} & \text{if } 0 \leq y_j \leq 0.5 \\
\frac{2}{n} & \text{if } 0.5 \leq y_j \leq 1.
\end{array}
\right.
\tag{5.4}
$$

Thus from eqn. (2.42) one obtains

$$
\Delta w_{ji} = \left\{
\begin{array}{ll}
\varepsilon_1 \left(-\frac{2}{n}\right) \frac{dy_j}{dx_j} y_i & \text{if } 0 \leq y_j \leq 0.5 \\
\varepsilon_1 \left(\frac{2}{n}\right) \frac{dy_j}{dx_j} y_i & \text{if } 0.5 \leq y_j \leq 1
\end{array}
\right.
\tag{5.5}
$$

or

$$\Delta w_{ji} = \begin{cases} -\varepsilon \frac{dy_j}{dx_j} y_i & \text{if } 0 \le y_j \le 0.5 \\ \varepsilon \frac{dy_j}{dx_j} y_i & \text{if } 0.5 \le y_j \le 1, \end{cases} \tag{5.6}$$

where $\varepsilon = \varepsilon_1 \times \frac{2}{n}$.

5.2.2.2 Weight correction for quadratic index of fuzziness
Let the error function E be chosen as

$$\begin{aligned} E &= g(\nu_q) \\ &= \nu_q{}^2, \end{aligned} \tag{5.7}$$

where the quadratic index of fuzziness [eqn. (2.16)] is expressed as

$$\nu_q = \frac{2}{\sqrt{n}} \sqrt{[\sum_{j=1}^{n} \{\min(y_j, \, 1 - y_j)\}^2]}. \tag{5.8}$$

Now

$$\nu_q^2 = \frac{4}{n} \left[\sum_{j=1}^{n} \{\min(y_j, \, 1 - y_j)\}^2 \right] \tag{5.9}$$

and

$$-\frac{\partial E}{\partial y_j} = \begin{cases} \frac{4}{n} \{-2y_j\} & \text{if } 0 \le y_j \le 0.5 \\ \frac{4}{n} \{2(1 - y_j)\} & \text{if } 0.5 \le y_j \le 1.0 \end{cases} \tag{5.10}$$

Thus

$$\Delta w_{ji} = \begin{cases} \varepsilon_2 \frac{4}{n} (-2y_j) \frac{dy_j}{dx_j} y_i & \text{if } 0 \le y_j \le 0.5 \\ \varepsilon_2 \frac{4}{n} \{2(1 - y_j)\} \frac{dy_j}{dx_j} y_i & \text{if } 0.5 \le y_j \le 1.0 \end{cases} \tag{5.11}$$

In other words,

$$\Delta w_{ji} = \begin{cases} \varepsilon(-y_j) \frac{dy_j}{dx_j} y_i & \text{if } 0 \le y_j \le 0.5 \\ \varepsilon\{(1 - y_j)\} \frac{dy_j}{dx_j} y_i & \text{if } 0.5 \le y_j \le 1.0, \end{cases} \tag{5.12}$$

where $\varepsilon = \varepsilon_2 \times (4/n) \times 2$.

If the target output $\{d_j\}$ is defined as

$$d_j = \begin{cases} 0 & \text{if } 0 \le y_j \le 0.5 \\ 1 & \text{if } 0.5 \le y_j \le 1.0, \end{cases} \tag{5.13}$$

then this fuzziness measure becomes equivalent to the sum of the squared errors.

It may be noted here that $(\partial E/\partial y_j)$ is not defined when $y_j = 0.5$ for both ν_l and ν_q. Thus, when implementing the algorithm, if y_j takes a value of 0.5 for some node, then movement can be made in any one of the directions by a small amount.

5.2.2.3 Weight correction for logarithmic entropy   Now consider

$$E = g(H) \tag{5.14}$$
$$= H, \tag{5.15}$$

where H is the entropy of a fuzzy set, eqn. (2.17), defined as

$$H(A) = -\frac{1}{n\ln(2)} \sum_{j=1}^{n} \{y_j \ln y_j + (1 - y_j) \ln(1 - y_j)\}. \tag{5.16}$$

Thus

$$-\frac{\partial E}{\partial y_j} = \frac{1}{n\ln(2)} \ln \frac{y_j}{1 - y_j}. \tag{5.17}$$

Note that as $y_j \longrightarrow 0$ *or* 1, $\mathrm{abs}\{\ln[y_j/(1 - y_j)]\} \longrightarrow \infty$, whereas as $y_j \longrightarrow 0.5$, $\mathrm{abs}\{\ln[y_j/(1 - y_j)]\} \longrightarrow 0$.

For a fuzzy set, the fuzziness value is minimum when the membership values of all the elements are 0 or 1, and maximum when they all are 0.5. So for the network the error is minimum (*i.e.*, the network has stabilized) when all the output values are either 0 or 1, and is maximum when they all are 0.5 (the network is most unstable). Using eqns. (2.42)–(2.44) and (5.17) one notices that $\mathrm{abs}(\partial E/\partial y_j)$ is minimum (= 0) when all the output values are 0.5. If one uses the gradient descent search, the rate of learning becomes minimum at the most unstable state. However, to expedite the learning it is desirable to make the weight correction large when the network is most unstable (*i.e.*, when all the output values are 0.5). In other words, for a neuron, the weight correction for its links should be maximum when its output status is very close to 0.5 and is minimum when its output status is close to 0 or 1. This can be achieved by taking

$$\Delta w_{ji} \propto -\frac{\frac{\partial E}{\partial y_j}}{\left|\frac{\partial E}{\partial y_j}\right|^q} \qquad q > 1, \tag{5.18}$$

i.e.,

$$\Delta w_{ji} = -\varepsilon_3 \frac{\frac{\partial E}{\partial y_j}}{\left|\frac{\partial E}{\partial y_j}\right|^q} \frac{dy_j}{dx_j} y_i \qquad q > 1, \tag{5.19}$$

where $|(\partial E/\partial y_j)|$ represents the magnitude of the gradient.

Such a choice for Δw_{ij} does not violate the necessary requirements for gradient descent search. In any gradient descent search, the gradient vector determines the direction of movement, while the quantum of movement is controlled by a scalar multiplier which is generally preselected by the user. The magnitude of the gradient vector is not very important as far as the gradient descent search is concerned. In the present case since only the magnitude of movement is changed, keeping the direction the same, it is also equivalent to a scalar multiplication. However, if the scalar multiplier is too small, search would be slow, while if it is too large, it may result in oscillation.

Henceforth the discussion considers only $q = 2$. When $q = 2$, for the logarithmic entropy one gets

$$
\begin{aligned}
\Delta w_{ji} &= -\varepsilon_3 \frac{1}{\frac{\partial E}{\partial y_j}} \frac{dy_j}{dx_j} y_i = \varepsilon_3 (n \ln 2) \frac{1}{\ln \frac{y_j}{1-y_j}} \frac{dy_j}{dx_j} y_i \\
&= \varepsilon \frac{1}{\ln \frac{y_j}{1-y_j}} \frac{dy_j}{dx_j} y_i
\end{aligned} \tag{5.20}
$$

with $\varepsilon = \varepsilon_3 \times (n \ln 2)$. Thus

$$
\Delta w_{ji} = \begin{cases}
-\varepsilon \frac{1}{\ln \frac{1-y_j}{y_j}} \frac{dy_j}{dx_j} y_i & \text{if } 0 \le y_j \le 0.5 \\
\varepsilon \frac{1}{\ln \frac{y_j}{1-y_j}} \frac{dy_j}{dx_j} y_i & \text{if } 0.5 \le y_j \le 1.0
\end{cases} \tag{5.21}
$$

The expression of Δw_{ji} has been divided into two parts in order to keep analogy with that of index of fuzziness.

5.2.2.4 Weight correction for exponential entropy   If one considers

$$
\begin{aligned}
E &= g(H) \tag{5.22} \\
&= H, \tag{5.23}
\end{aligned}
$$

where H is the exponential entropy of a fuzzy set, eqn. (2.19), with

$$
H(A) = \frac{1}{n(\sqrt{e}-1)} \sum_{j=1}^{n} \{ y_j e^{1-y_j} + (1-y_j)e^{y_j} - 1 \}, \tag{5.24}
$$

then

$$
\frac{\partial H}{\partial y_j} = \frac{1}{n(\sqrt{e}-1)} \{ (1-y_j)e^{1-y_j} - y_j e^{y_j} \}. \tag{5.25}
$$

Applying similar argument as in the case of logarithmic entropy, for exponential entropy one obtains

$$
\begin{aligned}
\Delta w_{ji} &= -\varepsilon_4 \frac{1}{\frac{\partial E}{\partial y_j}} \frac{dy_j}{dx_j} y_i \\
&= -\varepsilon \frac{1}{(1-y_j)e^{1-y_j} - y_j e^{y_j}} \frac{dy_j}{dx_j} y_i
\end{aligned} \tag{5.26}
$$

with $\varepsilon = \varepsilon_4 \times n(\sqrt{e}-1)$.

In other words,

$$
\Delta w_{ji} = \begin{cases}
-\varepsilon \frac{1}{(1-y_j)e^{1-y_j} - y_j e^{y_j}} \frac{dy_j}{dx_j} y_i & \text{if } 0 \le y_j \le 0.5 \\
\varepsilon \frac{1}{y_j e^{y_j} - (1-y_j)e^{1-y_j}} \frac{dy_j}{dx_j} y_i & \text{if } 0.5 \le y_j \le 1.0
\end{cases} \tag{5.27}
$$

5.2.3   Learning rate for different error (fuzziness) measures

Considering eqns. (5.6), (5.12), (5.21), and (5.27), one can see that in each of the four cases, the expression for Δw_{ji} has a common factor $\varepsilon(dy_j/dx_j)y_i$. Therefore, for the sake of comparison of different learning rates the common factor $[\varepsilon(dy_j/dx_j)y_i]$ can be ignored. The remaining part of the expression for Δw_{ji} will be referred as the learning rate because only that factor is different for different measures of fuzziness. The learning rate for different error measures can, therefore, be written as

$$
\begin{aligned}
\Delta w_{ji}^{l} \quad &\propto \quad -1 \quad \text{for} \quad 0 \le y_j \le 0.5 \\
&\propto \quad 1 \quad \text{for} \quad 0.5 \le y_j \le 1.0
\end{aligned}
\tag{5.28}
$$

for *linear index of fuzziness*,

$$
\begin{aligned}
\Delta w_{ji}^{q} \quad &\propto \quad -y_j \quad \text{for} \quad 0 \le y_j \le 0.5 \\
&\propto \quad 1 - y_j \quad \text{for} \quad 0.5 \le y_j \le 1.0
\end{aligned}
\tag{5.29}
$$

for *quadratic index of fuzziness*,

$$
\begin{aligned}
\Delta w_{ji}^{le} \quad &\propto \quad -\frac{1}{\ln \frac{1-y_j}{y_j}} \quad \text{for} \quad 0 \le y_j \le 0.5 \\
&\propto \quad \frac{1}{\ln \frac{y_j}{1-y_j}} \quad \text{for} \quad 0.5 \le y_j \le 1.0
\end{aligned}
\tag{5.30}
$$

for the *logarithmic entropy* $(q = 2)$, and

$$
\begin{aligned}
\Delta w_{ji}^{ee} \quad &\propto \quad -\frac{1}{(1-y_j)e^{1-y_j} - y_j e^{y_j}} \quad \text{for} \quad 0 \le y_j \le 0.5 \\
&\propto \quad \frac{1}{y_j e^{y_j} - (1-y_j)e^{1-y_j}} \quad \text{for} \quad 0.5 \le y_j \le 1.0
\end{aligned}
\tag{5.31}
$$

for the *exponential entropy* $(q = 2)$.

A critical examination of eqns. (5.28)–(5.31) reveals that in each of the four cases the learning rate is ≤ 0 for $y_j \le 0.5$ and is ≥ 0 for $y_j \ge 0.5$. In other words, the direction of change is always same in all the four cases. Therefore, if one compares different learning rates separately for $y_j \in [0, 0.5]$ and $y_j \in [0.5, 1.0]$, one can forget about the sign (direction) of learning rate. For example, if $\Delta w_{ji}^{le} = -5$ and $\Delta w_{ji}^{ee} = -3$, then although $\Delta w_{ji}^{le} \le \Delta w_{ji}^{ee}$, the rate of learning is more for Δw_{ji}^{le}.

Figure 5.2 depicts the rates of learning for different error measures with variation of status value of an output neuron. Because of the reasons mentioned in the previous paragraph, only the magnitudes of Δw_{ji}^{*} (where $* = l/q/le/ee$) have been plotted. From the figure it is noticed that for all the error measures, the rate of learning is low when the neurons are very close to stable states (*i.e.*, status value 0/1) and is high when the neurons are highly unstable (*i.e.*, status value 0.5). The curves are also symmetric around 0.5 of the status value. For linear index of fuzziness the learning rate is constant.

A comparative study of the different curves shows that the learning rate is minimum (for all status values) for the quadratic index of fuzziness and its

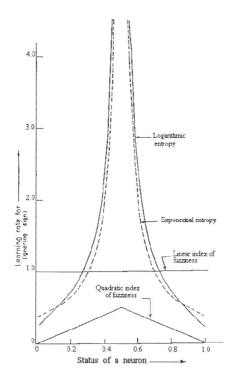

Fig. 5.2   Rate of learning with variation of output status for different error measures

absolute value is ≤ 0.5. For linear index of fuzziness it is constant and is equal to 1. On the other hand, for entropy measures the rates of learning are high. For status values very close to 0.5, learning rate is more for logarithmic entropy than that of the exponential entropy, whereas for output values close to $0/1$ learning rate is less for the logarithmic entropy. In other words, the change in rate of learning for exponential entropy is less than that of logarithmic entropy. So the outputs are expected to be more noise immune for the exponential entropy than for the logarithmic entropy; but will take more time to converge. Regarding learning rate the following proposition can be made.

Proposition. *The learning rate for quadratic index of fuzziness is the minimum.*

Proof. To prove the proposition, it suffices to prove

1. $\Delta w_{ji}^q < \Delta w_{ji}^l$
2. $\Delta w_{ji}^q < \Delta w_{ji}^{le}$
3. $\Delta w_{ji}^q < \Delta w_{ji}^{ee}$.

Proof of condition 1 ($\Delta w_{ji}^q < \Delta w_{ji}^l$). Leaving aside signs, $\Delta w_{ji}^q = \varepsilon \kappa$ with

$$\kappa = \begin{cases} y_j & \text{if } 0 \le y_j \le 0.5 \\ 1 - y_j & \text{if } 0.5 \le y_j \le 1.0 \end{cases}$$

But $\Delta w_{ji}^l = \varepsilon \times 1.0$.

Evidently $\Delta w_{ji}^q < \Delta w_{ji}^l$.

Proof of condition 2 ($\Delta w_{ji}^q < \Delta w_{ji}^{le}$). Leaving aside the signs

$$\Delta w_{ji}^{le} = \begin{cases} \varepsilon \dfrac{1}{\ln \frac{1-y_j}{y_j}} & \text{if } 0 \le y_j \le 0.5 \\[2ex] \varepsilon \dfrac{1}{\ln \frac{y_j}{1-y_j}} & \text{if } 0.5 \le y_j \le 1.0 \end{cases}$$

Proving the relation $\Delta w_{ji}^q < \Delta w_{ji}^{le}$ is equivalent to proving

$$\frac{1}{\ln \frac{1-y_j}{y_j}} > y_j \qquad \text{for} \qquad 0 \le y_j \le 0.5$$

$$\frac{1}{\ln \frac{y_j}{1-y_j}} > 1 - y_j \qquad \text{for} \qquad 0.5 \le y_j \le 1.0$$

Now to prove

$$\frac{1}{\ln \frac{1-y_j}{y_j}} > y_j \qquad \text{for} \quad 0 \le y_j \le 0.5, \text{ one obtains}$$

$$\ln \frac{1-y_j}{y_j} < \frac{1}{y_j}$$

or, $\ln \left(\frac{1}{y_j} - 1 \right) < \frac{1}{y_j}$

or, $\ln (x - 1) < x$ with $x = \frac{1}{y_j}$.

Suppose $y = \ln(x - 1)$. Then

$$\begin{aligned} x &= 1 + e^y \\ &= 1 + 1 + \frac{y}{1} + \frac{y^2}{2!} + \cdots \infty \\ &> y \qquad \qquad [\text{ since } x \ge 2 \text{ and thereby } y \ge 0]. \end{aligned}$$

Hence, $\ln (x - 1) < x$, thus proving the first part.

In order to prove the other part

$$\frac{1}{\ln \frac{y_j}{1-y_j}} > 1 - y_j \qquad \text{for} \qquad 0.5 \le y_j \le 1.0$$

or, $\ln \frac{y_j}{1-y_j} < \frac{1}{1-y_j}$

or, $\ln (x - 1) < x$ with $x = \frac{1}{1-y_j}$.

Rest of the proof is as in the previous case and hence the relation

$$\frac{1}{\ln \frac{1-y_j}{y_j}} > y_j \text{ for } 0 \le y_j \le 0.5, \text{ and } \frac{1}{\ln \frac{y_j}{1-y_j}} > 1 - y_j \text{ for } 0.5 \le y_j \le 1.0$$

Proof of condition 3 ($\Delta w_{ji}^q < \Delta w_{ji}^{ee}$). Leaving aside the signs

$$\Delta w_{ji}^{ee} = \begin{cases} \varepsilon \dfrac{1}{(1-y_j)e^{1-y_j} - y_j e^{y_j}} & \text{if } 0 \le y_j \le 0.5 \\[2ex] \varepsilon \dfrac{1}{y_j e^{y_j} - (1-y_j)e^{1-y_j}} & \text{if } 0.5 \le y_j \le 1.0 \end{cases}$$

To prove the relation $\Delta w_{ji}^q < \Delta w_{ji}^{ee}$, is equivalent to prove

$$\frac{1}{(1-y_j)e^{1-y_j} - y_j e^{y_j}} > y_j \qquad \text{for} \quad 0 \le y_j \le 0.5$$

$$\frac{1}{y_j e^{y_j} - (1-y_j)e^{1-y_j}} > 1 - y_j \qquad \text{for} \quad 0.5 \le y_j \le 1.0$$

Now to prove

$$\frac{1}{(1-y_j)e^{1-y_j} - y_j e^{y_j}} > y_j \qquad \text{for} \quad 0 \le y_j \le 0.5, \text{ one computes}$$

$(1 - x)e^{1-x} - xe^x < \frac{1}{x}$ for $x \in [0, 0.5]$

(for notational simplicity x has been used in place of y_j)

or, $x(1 - x)e^{1-x} - x^2 e^x < 1$

or, $xe^{1-x} - x^2(e^{1-x} + e^x) < 1$

or, $xe^{1-x} < 1 + x^2(e^{1-x} + e^x)$.

Let $f(x) = xe^{1-x}$

$\qquad f'(x) = (1 - x)e^{1-x} > 0, x \in [0, 0.5]$

$\longrightarrow xe^{1-x}$ monotonically increases for x in$[0, 0.5]$

$\longrightarrow xe^{1-x}$ attains the maximum value at $x = 1/2$ for $x \in [0, 0.5]$.

Hence, $\max\{xe^{1-x}\} = \frac{1}{2}\sqrt{e} < 1, \quad x \in [0,\ 0.5]$.

On the other hand, $\min\{1 + x^2(e^{1-x} + e^x)\} = 1$. Hence the relation.

To prove the other part

$$\frac{1}{y_j e^{y_j} - (1-y_j)e^{1-y_j}} > 1 - y_j \qquad \text{for} \quad 0.5 \le y_j \le 1.0, \quad \text{one has}$$

$$y_j e^{y_j} - (1 - y_j)e^{1-y_j} < \frac{1}{1-y_j}$$

or, $(1 - x)e^{1-x} - xe^x < \frac{1}{x}$ with $x = 1 - y_j, \quad x \in [0, 0.5]$.

The rest of the proof is as in the previous case, and thus one can write

$$\frac{1}{(1 - y_j)e^{1-y_j} - y_j e^{y_j}} > y_j \qquad \text{for} \quad 0 \le y_j \le 0.5$$

$$\frac{1}{y_j e^{y_j} - (1 - y_j)e^{1-y_j}} > 1 - y_j \qquad \text{for} \quad 0.5 \le y_j \le 1.0$$

∎

5.2.4   Results

An application of the methodology for extracting objects, specially from noisy environments, is shown in Ref. [1]. Here, we present some of the results. The problem can be stated as follows: *Given a noisy realization of a scene, the objective is to estimate the original scene that has resulted in the observation.*

A three-layered network with N^2 was used. A neuron thus gets input from nine neurons in the previous layer. The threshold value θ in this case is $\frac{9}{2} = 4.5$. The input gray levels are mapped in [0,1] by a linear transformation and is given as input to the network. The network is then allowed to settle. When the network has stabilized, the neurons having the status value 0 constitute one region type, say, object (background) and the remaining neurons with output status 1 constitute another region type, say, background (object).

Fig. 5.3   Original synthetic image

In order to check the effectiveness of this technique, computer simulation was done on a synthetic bitonic image (Fig. 5.3) corrupted by noise. The corrupted versions were obtained by adding noise from $N(0, \sigma^2)$ distribution with different values of σ (10,20,32). Three noisy inputs are shown in Figs. 5.4(a), 5.5(a) and 5.6(a). The images are of dimension 128×128 and have 32 levels. Simulation study was also done on a real image of a *noisy tank* [Fig. 5.7(a)]. The noisy tank image is of size 64×64 with 64 gray levels. For the simulation study ε value was taken as 0.2.

The objects extracted by this technique, with different expressions of error for different noisy versions of the synthetic image, are included in Figs. 5.4–5.6. Figure 5.7 depicts the objects extracted from the *noisy tank* image with different error models.

Examining the results it can easily be inferred that, as the noise level increases, the quality of the output, as expected, deteriorates; but approximate shapes and outlines are maintained. Comparing results of different error models, it is noticed that outputs with index of fuzziness measures (linear and quadratic) are better than those obtained by entropy measures ($q = 2$). Among the two different entropy measures, the exponential function is found to be more immune to noise. This is possibly due to different learning rates. For a fixed value of ε, the learning rate is low for the indices of fuzziness, whereas it is higher for entropy measures. When the learning rate is high, a particular neuron influences its neighbors to a great extent; thus the noisy elements affect the results strongly. The system thus fails to remove all the noise. Of the two entropy measures, the exponential one is more noise-immune because of its lower learning rate at the initial stage of learning. A critical examination of the results reveals that the index of fuzziness (both linear and quadratic) is consistently better than entropy measures for maintaining the compactness of the extracted objects. But shapes of objects are better preserved by entropy measures. This observation can be explained as follows. Since for the index of fuzziness, the rate of learning is slow, it smoothes out

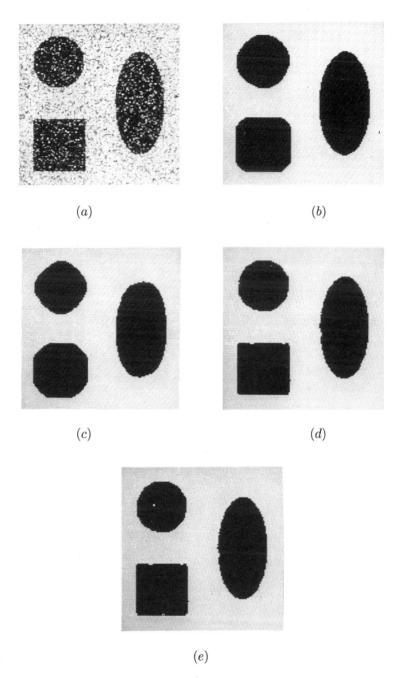

Fig. 5.4 Results for a noisy version ($\sigma = 10$) of synthetic image: (a) input; (b) extracted object with linear index of fuzziness; (c) extracted object with quadratic index of fuzziness; (d) extracted object with logarithmic entropy; (e) extracted object with exponential entropy

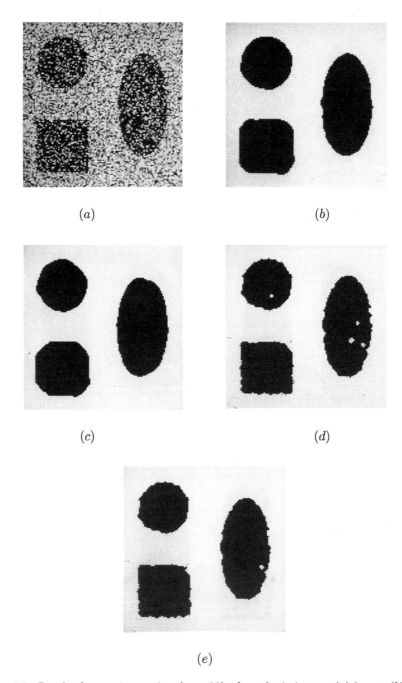

(a)

(b)

(c)

(d)

(e)

Fig. 5.5 Results for a noisy version ($\sigma = 20$) of synthetic image: (a) input; (b) extracted object with linear index of fuzziness; (c) extracted object with quadratic index of fuzziness; (d) extracted object with logarithmic entropy; (e) extracted object with exponential entropy

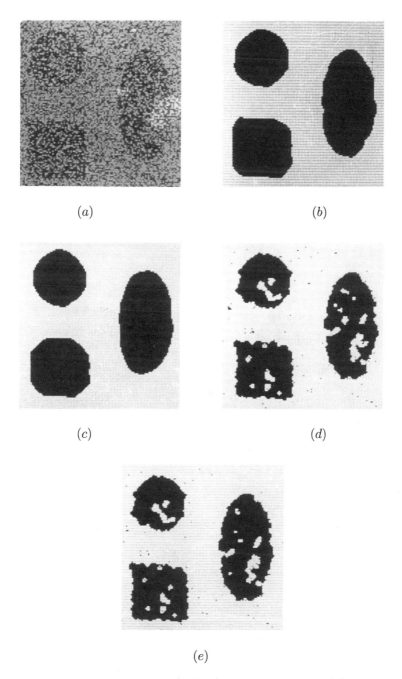

Fig. 5.6   Results for a noisy version ($\sigma = 32$) of synthetic image: (a) input; (b) extracted object with linear index of fuzziness; (c) extracted object with quadratic index of fuzziness; (d) extracted object with logarithmic entropy; (e) extracted object with exponential entropy

(a)

(b)

(c)

(d)

(e)

Fig. 5.7 Results for noisy tank image: (a) input; (b) extracted object with linear index of fuzziness; (c) extracted object with quadratic index of fuzziness; (d) extracted object with logarithmic entropy; (e) extracted object with exponential entropy

noises and creates compact regions. For entropy measures all noisy pixels may not be removed because of rapid learning, particularly when σ is large. On the other hand, entropy measures enable the network to preserve object boundaries as learning rate is very high near the most ambiguous region ($y_j \simeq 0.5$).

Some more results corresponding to first-order neighborhood (N^1) and higher values of q are available in an earlier work [1]. As expected, results corresponding to N^1 (Fig. 5.8) are worse than those for N^2. ♣

Ghosh [17] has also used the fuzzy correlation measure with this self-organizing MLP for object extraction. Fuzzy correlation provides a measure of the relationship between two membership functions representing fuzzy sets [18]. In other words, it gives a measure of information about the distance of a fuzzy set A from its nearest ordinary set $\underline{A}$ and is expressed as

$$C(A, \underline{A}) = 1 - \frac{4}{X_1 + X_2} \sum_{i=1}^{n} \{A(i) - \underline{A}(i)\}^2, \qquad (5.32)$$

with $X_1 = \sum_{i=1}^{n} \{2A(i) - 1\}^2$, $X_2 = \sum_{i=1}^{n} \{2\underline{A}(i) - 1\}^2$ and $0 \leq C(A, \underline{A}) \leq 1$. Choosing $E = 1 - C$, one obtains

$$\frac{\partial E}{\partial y_j} = \frac{8(X_1 + X_2)\{A(j) - \underline{A}(j)\} - 16X_3\{2A(j) - 1\}}{(X_1 + X_2)^2}, \qquad (5.33)$$

where $X_3 = \sum_j \{A(j) - \underline{A}(j)\}^2$. This is used for weight updating.

5.3 CELLULAR NETWORK AND GENETIC ALGORITHMS WITH FUZZINESS MEASURES

Setting up a cellular neural network (CNN) for a particular task needs a proper selection of circuit parameters (cloning template) that determines the dynamics of the network. In this section we describe a methodology of Pal and Bhandari [2] for demonstrating an application of genetic algorithms (GAs), whose basic operations are described in Appendix A, with fuzzy fitness function for object extraction from noisy images using a CNN. Here the required cloning templates are automatically selected. The algorithm uses both spatial [fuzzy compactness and index of area coverage (IOAC)] and grayness (entropy) ambiguity measures (as mentioned in Chapter 4) as the basis of the fitness function of GAs. This method is unsupervised and does not need any prior information of the desired (target) output. The results obtained using the heuristically selected cloning templates are compared with those obtained using the templates selected by GAs. It has been found that the performance of the latter is consistently better under different noisy conditions. Although this method has been developed for selection of cloning template and used for object extraction, it can also be applied to other image processing operations.

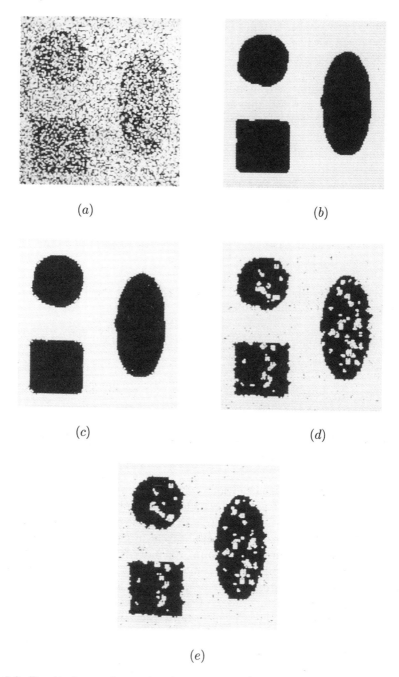

Fig. 5.8 Results for a noisy version ($\sigma = 20$ and N^1) of synthetic image: (a) input; (b) extracted object with linear index of fuzziness; (c) extracted object with quadratic index of fuzziness; (d) extracted object with logarithmic entropy; (e) extracted object with exponential entropy

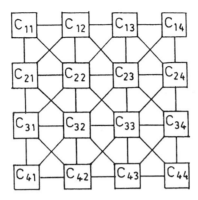

Fig. 5.9 Two-dimensional cellular neural network

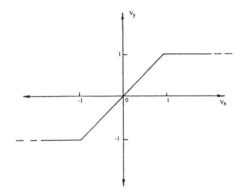

Fig. 5.10 Nonlinear input–output function

5.3.1 Cellular neural network

An $N_x \times N_y$ cellular neural network can be considered as an ordered set $\{C_{ij}\}$ of $N_x N_y$ cells that are arranged in a pattern as shown in Fig. 5.9. For a two-dimensional CNN, an r-neighborhood (N_{ij}^r) can be defined as $N_{ij}^r = \{C_{kl} \mid \max(\mid k - i \mid, \mid l - j \mid) \leq r, 1 \leq k \leq N_x; 1 \leq l \leq N_y\}$. The state v_{xij} of any cell C_{ij} in a CNN is described by the differential equation

$$C\frac{dv_{xij}(t)}{dt} = \frac{-1}{R_x}v_{xij}(t) + \sum_{C_{kl} \in N_{ij}^r} A_{ij;kl}v_{ykl}(t) + I_{ij}, 1 \leq i \leq N_x; 1 \leq j \leq N_y,$$

(5.34)

where $A_{ij;kl}$ represents the conductance of the link between C_{ij} and C_{kl}, and I_{ij} is the bias to the cell C_{ij}. Here R_x and C (constants for a CNN) are the resistance and capacitance of the cell, CR_x is the time constant of the circuit and R_x determines the power dissipation.

The output $v_{yij}(t)$ of the cell C_{ij} is a nonlinear function $f(v_{xij}(t))$, as shown in Fig. 5.10. It can be expressed as

$$v_{yij}(t) = f(v_{xij}(t)) = 0.5(|\, v_{xij}(t) + 1\,| - |\, v_{xij}(t) - 1\,|), \qquad (5.35)$$

for $1 \leq i \leq N_x$, $1 \leq j \leq N_y$, with the constraint $|\, v_{xij}(0)\,| \leq 1$, for $1 \leq i \leq N_x$, $1 \leq j \leq N_y$.

The state of each cell in a CNN is bounded and after the transients settle down, a CNN approaches a stable state [16]. Moreover, if the circuit parameters satisfy $A_{ij;ij} > (1/R_x)$, then

$\lim_{t \to \infty} |\, v_{xij}(t)\,| \geq 1, \qquad 1 \leq i \leq N_x; \quad 1 \leq j \leq N_y;$

or equivalently

$\lim_{t \to \infty} v_{yij}(t) = \pm 1, \qquad 1 \leq i \leq N_x; \quad 1 \leq j \leq N_y.$

5.3.2 Object extraction using CNN

As mentioned before, object extraction involves segmenting the whole image into two region types: object region and background region. Two adjacent pixels of an image belong to the same region if they have similar gray-value properties. So, both gray level and positional properties play an important role in making a decision as to whether a pixel belongs to object or background regions.

In order to explain the principle of object extraction using CNN, let us consider eqn. (5.34), which can be approximated, using eqn. (5.35), by a difference equation as

$$v_{xij}(n+1) = v_{xij}(n) + \frac{h}{C}\left[\frac{-1}{R_x}v_{xij}(n) + \sum_{C_{kl} \in N_{ij}^r} A_{ij;kl}\, f(v_{xkl}(n)) + I_{ij}\right]$$

$$(5.36)$$

for $1 \leq i \leq N_x$; $1 \leq j \leq N_y$, where h is a constant time step and $v_{xij}(n)$ is the state of the cell C_{ij} at the nth instant of time. Eqn. (5.36) can be interpreted as a two-dimensional filter for transforming an image $\mathbf{v}_x(n)$ into $\mathbf{v}_x(n+1)$. Usually, the filter is space invariant for image processing.

In the above definition $A_{ij;kl}$ is assumed to be position invariant. Now eqn. (5.36) can be written, for a unit time step $(h = 1)$, as

$$v_{xij}(n+1) = v_{xij}(n) - \frac{1}{R_x C}v_{xij}(n) + \frac{1}{C}[T * v_{yij}(n) + I_{ij}], \qquad (5.37)$$

where

$$T = \begin{bmatrix} T_{-r,-r} & \cdots & T_{-r,0} & \cdots & T_{-r,r} \\ \vdots & & \vdots & & \\ T_{0,-r} & \cdots & T_{0,0} & \cdots & T_{0,r} \\ \vdots & & \vdots & & \\ T_{r,-r} & \cdots & T_{r,0} & \cdots & T_{r,r} \end{bmatrix}$$

is the cloning template and * is a convolution operator. For any cloning template T, the convolution operator (*) is defined as

$$T * v_{ij} = \sum_{C_{kl} \in N_{ij}^r} T_{k-i,l-j} v_{kl}. \tag{5.38}$$

A CNN processes signals by mapping from one signal space to another. If the initial state space is $[-1.0, 1.0]^{N_x \times N_y}$ and the output space is $\{-1, 1\}^{N_x \times N_y}$, then the dynamic map F can be defined as

$$F : [-1.0, 1.0]^{N_x \times N_y} \to \{-1, 1\}^{N_x \times N_y}. \tag{5.39}$$

Object extraction in an image $X = \{x_{m,n} : m = 1, 2, \ldots, N_x;\ n = 1, 2, \ldots, N_y\}$ of size $N_x \times N_y$ can be considered as a mapping

$$E : [a, b]^{N_x \times N_y} \to \{A, B\}^{N_x \times N_y}, \tag{5.40}$$

where the range of gray levels of the image is $[a, b]$, and A, B are gray levels of object and background, respectively, or vice versa. Equations (5.39) and (5.40) are analogous. Thus if one can transform the gray level of the input image into $[-1.0, 1.0]$, it is possible to achieve a transformation of the image into $\{-1, 1\}$ by using a cellular neural network.

5.3.3 Selection of cloning template

The selection of cloning template T plays an important role in defining the dynamic rule of a CNN for performing a particular operation. The guidelines for selection of T for some operations such as noise removal, edge detection and line detection are mentioned in Ref. [16]. For example, in noise removal of an image, T can be expréssed as an averaging operator. For edge detection, T is expressed by a Laplacian or a difference operator so that the pixels of homogeneous and boundary regions can possess values -1 and +1, respectively, at the stable state of the net. The way one can select T for an object extraction problem is described below.

As mentioned earlier, in object extraction both gray level and positional properties should be taken into account and one way of achieving this operation is to use an weighted average operator. Therefore one can choose the weighted averaging operator in defining the dynamic rule of CNN in this regard. This operator can be expressed by a cloning template like C_1, C_2, C_3 and so on as shown below (the unit used here is $10^{-3}\ \Omega^{-1}$):

$$C_1 = \begin{bmatrix} 0.0 & 1.0 & 0.0 \\ 1.0 & 2.0 & 1.0 \\ 0.0 & 1.0 & 0.0 \end{bmatrix},$$

$$C_2 = \begin{bmatrix} 0.5 & 1.0 & 0.5 \\ 1.0 & 2.0 & 1.0 \\ 0.5 & 1.0 & 0.5 \end{bmatrix},$$

$$C_3 = \begin{bmatrix} 0.0 & 0.0 & 0.5 & 0.0 & 0.0 \\ 0.0 & 1.0 & 2.0 & 1.0 & 0.0 \\ 0.5 & 2.0 & 4.0 & 2.0 & 0.5 \\ 0.0 & 1.0 & 2.0 & 1.0 & 0.0 \\ 0.0 & 0.0 & 0.5 & 0.0 & 0.0 \end{bmatrix}.$$

Let us consider C_1, as an example, for explaining the object extraction operation in terms of the dynamic equation. Here for cell time constant $CR_x = 1$ μs (microsecond) and cell bias $I_{ij} = 0$ one has

$$\frac{dv_{xij}(t)}{dt} = 10^6[-v_{xij}(t) + v_{y(i-1)j}(t)+$$

$$v_{yi(j-1)}(t) + 2v_{yij}(t) + v_{yi(j+1)}(t) + v_{y(i+1)j}(t)], \tag{5.41}$$

$$v_{yij}(t) = 0.5(|\,v_{xij}(t) + 1\,| - |\,v_{xij}(t) - 1\,|), \qquad 1 \le i \le 8, \ 1 \le j \le 8. \tag{5.42}$$

Table 5.1   An 8×8 input image

-1.0	0.4	-0.8	-1.0	-0.6	-0.7	0.2	-0.8
-0.3	-0.7	-0.2	0.3	-0.7	-0.7	-1.0	-0.7
-0.1	-0.9	0.8	0.8	0.5	0.6	-0.9	-0.3
0.2	-1.0	1.0	0.8	0.6	0.3	-0.2	0.4
-0.3	0.1	0.8	0.1	0.7	0.4	0.2	-0.4
-0.7	-1.0	0.2	1.0	0.9	1.0	-0.2	-0.9
-0.5	0.2	-1.0	-0.6	-0.8	-0.7	0.2	-1.0
-0.2	0.1	-0.5	-1.0	-0.7	-1.0	-0.2	-0.6

Let the initial state of the CNN be the same as the pixel values shown in Table 5.1. Observe that for the pixel at (4,4) position, the derivative $dv_{xij}(t)/dt$ is positive, whereas the derivative at the point (2,2) is negative. As a result, the pixel values at (4,4) and (2,2) at the next iteration will tend to increase and decrease, respectively. After several iterations when the network becomes stable, these values will tend to +1 and -1, denoting object and background, respectively. The dynamic rule of eqn. (5.41) is therefore able to detect the homogeneous object and background regions in the image by making their values, +1 or -1 (Table 5.2). It is only the corner pixels of the object that may possess some intermediate value. It is therefore clear from the preceding discussion that different cloning templates are required for different image processing operations. Again, for a particular operation, the same cloning template may not be applicable for all kinds of images. For example, C_1 may not be applicable for segmenting thin or noisy image regions.

There is no standard method for selecting automatically a correct set of cloning template parameters in setting up the dynamics of CNN for a particular operation on a given image. Let us now describe the methodology of Pal and Bhandari [2] (using fuzziness measures and genetic algorithms) to provide a solution to this problem. Here, the problem of choosing correct parameters (for an r-neighborhood cloning template) of a CNN for object extraction has been considered to be equivalent to searching for an appropriate set of parameters $\{T_{ij} : -r \leq i \leq r; -r \leq j \leq r\}$ from a complex space that gives the best object background classification. (Note that the same framework may be used for other image processing operations.)

5.3.4   Optimum selection of cloning template

Determination of fitness function of GAs for selecting the optimum parameters of a CNN is an important task. Since image segmentation and object extraction are unsupervised problems, we need an evaluation function for quantifying the desired segmented output so that it can be used for defining the fitness function of GAs. The principle of minimization of fuzzy compactness ($Comp$), index of area coverage ($IOAC$), and entropy (H) is an established criterion for image enhancement and object extraction [19].

Table 5.2   Output image when the net reaches the stable state

-1.0	-1.0	-1.0	-1.0	-1.0	-1.0	-1.0	-1.0
-1.0	-1.0	-1.0	-1.0	-1.0	-1.0	-1.0	-1.0
-1.0	-1.0	0.7	1.0	1.0	-0.5	-1.0	-1.0
-1.0	-1.0	1.0	1.0	1.0	1.0	-1.0	-1.0
-1.0	-1.0	1.0	1.0	1.0	1.0	-1.0	-1.0
-1.0	-1.0	0.0	1.0	1.0	0.5	-1.0	-1.0
-1.0	-1.0	-1.0	-1.0	-1.0	-1.0	-1.0	-1.0
-1.0	-1.0	-1.0	-1.0	-1.0	-1.0	-1.0	-1.0

Entropy [eqn. (2.17)] of an image (X) considers the global information and provides an average amount of fuzziness in grayness of X, $i.e.$, the degree of difficulty (ambiguity) in deciding whether a pixel would be treated as black (dark) or white (bright). Compactness [eqn. (4.6)] and index of area coverage $IOAC$ [eqn. (4.15)], on the other hand, take into account the local information and reflect the amount of fuzziness in shape and geometry (spatial domain) of an image. Therefore, the concept of minimization of these ambiguity measures may be considered as the basis of a fitness (evaluation) function of GAs for object extraction. One may also use a composite measure ($e.g.$, product of

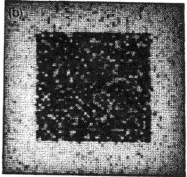

Fig. 5.11   Image of a squared object, with Gaussian noise: (*a*) $\sigma = 10$; (*b*) $\sigma = 20$

both grayness and spatial ambiguity measures) as the evaluation function, so that minimization of this composite measure implies achieving minimum ambiguity (fuzziness) in the resulting segmented image from both points of view.

This algorithm [2] uses the reciprocal of their product as the fitness function:

$$Fit(X) = \frac{1}{Comp(X).H(X)} \qquad (5.43)$$

or

$$Fit(X) = \frac{1}{IOAC(X).H(X)}, \qquad (5.44)$$

so that both grayness and spatial ambiguity of an image are taken care of in providing the quantitative indices for evaluating the quality of a segmented image output. The details of the algorithm are described in an earlier study [2].

5.3.5   Results

Some experimental results of the algorithm are shown on two 64×64 synthetic images (Figs. 5.11 and 5.12) of geometric objects corrupted by Gaussian noise of different standard deviations ($\sigma = 10$ and 20) and zero mean. (Note that the use of compactness and index of area coverage measures assumes that the input has single object region.) At first, the effectiveness of CNN has been demonstrated for C_1, C_2, C_3 cloning templates that were selected heuristically. Then the capability of GAs with fuzziness measures in automatically selecting the cloning templates is demonstrated. Throughout the experiment, it was assumed that CR_x (cell time constant) = 1 μs, R_x (resistance of a cell) = 10^3 Ω and I_{ij} (cell bias) = 0.

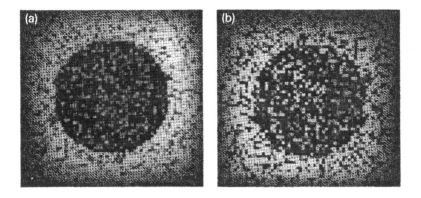

Fig. 5.12   Image of a circular object, with Gaussian noise: (*a*) $\sigma = 10$; (*b*) $\sigma = 20$

Fig. 5.13   Extracted square from its noisy ($\sigma = 10$) version, using (*a*) C_1, (*b*) C_2, (*c*) C_3

Fig. 5.14   Extracted square from its noisy ($\sigma = 20$) version, using (*a*) C_1, (*b*) C_2, (*c*) C_3

Fig. 5.15 Extracted square, using GA with *compactness* in fitness function, from its noisy versions having (*a*) $\sigma = 10$, (*b*) $\sigma = 20$

Fig. 5.16 Extracted square, using GA with *IOAC* in fitness function, from its noisy versions having (*a*) $\sigma = 10$, (*b*) $\sigma = 20$

Figsures 5.13 and 5.14 depict the outputs corresponding to the images (Fig. 5.11) with noise levels ($\sigma = 10$ and 20) when C_1, C_2, and C_3 have respectively been used to define the dynamic rule of CNN. The results, as expected, show that the performance of the algorithm deteriorates with increase of σ and improves with the increase of size of the cloning template. The template C_3 is less noise sensitive and provides better performance than do C_1 and C_2 because of the greater neighborhood effect.

For demonstrating the capability of genetic algorithms with fuzzy fitness function to obtain the optimum parameters of a cloning template, a template of size 3×3 ($r = 1$) was considered, with population size = 10, mutation probability = 0.005, crossover probability = 1, and number of iterations = 50. The output obtained for the square images with different noise levels are shown in Figs. 5.15 and 5.16, when eqns. (5.43) and (5.44), respectively, are

 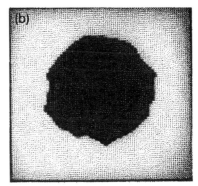

Fig. 5.17 Extracted circle, using GA with *compactness* in fitness function, from its noisy versions having (a) $\sigma = 10$, (b) $\sigma = 20$

 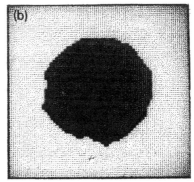

Fig. 5.18 Extracted circle, using GA with $IOAC$ in fitness function, from its noisy versions having (a) $\sigma = 10$, (b) $\sigma = 20$

used. The deterioration of output with noise is seen to be less than those of heuristic selection (Figs. 5.13 and 5.14). Note that the corner pixels of square images are affected when eqn. (5.43) is used, because it attempts to optimize the compactness by rounding the corners.

The results obtained for the circle images are shown in Figs. 5.17 and 5.18 respectively, when eqns. (5.43) and (5.44) are used as the fitness function. As expected, for the circle images the outputs obtained using eqn. (5.43) as the fitness function is better than those obtained using eqn. (5.44). The outputs obtained using the heuristically selected template C_2 are shown in Fig. 5.19. As in the case of the square image, the templates selected for circle image using genetic algorithms with fuzziness measures perform consistently well in different noise levels, as compared to those of heuristic selection. As a typical illustration of the cloning templates obtained by GA after 50 iterations, they

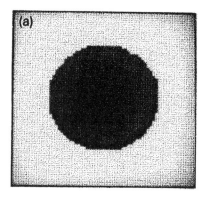 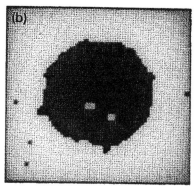

Fig. 5.19 Extracted circle, using C_3, from its noisy versions having (a) $\sigma = 10$, (b) $\sigma = 20$

are listed below (designated by C_{GA}^1 and C_{GA}^2):

$$C_{GA}^1 = \begin{bmatrix} 0.748 & 0.747 & 0.559 \\ 0.958 & 0.964 & 0.909 \\ 0.491 & 0.658 & 0.219 \end{bmatrix} 10^{-3}\,\Omega^{-1},$$

$$C_{GA}^2 = \begin{bmatrix} 0.897 & 0.827 & 0.314 \\ 0.680 & 0.995 & 0.758 \\ 0.249 & 0.749 & 0.192 \end{bmatrix} 10^{-3}\,\Omega^{-1}$$

for the circle image with $\sigma = 10$ when eqns. (5.43) and (5.44) are used for the fitness function.

REFERENCES

1. A. Ghosh, N. R. Pal, and S. K. Pal, "Self-organization for object extraction using multilayer neural network and fuzziness measures," *IEEE Transactions on Fuzzy Systems*, vol. 1, pp. 54–68, 1993.

2. S. K. Pal and D. Bhandari, "Genetic algorithms with fuzzy fitness function for object extraction using cellular neural networks," *Fuzzy Sets and Systems*, vol. 65, pp. 129–139, 1994.

3. R. C. Gonzalez and P. Wintz, *Digital Image Processing*. Reading, MA: Addison-Wesley, 1987.

4. A. Rosenfeld and A. C. Kak, *Digital Picture Processing*, vols. 1–2. New York: Academic Press, 1982.

5. S. K. Pal and D. Dutta Majumder, *Fuzzy Mathematical Approach to Pattern Recognition.* New York: Wiley (Halsted Press), 1986.

6. N. R. Pal and S. K. Pal, "A review on image segmentation techniques," *Pattern Recognition*, vol. 26, pp. 1277–1294, 1993.

7. K. S. Fu and J. K. Mui, "A survey on image segmentation," *Pattern Recognition*, vol. 13, pp. 3–16, 1981.

8. G. L. Bilbro, M. White, and W. Synder, "Image segmentation with neurocomputers," in *Neural Computers*, R. Eckmiller and C. V. D. Malsberg, eds. Berlin: Springer-Verlag, 1988.

9. A. Ghosh, N. R. Pal, and S. K. Pal, "Image segmentation using a neural network," *Biological Cybernetics*, vol. 66, pp. 151–158, 1991.

10. A. Ghosh and S. K. Pal, "Neural network, self-organization and object extraction," *Pattern Recognition Letters*, vol. 13, pp. 387–397, 1992.

11. A. Ghosh, N. R. Pal, and S. K. Pal, "Object background classification using Hopfield type neural network," *International Journal of Pattern Recognition and Artificial Intelligence*, vol. 6, pp. 989–1008, 1992.

12. S. K. Pal, S. De, and A. Ghosh, "Designing Hopfield type networks using genetic algorithms and its comparison with simulated annealing," *International Journal of Pattern Recognition and Artificial Intelligence*, vol. 11, pp. 447–461, 1997.

13. W. E. Blanz and S. L. Gish, "A real time image segmentation system using a connectionist classifier architecture," *International Journal of Pattern Recognition and Artificial Intelligence*, vol. 5, no. 4, pp. 603–617, 1991.

14. N. Babaguchi, K. Yamada, K. Kise, and Y. Tezuku, "Connectionist model binarization," *International Journal of Pattern Recognition and Artificial Intelligence*, vol. 5, no. 4, pp. 629–644, 1991.

15. B. S. Manjunath, T. Simchony, and R. Chellappa, "Stochastic and deterministic networks for texture segmentation," *IEEE Transactions on Acoustics, Speech, and Signal Processing*, vol. 38, no. 6, pp. 1039–1049, 1990.

16. L. O. Chua and L. Yang, "Cellular neural network: Theory," *IEEE Transactions on Circuits and Systems*, vol. 35, pp. 1257–1272, 1988.

17. A. Ghosh, "Use of fuzziness measures in layered networks for object extraction: A generalization," *Fuzzy Sets and Systems*, vol. 72, pp. 331–348, 1995.

18. C. A. Murthy, S. K. Pal, and D. Dutta Majumder, "Correlation between two fuzzy membership functions," *Fuzzy Sets and Systems*, vol. 7, pp. 23–38, 1985.

19. S. K. Pal and A. Ghosh, "Fuzzy geometry in image analysis," *Fuzzy Sets and Systems*, vol. 48, pp. 23–40, 1992.

6

Feature Evaluation

6.1 INTRODUCTION

Feature selection or extraction is a process of selecting a map of the form $\mathbf{F}' = f(\mathbf{F})$, by which a sample $\mathbf{F}(F_1, F_2, \ldots, F_n)$ in an n-dimensional measurement space $(\mathcal{R}^n)$ is transformed into a point $\mathbf{F}'(F_1', F_2', \ldots, F_{n'}')$ in an n'-dimensional $(n' < n)$ feature space $(\mathcal{R}^{n'})$. The problem of feature selection deals with choosing some of F_is from the measurement space to constitute the feature space. On the other hand, the problem of feature extraction deals with generating F_j's (constituting the feature space) based on some F_is in the measurement space. The main objective of these processes is to retain the optimum salient characteristics necessary for the recognition process and to reduce the dimensionality of the measurement space so that effective and easily computable algorithms can be devised for efficient categorization.

The criterion of a good feature is that it should be unchanging with any other possible variation within a class, while emphasizing differences that are important in discriminating between patterns of different types. In other words, those features for which the interclass or intraclass distances are maximized or minimized are considered to have optimal saliency. Different useful classical techniques to achieve this have been described [1, 2]. Several methods based on fuzzy set theory [3]–[6] and artificial neural networks (ANNs) [7]–[11] have also been reported. Fuzzy set theoretic approaches to feature selection are based mainly on measures of entropy and index of fuzziness [4, 5], fuzzy c-means [3], and fuzzy ISODATA [6] algorithms. Some of the recent attempts made for feature selection or extraction in the framework of ANNs are based mainly on multilayer feedforward networks [9]–[17] and self-organizing networks [13], [18]–[20]. The methods based on multilayer feedforward networks include, among others, determination of saliency (usefulness) of input features [14], development of Sammon's nonlinear discriminant analysis (NDA) network, and linear discriminant analysis (LDA) network [13], whereas those based on self-organizing networks include development of the nonlinear projection (NP-SOM)-based Kohonen self-organizing feature map [13], distortion tolerant Gabor transformations followed by minimum distortion clustering using multilayer self-organizing maps [18], a nonlinear projection method based on Kohonen's topology preserving maps [19], and principal component analysis (PCA) network [20].

Depending on whether the class information of the samples is known, these methods are classified as supervised or unsupervised. For example, the algorithms described in Refs. [4, 5, 9, 14] and [17] fall under the supervised category, whereas those in Refs. [6, 18] and [19] are unsupervised. In the area of neuro-fuzzy pattern recognition, one may note that the literature for feature selection or extraction is very scanty as compared to classification and clustering.

The present chapter describes some attempts, recently made, using neuro-fuzzy approaches for feature selection and extraction under both supervised and unsupervised modes of training. The underlying principle includes definition of a fuzzy feature evaluation index and its optimization in a connectionist framework. Depending on the task, different layered networks under supervised or unsupervised learning are formulated. Output of the network yields optimum weighting coefficients representing the individual importance of original or extracted features. For feature extraction, an optimum transformed space is similarly obtained. Theoretical analysis of the methodology is provided. Experimental results on speech (Section 3.3.4), medical (Section 4.2.1), and *iris* data, along with comparative studies, are also described.

6.2 SUPERVISED FEATURE SELECTION

A fuzzy feature evaluation index, based on the aggregated measure of compactness of the individual classes and the separation between the classes in terms of class membership functions, is defined in Section 6.2.1. The index value decreases with increase in both the compactness of individual classes and the separation between them. (One may use this index to find the best subset from a given set of features.) As Mahalanobis distance and divergence between the classes increase, the feature evaluation index decreases [21]–[23]. Weighting factors representing the feature importance are then incorporated into membership functions, giving rise to a transformation of the feature space, which provides a generalized framework for modeling class structures. Section 6.2.2 describes a method of minimization of the evaluation index through supervised learning of a layered network. This determines the optimum set of weighting coefficients, providing an ordering of the importance of the features individually. Here the interdependence of the features has been taken into account. Note that all these operations are embedded in a single-layered network. Section 6.2.3 deals with a theoretical analysis of the neuro-fuzzy methodology mentioned above. This includes derivation of a fixed upper bound and a varying lower bound of the feature evaluation index. Monotonically increasing behavior of the feature evaluation index, with respect to the lower bound, is established. A relation of the evaluation index with interclass distance and weighting coefficient is also derived. Finally, some results of the algorithm are shown in Section 6.2.4.

6.2.1   Fuzzy evaluation index and weighted membership function

Consider an n-dimensional feature space containing $F_1, F_2, \ldots, F_i, \ldots, F_n$ features (components). Let there be l classes $C_1, C_2, \ldots, C_k, \ldots, C_l$. The feature evaluation index for a subset (Ω_F) containing a few of these n features is defined as [21]

$$E = \sum_k \sum_{F \in C_k} \frac{s_k(F)}{\sum_{\substack{k' \neq k}} s_{kk'}(F)} \alpha_k, \tag{6.1}$$

where F is constituted by the features in Ω_F only. Here

$$s_k(F) = \mu_{C_k}(F) \times (1 - \mu_{C_k}(F)) \tag{6.2}$$

and

$$s_{kk'}(F) = \frac{1}{2}[\mu_{C_k}(F) \times (1 - \mu_{C_{k'}}(F))] + \frac{1}{2}[\mu_{C_{k'}}(F) \times (1 - \mu_{C_k}(F))], \tag{6.3}$$

where $\mu_{C_k}(F)$ and $\mu_{C_{k'}}(F)$ are the membership values of the pattern F in classes C_k and $C_{k'}$, respectively; and α_k is the normalizing constant for class C_k, which takes care of the effect of relative sizes of the classes.

Note that s_k is zero (minimum) if $\mu_{C_k} = 1$ *or* 0, and 0.25 (maximum) if $\mu_{C_k} = 0.5$. On the other hand, $s_{kk'}$ is zero (minimum) when $\mu_{C_k} = \mu_{C_{k'}} = 1$ *or* 0, and 0.5 (maximum) for $\mu_{C_k} = 1$, $\mu_{C_{k'}} = 0$ or vice versa.

Therefore, the term $\left(s_k / \sum_{k' \neq k} s_{kk'}\right)$ is minimum if $\mu_{C_k} = 1$ and $\mu_{C_{k'}} = 0$ for all $k' \neq k$, that is, if the ambiguity in the belongingness of a pattern F to classes C_k and $C_{k'}$ $\forall k' \neq k$ is minimum (the pattern belongs to only one class). It is maximum when $\mu_{C_k} = 0.5$ for all k. In other words, the value of E decreases as the belongingness of the patterns increases to only one class (*i.e.*, compactness of individual classes increases) and at the same time decreases for other classes (*i.e.*, separation between classes increases). E increases when the patterns tend to lie at the boundaries between classes (*i.e.*, $\mu \to 0.5$). Therefore, for the purpose of feature selection, one may choose those features for which the value of E is minimum. In eqn. (6.1), E

is computed over all the samples in the feature space irrespective of the size of the classes. Hence it is expected that the contribution of a class of greater size (*i.e.*, with larger number of samples) will be more in the computation of E. As a result, the index value will be more biased by the larger classes; this might affect the process of feature selection. In order to overcome this, *i.e.*, to normalize this effect of the size of the classes, a factor α_k corresponding to the class C_k is introduced; α_k can have an expression such as $\alpha_k = 1 - p_k$, $\alpha_k = (1/|C_k|)$ or $\alpha_k = (1/p_k)$, where p_k is the *a priori* probability for class C_k.

The membership $(\mu_{C_k}(\mathbf{F}))$ of a pattern $\mathbf{F}$ to a class C_k is defined with a multidimensional π function [eqn. (2.6)] expressed as [21]

$$
\begin{aligned}
\mu_{C_k}(\mathbf{F}) &= 1 - 2d_k^2(\mathbf{F}) & 0 \le d_k(\mathbf{F}) < \tfrac{1}{2}, \\
&= 2[1 - d_k(\mathbf{F})]^2 & \tfrac{1}{2} \le d_k(\mathbf{F}) < 1, \\
&= 0 & \text{otherwise.}
\end{aligned}
\tag{6.4}
$$

The distance $d_k(\mathbf{F})$ of the pattern $\mathbf{F}$ from $\mathbf{m}_k$ (the center of class C_k) is

$$
d_k(\mathbf{F}) = \left[\sum_i \left(\frac{F_i - m_{ki}}{\lambda_{ki}} \right)^{r_k} \right]^{1/r_k} , \quad r_k > 0,
\tag{6.5}
$$

where

$$
\lambda_{ki} = 2 \max_{\mathbf{F} \in C_k} [\|F_i - m_{ki}\|],
\tag{6.6}
$$

and

$$
m_{ki} = \frac{\sum\limits_{\mathbf{F} \in C_k} F_i}{|C_k|}.
\tag{6.7}
$$

Equations (6.4)–(6.7) are such that the membership $\mu_{C_k}(\mathbf{F})$ of a pattern $\mathbf{F}$ is 1 if it is located at the mean of C_k, and 0.5 if it is at the boundary (*i.e.*, ambiguous region) for a symmetric class structure.

In practice, the class structure may not be symmetric. In that case the membership values of some patterns at the boundary of the class will be greater than 0.5. Also, some patterns of other classes may have membership values greater than 0.5 for the class under consideration. In order to handle such an undesirable situation, the membership function corresponding to a class needs to be transformed so that it can model the real life class structures appropriately. For this purpose, one incorporates a weighting factor corresponding to a feature that transforms the feature space in such a way that the transformed membership functions model the class structures suitably. Note that this incorporation of weighting factors makes the method of modeling the class structures more generalized; a symmetric class structure is a special case.

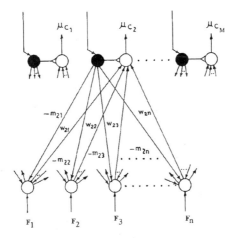

Fig. 6.1 Schematic diagram of the supervised neural network model; black circles represent auxiliary nodes, and white circles represent input and output nodes; small triangles attached to output nodes represent modulatory connections from respective auxiliary nodes

One may define weighted distance from eqn. (6.5) as [23]

$$d_k(\mathbf{F}) = \left[\sum_i w_i^{r_k} \left(\frac{F_i - m_{ki}}{\lambda_{ki}}\right)^{r_k}\right]^{1/r_k}, \quad w_i \in [0,1]. \qquad (6.8)$$

The membership values (μ) of the sample points of a class now become dependent on w_i. The values of w_i (< 1) make the function of eqn. (6.4) flattened along the axis of F_i. The lower the value of w_i, the higher is the extent of flattening. In an extreme case when $w_i = 0$, $d_k = 0$ and $\mu_{C_k} = 1$ for all the patterns.

In pattern recognition literature, the weight w_i [eqn. (6.8)] can be viewed as reflecting the relative importance of feature F_i in measuring the similarity (in terms of distance) of a pattern to a class. The higher the value of w_i, the greater is the importance of F_i in characterizing or discriminating a class or distinguishing between classes; $w_i = 1$ (0) indicates the maximum (minimum) importance of F_i.

Therefore, the compactness of the individual classes and the separation between them as measured by E [eqn. (6.1)] is now essentially a function of $\mathbf{w}$ ($= [w_1, w_2, \ldots, w_n]$), if one considers all the n features together. The problem of feature selection or ranking thus reduces to finding a set of w_i values for which E becomes minimum; w_i values indicate the relative importance of F_i values in characterizing or discriminating classes. The task of minimization may be performed with various techniques [24, 25]. Pal *et al.* [21] have used the gradient descent technique in a connectionist framework (because of its massive parallelism, fault tolerance, *etc.*) for minimizing E. This is described in the following section.

6.2.2   Connectionist realization

The network (Fig. 6.1) used for this purpose consists of two layers: input and output. The input layer represents the set of all features, and the output layer corresponds to the pattern classes. Input nodes accept activations corresponding to the feature values of the input patterns. The output nodes produce the membership values of the input patterns corresponding to the respective pattern classes. An auxiliary node is connected to each output node for controlling its activation through modulatory links. An output node can be activated from the input layer only when the corresponding auxiliary node remains active. Input nodes are connected to the auxiliary nodes through feedback links. The weight of the feedback link from the auxiliary node, connected to the kth output node (corresponding to class C_k), to the ith input node (corresponding to feature F_i) is equated to $-m_{ki}$. The weight of the feedforward link from the ith input node to the kth output node provides the degree of importance of the feature F_i, and is given by [21]

$$W_{ki} = \left(\frac{w_i}{\lambda_{ki}} \right)^{r_k}. \tag{6.9}$$

During training, the patterns are presented at the input layer and the membership values are computed at the output layer. The feature evaluation index for these membership values is computed [eqn. (6.14)] and the values of w_is are updated in order to minimize this index. Note that the λ_{ki} and m_{ki} values are directly computed from the training set and kept fixed during the updating of w_i values. The auxiliary nodes are activated (*i.e.*, activation values are equated to unity) one at a time while the others are rendered inactive (*i.e.*, activation values are fixed at 0). Thus, during training, only one output node is allowed to get activated at a time.

When the kth auxiliary node is activated, input node i has an activation value

$$u_{ik} = (x_{ik})^{r_k}, \tag{6.10}$$

where x_{ik} is the total activation received by the ith input node for pattern $\mathbf{F}$, when the auxiliary node k is active. x_{ik} is given by

$$x_{ik} = F_i - m_{ki}. \tag{6.11}$$

F_i is the external input (value of the ith feature for pattern $\mathbf{F}$) and $-m_{ki}$ is the feedback activation from the kth auxiliary node to the ith input node. The activation value of the kth output node is given as

$$v_k = g(y_k), \tag{6.12}$$

where $g(.)$, the activation function of each output node, is a π function as given in eqn. (6.4); y_k, the total activation received by the kth output node for pattern $\mathbf{F}$, is given by

$$y_k = \left(\sum_i u_{ik} \left(\frac{w_i}{\lambda_{ki}} \right)^{r_k} \right)^{1/r_k}. \tag{6.13}$$

Note that y_k is the same as d_k [eqn. (6.8)] for the given input pattern $\mathbf{F}$, and v_k is equal to the membership value of the input pattern $\mathbf{F}$ in class C_k.

The expression for $E(\mathbf{w})$ [from eqn. (6.1)], in terms of the output node activations, is given by [21]

$$E(\mathbf{w}) = \sum_k \sum_{\mathbf{F} \in C_k} \frac{v_k(1 - v_k)}{\sum_{k' \neq k} \frac{1}{2}[v_k(1 - v_{k'}) + v_{k'}(1 - v_k)]} \times \alpha_k. \tag{6.14}$$

The training phase of the network takes care of the task of minimization of $E(\mathbf{w})$ [eqn. (6.14)] with respect to $\mathbf{w}$, using gradient descent. The change in w_i (Δw_i) is computed as

$$\Delta w_i = -\varepsilon \frac{\partial E}{\partial w_i}, \forall i, \tag{6.15}$$

where ε is the learning rate.

For the computation of $(\partial E/\partial w_i)$, the following expressions are used [21]:

$$\frac{\partial s_{kk'}(\mathbf{F})}{\partial w_i} = \frac{1}{2} \left[[1 - 2v_{k'}] \frac{\partial v_k}{\partial w_i} + [1 - 2v_k] \frac{\partial v_{k'}}{\partial w_i} \right], \tag{6.16}$$

$$\frac{\partial s_k(\mathbf{F})}{\partial w_i} = [1 - 2v_k] \frac{\partial v_k}{\partial w_i}, \tag{6.17}$$

$$\begin{aligned} \frac{\partial v_k}{\partial w_i} &= -4y_k \frac{\partial y_k}{\partial w_i}, & 0 \leq y_k < \frac{1}{2} \\ &= -4[1 - y_k] \frac{\partial y_k}{\partial w_i}, & \frac{1}{2} \leq y_k < 1 \\ &= 0, & \text{otherwise} \end{aligned} \tag{6.18}$$

and

$$\frac{\partial y_k}{\partial w_i} = \left(\frac{w_i}{y_k} \right)^{r_k - 1} \left(\frac{F_i - m_{ki}}{\lambda_{ki}} \right)^{r_k}. \tag{6.19}$$

Alternately, one can also express E as a function of W_{ki}, where $W_{ki} = (w_i/\lambda_k)^{r_k}$ [eqn. (6.9)], and then minimize E with respect to W_{ki}. In this case, during the training phase the W_{ki} values can be updated using the same gradient descent technique. After training, the degree of importance of ith feature can be computed as $w_i = (W_{ki})^{1/r_k} \times \lambda_{ki}$.

The steps involved in the training phase of the network are as follows:

1. Calculate the mean vectors ($\mathbf{m}_k$) of all the classes from the data set and equate the weight of the feedback link from the auxiliary node corresponding to class C_k to the input node i as $-m_{ki}$ (for all i and k).

2. Compute λ_{ki} values from eqn. (6.6) and initialize the weight of the feedforward link from ith input node to kth output node (for all values of i and k). Set the value of r_k [eqn. (6.8] so that the membership values of all the patterns of the kth class are at least 0.5 for that class.

3. For each input pattern

   a. Present the pattern vector to the input layer of the network.

   b. Activate only one auxiliary node at a time. Whenever an auxiliary node is activated, it sends the feedback to the input layer. The input nodes in turn send the resultant activations to the output nodes. The activation of the output node (connected to the active auxiliary node) provides the membership value of the input pattern to the corresponding class. Thus, the membership values of the input pattern corresponding to all the classes are computed by sequentially activating the auxiliary nodes one at a time.

   c. Compute the desired change in w_is to be made, using the updating rule given in eqn. (6.15).

4. Compute total change in w_i for each i, over the entire set of patterns. Update w_i (for all i) with the average value of $\triangle w_i$.

5. Repeat the whole process until convergence, *i.e.*, the change in E, becomes less than a certain predefined small quantity.

After convergence, $E(\mathbf{w})$ attains a local minimum. In that case, the values of w_is indicate the order of importance of the features. Note that the method of individual feature ranking, explained in Section 6.2.1, considers each feature individually independent of others. On the other hand, the neuro-fuzzy method described in this section finds the set of w_i values (for which E is minimum) considering the effect of interdependencies of the features.

6.2.3 Theoretical analysis

Here, we provide the mathematical analysis [22] on the characteristics of the feature evaluation index (E) and the significance of weighting coefficients (w_i). This includes deriving a fixed upper bound and a varying lower bound of E [eqn. (6.1)], studying the variation of E with respect to the lower bound, and establishing a relation between E, w_i, and interclass distance. We use $\mathbf{x}$ in the sequel (of this section) to represent pattern vectors (instead of $\mathbf{F}$), for the ease of representation of various expressions.

6.2.3.1 Upper bound and lower bound of E   Equation (6.1) can be written as

$$E = \sum_k \sum_{\mathbf{x} \in C_k} \frac{\mu_k(1 - \mu_k)\alpha_k}{\frac{1}{2}\sum_{k' \neq k}[\mu_k(1 - \mu_{k'}) + \mu_{k'}(1 - \mu_k)]}, \tag{6.20}$$

where $\mu_k = \mu_{C_k}(\mathbf{x})$ and $\mu_{k'} = \mu_{C_{k'}}(\mathbf{x})$. Let $E = \sum_k E_k = \sum_k \sum_{\mathbf{x} \in C_k} E_k(\mathbf{x}|\mathbf{x} \in C_k)$, where

$$E_k = \sum_{\mathbf{x} \in C_k} \frac{\mu_k(1 - \mu_k)\alpha_k}{\frac{1}{2} \sum_{k' \neq k} [\mu_k(1 - \mu_{k'}) + \mu_{k'}(1 - \mu_k)]} \tag{6.21}$$

and

$$E_k(\mathbf{x}|\mathbf{x} \in C_k) = \frac{\mu_k(1 - \mu_k)\alpha_k}{\frac{1}{2} \sum_{k' \neq k} [\mu_k(1 - \mu_{k'}) + \mu_{k'}(1 - \mu_k)]}; \tag{6.22}$$

here E_k is the value of the evaluation index (E) corresponding to a class C_k and $E_k(\mathbf{x}|\mathbf{x} \in C_k)$ is the contribution of a pattern $\mathbf{x}$ in class C_k to E_k.

For a pattern $\mathbf{x}$ in class C_k, $\frac{1}{2} \sum_{k' \neq k} [\mu_k(1 - \mu_{k'}) + \mu_{k'}(1 - \mu_k)] =$

$$\frac{1}{2} \sum_{k' \neq k} [\mu_k(1 - \mu_k) + (\mu_k - \mu_{k'})^2 + \mu_{k'}(1 - \mu_{k'})].$$

Since $[(\mu_k - \mu_{k'})^2 + \mu_{k'}(1 - \mu_{k'})] \geq 0$,

$$\frac{1}{2} \sum_{k' \neq k} [\mu_k(1 - \mu_{k'}) + \mu_{k'}(1 - \mu_k)] \geq \frac{l-1}{2}\mu_k(1 - \mu_k),$$

where l is the number of classes. Since $0 < \alpha_k < 1$, one can write

$$E_k(\mathbf{x}|\mathbf{x} \in C_k) \leq \frac{2}{(l - 1)}. \tag{6.23}$$

Therefore

$$\mathcal{E}(E) \leq \frac{2l}{l - 1}, \tag{6.24}$$

where $\mathcal{E}$ denotes the "mathematical expectation" operator. ♣

Again, for a pattern $\mathbf{x}$ in class C_k, $\mu_k, \mu_{k'} \in [0, 1]$,

$$\frac{1}{2}[\mu_k(1 - \mu_{k'}) + \mu_{k'}(1 - \mu_k)] \leq \frac{1}{2},$$

$$\sum_{k' \neq k} \frac{1}{2}[\mu_k(1 - \mu_{k'}) + \mu_{k'}(1 - \mu_k)] \leq \frac{1}{2}(l - 1),$$

$$\frac{1}{\sum_{k' \neq k} \frac{1}{2}[\mu_k(1 - \mu_{k'}) + \mu_{k'}(1 - \mu_k)]} \geq \frac{2}{(l - 1)},$$

$$\sum_k \frac{\mu_k(1 - \mu_k)\alpha_k}{\sum_{k' \neq k} \frac{1}{2}[\mu_k(1 - \mu_{k'}) + \mu_{k'}(1 - \mu_k)]} \geq \frac{2}{(l - 1)} \sum_k \mu_k(1 - \mu_k)\alpha_k.$$

Thus

$$E_k(\mathbf{x}|\mathbf{x} \in C_k) \geq \frac{2}{(l-1)}\mu_k(1-\mu_k)\alpha_k.$$

That is,

$$\mathcal{E}(E) \geq \frac{2}{(l-1)}\mathcal{E}(\sum_k \mu_k(1-\mu_k)\alpha_k). \tag{6.25}$$

Therefore,

$$\frac{2}{(l-1)}\mathcal{E}(\sum_k \mu_k(1-\mu_k)\alpha_k) \leq \mathcal{E}(E) \leq \frac{2l}{(l-1)}. \tag{6.26}$$

Note that the upper bound of $\mathcal{E}(E)$ is fixed, whereas the lower bound is varying with $[2/(l-1)]\mathcal{E}(\sum_k \mu_k(1-\mu_k)\alpha_k)$. ♣

Let us now analyze the behavior of $E_k(\mathbf{x}|\mathbf{x} \in C_k)$ with respect to $\mu_k(1-\mu_k)$. For this purpose, substitute $\mu_k(1-\mu_k)$ by h_k in eqn. (6.22). In that case, $\frac{dE_k(\mathbf{x}|\mathbf{x}\in C_k)}{dh_k} =$

$$\frac{\alpha_k\left[\sum_{k'\neq k}[\mu_{k'}(1-\mu_k)+\mu_k(1-\mu_{k'})](1-2\mu_k) - \mu_k(1-\mu_k)\sum_{k'\neq k}(1-2\mu_{k'})\right]}{\frac{1}{2}\left[\sum_{k'\neq k}[\mu_{k'}(1-\mu_k)+\mu_k(1-\mu_{k'})]\right]^2 (1-2\mu_k)}$$

$$= \frac{\nu_k\alpha_k}{\frac{1}{2}\left[\sum_{k'\neq k}[\mu_{k'}(1-\mu_k)+\mu_k(1-\mu_{k'})]\right]^2}, \tag{6.27}$$

where

$$\nu_k = \frac{\sum_{k'\neq k}[\mu_{k'}(1-\mu_k)+\mu_k(1-\mu_{k'})](1-2\mu_k) - \mu_k(1-\mu_k)\sum_{k'\neq k}(1-2\mu_{k'})}{(1-2\mu_k)}.$$

$$\tag{6.28}$$

It is clear from eqn. (6.27) that $[dE_k(\mathbf{x}|\mathbf{x}\in C_k)/dh_k]$ is positive or negative if ν_k is positive or negative. In other words, $E_k(\mathbf{x}|\mathbf{x} \in C_k)$ increases or decreases monotonically with $\mu_k(1-\mu_k)$ if ν_k is positive or negative. Simplifying the expression on the right-hand side of eqn. (6.28) one may write [22]

$$\nu_k = \sum_{k'\neq k}\mu_{k'} - \frac{\mu_k^2\sum_{k'\neq k}(1-2\mu_{k'})}{(1-2\mu_k)}. \tag{6.29}$$

In order to show that $E_k(\mathbf{x}|\mathbf{x} \in C_k)$ monotonically increases with $\mu_k(1-\mu_k)$ for both *nonoverlapping* and *overlapping* class structures, consider the following cases.

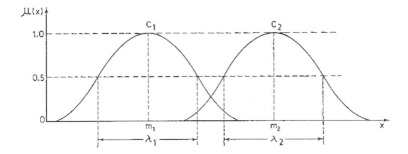

Fig. 6.2 Nonoverlapping pattern classes modeled by π function

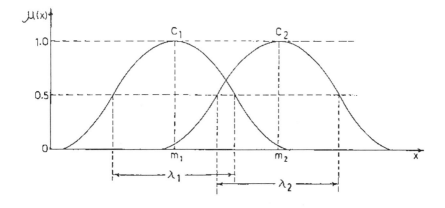

Fig. 6.3 Overlapping pattern classes modeled by π function

Case 1: Nonoverlapping (Fig. 6.2). Here, for a pattern **x**, if $|x_i - m_{ki}| \leq (\lambda_{ki}/2)$ holds for all values of i, $\mu_k \geq 0.5$, and $\mu_{k'} < 0.5$, $\forall k' \neq k$. Therefore, $\nu_k > 0$ [eqn. (6.29)], and as a result, $[dE_k(\mathbf{x}|\mathbf{x} \in C_k)/dh_k] > 0$. This indicates that $E_k(\mathbf{x}|\mathbf{x} \in C_k)$ is monotonically increasing with $\mu_k(1 - \mu_k)$.

Case 2: Overlapping (Fig. 6.3). In this case, for a pattern **x**, if $|x_i - m_{ki}| \leq (\lambda_{ki}/2)$ holds for all values of i, $\mu_k \geq 0.5$, and $\mu_{k'} \gtrsim 0.5$, $\forall k' \neq k$. Since the classes are overlapping, let us consider two different possibilities: **x** lying outside the overlapping zone (*i.e.*, $|x_i - m_{ki}| \leq (\lambda_{ki}/2)$, $\forall i$ and $|x_i - m_{k'i}| > (\lambda_{k'i}/2)$, $\forall i$), and **x** lying within the overlapping zone (*i.e.*, $|x_i - m_{ki}| < (\lambda_{ki}/2)$, $\forall i$ and $|x_i - m_{k'i}| < (\lambda_{k'i}/2)$, $\forall i$).

If the pattern $\mathbf{x}$ lies outside the overlapping zone, then $\mu_{k'} < 0.5$ and thereby $\nu_k > 0$ [eqn. (6.29)]. This indicates that $E_k(\mathbf{x}|\mathbf{x} \in C_k)$ monotonically increases with $\mu_k(1 - \mu_k)$.

If $\mathbf{x}$ lies within the overlapping zone, then both μ_k and $\mu_{k'}$ are greater than 0.5. Then there are three possibilities: (1) $\mu_k > \mu_{k'}$, (2) $\mu_k \approx \mu_{k'}$ and (3) $\mu_k < \mu_{k'}$.

1. $\mu_k > \mu_{k'}$. Let $\mu_{k'} = \mu_k - \varepsilon_{kk'}$, where $\varepsilon_{kk'} > 0$. Therefore, from eqn. (6.29),

$$\nu_k = \sum_{k' \neq k}(\mu_k - \varepsilon_{kk'}) - \frac{\mu_k^2 \sum_{k' \neq k}(1 - 2\mu_k + 2\varepsilon_{kk'})}{(1 - 2\mu_k)}, \qquad (6.30)$$

i.e.,

$$\nu_k = (l - 1)\mu_k - \sum_{k' \neq k}\varepsilon_{kk'} - \frac{2\mu_k^2 \sum_{k' \neq k}\varepsilon_{kk'} - \mu_k^2(2\mu_k - 1)(l - 1)}{1 - 2\mu_k}. \qquad (6.31)$$

Thus, $E_k(\mathbf{x}|\mathbf{x} \in C_k)$ increases monotonically with $\mu_k(1 - \mu_k)$ if

$$(l - 1)\mu_k - \sum_{k' \neq k}\varepsilon_{kk'} - \frac{2\mu_k^2 \sum_{k' \neq k}\varepsilon_{kk'} - \mu_k^2(2\mu_k - 1)(l - 1)}{1 - 2\mu_k} > 0, \qquad (6.32)$$

i.e., if

$$\frac{1}{l - 1}\sum_{k' \neq k}\varepsilon_{kk'} > -\frac{\mu_k(1 - \mu_k)(2\mu_k - 1)}{(1 - \mu_k)^2 + \mu_k^2}. \qquad (6.33)$$

Since $\varepsilon_{kk'} > 0$, this inequality always holds and therefore, in such cases, $E_k(\mathbf{x}|\mathbf{x} \in C_k)$ always increases monotonically with $\mu_k(1 - \mu_k)$.

2. $\mu_k \approx \mu_{k'}$. In this case, $\varepsilon_{kk'} \approx 0$, and therefore, the inequality (6.33) always holds. Thus here, too, one gets a monotonic increasing nature of $E_k(\mathbf{x}|\mathbf{x} \in C_k)$ with respect to $\mu_k(1 - \mu_k)$.

3. $\mu_k < \mu_{k'}$.

In this case, $\varepsilon_{kk'} < 0$. Now replace $\varepsilon_{kk'}$ by $-\varepsilon_{kk'}$, *i.e.*, $\mu_{k'} = \mu_k + \varepsilon_{kk'}$. Then the condition for $E_k(\mathbf{x}|\mathbf{x} \in C_k)$ becoming a monotonically increasing function with respect to $\mu_k(1 - \mu_k)$ becomes

$$\frac{1}{l - 1}\sum_{k' \neq k}\varepsilon_{kk'} < \frac{\mu_k(1 - \mu_k)(2\mu_k - 1)}{(1 - \mu_k)^2 + \mu_k^2}. \qquad (6.34)$$

This condition provides an upper bound on the average value of $\varepsilon_{kk'}$ (hence on the average value of $\mu_{k'}$) that can be allowed in order to get a monotonic increasing behavior of $E_k(\mathbf{x}|\mathbf{x} \in C_k)$ with respect to $\mu_k(1 - \mu_k)$.

First, the chance of $\mu_k < \mu_{k'}$ is low for a pattern in class C_k. Even if this happens (say, for overlapping cases), the chance of $[1/(l-1)] \sum_{k' \neq k} \varepsilon_{kk'} > [\mu_k(1-\mu_k)(2\mu_k-1)]/[(1-\mu_k)^2 + \mu_k^2]$ is very low (as illustrated in the following two examples). Therefore, $E_k(\mathbf{x}|\mathbf{x} \in C_k)$ is most likely monotonically increasing with $\mu_k(1-\mu_k)$.

Example 1. Let $\mu_1 = 0.6$ for a pattern $\mathbf{x}$ lying within the region $||\mathbf{x} - \mathbf{m}_1|| < (\lambda_1/2)$ in class C_1. Then the condition (6.34) becomes

$$\frac{1}{l-1} \sum_{k' \neq k} \varepsilon_{kk'} < 0.1.$$

In order to violate this condition, the average membership value of $\mathbf{x}$ (say, μ_2) to classes other than C_1 should be at least 0.7. It can also be seen that whatever be the value of μ_1 (> 0.5), the value of μ_2 should be greater than μ_1. This is unusual. Thus one can say that in this case the inequality in (6.34) will be satisfied and thereby, expect a monotonic increasing behavior of $E_1(\mathbf{x}|\mathbf{x} \in C_1)$ with respect to $\mu_1(1-\mu_1)$.

Example 2. Let $\mu_1 = 0.5$. Here, the condition (6.34) becomes

$$\frac{1}{l-1} \sum_{k' \neq k} \varepsilon_{kk'} < 0;$$

that is, the average membership value of $\mathbf{x}$ to classes other than C_1 should be greater than or equal to 0.5. This situation occurs when the classes are highly overlapping. In other words, if there is high amount of overlap, the behavior of $E_k(\mathbf{x}|\mathbf{x} \in C_k)$ becomes unpredictable for ambiguous patterns.   ♣

Thus we can say that, in almost all the cases, $E_k(\mathbf{x}|\mathbf{x} \in C_k)$ monotonically increases with $\mu_k(1-\mu_k)$. Therefore, one can expect that E_k [$= \sum_{\mathbf{x} \in C_k} E_k(\mathbf{x}|\mathbf{x} \in C_k)$] monotonically increases with $\sum_k \mu_k(1-\mu_k)$. In other words, almost in all the cases $\mathcal{E}(E)$ is a monotonically increasing function of $\mathcal{E}\left(\sum_k (\mu_k(1-\mu_k)\alpha_k\right)$, as the α_k values are positive constants.

6.2.3.2 Relation between E, interclass distance, and w_i   In order to derive a relation of lower bound $\mathcal{E}(E)$ with interclass distance and weighting coefficients for some well-defined class structures, one assumes the following [22]:

- The classes $C_1, C_2, \ldots, C_k, \ldots, C_l$ have independent, identical Gaussian distributions with respective means $\mathbf{m}_1, \mathbf{m}_2, \ldots, \mathbf{m}_k, \ldots, \mathbf{m}_l$ and the same variance σ^2. Let $\mathcal{P}(\mathbf{x}|C_k)$ be the class-conditional probability density function for class C_k. Then

$$\mathcal{P}(\mathbf{x}|C_k) = \frac{1}{\sqrt{2\pi}\sigma} \exp\left(-\sum_i \frac{(x_i - m_{ki})^2}{2\sigma^2}\right). \qquad (6.35)$$

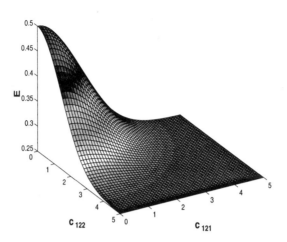

Fig. 6.4   Graphical representation of $\mathcal{E}(E)$ with respect to c_{121} and c_{122}, with $w_1 = w_2 = 1.0$

- The membership of a pattern $\mathbf{x}$ in a class C_k is given by

$$\mu_k \;\; = \;\; \mu_k(\mathbf{x}) \;\; = \;\; \exp\left(-\sum_i \frac{(x_i - m_{ki})^2 w_i^2}{2\lambda^2}\right), \qquad (6.36)$$

where λ is the bandwidth of the class C_k, and is the same for all the classes.

$\mathcal{E}(E)$ is given by

$$\mathcal{E}(E) = \int_{\mathbf{x}} E\mathcal{P}(\mathbf{x})d\mathbf{x}, \qquad (6.37)$$

where

$$\mathcal{P}(\mathbf{x}) = \sum_k p_k \mathcal{P}(\mathbf{x}|C_k), \qquad (6.38)$$

where p_k is the *a priori* probability of class C_k. Evaluating the right-hand side of eqn. (6.37) (see Appendix B for detailed computation), we obtain

$$\mathcal{E}(E) \approx \sum_k \frac{\alpha_k p_k}{l-1} \frac{\sum_i w_i^2}{2\rho^2}\left[1 + \sum_{k' \neq k} \exp\left(-\sum_i \frac{c_{kk'i}^2}{2\sigma^2\left(1 + \frac{\rho^2}{w_i^2}\right)}\right)\right], \qquad (6.39)$$

where $\rho = (\lambda/\sigma)$ and $c_{kk'i} = m_{ki} - m_{k'i}$ is a measure of interclass distance between the classes C_k and $C_{k'}$ along the feature axis x_i.

Now consider two classes C_1 and C_2, with two features x_1 and x_2. Let C_1 and C_2 have unit normal distribution, specifically, $\sigma = 1.0$. Let $\lambda = 1.0$

and $p_k = \alpha_k = 0.5$ $(\forall k)$. c_{121} and c_{122} are the interclass distances between classes C_1 and C_2 along the feature axes x_1 and x_2, respectively. Here we demonstrate graphically the variation of $\mathcal{E}(E)$ with respect to c_{121}, c_{122}, and w_1, w_2.

Figure 6.4 shows the variation of $\mathcal{E}(E)$ with respect to c_{121} and c_{122} with $w_1 = w_2 = 1$; $\mathcal{E}(E)$ is maximum when $c_{121} = c_{122} = 0$, that is, when the two classes completely overlap, and decreases with the increase in c_{121} and c_{122}. This variation is symmetric with respect to both c_{121} and c_{122}. The rate of decrease in $\mathcal{E}(E)$ also decreases as c_{121} (and c_{122}) increases. Finally, after a certain value of c_{121} (and c_{122}) the rate of decrease in $\mathcal{E}(\sum_k \mu_k(1 - \mu_k)\alpha_k)$ becomes infinitesimally small. This is also evident from the way of computing μ values, where μ_2 of a pattern $\mathbf{x}$ with fixed μ_1 decreases with increase in interclass distance. If the interclass distance exceeds a certain value, μ_2 becomes very small. Thus the contribution of the pattern to the evaluation index is not further affected by the extent of the class separation.

Figures 6.5 and 6.6 show the variation of $\mathcal{E}(E)$ with respect to w_1 and w_2 for different interclass distances, when $\sum_{i=1}^2 w_i^2 = 1$. Here $c_{122} = 0$ throughout, whereas c_{121} is considered to be 1.0, 3.0, 5.0, 7.0 and 9.0 respectively. It is seen from the figures that E decreases with w_1 (or increases with w_2) and attains a maximum (or minimum) when $w_1 = 0$ (or when $w_2 = 0$). This is due to the fact that the feature x_2 has no discriminating power as $c_{122} = 0$. On the other hand, the feature x_1 is necessary for classification as there is a separation ($c_{121} \neq 0$) between the classes along its axis. Note also from Figs. 6.5 and 6.6 that for higher values of c_{121}, the decrease (or increase) of E is sharper. This indicates that the rate of convergence of the network to a local minimum increases, as expected, with the decrease in overlap between the classes.

6.2.4 Results

The effectiveness of the algorithms both for feature subset selection using fuzzy feature evaluation index (Section 6.2.1) and individual feature ranking with neuro-fuzzy approach (Section 6.2.2) was demonstrated by Pal *et al.* [21] on three data sets: *vowel* (described in Section 3.3.4, Fig. 3.4), *iris* [26], and *hepato* (medical data, described in Section 4.2.1). Here we present some of the results related to the neuro-fuzzy method only.

Anderson's *iris* data [26] set contains three classes: three varieties of iris flowers, *Iris setosa, Iris versicolor, and Iris virginica*, consisting of 50 samples each. Each sample has four features: *sepal length (SL), sepal width (SW), petal length (PL),* and *petal width (PW)*. The nine input features of *hepato*– *GOT, GPT, LDH, GGT, BUN, MCV, MCH, TBil*, and *CRTNN*–are described in Section 4.2.1.

The relation of fuzzy feature evaluation index E [eqn. (6.1)] with Mahalanobis distance and divergence measure [21] is graphically depicted in

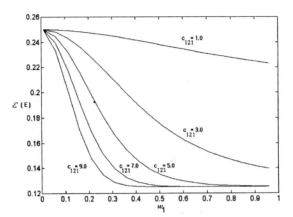

Fig. 6.5 Graphical representation of $\mathcal{E}(E)$ with respect to w_1, for different values of c_{121}, with $c_{122} = 0$ and $\sum_{i=1}^{2} w_i^2 = 1$

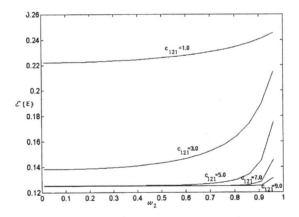

Fig. 6.6 Graphical representation of $\mathcal{E}(E)$ with respect to w_2, for different values of c_{121}, with $c_{122} = 0$ and $\sum_{i=1}^{2} w_i^2 = 1$

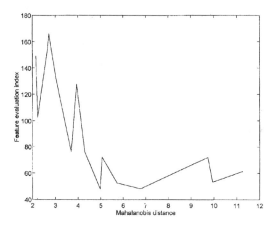

Fig. 6.7 Graphical representation of relationship between feature evaluation index and Mahalanobis distance for *vowel* data

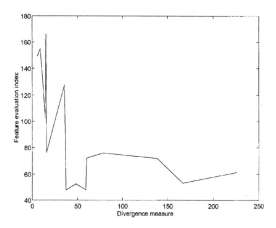

Fig. 6.8 Graphical representation of relationship between feature evaluation index and divergence measure for *vowel* data

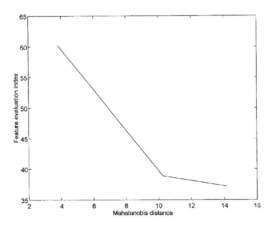

Fig. 6.9 Graphical representation of relationship between feature evaluation index and Mahalanobis distance for *iris* data

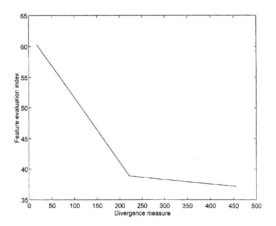

Fig. 6.10 Graphical representation of relationship between feature evaluation index and divergence measure for *iris* data

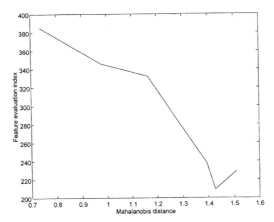

Fig. 6.11 Graphical representation of relationship between feature evaluation index and Mahalanobis distance for *hepato* data

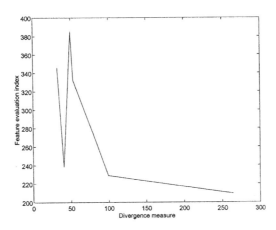

Fig. 6.12 Graphical representation of relationship between feature evaluation index and divergence measure for *hepato* data

Figs. 6.7 and 6.8 (for *vowel* data), Figs. 6.9 and 6.10 (for *iris* data), and Figs. 6.11 and 6.12 (for *hepato* data). They are computed over every pair of classes. As expected, Figs. 6.7–6.12 show a decrease in feature evaluation index with increase in Mahalanobis distance and divergence measure between the classes.

Tables 6.1–6.3 provide the degrees of importance (w) of different features corresponding to the *vowel*, *iris*, and *hepato* data, obtained by the neuro-fuzzy method described in Section 6.2.2. The values of r_k in eqn. (6.8) were found to be 28.8, 78.5, 21.4, 74.0, 20.4, and 47.8 for the six-class *vowel* data, 71.7, 241.3, and 193.9 for the three-class *iris* data, and 65.0, 38.5, 12.8, and 163.2 for the four-class *hepato* data. Three different initializations of w were used in order to train the network:

1. $w_i = 1$, for all i, *i.e.*, all the features are considered to be equally important.

2. $w_i \in [0, 1]$, for all i, *i.e.*, the network starts searching for a suboptimal set of weights from an arbitrary point in the search space.

3. $w_i = 0.5 \pm \varepsilon$, for all i, $\varepsilon \in [0, 0.01]$, *i.e.*, the features are considered to be almost equally, but not fully, important.

Note that $w_i = 1$ implies that feature F_i is most important; that is, its presence is necessary for characterizing the pattern classes. Similarly, $w_i = 0$ means that F_i has no importance and, therefore, its presence in the feature vector is not required. However, $w_i = 0.5$ indicates an ambiguous situation about the presence of F_i, and ε adds a small perturbation to the degree of presence or importance.

Table 6.1 Importance of different features on *vowel* data (supervised)

	Initial w					
	$= 1.0$		in $[0, 1]$		$= 0.5 \pm \varepsilon$	
Feature	w	Rank	w	Rank	w	Rank
F_1	0.640382	2	0.257358	2	0.213647	2
F_2	0.759389	1	0.437536	1	0.342621	1
F_3	0.435496	3	0.154319	3	0.123651	3

Table 6.2 Importance of different features on *iris* data (supervised)

	Initial w					
	$= 1.0$		in $[0, 1]$		$= 0.5 \pm \varepsilon$	
Feature	w	Rank	w	Rank	w	Rank
SL	0.480797	4	0.203230	4	0.229066	4
SW	0.572347	3	0.302529	3	0.374984	3
PL	0.617570	1	0.422186	1	0.420367	1
PW	0.617173	2	0.402027	2	0.402833	2

It is seen from Table 6.1 that the order of importance of features of the *vowel* data, in all the cases, is F_2, F_1, F_3. This conforms to those obtained by several earlier investigations involving pattern classification and feature evaluation [4, 5, 21, 27, 28]. Similarly, for *iris* data (Table 6.2) the order is seen to be PL, PW, SW, SL. Here the best two features are PL and PW, confirming earlier experiments using neural method [29], fuzzy feature subset selection method [21], and *k*-NN classifier [23]. In the case of *hepato* data (Table 6.3), the set of best four features is found to be $\{MCV, GOT, GPT, LDH\}$. Some more detailed results and comparison with other related methods have been reported [21].

Table 6.3 Importance of different features on *hepato* data (supervised)

Feature	Initial w					
	$= 1.0$		in $[0, 1]$		$= 0.5 \pm \varepsilon$	
	w	Rank	w	Rank	w	Rank
GOT	0.576090	2	0.601643	2	0.613058	2
GPT	0.300417	3	0.529896	3	0.534147	3
LDH	0.181370	4	0.341677	4	0.322765	4
GGT	0.133649	5	0.300638	5	0.235711	6
BUN	0.070480	9	0.142536	8	0.123007	9
MCV	0.735713	1	0.748205	1	0.747224	1
MCH	0.128931	6	0.101046	7	0.300428	5
$TBil$	0.123402	7	0.204479	6	0.201762	7
$CRTNN$	0.103465	8	0.125008	9	0.149290	8

In order to demonstrate the validity of the ranking from the point of structural description of classes, the different scatterplots of *iris* data (Figs. 6.13–6.18) are considered here as an example. The symbols ".," "+," and "o" represent the classes *Iris setosa, Iris versicolor,* and *Iris virginica,* respectively, in the figures.

Let us now demonstrate the structural description of various classes in the transformed feature space, which is obtained by multiplying the original feature values with their respective (optimum) weighting coefficients (Section 6.2.1). Figure 6.19 depicts the scatterplot, as an illustration [23], in the two-dimensional PL–PW transformed space for *iris* data. Note that the scales along both the transformed axes are kept identical to those of the original one (Fig. 6.18), for ease of comparison. It is seen from Figs. 6.18 and 6.19 that the classes in the transformed feature space are more compact than those in the original space, thereby validating one of the objectives of the algorithm. In order to support this finding, one may refer to the results of *k*-NN classifier [23] used on the transformed space. It was found for the pair $\{PL, PW\}$ that the *k*-NN classifier results in 94%, 94%, 96%, 96.67%, and 97.33% in the transformed space as compared to 93.33%, 94%, 96%, 96%, and 96.67% in the original space for $k = 1, 2, 3, 5, 9$, respectively.

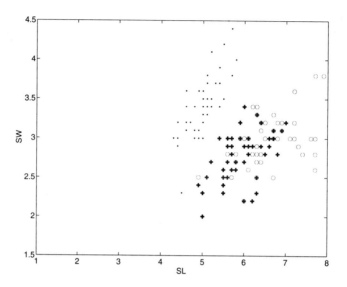

Fig. 6.13   Scatterplot $SL - SW$ for *iris* data

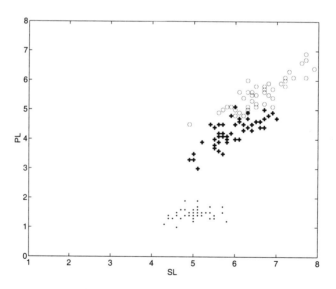

Fig. 6.14   Scatterplot $SL - PL$ for *iris* data

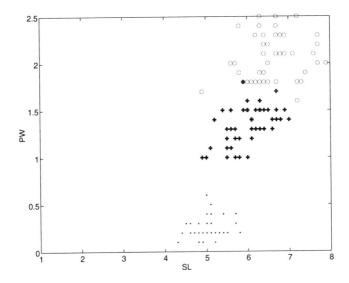

Fig. 6.15 Scatterplot $SL - PW$ for *iris* data

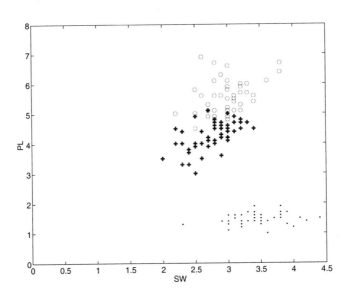

Fig. 6.16 Scatterplot $SW - PL$ for *iris* data

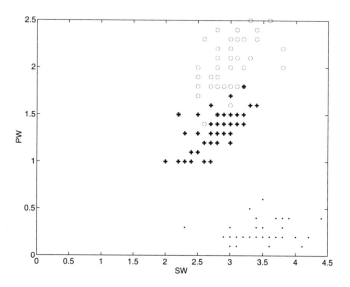

Fig. 6.17   Scatterplot $SW - PW$ for *iris* data

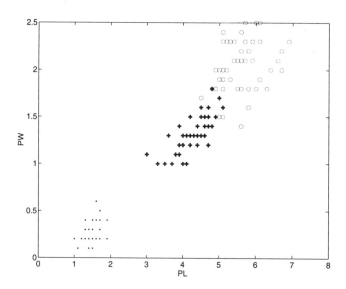

Fig. 6.18   Scatterplot $PL - PW$ for *iris* data

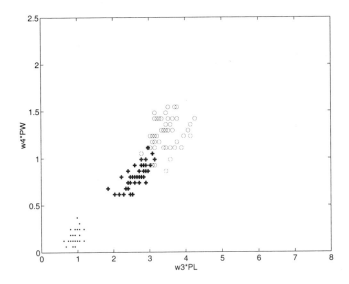

Fig. 6.19 Scatterplot $PL - PW$ for *iris* data, in transformed space

It has been observed experimentally that the network converges much slower with the initialization $w_i = 1$, for all i, as compared to the others. For example, the number of iterations required by the network (corresponding to the initializations $w_i = 1$, $[0,1]$ and $0.5 \pm \varepsilon$) to converge are $17,300$, $10,000$, and $11,500$ for *vowel* data; 9400, 7000, and 5600 for *iris* data; and 4700, 3000, and 1900 for *hepato* data.

6.3 UNSUPERVISED FEATURE SELECTION

This section describes an unsupervised neuro-fuzzy approach developed by Basak *et al.* [30] for feature selection. A fuzzy feature evaluation index [different from that of eqn. (6.1)] is defined for a set of features in terms of membership values denoting the degree of similarity between two patterns, measured by a weighted distance between them. As in Section 6.2, the weighting coefficients are used to denote the degree of importance of the individual features in characterizing or discriminating different clusters and provide flexibility in modeling various clusters. The lower the value of the evaluation index, the higher is the importance of the feature(s). The evaluation index is minimized through unsupervised learning of the network, thereby determining the optimum weighting coefficients providing an ordering of the individual features. All these operations are embedded in a single-layered network.

As in Section 6.2, one may also use the above-mentioned fuzzy evaluation index alone to find the best subset of features under unsupervised mode, by computing the evaluation index (where the weighting coefficients are unity) on different subsets of features and then ordering them accordingly. Details of such an algorithm with experimental results on *vowel*, *iris*, and *hepato* data have been described [30].

6.3.1 Feature evaluation index

6.3.1.1 Definition   Let μ_{pq}^{O} be the degree that both the pth and qth patterns belong to the same cluster in the n-dimensional original feature space, and μ_{pq}^{T} be that in the n'-dimensional ($n' < n$) transformed feature space. The μ values determine how similar a pair of patterns are in the respective features spaces; that is, μ may be interpreted as the membership value of a pair of patterns belonging to the fuzzy set "similar." Let s be the number of samples on which the feature evaluation index is computed.

The feature evaluation index for a set (Ω) of transformed features is defined as [30]

$$E = \frac{2}{s(s-1)} \sum_{p} \sum_{q \neq p} \frac{1}{2} [\mu_{pq}^{T}(1 - \mu_{pq}^{O}) + \mu_{pq}^{O}(1 - \mu_{pq}^{T})]. \qquad (6.40)$$

It has the following characteristics:

1. If $\mu_{pq}^{O} = \mu_{pq}^{T} = 0$ or 1, the contribution of the pair of patterns to the evaluation index E is zero (minimum).

2. If $\mu_{pq}^{O} = \mu_{pq}^{T} = 0.5$, the contribution of the pair of patterns to E becomes 0.25 (maximum).

3. For $\mu_{pq}^{O} < 0.5$ as $\mu_{pq}^{T} \to 0$, E decreases.

4. For $\mu_{pq}^{O} > 0.5$ as $\mu_{pq}^{T} \to 1$, E decreases.

Therefore, the feature evaluation index decreases as the membership value representing the degree of belonging of pth and qth patterns to the same cluster in the transformed feature space tends to either 0 (when $\mu^{O} < 0.5$) or 1 (when $\mu^{O} > 0.5$). In other words, the feature evaluation index decreases as the decision on the similarity between a pair of patterns (*i.e.*, whether they lie in the same cluster) becomes more and more crisp. This means, if the intercluster or intracluster distances in the transformed space increase or decrease, that the feature evaluation index of the corresponding set of features decreases. The objective, therefore, is to select those features for which the evaluation index becomes minimum, thereby optimizing the decision on the similarity of a pair of patterns with respect to their belonging to a cluster.

6.3.1.2 Computation of membership function   In order to satisfy the characteristics of E [eqn. (6.40)], the membership function (μ) in a feature space may be defined as [30]

$$\begin{aligned} \mu_{pq} &= 1 - \tfrac{d_{pq}}{D}, && \text{if } d_{pq} \leq D, \\ &= 0, && \text{otherwise,} \end{aligned} \qquad (6.41)$$

where d_{pq} is a distance measure that provides similarity (in terms of proximity) between the pth and qth patterns in the feature space. Note that the higher the value of d_{pq}, the lower is the value of μ_{pq}, and vice versa. D is a parameter that reflects the minimum separation between a pair of patterns belonging to two different clusters. When $d_{pq} = 0$ and $d_{pq} = D$, one has $\mu_{pq} = 1$ and 0, respectively. If $d_{pq} = (D/2)$, then $\mu_{pq} = 0.5$; that is, when the distance between the patterns is just half the value of D, the difficulty in making a decision as to whether both the patterns are in the same cluster becomes maximum, thereby making the situation most ambiguous. One can take $D = \beta d_{\max}$, where $d_{\max}$ is the maximum separation between a pair of patterns in the entire feature space and $0 < \beta \leq 1$ is a user-defined constant.

The distance d_{pq} [eqn. (6.41)] can be expressed in many ways. Consider, for example, the Euclidean distance between the two patterns. Then

$$d_{pq} = [\sum_i (F_{pi} - F_{qi})^2]^{1/2}, \qquad (6.42)$$

where F_{pi} and F_{qi} are values of ith feature of pth and qth patterns, respectively; $d_{\max}$ is defined as

$$d_{\max} = [\sum_i (F_{i_{\max}} - F_{i_{\min}})^2]^{1/2}, \qquad (6.43)$$

where $F_{i_{\max}}$ and $F_{i_{\min}}$ are respectively the maximum and minimum values of the ith feature.

Incorporating weighting coefficients   The similarity between two patterns is measured in terms of proximity, as conveyed by the expression for d_{pq} [eqn. (6.42)]. Since d_{pq} is an Euclidean distance, the methodology implicitly assumes that the clusters are hyperspherical. But in practice, this may not necessarily be the case. To model the practical situation, the concept of weighted distance is introduced such that

$$\begin{aligned} d_{pq} &= [\sum_i w_i^2 (F_{pi} - F_{qi})^2]^{1/2}, \\ &= [\sum_i w_i^2 \chi_i^2]^{\frac{1}{2}}, \quad \chi_i = (F_{pi} - F_{qi}), \end{aligned} \qquad (6.44)$$

where $w_i \in [0,1]$ represents the weighting coefficient corresponding to ith feature.

The membership value μ_{pq} is now computed by eqns. (6.41), (6.43), and (6.44), and becomes dependent on w_i. The values of w_i (< 1) make μ_{pq} of eqn. (6.41) flattened along the axis of d_{pq}. The lower the value of w_i, the higher is the extent of flattening. In the extreme case, when $w_i = 0$, $\forall i$, $d_{pq} = 0$, and $\mu_{pq} = 1$ for all pair of patterns, $i.e.$, all the patterns lie on the same point, rendering them indiscriminable.

In pattern recognition literature, the weight w_i [eqn. (6.44)] can be viewed as reflecting the relative importance of feature F_i in measuring the similarity (in terms of distance) of a pair of patterns. It is such that the higher the value of w_i, the more important is F_i in characterizing a cluster or discriminating between various clusters; $w_i = 1$ (0) indicates most (least) importance of F_i.

Note that one may define μ_{pq} in a different way satisfying the above-mentioned characteristics. The computation of μ_{pq} in eqn. (6.41) does not require information about class label of the patterns.

6.3.2   Connectionist minimization of E

The objective is to minimize the evaluation index E [eqn. (6.40)], which involves the terms μ^O and μ^T. Note that the n-dimensional transformed space is obtained by introducing $\mathbf{w}$ $(= [w_1, w_2, \ldots, w_n])$ on the n-dimensional original space. The computation of μ^O requires eqns. (6.41)–(6.43), while μ^T needs eqns. (6.41), (6.43), and (6.44). Therefore, the evaluation index E [eqn. (6.40)] becomes a function of $\mathbf{w}$, if one considers ranking of n features in a set.

The problem of feature selection or ranking of individual features thus reduces to finding a set of w_i values for which E becomes minimum; w_i values indicate the relative importance of F_i values. The task of minimization is performed, as in Section 6.2.2, using the gradient descent technique in a connectionist framework under unsupervised mode.

The network (Fig. 6.20) designed for performing all these operations ($i.e.$, computation of μ^O and μ^T, and minimization) consists of input, hidden, and output layers. The input layer has a pair of nodes corresponding to each feature, $i.e.$, the number of nodes in the input layer is $2n$ for an n-dimensional (original) feature space. The hidden layer consists of n nodes that compute the part χ_i^2 of eqn. (6.44) for each pair of patterns. The output layer consists of two nodes, computing μ^O and μ^T. The feature evaluation index E [eqn. (6.53)] is evaluated from these μ values off the network.

Input nodes receive activations corresponding to feature values of each pair of patterns. The jth node in the hidden layer is connected only to the ith and $(i + n)$th input nodes via connection weights $+1$ and -1, respectively, where $j, i = 1, 2, \ldots, n$ and $j = i$. The output node computing μ^T values is connected to the jth node in the hidden layer via connection weight W_j $(= w_j^2)$, whereas that computing μ^O values is connected to all the nodes in the hidden layer via connection weights $+1$ each.

During training each pair of patterns is presented at the input layer and the evaluation index computed. The weights W_j are updated using gradient descent technique, in order to minimize the index E. Note that $d_{\max}$ is directly computed from the unlabeled training set. The values of $d_{\max}$ and β are stored

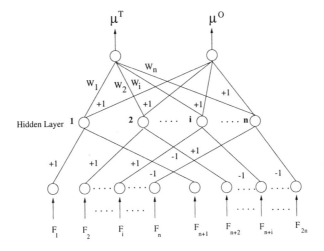

Fig. 6.20 Schematic diagram of unsupervised neural network model for feature selection

in both the output nodes for the computation of D. When the pth and qth patterns are presented to the input layer, the activation produced by the ith $(1 \leq i \leq 2n)$ input node is

$$v_i^0 = y_i^0, \qquad (6.45)$$

where

$$\begin{aligned} y_i^0 &= F_{pi}, \quad \text{for } 1 \leq i \leq n \\ y_{i+n}^0 &= F_{qi}, \quad \text{for } 1 \leq i \leq n, \end{aligned} \qquad (6.46)$$

are the total activations received by the ith and $(i+n)$th $(1 \leq i \leq n)$ input nodes, respectively. The total activation received by the jth hidden node [connecting the ith and $(i+n)$th, $1 \leq i \leq n$, input nodes] is given by

$$y_j^1 = 1 \times v_i^0 + (-1) \times v_{i+n}^0, \quad \text{for } 1 \leq i \leq n, \qquad (6.47)$$

and the activation produced by it is

$$v_j^1 = (y_j^1)^2. \qquad (6.48)$$

Total activation received by the output node that computes μ^T values is

$$y_T^2 = \sum_j W_j v_j^1, \qquad (6.49)$$

and that received by the other output node that computes μ^O values is

$$y_O^2 = \sum_j v_j^1. \qquad (6.50)$$

Therefore, y_T^2 and y_O^2 represent d_{pq}^2 as given by eqns. (6.44) and (6.42), respectively. The activations, v_T^2 and v_O^2, of the output nodes represent μ_{pq}^T and μ_{pq}^O for the pth and qth pattern pairs, respectively. Thus

$$
\begin{aligned}
v_T^2 &= 1 - \frac{(y_T^2)^{1/2}}{D}, && \text{if } (y_T^2)^{1/2} \le D, \\
&= 0, && \text{otherwise,}
\end{aligned}
\tag{6.51}
$$

and

$$
\begin{aligned}
v_O^2 &= 1 - \frac{(y_O^2)^{1/2}}{D}, && \text{if } (y_O^2)^{1/2} \le D, \\
&= 0, && \text{otherwise.}
\end{aligned}
\tag{6.52}
$$

The evaluation index (which is computed off the network), in terms of these activations, is then written [from eqn. (6.40)] as

$$
E(\mathbf{W}) = \frac{2}{s(s-1)} \sum_p \sum_{q \ne p} \frac{1}{2} [v_T^2(1 - v_O^2) + v_O^2(1 - v_T^2)]. \tag{6.53}
$$

As mentioned before, the task of minimization of $E(\mathbf{W})$ [eqn. (6.53)] with respect to $\mathbf{W}$ is performed using gradient descent, where the change in W_j ($\triangle W_j$) is computed as

$$
\triangle W_j = -\varepsilon \frac{\partial E}{\partial W_j}, \quad \forall j, \tag{6.54}
$$

with ε as the learning rate.

For computation of $(\partial E / \partial W_j)$ corresponding to a pair of patterns, the following expressions are used:

$$
\frac{\partial E(\mathbf{W})}{\partial W_j} = \frac{1}{2} \left[1 - 2v_O^2\right] \frac{\partial v_T^2}{\partial W_j}, \tag{6.55}
$$

$$
\begin{aligned}
\frac{\partial v_T^2}{\partial W_j} &= -\frac{\frac{1}{2} \frac{\partial y_T^2}{\partial W_j} (y_T^2)^{-(1/2)}}{D}, && \text{if } (y_T^2)^{1/2} \le D \\
&= 0, && \text{otherwise,}
\end{aligned}
\tag{6.56}
$$

and

$$
\frac{\partial y_T^2}{\partial W_j} = v_j^1. \tag{6.57}
$$

The steps of the algorithm for learning $\mathbf{W}$ are as follows:

1. Calculate $d_{\max}$ from the unlabeled training set. Store $d_{\max}$ and β (user specified) in the output nodes.

2. Initialize W_j with small random values in $[0, 1]$.

3. Repeat until convergence, i.e., until the value of E becomes less than or equal to a certain predefined small quantity, or number of iterations reaches a certain predefined number of iterations.

a. For each pair of patterns

    i. Present the pattern pair to the input layer.

    ii. Compute ΔW_j for each j using the updating rule of eqn. (6.54).

b. Update W_j for each j with ΔW_j averaged over all the pairs.

After convergence, $E(\mathbf{W})$ attains a local minimum. Then the weights $(W_j = w_j^2)$ of the links, connecting hidden nodes and the output node computing μ^T values, indicate the order of importance of the features. Note that this unsupervised method performs the task of feature selection without clustering the feature space explicitly, and does not need to know the number of clusters present in the feature space. ♣

As mentioned before, one can use eqns. (6.40)–(6.43) only for feature subset selection [30] without using neural nets. Then each feature is considered to be independent of each other. On the other hand, the neuro-fuzzy method described here for individual feature ranking finds the set of w_i values (for which E is minimum) considering the effect of interdependence of the features.

6.3.3   Results

Some of the results demonstrating the effectiveness of the neuro-fuzzy algorithm on three real life data sets–*vowel* (Section 3.3.4), *iris* (Section 6.2.4), and *hepato* (Section 4.2.1)–are presented here.

Table 6.4 w values of *vowel* data (unsupervised)

Feature	w	Order
F_1	0.590065	2
F_2	0.896044	1
F_3	0.120944	3

Table 6.5 w values of *iris* data (unsupervised)

Feature	w	Order
SL	0.058414	4
SW	0.194421	3
PL	0.965575	1
PW	0.603508	2

Table 6.6 w values of *hepato* data (unsupervised)

Feature	w	Order
GOT	0.851015	1
GPT	0.665853	8
LDH	0.733647	2
GGT	0.055946	9
BUN	0.704469	6
MCV	0.704249	7
MCH	0.706765	4
TBil	0.706562	5
CRTNN	0.707109	3

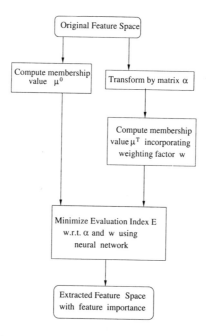

Fig. 6.21 Different tasks for feature extraction in a connectionist framework (w.r.t. = with respect to)

Tables 6.4–6.6 provide the degrees of importance (w value) of different features, corresponding to these data sets. The value of β was taken to be 2.0 throughout the experiment. In the case of *vowel* and *iris* data, the order of importance of the features is found, as in the supervised method of Section 6.2.4, to be $F_2 > F_1 > F_3$ (Table 6.4) and $PL > PW > SW > SL$ (Table 6.5), respectively. For the medical data *hepato*, the best two features (unlike Section 6.2.4) are GOT and LDH (Table 6.6). These were also found to be the best two individual features by the unsupervised feature subset selection algorithm [30].

6.4   UNSUPERVISED FEATURE EXTRACTION

In this section we describe a feature extraction algorithm that provides an optimum transformed space along with the relative importance of the transformed (extracted) features [31]. This transformed space is obtained through a set of linear transformations embedded in a layered network. Computation of the membership values in the transformed space involves a set of weighting coefficients, which provides flexibility in modeling various clusters and reflects the degree of individual importance of the transformed features. The network performs the task of minimization of the above-mentioned index through unsupervised learning process, thereby extracting the optimum transformed space along with the weighting coefficients. This is described in Fig. 6.21. Like the feature selection algorithm of Section 6.3, it considers interdependence of the original features. The architecture of the network is such that the number of nodes in its second hidden layer determines the desired number of extracted features.

In the process of feature extraction, the input feature space ($\mathbf{F}$) is transformed to $\mathbf{F}'$ by a matrix α $(= [\alpha_{ji}]_{n' \times n})$:

$$\mathbf{F} \xrightarrow{\alpha} \mathbf{F}'.$$

The jth transformed feature is, therefore

$$F'_j = \sum_i \alpha_{ji} F_i, \tag{6.58}$$

where α_{ji} ($j = 1, 2, \ldots, n'$, $i = 1, 2, \ldots, n$ and $n > n'$) is a set of coefficients. The membership values (μ) are computed using eqn. (6.41) on the basis of the derived feature values. The distance d_{pq} between the pth and qth patterns, in the transformed space, is

$$
\begin{aligned}
d_{pq} &= \left[\sum_j w_j^2 \left(\sum_i \alpha_{ji}(F_{pi} - F_{qi}) \right)^2 \right]^{1/2}, \\
&= \left[\sum_j w_j^2 \left(\sum_i \alpha_{ji}\chi_i \right)^2 \right]^{1/2}, \qquad \chi_i = F_{pi} - F_{qi}, \\
&= \left[\sum_j w_j^2 \psi_j^2 \right]^{1/2}, \qquad \psi_j = \sum_i \alpha_{ji}(F_{pi} - F_{qi}),
\end{aligned}
$$

$$(6.59)$$

and the maximum distance $d_{\max}$ is computed as

$$
\begin{aligned}
d_{\max} &= \left[\sum_j \left(\sum_i |\alpha_{ji}|(F_{i_{\max}} - F_{i_{\min}}) \right)^2 \right]^{1/2}, \\
&= \left[\sum_j \phi_j^2 \right]^{1/2}, \qquad \phi_j = \sum_i (|\alpha_{ji}|(F_{i_{\max}} - F_{i_{\min}})).
\end{aligned}
$$

$$(6.60)$$

As in the case of feature selection, weighting coefficients (w_j) representing the importance of the transformed features make the shape of clusters in the transformed space hyperellipsoidal.

The membership μ^T is computed using d_{pq} and $d_{\max}$ [eqns. (6.41), (6.59), and (6.60)], while μ^O is obtained from eqns. (6.41)–(6.43) of the feature selection algorithm. The problem of feature extraction therefore reduces to finding a set of α_{ji} and w_j for which E [eqn. (6.40)] becomes a minimum. This is schematically explained in Fig. 6.21. The task of minimization has been performed by gradient descent technique under unsupervised learning. Like the feature selection method of Section 6.3, all these operations (*i.e.*, computation of μ^O and μ^T, and minimization for learning α and $\mathbf{w}$) are performed in a single network [31]. This is described below.

6.4.1   Connectionist model

The network (Fig. 6.22) consists of one input, two hidden, and one output layers. The input layer consists of a pair of nodes corresponding to each feature. The first hidden layer has $2n$ (for n-dimensional original feature space) nodes. Each of the first n nodes computes the part χ_i of eqn. (6.59) and the rest compute χ_i^2. The value of $(F_{i_{\max}} - F_{i_{\min}})$ is stored in each of the first n nodes. The number of nodes in the second hidden layer is taken as n', in order to extract n' features. Each of these nodes has two parts; one computing ψ_j^2 of eqn. (6.59) and the other ϕ_j^2 of eqn. (6.60). The output

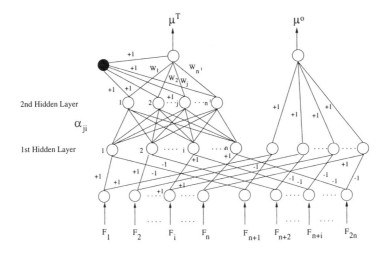

Fig. 6.22 Connectionist model for feature extraction

layer consists of two nodes that compute μ^T and μ^O values. There is a node (represented by black circle) in between the output node computing μ^T values and the second hidden layer. This node computes $d_{\max}$ [eqn. (6.60)] in the transformed feature space and sends it to the output node for computing μ^T. The value of β is stored in both the output nodes. The feature evaluation index E [eqn. (6.71)] is computed from these μ values off the network.

Input nodes receive activations corresponding to feature values of each pair of patterns. A (j_1)th node in the first hidden layer is connected to an ith $(1 \leq i \leq n)$ input node via connection weight $+1$, and to the $(i+n)$th $(1 \leq i \leq n)$ input node via connection weight -1. A (j_2)th node in the second hidden layer is connected to a (j_1)th node in the first hidden layer via connection weight $\alpha_{j_2 j_1}$. The output node computing μ^T values is connected to a (j_2)th node in the second hidden layer via connection weight W_{j_2} $(= w_{j_2}^2)$, and that computing μ^O values is connected to a (j_1)th $(n+1 \leq j_1 \leq 2n)$ node in the first hidden layer via connection weight $+1$ each. The node represented by the black circle is connected via weights $+1$ with the second hidden layer and also with the output node computing μ^T values.

During training, each pair of patterns is presented to the input layer and the evaluation index is computed. The weights $\alpha_{j_2 j_1}$ and W_{j_2} values are updated, using gradient descent, in order to minimize the index E. When the pth and qth patterns are presented to the input layer, the activation produced by the ith $(1 \leq i \leq 2n)$ input node is

$$v_i^0 = y_i^0, \tag{6.61}$$

where

$$\begin{aligned} y_i^0 &= F_{pi}, \quad \text{for} \quad 1 \leq i \leq n \\ y_{(i+n)}^0 &= F_{qi}, \quad \text{for} \quad 1 \leq i \leq n. \end{aligned} \tag{6.62}$$

Here y_i^0 $(1 \le i \le 2n)$ is the total activation received by an ith input node. The total activation received by the (j_1)th node in the first hidden layer (connecting ith and $(i+n)$th input nodes) is given by

$$y_{j_1}^{1'} = 1 \times v_i^0 + (-1) \times v_{i+n}^0, \quad \text{for} \quad 1 \le i \le n, \tag{6.63}$$

and the activation produced by it is

$$\begin{aligned} v_{j_1}^1 &= (y_{j_1}^1), && \text{for} \quad 1 \le j_1 \le n, \\ &= (y_{j_1}^1)^2, && \text{for} \quad n+1 \le j_1 \le 2n. \end{aligned} \tag{6.64}$$

Total activation received by (j_2)th node in the second hidden layer is given by

$$y_{j_2}^2 = \sum_{j_1} \alpha_{j_2 j_1} v_{j_1}^1, \tag{6.65}$$

and the activation produced by it is

$$v_{j_2}^2 = (y_{j_2}^2)^2. \tag{6.66}$$

Total activation received by the output node that computes μ^T values is

$$y_T^3 = \sum_{j_2} W_{j_2} v_{j_2}^2, \tag{6.67}$$

and that received by the other output node computing μ^O values is

$$y_O^3 = \sum_{j_2} v_{j_2}^2. \tag{6.68}$$

Therefore, y_T^3 and y_O^3 represent d_{pq}^2 as given by eqns. (6.59) and (6.42), respectively. The activations, v_T^3 and v_O^3, of the output nodes represent μ_{pq}^T and μ_{pq}^O for the pth and qth pattern pair, respectively. Thus

$$\begin{aligned} v_T^3 &= 1 - \frac{(y_T^3)^{1/2}}{D}, && \text{if} \quad (y_T^3)^{1/2} \le D, \\ &= 0, && \text{otherwise}, \end{aligned} \tag{6.69}$$

and

$$\begin{aligned} v_O^3 &= 1 - \frac{(y_O^{(3)})^{\frac{1}{2}}}{D}, && \text{if} \quad (y_O^3)^{1/2} \le D, \\ &= 0, && \text{otherwise}. \end{aligned} \tag{6.70}$$

The evaluation index, in terms of these activations, is then written [from eqn. (6.40)] as

$$E(\alpha, \mathbf{W}) = \frac{2}{s(s-1)} \sum_p \sum_{q \ne p} \frac{1}{2} [v_T^3 (1 - v_O^3) + v_O^3 (1 - v_T^3)]. \tag{6.71}$$

The task of minimization of $E(\alpha, \mathbf{W})$ [eqn. (6.71)] with respect to $\alpha_{j_2 j_1}$ and W_{j_2} for all j_1 and j_2 is performed using gradient descent, where the changes in $\alpha_{j_2 j_1}$ ($\Delta\alpha_{j_2 j_1}$) and W_{j_2} (ΔW_{j_2}) are computed as

$$\Delta\alpha_{j_2 j_1} = -\varepsilon_1 \frac{\partial E}{\partial \alpha_{j_2 j_1}}, \forall j_1, j_2 \tag{6.72}$$

and

$$\Delta W_{j_2} = -\varepsilon_2 \frac{\partial E}{\partial W_{j_2}}, \forall j_2, \tag{6.73}$$

with ε_1 and ε_2 as the learning rates.

For computation of $(\partial E/\partial\alpha_{j_2 j_1})$ and $(\partial E/\partial w_{j_2})$ corresponding to a pair of patterns, the following expressions are used:

$$\frac{\partial E}{\partial \alpha_{j_2 j_1}} = \frac{1}{2}\left[1 - 2v_O^3\right]\frac{\partial v_T^3}{\partial \alpha_{j_2 j_1}}, \tag{6.74}$$

$$\frac{\partial v_T^3}{\partial \alpha_{j_2 j_1}} = -\frac{\frac{1}{2}D\frac{\partial y_T^3}{\partial \alpha_{j_2 j_1}}(y_T^3)^{-(1/2)} - \frac{\partial D}{\partial \alpha_{j_2 j_1}}(y_T^3)^{(1/2)}}{D^2}, \quad \text{if } (y_T^3)^{1/2} \leq D, \tag{6.75}$$
$$= 0, \qquad\qquad\qquad\qquad\qquad\qquad\qquad \text{otherwise,}$$

$$\frac{\partial y_T^3}{\partial \alpha_{j_2 j_1}} = W_{j_2}\frac{\partial v_{j_2}^2}{\partial \alpha_{j_2 j_1}}, \tag{6.76}$$

$$\frac{\partial v_{j_2}^2}{\partial \alpha_{j_2 j_1}} = 2y_{j_2}^2\frac{\partial y_{j_2}^2}{\partial \alpha_{j_2 j_1}}, \tag{6.77}$$

$$\frac{\partial y_{j_2}^2}{\partial \alpha_{j_2 j_1}} = v_{j_1}^1, \tag{6.78}$$

$$\frac{\partial D}{\partial \alpha_{j_2 j_1}} = \frac{\beta}{d_{\max}}\left(\sum_i |\alpha_{j_2 i}|(F_{i_{\max}} - F_{i_{\min}})\right)(F_{j_{1\max}} - F_{j_{1\min}}), \tag{6.79}$$

$$\frac{\partial E}{\partial W_{j_2}} = \frac{1}{2}\left[1 - 2v_O^3\right]\frac{\partial v_T^3}{\partial W_{j_2}}, \tag{6.80}$$

$$\frac{\partial v_T^3}{\partial W_{j_2}} = -\frac{\frac{1}{2}\frac{\partial y_T^3}{\partial W_{j_2}}(y_T^3)^{-(1/2)}}{D}, \quad \text{if } (y_T^3)^{\frac{1}{2}} \leq D, \tag{6.81}$$
$$= 0, \qquad\qquad\qquad\qquad \text{otherwise,}$$

and

$$\frac{\partial y_T^3}{\partial W_{j_2}} = v_{j_2}. \tag{6.82}$$

6.4.2   Algorithm for learning α and $\mathbf{W}$

1. Calculate $d_{\max}$ (eqn. (6.43)) from the unlabeled training set and store it in the output node computing μ^O values. Store β (user specified) in both the output nodes.

2. Initialize $\alpha_{j_2 j_1}$ and W_{j_2} with small random values in $[0, 1]$.

3. Repeat until convergence, *i.e.*, until the value of E becomes less than or equal to a certain predefined small quantity, or number of iterations attains a certain predefined number of iterations.

   a. For each pair of patterns
      i. Present the pattern pair to the input layer.
      ii. Compute $\triangle \alpha_{j_2 j_1}$ and $\triangle W_{j_2}$ for each j_1 and j_2, using the updating rules in eqns. (6.72) and (6.73).
   b. Update $\alpha_{j_2 j_1}$ and W_{j_2} for each j_1 and j_2 with $\triangle \alpha_{j_2 j_1}$ and $\triangle W_{j_2}$ averaged over all the pairs.

After convergence, $E(\alpha, \mathbf{W})$ attains a local minimum. Then the extracted features are obtained by eqn. (6.58) using the optimum α values. The weights of the links, connecting the output node computing μ^T values to the nodes in the second hidden layer, indicate the order of importance of the extracted features. One may note that like feature selection, this method considers interdependence of original features, performs the task without clustering the feature space explicitly, and does not need to factor in the number of clusters present in the feature space.

6.4.3   Results

Here we provide some of the results [31] on three real life data sets–*iris* (Section 6.2.4), *vowel* (Section 3.3.4), and *hepato* (Section 4.2.1)–to demonstrate the effectiveness of the algorithm. As mentioned before, the number of nodes in the second hidden layer determines the desired number of extracted features; that is, in order to extract n' features, one needs to employ exactly n' nodes in the second hidden layer. The method therefore consists of performing experiments for different number of nodes in the second hidden layer, and selecting the one for which the E value is minimum in a fixed number of iterations to correspond to the best set of extracted features.

Let us consider the case of *iris* data, as an example. Table 6.7 shows the values of α_{ji} [in eqn. (6.58)] for different sets of extracted features along with their E values. The extracted features are obtained by eqn. (6.58). Note that the set containing two extracted features results in minimum E value, and therefore is considered to be the best. The expressions for these two extracted features are then written, from eqn. (6.58), as

$$I_1 = 0.001188 * SL + 0.000859 * SW - 0.003088 * PL - 0.051099 * PW$$

Table 6.7 α values corresponding to different sets of extracted features, with their E values, on *iris* data

Extracted	Coefficients (α) of				E
feature set containing	SL	SW	PL	PW	[eqn. (6.40)]
One feature	0.071854	-0.028614	0.195049	0.139982	0.102437
Two features	0.001188	0.000859	-0.003088	-0.051099	0.101643
	0.008649	0.024023	-0.269199	-0.066076	
Three features	-0.017140	0.005148	-0.123089	-0.152892	
	-0.003976	-0.024542	-0.005904	-0.084350	0.104762
	0.023984	-0.004368	0.237469	0.199510	

Table 6.8 α values corresponding to the best set of extracted features, with their w values, on *vowel* data

Extracted features	Coefficients (α) of			w	Rank
	F_1	F_2	F_3		
V_1	-0.005676	0.050687	0.000573	0.710050	2
V_2	0.000755	-0.159839	0.000934	0.737597	1

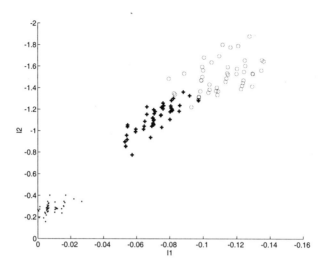

Fig. 6.23 Scatterplot $I_1 - I_2$, in the extracted plane obtained by neuro-fuzzy method, for *iris* data

and

$$I_2 = 0.008649 * SL + 0.024023 * SW - 0.269199 * PL - 0.066076 * PW.$$

The w values representing the importance of the features I_1 and I_2 were found to be 0.712669 and 0.889967, respectively.

Similarly, the dimension of the best extracted feature space was found to be 2 for *vowel* data, and 8 for medical data *hepato*. Tables 6.8 and 6.9 show the α and w-values for the best extracted feature sets corresponding to *vowel* and *hepato* data.

In order to demonstrate the effectiveness of the feature extraction method, the discriminating capability of the extracted features was compared with that of the original ones, using k-NN classifier for $k = 1, 3, 5$ [31]. In the case of *iris* data, the recognition score using the extracted feature set was found to be greater than or equal to that obtained using any set of original features, except for one case [*e.g.*, the set $\{SL, SW, PL, PW\}$ with $k = 5$]. Similar to this was the case with *vowel* data, where the extracted feature pair performed better than any other set of original features, except the set $\{F_1, F_2, F_3\}$.

This algorithm for feature extraction was compared [31] with the well-known principal component analysis in a connectionist framework, called *principal component analysis network* (PCAN) [20]. Scatterplots in Figs. 6.23 and 6.24 show the class structures of *iris* data in the two-dimensional extracted planes, obtained by the neuro-fuzzy method and the PCAN, respectively. The number of samples lying in the overlapping region is seen to be higher in the latter case. This is also verified from the results of fuzzy c-means clustering

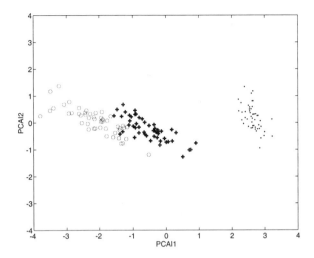

Fig. 6.24 Scatterplot $PCA_1 - PCA_2$, in the extracted plane obtained by PCA network, for *iris* data

algorithm (for $c = 3$), where the number of misclassified samples (lying in other regions) is 14 for the former case, as compared to 17 in the latter.

In order to compare the above-mentioned class structures of the extracted planes with that of the original feature space, one may refer to the *PL-PW* plane of Fig. 6.18. (Note that $\{PL, PW\}$ is found in Sections 6.2.4 and 6.3.3 to be the best feature pair for *iris* data.) The extracted feature plane $I_1 - I_2$ (Fig. 6.23) is seen to bear more resemblance to Fig. 6.18, as compared to Fig. 6.24. It preserves the data structure, cluster shape, and interpattern distances better than does PCAN.

Note that both the neuro-fuzzy method and PCAN extract features without clustering the feature space explicitly, and do not require one to assume the number of clusters. Moreover, the task of feature extraction by the neuro-fuzzy method involves projection of an n-dimensional original space directly to an n'-dimensional transformed space. On the other hand, in the case of PCAN, this task involves projection of an n-dimensional original space to an n-dimensional transformed space, followed by a selection of the best n'-transformed components.   ♣

So far we have explained, in Chapters 3–6, various neuro-fuzzy models mainly for performing pattern classification and feature evaluation. The tasks of rule generation, inferencing, and querying will be described in the following three chapters.

Table 6.9 α values corresponding to the best set of extracted features, with their w values, on *hepato* data

Extracted features	Coefficients (α) of									w	Rank
	GOT	GPT	LDH	GGT	BUN	MCV	MCH	TBil	CRTNN		
H_1	-0.193	-0.020	-0.155	-0.059	-0.081	0.096	0.135	0.193	-0.096	0.705	4
H_2	-0.046	0.097	0.035	-0.045	0.070	0.082	0.042	0.088	-0.136	0.711	1
H_3	-0.163	0.102	-0.122	-0.124	-0.155	-0.106	-0.110	0.101	-0.004	0.703	6
H_4	0.123	-0.170	-0.028	-0.107	0.142	0.043	-0.194	0.162	0.035	0.706	3
H_5	0.142	0.173	0.132	0.073	-0.045	-0.177	-0.188	-0.032	-0.030	0.705	4
H_6	-0.208	-0.003	0.083	0.102	0.013	-0.030	0.132	0.032	-0.081	0.707	2
H_7	-0.160	0.116	-0.163	0.082	-0.146	0.094	0.052	-0.142	-0.078	0.704	5
H_8	0.137	0.002	0.125	0.047	-0.078	-0.047	-0.164	0.125	0.053	0.707	2

REFERENCES

1. J. T. Tou and R. C. Gonzalez, *Pattern Recognition Principles*. London: Addison-Wesley, 1974.

2. P. A. Devijver and J. Kittler, *Pattern Recognition, A Statistical Approach*. London: Prentice–Hall, 1982.

3. J. C. Bezdek, *Pattern Recognition with Fuzzy Objective Function Algorithms*. New York: Plenum Press, 1981.

4. S. K. Pal and B. Chakraborty, "Fuzzy set theoretic measure for automatic feature evaluation," *IEEE Transactions on Systems, Man, and Cybernetics*, vol. 16, pp. 754–760, 1986.

5. S. K. Pal, "Fuzzy set theoretic measures for automatic feature evaluation: II," *Information Sciences*, vol. 64, pp. 165–179, 1992.

6. J. C. Bezdek and P. F. Castelaz, "Prototype classification and feature selection with fuzzy sets," *IEEE Transactions on Systems, Man, and Cybernetics*, vol. 7, pp. 87–92, 1977.

7. Y. H. Pao, *Adaptive Pattern Recognition and Neural Networks*. Reading, MA: Addison-Wesley, 1989.

8. R. Battiti, "Using mutual information for selecting features in supervised neural net learning," *IEEE Transactions on Neural Networks*, vol. 5, pp. 537–550, 1994.

9. D. W. Ruck, S. K. Rogers, and M. Kabrisky, "Feature selection using a multilayer perceptron," *Neural Network Computing*, vol. 20, pp. 40–48, 1990.

10. A. Kowalczyk and H. L. Ferra, "Developing higher-order neural networks with empirically selected units," *IEEE Transactions on Neural Networks*, vol. 5, pp. 698–711, 1994.

11. L. M. Belue and K. W. Bauer, "Determining input features for multilayer perceptrons," *Neurocomputing*, vol. 7, pp. 111–121, 1995.

12. D. Lowe and A. R. Webb, "Optimized feature extraction and Bayes decision in feedforward classifier networks," *IEEE Transactions on Pattern Analysis and Machine Intelligence*, vol. 13, pp. 355–364, 1991.

13. J. Mao and A. K. Jain, "Artificial neural networks for feature extraction and multivariate data projection," *IEEE Transactions on Neural Networks*, vol. 6, pp. 296–317, 1995.

14. K. L. Priddy, S. K. Rogers, D. W. Ruck, G. L. Tarr, and M. Kabrisky, "Bayesian selection of important features for feedforward neural networks," *Neurocomputing*, vol. 5, pp. 91–103, 1993.

15. E. Saund, "Dimensionality-reduction using connectionist networks," *IEEE Transactions on Pattern Analysis and Machine Intelligence*, vol. 11, pp. 304–314, 1989.

16. W. A. C. Schmidt and J. P. Davis, "Pattern recognition properties of various feature spaces for higher order neural networks," *IEEE Transactions on Pattern Analysis and Machine Intelligence*, vol. 15, pp. 795–801, 1993.

17. R. K. De, N. R. Pal, and S. K. Pal, "Feature analysis: Neural network and fuzzy set theoretic approaches," *Pattern Recognition*, vol. 30, pp. 1579–1590, 1997.

18. J. Lampinen and E. Oja, "Distortion tolerant pattern recognition based on self-organizing feature extraction," *IEEE Transactions on Neural Networks*, vol. 6, pp. 539–547, 1995.

19. M. A. Kraaijveld, J. Mao, and A. K. Jain, "A non-linear projection method based on Kohonen's topology preserving maps," *IEEE Transactions on Neural Networks*, vol. 6, pp. 548–559, 1995.

20. J. Rubner and P. Tavan, "A self-organizing network for principal component analysis," *Europhysics Letters*, vol. 10, pp. 693–698, 1989.

21. S. K. Pal, J. Basak, and R. K. De, "Fuzzy feature evaluation index and connectionist realization," *Information Sciences*, vol. 105, pp. 173–188, 1998.

22. J. Basak, R. K. De, and S. K. Pal, "Fuzzy feature evaluation index and connectionist realization–II: Theoretical analysis," *Information Sciences*, vol. 111, pp. 1–17, 1998.

23. R. K. De, J. Basak, and S. K. Pal, "Neuro-fuzzy feature evaluation with theoretical analysis," *Neural Networks* (in press).

24. D. M. Himmelblau, *Applied Nonlinear Programming.* New York: McGraw-Hill, 1976.

25. L. Davis, ed., *Genetic Algorithms and Simulated Annealing.* Los Altos: Morgan-Kaufmann, 1987.

26. R. A. Fisher, "The use of multiple measurements in taxonomic problem," *Annals of Eugenics*, vol. 7, pp. 179–188, 1936.

27. S. K. Pal and D. Dutta Majumder, *Fuzzy Mathematical Approach to Pattern Recognition.* New York: Wiley (Halsted Press), 1986.

28. S. K. Pal and D. Dutta Majumder, "Fuzzy sets and decision making approaches in vowel and speaker recognition," *IEEE Transactions on Systems, Man, and Cybernetics*, vol. 7, pp. 625–629, 1977.

29. J. M. Steppe and K. W. Bauer (Jr.), "Improved feature screening in feedforward neural networks," *Neurocomputing*, vol. 13, pp. 47–58, 1996.

30. J. Basak, R. K. De, and S. K. Pal, "Unsupervised feature selection using neuro-fuzzy approach," *Pattern Recognition Letters*, vol. 19, pp. 997–1006, 1998.

31. R. K. De, J. Basak, and S. K. Pal, "Unsupervised feature extraction using neuro-fuzzy approach," *Fuzzy Sets and Systems* (in press).

7

Rule Generation and Inferencing

7.1 INTRODUCTION

Artificial intelligence is the field that investigates how computers can be made to exhibit intelligence in different aspects of thinking, reasoning, perception, or action. In other words, it involves the study of the mental faculties using computational models [1]. A key observation in this direction is that knowledge should not be represented in heavily encoded forms that suppress the structure and constraints. This has led to the development of more explicit, symbolic, highly flexible forms of representation of knowledge, such as semantic nets, frames, and production rules that can be efficiently processed.

An expert system can be viewed as a rule-based application program that provides the user with the facility for posing and obtaining answers (that require expertise) to questions related to the information stored in its knowledge base [2, 3]. Basically it consists of the knowledge base, the inference engine, and a user interface linking the external environment to the system. The model typically functions in a narrow domain dealing with specialized knowledge generally possessed by human experts. Such systems possess a nontrivial inferential capability and are expected to be capable of directing the acquisition of new information in an efficient manner. The knowledge base of an expert system is problem-dependent and contains information that controls inferencing. Traditional rule-based models encode this information as IF–THEN rules. In *classification expert systems* [4], the outputs are represented by class variables that each can assume continuous values. Programs for diagnosis, fault detection, and pattern recognition are examples of applications that can be represented as classification problems and are handled by this type of expert system.

Neural networks can also be used for this purpose. Such models use the set of connection weights and/or node activations of a trained network for encoding the domain knowledge in a distributed fashion. These are called *connectionist expert systems* [4] and are usually suitable in data-rich environments. They help in minimizing human interaction and associated inherent bias during the phase of knowledge base formation (which is time-consuming in the case of traditional models) and also reduce the possibility of generating contradictory rules. The extracted rules help in alleviating the knowledge acquisition *bottleneck*, refining the initial domain knowledge, and providing reasoning and explanation facilities. Fuzzy neural networks can also be used for the same purpose, and can also handle uncertainty at various stages and levels.

The present chapter deals with the rule generation and inferencing aspects of neuro-fuzzy recognition models. Knowledge is acquired from the data domain, taking advantage of the neural learning techniques. This knowledge, often in fuzzy terminology, is represented or encoded among the connection weights of the trained neural nets. The models are capable of dealing with nonavailability of data, and can enquire the user for additional data when necessary. In the medical domain, for instance, data may be missing for various reasons; for example, some examinations can be risky for the patient or contraindications can exist, an urgent diagnostic decision may need to be made and some very informative but prolonged test results may have to be excluded from the feature set, or appropriate technical equipment may not be available. In such cases, the network can query the user for additional information only when it is particularly necessary to infer a decision.

Again, one realizes that the final responsibility for any diagnostic decision always has to be accepted by the medical practitioner. So the physician may want to verify the justification behind the decision reached, based on personal expertise. This requires the system to be able to explain its mode of reasoning for any inferred decision or recommendation, preferably in rule form, to convince the user that its reasoning is correct.

In this chapter we first (in Section 7.2) review the different neuro-fuzzy models for rule generation, inferencing, and querying, along with their salient features. These are provided under different integration categories, as mentioned in Section 2.5.1 of Chapter 2. These include the nonfuzzy models of Gallant [4], Saito and Nakano [5], Taha and Ghosh [6], Poli *et al.* [7], Omlin and Lee Giles [8], and Ishikawa [9]; the neuro-fuzzy models by Hayashi *et al.* [10, 11], Hudson *et al.* [12], Umano *et al.* [13], and Mitra and Pal [14, 15] (under category 1); the neuro-fuzzy algorithms used by Keller *et al.* [16, 17], Ishibuchi *et al.* [18]–[20], Takagi and Hayashi [21], and Nie [22] (under category 2); and the neuro-fuzzy models of Keller *et al.* [23], Rhee and Krishnapuram [24], Zurada and Lozowski [25], Mitra and Pal [26], Yager [27, 28],

Lin and Lu [29], Zhou and Quek [30], Romaniuk and Hall [31], and Sanchez [32, 33] (under category 3). Some of them are emphasized.

Sections 7.3–7.5 are devoted to describing, in detail, the algorithms for inferencing, querying, and rule generation using the fuzzy MLP [14, 34], fuzzy logical MLP [26, 35, 36], and the fuzzy Kohonen network [15], along with some experimental results. In these models the input, besides being in quantitative, linguistic, or set forms, or a combination of these, can also be missing. The connection weights of the trained network constitute the knowledge base for the problem under consideration. When partial information about a test pattern is presented at the input, the model either infers its category or queries the user for *relevant* information in the order of their relative importance (decided from the *learned* connection weights). If asked by the user, the network is capable of justifying its decision in rule form (relevant to a presented pattern) with the antecedent and consequent parts produced in linguistic and *natural* terms. The antecedent clauses are derived from the trained network by backtracking along *maximum-weighted* paths (through active nodes), whereas the consequent part is generated using a certainty measure. The effectiveness of the algorithms is demonstrated on vowel and synthetic data (of Chapter 3) and medical data (of Chapter 4).

7.2 NEURO-FUZZY MODELS

In this section we review various approaches for rule generation, mainly falling under categories 1, 2, and 3 of the neuro-fuzzy integration methodologies of Section 2.5.1. Before that some connectionist (nonfuzzy) models for rule generation are described to enable the readers in better understanding the significance of the neuro-fuzzy approach.

7.2.1 Connectionist (nonfuzzy) models

Let us first consider a few of the existing layered connectionist models by Gallant [4], Saito and Nakano [5], Taha and Ghosh [6], and Poli *et al.* [7] used for rule generation in the medical domain. The inputs and outputs consist of *crisp* variables in all cases. Generally the symptoms are represented by the input nodes while the diseases and possible treatments correspond to the intermediate and/or output nodes [4]–[6]. The multilayer network described by Saito and Nakano [5] is designed for detecting *headache*. A patient responds to a questionnaire regarding the perceived symptoms and these constitute the input to the network.

The model by Gallant [4], dealing with *sacrophagal* problems, uses a linear discriminant network (with no hidden nodes) that is trained by the simple *pocket algorithm*. The absence of the hidden nodes and nonlinearity limits the utility of the system in modeling complex decision surfaces [37]. Dependency information regarding the variables, in the form of an adjacency matrix, is provided by the expert. Every input variable x is approximated by three Boolean variables x_1', x_2', x_3' such that

If $x \geq \frac{1}{4}$, then $x_1' = 1$ else $x_1' = -1$,
If $x \geq \frac{1}{2}$, then $x_2' = 1$ else $x_2' = -1$,
If $x \geq \frac{3}{4}$, then $x_3' = 1$ else $x_3' = -1$.

Cell activations are discrete, taking on values $+1$, -1, or 0, corresponding to logical values of *true, false,* or *unknown.* Each cell computes its new activation y_i' as a linear discriminant function

$$S_i = \sum_{j \geq 0} w_{ij} y_j,$$

such that

$$y_i' = \begin{cases} +1 \text{ or } \text{true} & \text{if } S_i > 0 \\ -1 \text{ or } \text{false} & \text{if } S_i < 0 \\ 0 \text{ or } \text{unknown} & \text{otherwise.} \end{cases} \quad (7.1)$$

Here w_{ij} is the connection weight between cells i and j, such that $i > j$ and y_j is the activation of cell j.

A novel approach to designing a *modular* system, called *hypernet,* has been reported by Poli et al. [7]. This feedforward network consists of a reference-generating module, a drug compatibility module, and a therapy-selecting module in order to simulate the physician's reasoning as closely as possible. The user-friendly system provides graphics interface for easy handling as well as verification of decisions. The model is implemented for diagnosing and treating hypertension. The performance is good due to the embedded modularity of the network.

Rule generation is possible for the models described in Refs. [4]-[6]. In Ref. [5] the system supplies the doctor with information regarding possible diagnoses on the basis of its output node values. Relation factors, estimating the strength of the relationship between symptom(s) and disease(s), are extracted from the network. Rules are generated from the changes in levels of input and output units; the connection weights are not involved in the process. These rules are then used to allow patients to confirm the symptoms initially provided by them to the system, in order to eliminate noise from the answers.

Gallant's model [4] incorporates inferencing and forward chaining, confidence estimation, backward chaining, and explanation of conclusions by IF-THEN rules. In order to generate a rule, the attributes with greater inference strength (magnitude of connection weights) are selected and a conjunction of the more significant premises is formed to justify the output concept. Here, the user can also be queried to supplement incomplete input information. Let us describe the algorithm in detail. For each cell i, one computes

$$known_i = \sum_{j:y_j \ known} w_{ij} y_j$$

and

$$maxunknown_i = \sum_{j:y_j\ unknown} |w_{ij}|.$$

Whenever

$$|known_i| > maxunknown_i, \tag{7.2}$$

any additional information will not change the sign of the discriminant for y_i so that one can conclude

$$y_i = \begin{cases} +1 & \text{if } known_i > 0 \\ -1 & \text{if } known_i < 0. \end{cases} \tag{7.3}$$

The confidence of a cell is estimated as follows. For a known cell $conf(y_i) = y_i$. For an unknown input cell $conf(y_i) = 0$. For other unknown cells the computation is made in index order as

$$conf(y_i) = \frac{\sum_{j=0}^{i-1} w_{ij} conf(y_j)}{\sum_{j:y_j\ unknown} |w_{ij}|}. \tag{7.4}$$

During question generation, the system selects the unknown output variable y_i such that $|conf(y_i)|$ is maximum. Then it finds a j yielding $\max_j |w_{ij}|$: y_j unknown. If y_j is an input variable, the system asks the user for its value. Otherwise, this step is repeated. Rules are generated by traversing the trained connection weights as follows:

1. List all inputs that are known and have contributed to the ultimate positivity of a discriminant.

2. Arrange the list by decreasing absolute value of the weights.

3. Generate clauses for an IF–THEN rule from this ordered list until one satisfies

$$\left\{ \sum_{y_j\ used\ for\ clause} |w_{ij}| \right\} > \left\{ \sum_{remaining\ inputs\ to\ y_j} |w_{ij}| \right\}.$$

Taha and Ghosh [6] have introduced a *greedy* rule evaluation and ordering mechanism. It orders rules extracted from feedforward networks (in a rulebase) on the basis of three performance measures: soundness, completeness, and false-alarm measures. A method of integrating the output decisions of both the extracted rulebase and the corresponding trained network is described, with a goal of improving the overall performance of the system. The algorithm is implemented on the *Wisconsin breast cancer database*.

Omlin and Lee Giles [8] use trained discrete-time recurrent neural networks to correctly classify strings of a regular language. Rules defining the learned grammar can be extracted from networks in the form of deterministic finite-state automata (DFAs) by applying clustering algorithms in the output space of recurrent state neurons. A heuristic is used to choose among the consistent DFAs that model, that best approximates the learned regular grammar.

Ishikawa [9] demonstrates the training of a network using *structural learning with forgetting*. An examination of the resultant simplified and nonredundant network architecture leads to easy extraction of rules. The positive weights are reduced and negative weights increased using

$$\Delta w_{kj} = -\varepsilon \frac{\partial E}{\partial w_{kj}} - \eta \, \varepsilon \, sgn(w_{kj}),$$

where η is a forgetting constant (> 0) empirically selected. A total of 8124 samples of mushrooms, with 22 attributes each, have been studied for the two-class (edible or poisonous) problem. The method selects two or four most relevant attributes. For the two-attribute case, odor and spore–print–color were found to be important. The values for these two attributes were

- *Odor:* almond, anise, creosote, fishy, foul, musty, none, pungent and spicy,

- *Spore–print–color:* black, brown, buff, green, chocolate, orange, purple, white, yellow.

A sample of the antecedent part of an extracted rule for edible mushroom is (almond OR anise OR none) AND (spore–print–color $\neq$ green).   ♣

In the following sections we describe various approaches to rule generation and inferencing under different frameworks of neuro-fuzzy integration.

7.2.2   Incorporating fuzziness in neural net framework

As an illustration of the characteristics of layered fuzzy neural networks for inferencing and rule generation, the models by Hayashi and others [10, 11], and Hudson *et al.* [12] are described here. A *distributed single layer perceptron-based* model trained with the *pocket algorithm* has been used [10, 11] for diagnosing *hepatobiliary disorders*. All contradictory training data are excluded, as these cannot be tackled by the model. The input layer consists of fuzzy and crisp cell groups while the output is modeled only by fuzzy cell groups. The crisp cell groups are represented by m cells taking on two values in $\{(+1, +1, \ldots, +1), (-1, -1, \ldots, -1)\}$. Fuzzy cell groups, on the other hand, use binary m-dimensional vectors, each taking on values in $\{+1, -1\}$. Linguistic relative importance terms such as *very important* and *moderately important* are allowed in each proposition; linguistic truth values like *completely true, true, possibly true, unknown, possibly false, false,* and *completely false* are also assigned by the domain experts, depending on the output values. Provision is kept, using different linguistic truth values, for modeling the belonging of a pattern to more than one class. Extraction of fuzzy IF–THEN production rules is possible [11] using a top–down traversal involving analysis of the node activations, their bias and the associated link weights.

Hudson *et al.* [12] used a feedforward network for detecting *carcinoma of the lung*. The input nodes represent the data values for signs, symptoms, and test results (may be continuous or discrete) while the interactive nodes account for the interactions that may occur between these parameters. Information is extracted directly from the accumulated data and then combined with a rule-based system incorporating approximate reasoning techniques. The learning method is an adaptation of the *potential function* approach to pattern recognition and is used to determine the weighting factors as well as the relative strengths of rules for the two-class problem.

Recently, Umano *et al.* [13] have used Kohonen's self-organizing algorithm for extracting fuzzy rules from the data set. These are mapped to a layered fuzzy neural network structure, which is then tuned and pruned using *structural learning with forgetting* [9].

The fuzzy MLP and fuzzy Kohonen network, described in Sections 3.3 and 3.5, are also used for linguistic rule generation and inferencing. The details of the methods along with experimental results are provided in Sections 7.3 and 7.5. Note that these models extend the concept of Gallant's method (which is derived for a perceptron) [4] to an MLP and a Kohonen network, by incorporating fuzzy set theory at various levels.

7.2.3   Designing neural net by fuzzy logic formalism

The MLP-based approach reported by Keller and Tahani [16] falls under this category. It receives the possibility distributions of the antecedent clauses at the input, uses a hidden layer to generate an internal representation of the relationship, and finally produces the possibility distribution of the consequent at the output. The model is expected to function as an inference engine with each small subnetwork learning the functional input–output relationship of a rule. Trapezoidal possibility distributions, sampled at discrete points, are used to represent fuzzy linguistic terms and modifiers. The network is supposed to be able to extrapolate to other inputs (for a rule) following *modus ponens*. Conjunctive antecedent clauses are also modeled using separate groups of hidden nodes for each clause. Keller *et al.* [17] explicitly encode each rule in the structure of the network. A measure of disagreement between the input possibility distribution and the antecedent clause distribution is used at the *clause-checking* and *combination* layers to determine the uncertainty in the consequent part of the *fired* rule. Theoretical properties of various combination schemes are also investigated.

Ishibuchi *et al.* [18], on the other hand, use interval vectors to represent fuzzy input and output in an MLP. A backpropagation algorithm is applied on a cost function defined by α-level sets of actual and target fuzzy outputs, using the principles of interval arithmetic. Different fuzzy IF–THEN rules are interpolated from a few sample rules (used during training). Ishibuchi *et al.* [19, 20] have also reported learning methods of neural networks for utilizing expert knowledge represented by fuzzy IF–THEN rules. Both numeric and linguistic inputs are represented in terms of fuzzy numbers and intervals, which can be learned by the fuzzy neural network model. Here the connection weights are also modeled as fuzzy numbers represented by α-level sets. Note that a detailed description of this model has been provided in Section 3.2.1, where its classification aspect has been considered [38]. It is worth mentioning that the use of interval arithmetic operations causes the computations to be complex and time-consuming. Since fuzzy numbers are propagated through the whole network, the computation time and required memory capacities are $2h'$ times of those in the traditional neural networks of comparable size, where h' represents the number of quantized membership grades.

The neural-network-based fuzzy reasoning scheme by Takagi and Hayashi [21] is capable of learning the membership function of the IF part and determining the amount of control in the THEN part of the inference rules. The input data are clustered to find the best number of partitions corresponding to the number of inference rules applicable to the reasoning problem, with a single neural net block modeling one rule. The optimum number of cycles required is determined to avoid *overlearning* and the minimal number of input variables selected for inferring the control values.

Nie [22] has developed a general and systematic approach for constructing a multivariable fuzzy model from numerical data using a self-organizing counterpropagation network. Both supervised and unsupervised algorithms are used. Knowledge can be extracted from the data in the form of a set of rules. This rulebase is then utilized by a fuzzy reasoning model. Moreover, an online adaptive fuzzy model updates the rulebase (in terms of connection weights) in response to the incoming data. The model claims a simple structure, fast learning speed and good modeling accuracy.

7.2.4   Changing basic characteristics of neurons

The work of Keller *et al.* [16, 17], which falls under the previous category (Section 7.2.3), is extended [23] in the present framework of neuro-fuzzy integration. The model uses a fixed network architecture that employs parametrized families of operators, such as the generalized mean and multiplicative hybrid operators. The hybrid operator can behave as union, intersection, or mean operator for different sets of parameters, which can be learned during training. These networks possess extra predictable properties and admit a training algorithm that produces sharper inference results.

Rhee and Krishnapuram [24] have reported a method for rule generation from minimal approximate fuzzy aggregation networks, using the node activations and link weights. They estimate the linguistic labels and the corresponding triangular membership functions for the input features from the training data. Hybrid operators with compensatory behavior, whose parameters can be learned during gradient descent to estimate the type of aggregation, are employed at the neuronal level. Pruning of redundant features and/or hidden nodes helps in generating appropriate rules in terms of AND–OR operators that are represented by these hybrid functions. Zurada and Lozowski [25] have applied T- and S-norms on input membership functions *negative, zero,* and *positive* to extract linguistic rules for pattern classes. Mitra and Pal have used the fuzzy logical MLP (described in Section 3.4) for inferencing and rule generation [26]. This will be explained in detail, with experimental results, in Section 7.4.

A neural network for formulating fuzzy production rules has been constructed by Yager [27]. Numerical information is used to find the preliminary partitioning of the input–output joint space. The linguistic variables associated with the antecedent and consequent parts of the rules are represented as weights in the neural structure. The membership values of these linguistic variables can be learned. The determination of the firing level of a neuron is viewed as a measure of possibility between two fuzzy sets: the connection weights and the input. Unlike Keller *et al.* [17], here a self-organizing procedure is used to determine the structure and initial weights of the network, and obtain the nucleus of rules for a fuzzy knowledge base. This procedure is suitable in data-rich situations, where one is unable to find experts who can provide an organized description of the system. However, in the absence of expert opinions, the training data must be representative of the system's behavior and the unsupervised learning algorithm needs to be properly selected. Yager [28] has also employed neural modules for modeling the rules of fuzzy logic controllers with a combiner (using *min* or *product* functions). The various weights are learned and the importance of the antecedent clauses simulated.

Lin and Lu [29] have designed a five-layered network capable of processing both numerical and linguistic information. Fuzzy rules and membership functions are encoded for fuzzy inferencing. The inputs, outputs, and connection weights can be fuzzy numbers of any shape, represented by α-level fuzzy sets. Min and max operators are used to perform condition matching of fuzzy rules and integration of fired rules having the same consequent. Fuzzy supervised learning and fuzzy reinforcement learning are developed using interval arithmetic and fuzzy input–output pairs and/or linguistic information. The reinforcement signal from the environment involves linguistic information (fuzzy critic signal) such as *good, very good,* or *bad* instead of the normal numerical critic values like 0 (success) or -1 (failure). The system is used for reducing the number of rules in a fuzzy rulebase, and learning proper fuzzy control rules and membership functions.

The inferencing in the pseudo outer-product-based fuzzy neural network (POPFNN) [30] uses fuzzy rule-based systems that employ the *truth value restriction* method. There are five layers, termed the input, condition, rulebase, consequence, and output layers. The fuzzification of the input and the defuzzification of the output are automatically accomplished. The learning process consists of three phases: self-organization, POP learning, and supervised learning. A self-organizing algorithm [39] is employed in the first phase to initialize the membership functions of both the input and output variables by determining their centroids and widths. In the second phase, the POP algorithm is run in one pass to identify the fuzzy rules that are supported by the training set. The derived structure and parameters are then fine-tuned using the backpropagation algorithm.

A *cell recruitment* learning algorithm that is capable of forgetting previously learned facts by learning new information has been employed by Romaniuk and Hall [31] to build a neuro-fuzzy system for determining the *credit-worthiness of credit applicants*. The network consists of *positive* and *negative collector cells* along with *unknown* and *intermediate* cells, and can handle *fuzzy* or *uncertain* data. Fuzzy functions such as *maximum, minimum,* and *negation* are applied at the neuronal levels depending on the corresponding bias values. This incremental learning algorithm can be used either in conjunction with an existing knowledge base or alone. Extraction of fuzzy IF–THEN rules is also possible.

Let us now describe in detail a model by Sanchez [32, 33]. He has associated two types of connection weights–primary linguistic weights and secondary numerical weights–to generate the knowledge base for a *biomedical application* (*inflammatory protein variations*) using a feedforward network. Triangular membership functions such as (1) *negative large, negative medium, negative small, approximately zero, positive small, positive medium,* and *positive large* or, (2) *decreased, normal,* and *increased* account for the linguistic weights while the quantitative weights lie in the range [0,1]. The linguistic weights are tuned according to the information provided from the input–output examples, while the numeric weights and the network topology are determined by solving *fuzzy relation equations.*

The training phase uses fuzzy *min* and *max* operators. *Learning* consists of finding the numerical secondary weights and the network topology. The primary linguistic weights are adjusted by moving the slopes of the curves in the intrinsically fuzzy membership zone. There exist connections between input cells (S_j), output cells ($\triangle_i$), and possible hidden cells (H_{ij}). Primary weights (w_{ij}) are linguistic labels of fuzzy sets, characterizing the variations of the input cells ("S_j is w_{ij}") in relation to the output cells.

One assumes, depending on the context, that w_{ij} denotes either a linguistic weight or the associated fuzzy set. Secondary weights (v_{ij}) are numbers in the unit interval. Input cells have connections pointing either to hidden cells and followed by connections toward output cells (Fig. 7.1), or, directly to output cells (a numerical weight equal to zero). Hidden cells have only numerical weights associated with connections towards output cells. Input cells can take on numerical values or fuzzy numbers, in their underlying universe of discourse. When the activation of input cells S_j are given, the activations of output cells $\triangle_i$ are computed as follows:

$\min_j \ \max[v_{ij}, \mu_{w_{ij}}(x_j)]$ for numerical x_j

or

$\min_j \ \max[v_{ij}, \pi(w_{ij}, X_j)]$ for fuzzy number X_j,

where the terms x_j are numerical values assigned to S_j terms, X_j values are

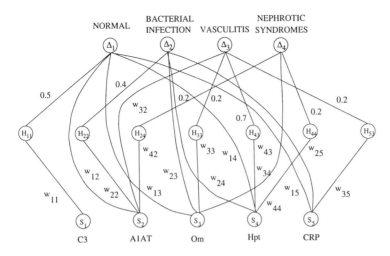

Fig. 7.1 Neuro-fuzzy model of Sanchez

fuzzy numbers meaning "around x_j" terms, $\mu_{w_{ij}}(x_j)$ is the grade of membership of x_j in w_{ij}, and $\pi(w_{ij}, X_j)$ is the possibility measure of X_j, given w_{ij}.

Of course, a mixed formula for output activation can involve both numerical x_js and fuzzy numbers X_js, and t-norms and t-conorms could replace *min* and *max* operators, respectively. Considering training input-output pairs, one proceeds as follows:

Case 1. The w_{ij} values are assumed to be known, at least as a rough approximation, so that the only unknown are the v_{ij} values. To solve this type of equation in the general case of complete dually Brouwerian lattices, in which the set of x values such that $\max(a, x) \geq b$ contains a least element, the technique of Di Nola *et al.* [40] is used. In the case of poor solutions, membership functions of the w_{ij} terms are adjusted by tuning the slope.

Case 2. Neither the w_{ij} nor the v_{ij} values are known, but the w_{ij} values are supposed to be members of a known finite fuzzy partition of $[-1, +1]$, as in fuzzy logic control. Again, for each w_{ij} of the fuzzy partition, the preceding equation has to be solved.

The biomedical application consists of five proteins, *C3-complement fraction (C3)*, *α-1-antitrypsine (A1AT)*, *orosomucoid (Om)*, *haptoglobin (Hpt)*, *C-reactive protein (CRP)*; and four diagnostic groups corresponding to the *normal* condition and three biological inflammatory syndromes, *bacterial infection, vasculitis, nephrotic syndromes*. Seven hidden units were needed.

A sample of the antecedent part of a rule for vasculitis ($\triangle_3$) is

A1AT(S_2): decreased-or-normal (w_{32})
Om(S_3): increased (w_{33}), with weight 0.2 (v_{33})

Hpt(S_4): veryincreased (w_{34}), with weight 0.7 (v_{34})
CRP (S_5): veryincreased (w_{35}), with weight 0.2 (v_{35}).

There exists no connection with $C3$ (S_1), indicating a numerical weight of one (v_{31}).   ♣

So far we have provided, in this section, an overview of various neuro-fuzzy models used for rule generation. In Sections 7.3–7.5 we shall describe in detail some of them [14, 15, 26], [34]–[36] along with their experimental results.

7.3   FUZZY MLP

Here we consider an $(H + 1)$-layered fuzzy MLP [41] (as introduced in Section 3.3) with $3n$ neurons in the input layer and l neurons in the output layer, and describe a method of rule generation [14]. The input vector with components x_j^0 represented as $\boldsymbol{F}$ by eqn. (3.28) is clamped at the input layer while the desired l-dimensional output vector with components d_j by eqn. (3.35) is clamped during training at the output layer. At the end of the training phase the model is supposed to have encoded the input–output information distributed among its connection weights. This constitutes the *knowledge base* of the desired decision making system. Handling of imprecise inputs is possible and natural decision is obtained associated with a certainty measure denoting the confidence in the decision. The model is capable of

- Inferencing based on complete and/or partial information

- Querying the user for unknown input variables that are key to reaching a decision

- Producing justification for inferences in the form of IF–THEN rules.

Figure 7.2 gives an overall view of the various stages involved in the process of inferencing and rule generation. Notations used here are the same as those in Chapter 3.

7.3.1   Input representation

The input can be in quantitative, linguistic or set forms or a combination of these. It is represented as a combination of memberships to the three primary linguistic properties *low, medium,* and *high*, modeled as π functions, in the three-dimensional space of eqn. (3.28). The details are available in [14, 42, 43]. Here we describe them in brief.

7.3.1.1   Quantitative form   As mentioned in Section 3.3.1, when the information is in exact numerical form such as F_j *is* r_1, say, the membership values for the different linguistic feature properties *low, medium,* and *high* are determined by the π function using eqns. (2.6) and (3.30)–(3.31).

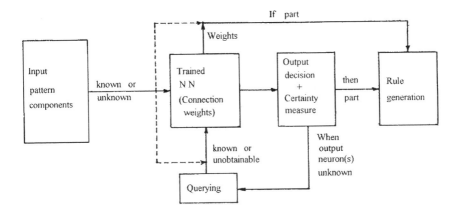

Fig. 7.2 Block diagram of inferencing and rule generation phases of fuzzy MLP

7.3.1.2 *Linguistic form* When the input is given as F_j *is prop* (say), where *prop* stands for any of the primary linguistic properties *low, medium,* or *high,* the membership values are assigned using the π sets of eqn. (3.29). The model can also handle [43] the linguistic hedges *very, more or less,* and *not,* using the *Con* and *Dil* operators of eqn. (2.7).

The modifiers *very* and *more or less (Mol)* may be defined in terms of *low* (L), *medium* (M), and *high* (H) as

$$V ery \ low \ \equiv \ \{Con(L), Con(M), Con(H)\}$$
$$V ery \ medium \ \equiv \ \{Con(L), Dil(M), Con(H)\} \qquad (7.5)$$
$$V ery \ high \ \equiv \ \{Con(L), Con(M), Con(H)\}$$

and

$$More \ or \ less \ low \ \equiv \ \{Con(L), Dil(M), Dil(H)\}$$
$$More \ or \ less \ medium \ \equiv \ \{Dil(L), Con(M), Dil(H)\} \qquad (7.6)$$
$$More \ or \ less \ high \ \equiv \ \{Dil(L), Dil(M), Con(H)\}.$$

The sets *very low* and *low* or, say, *very high* and *high* are considered to be pairs of different but overlapping sets [43], such that the *minimum (maximum)* feature value has a higher membership to the set *very low (very high)* as compared to that in the set *low (high)*. Hence π functions are found to be appropriate for modeling these linguistic sets.

The modifier *not* is defined as

$$\mu_{not(A)}(r) = 1 - \mu_A(r). \qquad (7.7)$$

7.3.1.3 *Set form* Here the input is a mixture of linguistic hedges and quantitative terms. Since the linguistic term increases the impreciseness in the information, the membership value of a quantitative term should be lower when modified by a hedge [43]. The modifiers used are *about, less than, greater than,* and *between.*

For an input F_j *is about* r_1, define

$$\mu \left(about \ \ r_1 \right) = \{ \mu \left(r_1 \right) \}^{1.25} , \tag{7.8}$$

where $F_j = r_1$ is the quantitative input.

When the input under consideration is F_j *is less than* r_1, the expression becomes

$$\mu \left(less \ \ than \ \ r_1 \right) = \begin{cases} \{ \mu \left(r_1 \right) \}^{1/2} & \text{if } r_1 \geq c_{prop} \\ \{ \mu \left(r_1 \right) \}^2 & \text{otherwise.} \end{cases} \tag{7.9}$$

Here c_{prop} denotes c_{low}, c_{medium}, and c_{high} given by eqns. (3.30)–(3.31), respectively, for each of the corresponding three overlapping partitions.

Similarly, for an input F_j *is greater than* r_1, the expression becomes

$$\mu \left(greater \ \ than \ \ r_1 \right) = \begin{cases} \{ \mu \left(r_1 \right) \}^{1/2} & \text{if } r_1 \leq c_{prop} \\ \{ \mu \left(r_1 \right) \}^2 & \text{otherwise.} \end{cases} \tag{7.10}$$

This also holds for the modifier *more than.*

Input information of the form F_j *is between* r_1 *and* r_2 or F_j *is less than* r_2 *and/but greater than* r_1 may be modeled as the geometric mean of the two component membership values as

$$\mu \left(between \ \ r_1 \ \ and \ \ r_2 \right) = \{ \mu \left(less \ \ than \ \ r_2 \right) * \mu \left(greater \ \ than \ \ r_1 \right) \}^{1/2} . \tag{7.11}$$

♣

If any input feature F_j is *not available* or *missing (missg)*, one may clamp the three corresponding neurons $x_k^0 = x_{k+1}^0 = x_{k+2}^0 = 0.5$, such that $k = (j-1) * 3 + 1$. Here $1 \leq k \leq 3n$ and $1 \leq j \leq n$, n being the dimension of the input vector. Thus

$$no \ \ information \equiv \left\{ \frac{0.5}{L}, \frac{0.5}{M}, \frac{0.5}{H} \right\}, \tag{7.12}$$

as 0.5 represents the *most ambiguous* value in the fuzzy membership concept. These input neurons are also tagged with $noinf_k^0 = noinf_{k+1}^0 = noinf_{k+2}^0 = 1$. For the remaining input neurons, $noinf_k^0$ is clamped with zero, indicating absence of ambiguity in the input information.

The appropriate input membership values so obtained, with or without the modifiers, are clamped at the corresponding input neurons.

7.3.2 Forward pass

The l-dimensional output vector with components y_j^H is computed using eqn. (2.38) in a single forward pass. This output vector, with components in the range $[0, 1]$, gives the inferred membership values of the test pattern to the l output classes. Associated with each neuron j in layer $h + 1$ are also

- Its confidence estimation factor $conf_j^{h+1}$

- A variable $unknown_j^{h+1}$ providing the sum of the weighted information from the preceding *ambiguous* neurons i in layer h having $noinf_i^h = 1$

- A variable $known_j^{h+1}$ giving the sum of the weighted information from the (remaining) *nonambiguous* preceding neurons with $noinf_i^h = 0$

For a neuron j in layer $h + 1$ with no preceding neurons i tagged with $noinf_i^h = 1$, the system considers $unknown_j^{h+1} = 0$. Otherwise

$$unknown_j^{h+1} = \sum_i w_{ji}^h y_i^h,$$

$$unden_j^{h+1} = \sum_i |w_{ji}^h|, \qquad (7.13)$$

for all i having $noinf_i^h = 1$. Similarly

$$known_j^{h+1} = \sum_i w_{ji}^h y_i^h \qquad (7.14)$$

for all i with $noinf_i^h = 0$. For neurons in layer $h > 0$, define [14]

$$noinf_j^h = \begin{cases} 1 & \text{if } |known_j^h| \leq |unknown_j^h| \\ 0 & \text{otherwise.} \end{cases} \qquad (7.15)$$

Neuron j with $noinf_j^h = 1$ signifies a lack of meaningful information. Using eqns. (2.37)–(2.38) and (7.13)–(7.15), define [14]

$$conf_j^h = \begin{cases} \left| \dfrac{\sum_i y_i^{h-1} w_{ji}^{h-1}}{unden_j^h} \right| & \text{if } noinf_j^h = 1 \text{ and } h > 0 \\ y_j^h & \text{otherwise.} \end{cases} \qquad (7.16)$$

Note that $conf_j^h$ is comparable either among the set of neurons having $noinf_j^h = 1$, or among those with $noinf_j^h = 0$, but not between the neurons belonging to these two different sets. In the output layer ($h = H$) if $noinf_j^H = 0$ then $conf_j^H$ is higher for neurons having larger y_j^H, implying a greater belongingness to output class j. If $noinf_j^H = 1$, then as $unden_j^H$ by eqn. (7.13) (absolute sum of connection weights from *ambiguous* preceding layer neurons) increases, the confidence $conf_j^H$ decreases and vice versa.

If there is no output neuron j with $noinf_j^H = 1$, then the system finalizes the decision inferred irrespective of whether the input information is complete or partial. In case of partial inputs, this implies presence of all the *necessary* features required for taking the decision. It may be mentioned that the weights (learned during training), that constitute the *knowledge base*, play an important part in determining whether a missing input feature information is *essential* to the final inferred decision or not.

It is to be noted that the difficulty in arriving at a particular decision in favor of class j is dependent not only on the membership value y_j^H but also on its differences with other class membership values y_i^H, where $i \neq j$. To take this factor into account, a certainty measure (for each output neuron) is defined as [14]

$$bel_j^H = y_j^H - \sum_{i \neq j} y_i^H, \qquad (7.17)$$

where $bel_j^H \leq 1$.

7.3.3 Querying

If there is any neuron j in the output layer H with $noinf_j^H = 1$ by eqn. (7.15), then begin the querying phase with backtracking [14]. Select the *unknown* output neuron j_1 from among the neurons with $noinf_j^H = 1$ such that $conf_{j_1}^H$ by eqn. (7.16) (among them) is maximum. This enables starting the process at an output neuron that is *most certain* among the *ambiguous* neurons. The path from neuron j_1 in layer H is pursued in a *top–down* manner, to find the *ambiguous* neuron i_1 in the preceding layer ($h = H - 1$) such that

$$|w_{j_1 i_1}^h * y_{i_1}^h| = \max_i |w_{j_1 i}^h * y_i^h|, \text{ where } noinf_i^h = 1. \qquad (7.18)$$

This process is repeated until the input layer ($h = 0$) is reached. Then the model queries the user for the value of the corresponding input feature u_1 such that

$$u_1 = (i_1 - 1) \bmod 3 + 1, \qquad (7.19)$$

where $1 \leq i_1 \leq 3n$, $1 \leq u_1 \leq n$ and n is the dimension of the input pattern vector.

When asked for the value of a *missing* variable, the user can respond in any of the forms stated in Section 7.3.1. However, if a *missing* input variable of eqn. (7.12) is found to be missing once again, the system tags it as *unobtainable*. This implies that the value of this variable will not be available for the remainder of this session. The inferencing mechanism treats such variables as *known* with *final* values $x_{k_1}^0 = x_{k_1+1}^0 = x_{k_1+2}^0 = 0.5$, with $noinf_{k_1}^0 = noinf_{k_1+1}^0 = noinf_{k_1+2}^0 = 0$, such that

$$information \equiv \left\{ \frac{0.5}{L}, \frac{0.5}{M}, \frac{0.5}{H} \right\}. \qquad (7.20)$$

The response from an *unobtainable* (*unobt*) input variable might allow the neuron activations in the following layers to be inferred, unlike that of a *missing* (*missg*) variable.

Once the requested input variable is supplied by the user, the procedure in Section 7.3.2 is followed either to infer a decision or to continue with further querying. On completion of this phase, all neurons in the output layer have $noinf_j^H = 0$ by eqn. (7.15).

7.3.4 Justification

The user can ask the system why it inferred a particular conclusion. The system answers with an IF–THEN rule applicable to the case at hand. Note that these IF–THEN rules are not represented explicitly in the knowledge base; they are generated by the *inferencing system*, by backtracking, from the connection weights as needed for explanation. As the model has already inferred a conclusion (at this stage), a subset of the currently known information is selected to justify this decision. It is ensured that output nodes j with $bel_j^H > 0$ (or, large y_j^H values) are chosen for obtaining the justification.

7.3.4.1 Output layer Let the user ask for the justification about a conclusion regarding class j. Starting from the output layer $h = H$, the process continues in a *top–down* manner until the input layer $h = 0$ is reached. In the first step, those neurons i in the preceding layer that have a positive impact on the conclusion at output neuron j are selected, such that $w_{ji}^{H-1} > 0$. Let the set of m_{H-1} neurons so chosen, be $\left\{ a_1^{H-1}, a_2^{H-1}, \ldots, a_{m_{H-1}}^{H-1} \right\}$ and let their connection weights to neuron j in layer H be given as $\left\{ wet_{a_1^{H-1}} = w_{ja_1}^{H-1}, \ldots, wet_{a_{m_{H-1}}^{H-1}} = w_{ja_{m_{H-1}}}^{H-1} \right\}$. For the remaining layers one obtains the *maximum weighted* paths through these neurons down to the input layer.

7.3.4.2 Intermediate layers Select neuron i in layer $0 < h < H - 1$ if

$$y_i^h > 0.5,$$
$$wet_{i^h} = \max_{a_k^{h+1}} \left[wet_{a_k^{h+1}} + w_{a_k i}^h \right], \tag{7.21}$$

such that $wet_{i^h} > 0$ [14]. This implies choosing a path with neurons that are currently active, for deciding the conclusion that is being justified. It also enables each neuron i to lie along one of the *maximum weighted* paths from the input layer ($h = 0$) to the output node j in $h = H$, by choosing only one of the m_{h+1} previously selected paths that provides the largest net weight wet_{i^h}. Let the set of m_h neurons so chosen be $\{a_1^h, a_2^h, \ldots, a_{m_h}^h\}$ and their cumulative link weights to neuron j in layer H be $\left\{ wet_{a_1^h}, wet_{a_2^h}, \ldots, wet_{a_{m_h}^h} \right\}$, respectively.

7.3.4.3 Input layer Let the process of eqn. (7.21) result in m_0 chosen neurons (paths) in (from) the input layer ($h = 0$). These neurons indicate inputs that are *known* and have contributed to the ultimate positivity of the conclusion at neuron j in the output layer H. It may happen that $m_0 = 0$, such that no clear justification may be provided for a particular input–output case. This implies that no suitable path can be selected by eqn. (7.21) and the process terminates.

Let the set of selected m_0 input neurons and the corresponding path weights to neuron j in layer H be $\{a_1^0, a_2^0, \ldots, a_{m_0}^0\}$ and $\{wet_{a_1^0}, wet_{a_2^0}, \ldots, wet_{a_{m_0}^0}\}$, respectively. These neurons are arranged in the decreasing order of their *net impacts*, where

$$net\ impact_i = y_i^0 * wet_{i^0}. \tag{7.22}$$

Then the clauses for an IF-THEN rule are generated from this ordered list until

$$\sum_{i_s} wet_{i_s^0} > 2 \sum_{i_n} wet_{i_n^0}, \tag{7.23}$$

where i_s indicates the input neurons selected for the clauses and i_n denotes the input neurons remaining from the set $\{a_1^0, a_2^0, \ldots, a_{m_0}^0\}$, such that

$$|i_s| + |i_n| = m_0.$$

Here $|i_s|, |i_n|$ refer respectively to the number of neurons selected and remaining from the aforementioned set. This heuristic [14] allows the *currently active* test pattern inputs (current evidence) to influence the generated *knowledge base* (connection weights learned during training) in producing the antecedent part of a rule to justify the *current* inference.

7.3.4.4 Antecedent clause generation   For a neuron i_{s_1} in the input layer, selected for clause generation, the corresponding input feature u_{s_1} is obtained as in eqn. (7.19). The antecedent of the rule is given in linguistic form with [14]

$$prop = \begin{cases} low & \text{if } i_{s_1} - 3(u_{s_1} - 1) = 1 \\ medium & \text{if } i_{s_1} - 3(u_{s_1} - 1) = 2 \\ high & \text{otherwise.} \end{cases} \tag{7.24}$$

Suppose that an input feature (of a test pattern) is supplied in linguistic form as *medium* and that the individual components are $\{0.7, 0.95, 0.7\}$. The neuron i_{s_1} selected for clause generation by eqns. (7.21)–(7.23) can, however, result in feature u_{s_1} corresponding to any of the three properties *low*, *medium*, or *high* by eqn. (7.24). This is because the path generated during backtracking is determined primarily by the connection weight magnitudes encoded during training, although the test pattern also plays a minor part.

A linguistic hedge *very, more or less* or *not* may be attached to the linguistic property in the antecedent part, if necessary. For this purpose, the mean square distance $d(u_{s_1}, pr_m)$ between the three components of feature u_{s_1} and *prop* [of eqn. (7.24)] with or without modifiers, represented as pr_m, is used. The corresponding three-dimensional values for pr_m are given by eqn. (3.29) (with no modifiers) and by eqns. (7.5)–(7.7) with the modifiers *very, more or less* and *not*, respectively. The pr_m for which $d(u_{s_1}, pr_m)$ is the *minimum* is selected as the antecedent clause corresponding to feature u_{s_1} (neuron i_{s_1}) for the rule justifying the conclusion regarding output neuron j.

This procedure is repeated for all the $|i_s|$ neurons selected by eqn. (7.23) to generate a set of conjunctive antecedent clauses for the rule. Note that all input features (of the test pattern) need not necessarily be selected for antecedent clause generation.

7.3.4.5 *Consequent deduction*

The consequent part of the rule can be stated in quantitative form as membership value y_j^H to class j. However, a more *natural* form of decision can also be provided for the class j, considering the value of bel_j^H of eqn. (7.17). For the linguistic output form, one may use

1. *Very likely* for $0.8 \leq bel_j^H \leq 1$

2. *Likely* for $0.6 \leq bel_j^H < 0.8$

3. *More or less likely* for $0.4 \leq bel_j^H < 0.6$

4. *Not unlikely* for $0.1 \leq bel_j^H < 0.4$

5. *Unable to recognize* for $bel_j^H < 0.1$

In principle, it should be possible to examine a network and produce every such IF–THEN rule. (These rules can also be used to form the knowledge base of a traditional expert system.)

7.3.4.6 *Example*

Consider the simple three-layered network given in Fig. 7.3, demonstrating a simple rule generation instance regarding class 1. Let the paths be generated by eqn. (7.21). A sample set of connection weights w_{ji}^h, input activation y_i^0 and the corresponding linguistic labels are depicted in the figure. The solid and dotted–dashed paths (that have been selected) terminate at input neurons i_s and i_n respectively, as determined by eqn. (7.23). The dashed lines indicate the paths not selected by eqn. (7.21), using the w_{ji}^h and y_i^h values in the process. Let the certainty measure for the output neuron under consideration be 0.7. Then the rule generated by the model in this case to justify its conclusion regarding class 1 would be

> If F_1 is *very medium* AND F_2 is *high*
> then *likely* class 1.

In this case, the *net path weights* by eqn. (7.23) at the end of the clause selection process are found to be 2.7 $(= 1.6 + 1.1)$ and 1.05 for the *selected* i_s and *not selected* i_n neurons respectively, such that $2.7 > 2*1.05$. The modifier *very* is obtained by applying appropriate operators [eqns. (7.5)–(7.7)], and this is found to result in the *minimum* value for $d(u_{s_1}, pr_m)$.

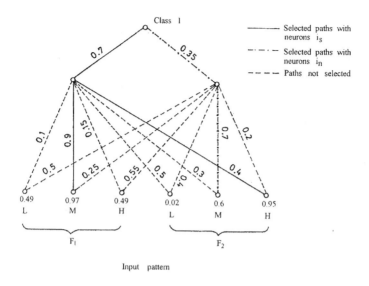

Fig. 7.3 Example demonstrating rule generation scheme by backtracking

To demonstrate querying, let us consider F_1 to be initially *unknown*. Then $y_1^0 = y_2^0 = y_3^0 = 0.5$, with the other values corresponding to those given in Fig. 7.3. From eqns. (7.13)–(7.15), one obtains $known_1^1 = 0.57$, $known_2^1 = 0.618$, $unknown_1^1 = 0.575$, $unknown_2^1 = 0.65$, and therefore $noin f_1^1 = noin f_2^1 = noin f_1^2 = 1$. As the system cannot reach any conclusion in this state, the querying phase is started. In this case, the only *unknown* input feature is F_1, and it can be supplied in any of the forms mentioned in Section 7.3.1.

7.3.5 Results

Here we present some results of the algorithm for inferencing and rule generation on the vowel data (Fig. 3.4, Chapter 3), three sets (A, B, C) of artificially generated nonconvex (linearly nonseparable) pattern classes (Figs. 3.5–3.7) and some medical data–*hepato*, *kala-azar*, and *electroencephalography* (EEG)– of Section 4.2. (Note that the classification aspect of these data has been dealt with in Chapters 3 and 4.)

7.3.5.1 Vowel data Here the sample results correspond to a five-layered fuzzy MLP having $m = 10$ nodes per hidden layer and 50% training set. Table 7.1 illustrates the inferred output responses (in terms of class j and membership y_j^H, for both the best and significant second best choices) of the model on a set of partial and complete input feature vectors. It is observed that often the two features F_1 and F_2 are sufficient for reaching a conclusion. In the table, the entry (row) 2 corresponds to no particular vowel class and hence the certainty measure is appreciably low with both classes e and i registering *ambiguous* output membership values slightly less than 0.5. Note that $F_3 = unobtainable$ is generated by eqn. (7.20). Entry 4a maps to a line parallel to the F_2 axis at $F_1 = 700$ in Fig. 3.4. Note that both classes a and ∂ register positive belongingness, although class a is the *more likely* winner. On the other hand entry 3, with a complete feature vector, specifies a more certain decision in favor of class a. In entry 4b, with a *certain* value for F_2, the decision shifts in favor of class e. Entry 5 also possesses finite belongingness to classes e and i, but the certainty measure is indicative of the *uncertainty* in the decision. The *ambiguity* of entries 6 and 7 is evident from Fig. 3.4 as well as from the two highest output membership values and the certainty measures. Entry 11a corresponds to a horizontal band across Fig. 3.4 around $F_1 = 350$. The classes e and i, which have the highest horizontal coverage in this region, correspond to the significant responses obtained. In entry 11b, as F_2 becomes set at *high*, the response in favor of class i increases. However, the *ambiguity* in the decision is still evident.

Table 7.1   Inferred output response on *vowel* data, with fuzzy MLP

Serial	Input features			Highest output		2nd choice		
no.	F_1	F_2	F_3	j_1	$y_{j_1}^H$	j_2	$y_{j_2}^H$	$bel_{j_1}^H$
1	300	900	*Missg*	u	0.89	–	–	0.88
2	250	1550	*Unobt*	e	0.49	i	0.47	0.02
3	700	1000	2600	a	0.89	–	–	0.89
4a	700	*Missg*	*Missg*	a	0.85	∂	0.14	0.71
4b	700	2300	*Missg*	e	0.77	–	–	0.66
5	450	2400	*Missg*	e	0.70	i	0.11	0.47
6	600	1200	*Missg*	∂	0.71	o	0.27	0.39
7	*Low*	*Very low*	*Missg*	u	0.48	o	0.35	0.10
8	*High*	*Mol low*	*Missg*	a	0.91	–	–	0.91
9	*Between* 500 and 600	1600	*Missg*	e	0.75	–	–	0.72
10	*Greater* than 650	*High*	*Missg*	e	0.75	–	–	0.60
11a	*About 350*	*Missg*	*Missg*	e	0.70	i	0.10	0.50
11b	*About 350*	*High*	*Missg*	e	0.65	i	0.34	0.31

Table 7.2 demonstrates a sample of the partial input feature combinations that are insufficient for inferring any particular decision. The *more essential* of the feature value(s) is queried for by eqns. (7.18)–(7.19). Entries 3 and 5 are seen to lack *essential* information despite having specific values corresponding to two features. This can be explained from the ambiguity of decision (with respect to a class) observed for these pattern points in Fig. 3.4.

Table 7.2   Querying on *vowel* data, with fuzzy MLP

Serial	Input features			Query
no.	F_1	F_2	F_3	for
1a	700	*Missing*	*Missing*	F_2
1b	700	2300	*Missing*	–
2a	*About 350*	*Missing*	*Missing*	F_2
2b	*About 350*	*High*	*Missing*	–
3	400	800	*Missing*	F_3
4	400	*Missing*	*Missing*	F_3
5	250	1550	*Missing*	F_3

Table 7.3 shows the rules generated from the *knowledge base* by presenting a sample set of test patterns. The antecedent parts are obtained using eqns. (7.21)–(7.24) while the consequent parts are deduced from the values of the certainty measure $bel_{j_1}^H$. The rules obtained may be verified by comparing with Fig. 3.4. Note that entries 5, 6, and 9 generate no justification.

Table 7.3   Rules generated on *vowel* data, with fuzzy MLP

Serial	Input features			Justification/rule generation	
no.	F_1	F_2	F_3	IF clause	THEN part
1	300	900	*Missing*	F_2 and F_1 very low	*Very likely* class *u*
2	250	1550	*Unobt*	F_1 very low, F_2 Mol low	*Unable to recognize*
3	700	1000	2600	F_2 very low, F_1 and F_3 Mol high	*Very likely* class *a*
4	700	*Unobt*	*Missing*	F_1 Mol high	*Likely* class *a*
5	450	2400	*Missing*	No explanation	–
6	700	2300	*Missing*	No explanation	–
7	*High*	*Mol low*	*Missing*	F_1 high, F_2 Mol low	*Very likely* class *a*
8	*Between 500 and 600*	1600	*Missing*	F_2 and F_1 very medium	*Likely* class *e*
9	*Greater than 650*	*High*	*Missing*	No explanation	–
10	*About 350*	*High*	*Missing*	F_2 high, F_1 very low	*Not unlikely* class *e*

7.3.5.2 Synthetic data (A, B, C) Tables 7.4, 7.7, and 7.10 demonstrate the inferred output responses for the three pattern sets A, B, C (Figs. 3.5–3.7). The querying phase is demonstrated in Tables 7.5,   7.8, and   7.11, while Tables 7.6,   7.9, and   7.12 illustrate the generation of a few rules from the above-mentioned three *knowledge bases*. These results correspond to three-layered networks, with 10% training set, using 17, 11, and 13 hidden nodes for data A, B, C respectively. The disjunctive (OR) terms in the antecedent part are obtained by combining the various clauses generated for the *same* feature corresponding to a single rule. The disjunctions (/) occur as a result of the concave and/or disjoint nature of the pattern class(es). The remaining clauses are combined conjunctively.

Table 7.4 Inferred output response on pattern set A, with fuzzy MLP

Serial	Input features		Highest output		2nd choice		Certainty
no.	F_1	F_2	j_1	$y_{j_1}^H$	j_2	$y_{j_2}^H$	$bel_{j_1}^H$
1	*Low*	*Missing*	1	1.0	–	–	0.99
2	*Very low*	*Low*	1	1.0	–	–	1.0
3	*Mol low*	*Low*	*None*	1.0	2	0.02	0.99
4	*Not low*	*Missing*	*None*	1.0	–	–	–
	Not low	*Low*	1	0.97	2	0.02	0.95
5	*Medium*	*Missing*	2	0.83	*None*	0.16	0.66
6	*Very medium*	*Missing*	2	0.96	*None*	0.01	0.95
7	*Mol medium*	*Missing*	*None*	0.68	2	0.41	0.27
8	*Not medium*	*Low*	1	1.0	–	–	1.0
9	*Low*	*High*	1	1.0	2	0.02	0.97
10	*Medium*	*Medium*	*None*	0.93	2	0.13	0.73
11	*High*	*High*	1	1.0	2	0.03	0.97

Entries 1 and 5–7 in Table 7.4 correspond to horizontal bands across Fig. 3.5 around the regions of the given F_1 values. Class 1, which has the highest horizontal coverage at $F_1 = low$ in entry 1, produces a *significant* response. As F_1 changes from *medium* (entry 5) to *very medium* (entry 6), the response to class 2 increases and the corresponding ambiguity in the certainty factor decreases. With $F_1 = Mol\ medium$ (in entry 7), class *none* produces a relatively larger response, although the result is *more ambiguous* as observed from the certainty measure. Comparing entries 2 and 8 with entry 3, it is observed that as F_1 changes from *very low* or *not medium* to *Mol low*, the response for class 1 decreases in favor of that for class *none*. All results of Tables 7.4–7.6 may be verified by comparing with Fig. 3.5, which depicts pattern set A. Note from Table 7.6 that entries 1, 5, and 8 generate *no justification*.

In Table 7.7, entries 1, 4, 5, and 7 correspond to horizontal bands across Fig. 3.6 showing pattern set B. Class *none*, having the largest horizontal coverage at $F_1 = low$ in entry 1, produces a *significant* response. Note that

Table 7.5 Querying on pattern set A, with fuzzy MLP

Serial	Input features		Query
no.	F_1	F_2	for
1	*Low*	*Missing*	–
2	*Very low*	*Missing*	F_2
3	*Mol low*	*Missing*	F_2
4	*Not low*	*Missing*	F_2
5	*Medium*	*Missing*	–
6	*Very medium*	*Missing*	–
7	*Mol medium*	*Missing*	–
8	*Not medium*	*Missing*	F_2
9	*High*	*Missing*	–
10	*Very high*	*Missing*	F_2
11	*Mol high*	*Missing*	F_2

Table 7.6 Rules generated on pattern set A, with fuzzy MLP

Serial	Input features		Justification/rule generation	
no.	F_1	F_2	IF clause	THEN part
1	*Low*	*Missing*	*No explanation*	–
2	*Mol low*	*Low*	F_1 *very medium,* F_2 *low/very medium*	*Very likely* *no class*
3	*Medium*	*Missing*	F_1 *medium*	*Likely* class 2
4	*Very medium*	*Missing*	F_1 *very medium*	*Very likely* class 2
5	*Not medium*	*Low*	*No explanation*	–
6	*Mol medium*	*Low*	F_1 *Mol medium/Mol high,* F_2 *very medium*	*Very likely* *no class*
7	*Mol high*	*Low*	F_1 *very medium/Mol high,* F_2 *very medium*	*Very likely* *no class*
8	*Low*	*High*	*No explanation*	–
9	*Medium*	*Medium*	F_1 and F_2 *medium*	*Likely* *no class*
10	*High*	*Medium*	F_2 *medium,* F_1 *high/very medium*	*Very likely* *no class*
11	*Mol medium*	*Missing*	F_1 *Mol medium/not high*	*Not unlikely* *no class*

Table 7.7 Inferred output response on pattern set B, with fuzzy MLP

Serial no.	Input features		Highest output		2nd choice		Certainty
	F_1	F_2	j_1	$y_{j_1}^H$	j_2	$y_{j_2}^H$	$bel_{j_1}^H$
1	*Low*	*Missing*	*None*	1.0	–	–	1.0
2	*Very low*	*Missing*	1	0.60	*None*	0.41	0.19
	Very low	*Low*	*None*	1.0	–	–	1.0
3	*Mol low*	*Low*	2	1.0	–	–	1.0
4	*Medium*	*Missing*	1	0.67	*None*	0.34	0.32
5	*Mol medium*	*Missing*	*None*	0.72	1	0.32	0.4
6	*Not medium*	*Missing*	2	0.73	*None*	0.27	0.47
	Not medium	*Low*	2	1.0	–	–	1.0
7	*Mol high*	*Missing*	1	1.0	–	–	1.0
8	*Not high*	*Missing*	*None*	0.8	1	0.2	0.62
	Not high	*Low*	*None*	1.0	2	0.01	0.99
9	*Low*	*High*	*None*	1.0	–	–	1.0
10	*Medium*	*Medium*	*None*	1.0	–	–	1.0

entry 4 (with $F_1 = medium$ and inferring class 1) and entry 5 (with $F_1 = Mol$ *medium* and inferring class *none*) denote *ambiguous* decisions as observed from the certainty measure. However, entry 7, with $F_1 = Mol\ high$, produces a *more*

Table 7.8 Querying on pattern set B, with fuzzy MLP

Serial no.	Input features		Query for
	F_1	F_2	
1	*Very low*	*Missing*	F_2
2	*Mol low*	*Missing*	F_2
3	*Medium*	*Missing*	–
4	*Mol medium*	*Missing*	–
5	*Not medium*	*Missing*	F_2
6	*Very high*	*Missing*	F_2
7	*Mol high*	*Missing*	–
8	*Not high*	*Missing*	F_2

definite response in favor of class 1. As F_2 becomes *known* as *low* in entry 2, the response changes from class 1 to class *none*. This is due to the fact that along the horizontal band at $F_1 = very\ low$, class 1 has the largest horizontal coverage. However, when the smaller region of interest is specified at $F_2 = low$, the decision shifts in favor of class *none* and the *ambiguity* in decision decreases drastically as the certainty increases ($bel_{j_1}^H = 1$ here). In the cases of entries 6 and 8, the corresponding responses in favor of classes 2 and *none* become *more certain* as F_2 becomes specified. All results of Tables 7.7–7.9 may be verified by comparing with Fig. 3.6. Note that in Table 7.9, entries 2 and 4 generate *no justification.*

Table 7.9 Rules generated on pattern set B, with fuzzy MLP

Sr.	Input features		Justification/Rule generation	
no.	F_1	F_2	IF clause	THEN part
1	*Mol high*	*Missing*	F_1 *Mol high/very medium*	*Very likely* class 1
2	*Medium*	*Missing*	*No explanation*	–
3	*Medium*	*Low*	F_1 *medium/Mol high,*	
			F_2 *very medium*	*Mol likely* class 1
4	*Mol medium*	*Missing*	*No explanation*	–
5	*Medium*	*High*	F_1 *medium,*	
			F_2 *high/very medium*	*Very likely no class*
6	*High*	*Medium*	F_2 *medium/Mol high,*	
			F_1 *high*	*Mol likely no class*

Table 7.10 Inferred output response on pattern set C, with fuzzy MLP

Serial	Input features		Highest output		2nd choice		Certainty
no.	F_1	F_2	j_1	$y_{j_1}^H$	j_2	$y_{j_2}^H$	$bel_{j_1}^H$
1	*Not low*	*Missing*	1	0.81	*None*	0.19	0.61
2	*Medium*	*Missing*	2	0.92	*None*	0.07	0.93
3	*Mol medium*	*Missing*	*None*	0.97	2	0.07	0.90
	Mol medium	*Low*	2	0.88	*None*	0.11	0.77
4	*Not medium*	*Low*	1	0.82	*None*	0.18	0.63
5	*Very high*	*Missing*	1	0.82	*None*	0.17	0.64
6	*Medium*	*High*	2	1.0	–	–	1.0

In Table 7.10, entries 1, 2 and 5 correspond to horizontal bands across Fig. 3.7 showing pattern set C. Entries 1 and 5, for $F_1 = $ *not low* and *very high*, respectively, generate comparatively *less certain* decisions in favor of class 1. Entry 2, with $F_1 = $ *medium*, produces a *decisive* response in favor of class 2. As F_2 becomes *known* as *low* in entry 3, the response changes from class *none* to class 2 as the region of interest becomes more localized. But the *ambiguity* in decision is observed to be more in the case of the complete input specification. All results of Tables 7.10–7.12 may be verified by comparing with Fig. 3.7.

Table 7.11   Querying on pattern set C, with fuzzy MLP

| Serial | Input features | | Query |
no.	F_1	F_2	for
1	*Low*	*Missing*	F_2
2	*Very low*	*Missing*	F_2
3	*Not low*	*Missing*	–
4	*Medium*	*Missing*	–
5	*Mol medium*	*Missing*	F_2
6	*Not medium*	*Missing*	F_2
7	*High*	*Missing*	F_2
8	*Very high*	*Missing*	–
9	*Not high*	*Missing*	F_2

Table 7.12   Rules generated on pattern set C, with fuzzy MLP

| Sr. | Input features | | Justification/rule generation | |
no.	F_1	F_2	IF clause	THEN part
1	*Very low*	*Low*	F_1 *very low,*	
			F_2 *low/very medium*	*Very likely no class*
2	*Not low*	*Missing*	F_1 *very high*	*Likely* class 1
3	*Medium*	*Missing*	F_1 *medium/Mol low*	*Very likely* class 2
4	*Mol medium*	*Low*	F_1 *Mol medium/Mol low,*	
			F_2 *low*	*Likely* class 2
5	*Not medium*	*Low*	F_2 *low/very medium*	*Likely* class 1
6	*High*	*Low*	F_1 *high,* F_2 *low*	*Very likely no class*
7	*Medium*	*High*	F_1 *medium/Mol low,*	
			F_2 *high*	*Very likely* class 2

7.3.5.3 Medical data

Hepatobiliary disorders Table 7.13 depicts the rule generation and querying phases of the fuzzy MLP (trained using $perc = 70\%$ with 40 nodes in each of the three hidden layers) for a sample set of partially known input features of the *hepato* data (Section 4.2.1). Columns 3 and 4 refer respectively to the input feature supplied by the user after querying and the resulting output membership value of the neuron corresponding to the hepatobiliary disorder supported by the THEN part of the generated rule in column 6. The last column indicates the rules obtained from the initially supplied feature set in column 1 [44]. There were only two types of such rules in Hayashi's report [44]: the ones excluding a disease and the ones confirming a disease. The fuzzy MLP, on the other hand, resorts to querying and further updating to obtain rules that are more specifically indicative of a disease. Note that querying should be resorted to at a particular stage, and therefore querying is not required in all cases with a partial set of input features (*e.g.*, see row 1 of the table).

Kala-azar Tables 7.14 and 7.15 show the inferencing ability of a three-layered fuzzy MLP with 10 hidden nodes on a sample set of *kala-azar* data (Section 4.2.2). In Table 7.14 class 1 corresponds to *diseased* while class 2 refers to *cured*. Entries 1 and 6 correspond to patients experiencing speedy recovery during the course of treatment, while entry 2 refers to a patient who was gradually cured. The certainty measure and output membership values bear testimony to this. Note that the first and second rows for each entry refer respectively to the status of the patient at the end of 10 and 20 days. Entries 3 and 4 correspond to patients who expired after 10 days of treatment. Entries 5 and 7 refer to patients whose conditions deteriorated during treatment. All these cases may be verified from the patient records listed in Biswas' study [45]. Table 7.15 illustrates a few of the rules generated from the knowledge base. The serial numbers refer to the corresponding test cases provided in Table 7.14.

Electroencephalography Classification and rule generation using EEG data [46] involved the use of 30 input features, which were later reduced to 3 without appreciable deterioration in performance. Let the 3 features be represented as F_1, F_2, and F_3 corresponding to EEG activity levels *slow*, *medium*, and *fast*, respectively. The rules obtained are enumerated as follows:

- If F_1 is *large* and $F_2 > 0$ and F_3 is *small*, then class 1 (depressed).

- If F_1 is *small* and $F_2 < 0$ and F_3 is *large*, then class 2 (normal).

In the Mitra *et al.* study [46], the conventional approach of n input nodes is used instead of the $3n$ linguistic input nodes. Therefore, the *net impact$_i$* values of eqn. (7.22) corresponding to F_1 and F_3 are compared, such that the feature providing a relatively lower value is assigned a linguistic label *small* while the other is defined as *large*.

Table 7.13 Rule generation and querying phases of *hepato* data

Input features			$y_{j_1}^H$	Rule generated		Ini-
Initially supplied	Initially unknown	Query for		IF clause	THEN part	tial rule
$GOT > 100$ $GPT < 40$ $LDH > 700$ $GGT < 60$ $15 < BUN$ < 20 $30 < MCH$ < 36 *male*	$MCV, TBil,$ $CRTNN$	–	.77	GOT *medium,* GPT *low,* GGT *very low,* BUN *very med.*	*Likely* PH	ALD *false*
$MCV > 100$ *male*	$GOT, GPT,$ $LDH, GGT,$ $BUN, MCH,$ $TBil,$ $CRTNN$	GOT GPT MCH BUN LDH	.0 .1 .07 .26 .74 1.0	GOT *very low,* GPT *very low,* LDH *very low,* MCV *very high,* MCH *Mol med.,* MCH *Mol high*	*Very likely* LC	PH *false*
$GOT < 40$ *female*	$GPT, LDH,$ $GGT, BUN,$ $MCV, MCH,$ $TBil,$ $CRTNN$	GPT GGT BUN LDH MCV	.04 .07 .62 .53 .67 .72	GOT *very low,* GPT *very low,* LDH *low,* GGT *very low,* BUN *Mol med.,* MCV *Mol med.*	*Likely* LC	PH *false*
$GOT < 40$ $40 < GPT$ < 100 $MCV < 90$ *female*	$LDH, GGT,$ $BUN, MCH,$ $TBil$ $CRTNN$	MCH	.75 .8	GOT *very low,* MCV *very low,* MCH *Mol med.,* MCH *Mol low*	*Likely* C	PH *false*
$LDH > 700$ $MCV < 90$ *male*	$GOT, GPT,$ $GGT, BUN,$ $MCH, TBil,$ $CRTNN$	GOT GPT MCH GGT BUN	.87 .91 .94 .94 .87 .84	GOT *low,* GPT *Mol low,* BUN *very med.,* MCV *very low,* MCH *Mol med.*	*Very likely* PH	LC *false*
$BUN > 20$ $MCV > 100$ *male*	$GOT, GPT,$ $LDH, GGT,$ $MCH, TBil,$ $CRTNN$	GOT GPT MCH	.85 .85 .9 .84	GOT *high,* BUN *Mol high,* MCV *high,* MCH *Mol med.,* MCH *Mol high*	*Very likely* PH	C *false*
$GOT < 40$ $40 < GPT$ < 100 *male*	$LDH, GGT,$ $BUN, MCV,$ $MCH, TBil,$ $CRTNN$	MCH $CRTNN$ GGT BUN MCV	.01 .59 .77 .88 .78 .89	GOT *very low,* BUN *very low,* MCV *very high,* MCH *high,* $CRTNN$ *low,* $CRTNN$ *very medium*	*Very likely* ALD	PH *false*

Table 7.14 Inferred output response on *kala-azar* data

Sr. no.	Input features				Highest output		2nd choice	Certainty
	F_1	F_2	F_3	F_4	j_1	$y_{j_1}^H$	$y_{j_2}^H$	$bel_{j_1}^H$
1	20.0	0.8	56.48	71.3	2	0.75	0.24	0.52
	22.5	0.87	61.21	60.5	2	0.91	–	0.83
2	26.0	0.9	51.45	76.6	1	0.50	0.49	0.01
	29.0	0.97	48.89	64.0	2	0.51	0.49	0.03
3	45.0	1.2	75.0	65.0	1	0.76	0.26	0.5
4	52.0	1.4	35.7	64.5	1	1.0	–	1.0
5	25.0	1.1	86.85	90.0	1	0.59	0.4	0.19
	27.0	1.3	117.27	89.3	1	1.0	–	1.0
6	18.0	0.83	78.8	65.5	2	0.75	0.25	0.5
	19.0	0.9	71.02	64.0	2	0.97	–	0.94
7	21.0	0.8	72.46	96.0	1	0.87	0.13	0.73
	30.0	1.1	96.4	85.0	1	1.0	–	1.0

Table 7.15 Rules generated on *kala-azar* data

Serial no.	IF clause	THEN part
1	F_3 *very medium,* F_4 *and* F_1 *very low*	*More or less likely* cured
	F_3 *very medium,* F_2 *very medium,* F_1 *Mol low*	*Very likely* cured
2	F_4 *very low,* F_2 *and* F_1 *very medium,* F_3 *low*	*Unable to recognize*
	F_3 *very medium,* F_2 *Mol high*	*Unable to recognize*
3	F_4 *very low,* F_3 *Mol high*	*More or less likely* diseased
4	F_4 *and* F_3 *very low*	*Very likely* diseased
5	F_4 *and* F_1 *very medium*	*Not unlikely* diseased
	F_4 *very medium,* F_1 *Mol high*	*Very likely* diseased
6	F_3 *and* F_2 *very medium*	*More or less likely* cured
7	F_4 *Mol high,* F_2 *low*	*Likely* diseased
	F_1 *high,* F_4 *Mol low*	*Very likely* diseased

It is observed that the two rules match partly with the statistical analysis of the data [47, 48]. In depression, the slow wave (δ) EEG activity is increased and the fast wave (β) EEG activity is reduced. Incidentally, the role of F_2 cannot be explained from the existing clinical ideas and the experimental findings. The reasons for this may lie in the fact that the medium EEG activity defined here encompasses two bands θ and α, and a subband β_1 (*i.e.*, slow β activity).

7.4 FUZZY LOGICAL MLP

The inferencing and rule generation part of the fuzzy logical MLP described earlier [26], which will be described in this section, is somewhat analogous to that described in Section 7.3. Hence only the relevant distinctive features essential for accommodating the logical operators, are explained.

7.4.1 Forward pass

Let us refer to Fig. 3.11 of Chapter 3 while considering the following definitions [26]. For each neuron j in layer h, the operators T and S stand for the conjugate pair of *t-norm* and *t-conorm* defined by T^m and T^p in Section 2.2.4. Therefore

$$unknown_j^h = \begin{cases} T\left[S\left(y_1^{h-1}, w_{j1}^{h-1}\right), \ldots, S\left(y_{n_1}^{h-1}, w_{jn_1}^{h-1}\right)\right] & \text{for } h = 1 \\ S\left[T\left(y_1^{h-1}, w_{j1}^{h-1}\right), \ldots, T\left(y_{n_2}^{h-1}, w_{jn_2}^{h-1}\right)\right] & \text{otherwise,} \end{cases}$$

(7.25)

and

$$unden_j^h = \sum_i w_{ji}^{h-1}$$

(7.26)

for all i having $noinf_i^{h-1} = 1$, where $i = 1, \ldots, n_1(n_2)$ for $h = 1(2)$. Analogously,

$$known_j^h = \begin{cases} T\left[S\left(y_1^{h-1}, w_{j1}^{h-1}\right), \ldots, S\left(y_{n_1}^{h-1}, w_{jn_1}^{h-1}\right)\right] & \text{for } h = 1 \\ S\left[T\left(y_1^{h-1}, w_{j1}^{h-1}\right), \ldots, T\left(y_{n_2}^{h-1}, w_{jn_2}^{h-1}\right)\right] & \text{otherwise,} \end{cases}$$

(7.27)

for all i with $noinf_i^{h-1} = 0$. Here the T or S operation at layer h is performed over all n_1 S or n_2 T operation outputs from the neurons in the preceding layer $h - 1$ for $h = 1$ or 2 respectively. This is done keeping in mind the *And-Or* structure of the nodes in the hidden and output layers as given by eqns. (3.40)–(3.41). For $h > 0$,

$$noinf_j^h = \begin{cases} 1 & \text{if } known_j^h > unknown_j^h & \text{for } h = 1 \\ 1 & \text{if } known_j^h < unknown_j^h & \text{for } h = 2 \\ 0 & \text{otherwise.} \end{cases}$$

(7.28)

Note that the relations in eqn. (7.28) are opposite for $h = 1$ and 2. This is because the T and S operators are applied in opposite sequences for the two layers in eqns. (7.25) and (7.27), while deriving $unknown_j^h$ and $known_j^h$, respectively.

Using eqns. (3.40)–(3.41) and (7.25)–(7.28), one has

$$conf_j^h = \begin{cases} \frac{y_j^h}{unden_j^h} & \text{if } noinf_j^h = 1 \text{ and } h > 0 \\ y_j^h & \text{otherwise.} \end{cases} \quad (7.29)$$

A certainty measure (for each output neuron) is defined as

$$cert_j^H = \frac{y_j^H}{\sum_i y_i^H}, \quad (7.30)$$

where $0 \le cert_j^H \le 1$. Depending on the value of $cert_j^H$, the final inferred output may be given in natural form irrespective of whether the input is fuzzy or deterministic and complete or partial.

Table 7.16 Output response on *vowel* data, with model P

Serial	Input features			Highest outp.		2nd choice		
no.	F_1	F_2	F_3	j_1	$y_{j_1}^H$	j_2	$y_{j_2}^H$	$cert_{j_1}^H$
1	700	1000	2600	a	0.96	–	–	0.99
2	400	800	Unobt	o	0.27	–	–	0.89
3	400	Unobt	Unobt	e	0.17	i	0.17	0.4
4	700	1300	Unobt	a	0.73	–	–	0.98
5	700	1000	Unobt	a	0.84	–	–	1.0
6	450	2400	Unobt	i	0.38	e	0.2	0.65
7	900	1400	Unobt	a	0.44	–	–	1.0
8	600	1200	Unobt	a	0.4	o	0.3	0.57
9	Between 500 and 600	1600	Missg	e	0.61	o	0.2	0.62
10	High	Mol low	Unobt	a	0.75	–	–	1.0
11	Greater than 650	High	Unobt	e	0.37	–	–	1.0
12	About 350	Unobt	Unobt	i	0.16	–	–	0.81

7.4.2 Querying

If there is any neuron j in the output layer H with $noinf_j^H = 1$ by eqn. (7.28), the querying phase begins. The *unknown* output neuron j_1 is selected from the neurons with $noinf_j^H = 1$, such that $conf_{j_1}^H$ by eqn. (7.29) (among them) is maximum.

Table 7.17 Querying on *vowel* data, with model P

Serial	Input features			Query
no.	F_1	F_2	F_3	for
1	*About* 350	*Missing*	*Missing*	F_2
2	400	800	*Missing*	F_3
3	700	*Missing*	*Missing*	F_2
4	450	2400	*Missing*	F_3
5	900	1400	*Missing*	F_3
6	600	1200	*Missing*	F_3
7	*High*	*Mol low*	*Missing*	F_3
8	*Greater than* 650	*High*	*Missing*	F_3
9	*Between* 500 and 600	1600	*Missing*	–

Table 7.18 Rules generated on *vowel* data, with model P

Sr.	Input features			Justification/rule generation	
no.	F_1	F_2	F_3	IF clause	THEN part
1	300	900	*Unobt*	F_1 *or* F_2 *very low*	*Very likely* class u
2	700	1000	2600	F_3 *and* F_1 *very med.*	
				or F_1 *Mol high*	
				or F_2 *very low*	*Very likely* class a
3	700	*Unobt*	*Missg*	F_1 *very med.*	*Likely* class a, but
				or Mol high	*not unlikely* e
4	400	800	*Unobt*	F_1 *and* F_2 *very low*	*Very likely* class o,
					but *not unlikely* u
5	400	*Unobt*	*Unobt*	F_1 *very low*	*Mol likely* class e/i,
					but *not unlikely* o
6	700	1300	*Unobt*	F_2 *and* F_1 *very med.*	
				or F_1 *Mol high*	*Very likely* class a
7	600	1200	*Unobt*	F_1 *and* F_2 *very med.*	
				or F_2 *low*	*Mol likely* class a/o
8	450	2400	*Unobt*	F_2 *very high,*	
				F_1 *Mol low*	*Likely* class i, but
				or F_1 *very med.*	*not unlikely* e
9	900	1400	*Unobt*	F_2 *very med.*	
				or F_1 *very high*	*Very likely* class a
10	*Between* 500, 600	1600	*Missg*	F_2 *very med. or* F_1 *very med./Mol low*	*Likely* class e, but *not unlikely* o
11	*Greater than* 650	*High*	*Missg*	F_2 *high,* F_1 *Mol high*	
				or F_1 *very med.*	*Very likely* class e
12	*About* 350	*Unobt*	*Unobt*	F_1 *very low*	*Very likely* class i, but *not unlikely* e

Select $i = i_1$ such that with $noinf_i^h = 1$, for $0 \le h < H - 1$,

$$
\begin{aligned}
S\left(w_{j_1 i_1}^h, y_{i_1}^h\right) &= \min_i \left[S\left(w_{j_1 i}^h, y_i^h\right)\right] \quad \text{for } h = 0 \\
T\left(w_{j_1 i_1}^h, y_{i_1}^h\right) &= \max_i \left[T\left(w_{j_1 i}^h, y_i^h\right)\right] \quad \text{otherwise.}
\end{aligned}
\tag{7.31}
$$

For node i_1 in the input layer ($h = 0$), the model queries the user for the value of the corresponding input feature u_1.

7.4.3 Justification

The antecedent and consequent parts of the justifying rules are obtained by an algorithm analogous to that described earlier in Section 7.3.4 for the fuzzy MLP (with no logical operators). The clauses are conjunctive when the corresponding generated paths bifurcate at layer 1 nodes, and are disjunctive when this bifurcation occurs at layer 2 nodes. This follows from the AND-OR structure of the network given by eqns. (3.40)–(3.41). The selected clauses correspond to the *salient* input features (determined both by the connection weight magnitudes learned during training and the input feature components of the test pattern under consideration).

7.4.4 Results

Some results of the algorithm when implemented on the vowel data (Fig. 3.4) and two sets (D, E) of artificially generated patterns (Figs. 3.12 and 3.13) using a three-layered network, trained with 10% samples from each class, are provided here. The details regarding the intermediate stages involving the inferred output response, querying and rule generation have been reported for the *vowel* data only, as an illustration. The comparison of the rules generated by the various models P, KDL, and O (as described in Section 3.4.3) are also provided.

7.4.4.1 Vowel data   Results for model P [conjugate pair (T^p, S^p)], with $m = 20$, are shown in Tables 7.16–7.18. Table 7.16 provides a sample of the inferred output response of the model using partial and complete sets of input features. Tables 7.17 and 7.18 demonstrate the querying and rule generation phases of the said model.

7.4.4.2 Synthetic data (D, E)   Results depicted here correspond to $m = 12$ for pattern set D (Fig. 3.12) and $m = 10$ for pattern set E (Fig. 3.13) for networks trained using 10% samples from each class.

Some sample rules generated from a set of test patterns using the model P for pattern sets D and E are depicted in Tables 7.19 and 7.20, respectively, while Table 7.21 demonstrates the rules obtained using model KDL [conjugate pair (T^m, S^m) of eqn. (2.31)] for pattern set E. (As mentioned in Section 3.4.3,

Table 7.19 Rules generated on pattern set D, with model P

Sr.	Input features		Justification/rule generation	
no.	F_1	F_2	IF clause	THEN part
1	*Medium*	*Low*	F_1 *medium* to *Mol high*, F_2 *very med.* or F_2 *low*	*Mol likely* class 2, but *not unlikely* 1/3/*no class*
2	*Low*	*Very high*	F_1 *low/very med.* or F_2 *very high*	*Likely* class 5, *Mol likely* 4/*no class*
3	*Low*	*Mol high*	F_2 *very med./Mol high* or F_1 *low*	*Mol likely no class*, but *not unlikely* 5/4
4	*Low*	*Not high*	F_1 *low/very med.* or F_2 *very low*	*Likely* class 1, *not unlikely no class*/2
5	*Medium*	*Medium*	F_1 *medium* to *Mol high* or F_2 *medium/Mol low*	*Not unlikely no class*/3/2/4/1
6	*Medium*	*High*	F_1 *Mol low* to *medium*, F_2 *high*	*Mol likely* class 4, but *not unlikely* 5/*noclass*/3
7	*High*	*Low*	F_1 *high*, F_2 *very med.* or F_2 *low*	*Mol likely* class 2/3
8	*High*	*High*	F_2 *high*, F_1 *very med.* to *high*	*Likely* class 4, but *not unlikely* 3

model KDL could not yield good classification performance in case of pattern set D, and therefore the corresponding results for rule generation are not included here). Note that model KDL uses the same network architecture and initial connection weights as model P.   ♣

The built-in AND–OR structure of the fuzzy logical MLP helps it to generate more appropriate rules in AND–OR form, expressed as disjunction of conjunctive clauses. The sigmoidal nonlinearities of the fuzzy MLP approximate the AND or OR functions in special cases, depending on the values of the thresholds learned. Hence the clauses of the rules in AND-OR forms cannot be generated with comparable efficiency. However, it is worth mentioning that more meaningful rules can be generated by the fuzzy logical MLP only in case of problem domains that can be represented in terms of AND-OR combinations of the features, like synthetic data (D, E) of Figs. 3.12 and 3.13. For complex feature spaces, such as real life medical data, it is seen that the fuzzy MLP produces better results.

7.5 FUZZY KOHONEN NETWORK

Here we explain the inferencing ability [15] of the fuzzy Kohonen network [49], described in Section 3.5. To avoid repetitions, only those portions of

Table 7.20 Rules generated on pattern set E, with model P

Serial no.	Input features		Justification/rule generation	
	F_1	F_2	IF clause	THEN part
1	*Low*	*Low*	F_2 *low* to *very medium*, F_1 *low*	*Likely* class 2, but *not unlikely* 1
2	*Low*	*Medium*	F_2 *Mol low* to *medium*, F_1 *low* or F_2 *Mol high*	*Likely* class 2, but *not unlikely* 1
3	*Low*	*High*	F_2 *high* or F_1 *low*, F_2 *very medium*	*Very likely* class 2
4	*Medium*	*Low*	F_1 *Mol low* to *medium*, F_2 *low* or F_2 *very medium*	*Likely* class 1, but *not unlikely* 2
5	*Medium*	*High*	F_1 *medium*, F_2 *high* or F_1 *Mol high*, F_2 *very med.*	*Likely* class 2, but *not unlikely* 1
6	*High*	*Low*	F_2 *low*, F_1 *very medium* or F_1 *high*	*Very likely* class 1
7	*High*	*Medium*	F_2 *medium* to *Mol high*, F_1 *high* or F_2 *Mol low*	*Very likely* class 1, but *not unlikely* 2
8	*High*	*High*	F_2 *high*, F_1 *high* or F_1 *very medium*	*Likely* class 1, but *not unlikely* 2
9	*Medium*	*Medium*	F_1 *Mol low* to *medium*, F_2 *Mol low* or F_2 *medium*	*Mol likely* class 1/2

Table 7.21 Rules generated on pattern set E, with model KDL

Serial no.	Input features		Justification/rule generation	
	F_1	F_2	IF clause	THEN part
1	*Low*	*Low*	F_2 *low* to *very medium*, F_1 *low*	*Likely* class 2, but *not unlikely* 1
2	*Low*	*Medium*	F_2 *Mol low* to *medium*, F_1 *low* or F_1 *very medium*	*Likely* class 2, but *not unlikely* 1
3	*Low*	*High*	F_2 *high* or F_1 *low*, F_2 *very medium*	*Very likely* class 2
4	*Medium*	*Low*	F_1 *Mol low* to *medium*, F_2 *low* or F_2 *very medium*	*Mol likely* class 1/2
5	*Medium*	*High*	F_1 *medium* or F_2 *high* or F_1 *Mol high*, F_2 *very med.*	*Mol likely* class 2/1
6	*High*	*Low*	F_2 *low*, F_1 *very medium* or F_1 *high*	*Very likely* class 1
7	*High*	*Medium*	F_2 *medium*, F_1 *high* or F_2 *Mol high*, F_1 *very med.*	*Likely* class 1, but *not unlikely* 2
8	*High*	*High*	F_2 *high*, F_1 *very medium* or F_1 *high*	*Likely* class 1, but *not unlikely* 2

this partially supervised fuzzy Kohonen network that are specifically different from the fully supervised fuzzy MLP will be discussed. Besides, it is
worth noting that the fuzzy Kohonen model uses a $(3n + l)$-dimensional input
space consisting of the contextual class information along with the linguistic
features.

The input feature F_j may be provided in quantitative, linguistic, and/or
set forms, as described in Section 7.3.1. However, if any input feature F_j is *not
available* or *missing*, the system clamps the three corresponding input vector
components of eqn. (7.12) (incident on the neurons) $x_k = x_{k+1} = x_{k+2} = 0.5$,
such that $k = (j - 1) * 3 + 1$. Here $1 \leq k \leq 3n + l$ and $1 \leq j \leq n$, where
n is the dimension of the input pattern vector. Note that the system deals
with the $3n$-dimensional x' constituent (feature information) of the input
vector x [eqn. (3.54)]. These vector components are also tagged with values
$ininf_k = ininf_{k+1} = ininf_{k+2} = 1$. The tag is used for determining whether
the corresponding neuron is *known* or *unknown* by eqns. (7.32)–(7.33). It is to
be mentioned that for the remaining $\{3(n - |j|) + l\}$ input vector components
of x [eqn. (3.54)], the corresponding variables $ininf_k$ are tagged with zero
(where $|j|$ denotes the number of *missing* input features).

7.5.1 Forward pass

Initially the system prompts the user for the input feature information that
may be provided in any of the forms listed earlier (Section 7.3.1). The components of the l-dimensional contextual class information part x'' of the input
vector x [of eqn. (3.54)] along with the corresponding $ininf_k$ terms are kept
clamped at zero. The N^2 neuron outputs η_i are computed using eqns. (2.45)
and (3.59). Analogous to the procedure discussed in Section 7.3.2, here each
neuron i is associated with

- Its confidence estimation factor $conf_i$

- A variable $unknown_i$ providing the sum of the weighted information
  from the input components x_k having $ininf_k = 1$

- A variable $known_i$ giving the sum of the weighted information from the
  (remaining) *nonambiguous* input constituents with $ininf_k = 0$

Note that when there are no input components x_k tagged with $ininf_k = 1$,
one may clamp $unknown_i = 0$ for all the N^2 neurons. The contextual class
information part x'' of x is kept clamped at zero and therefore produces no
contribution in this stage. For neuron i, define [15]

$$unknown_i = \sum_k m_{ik} x_k,$$

$$unden_i = \sum_k |m_{ik}|, \tag{7.32}$$

for all k having $ininf_k = 1$. Similarly

$$known_i = \sum_k m_{ik}x_k, \tag{7.33}$$

for all k with $ininf_k = 0$. For the N^2 neurons, let

$$noinf_i = \begin{cases} 1 & \text{if } |known_i| \leq |unknown_i| \\ 0 & \text{otherwise,} \end{cases} \tag{7.34}$$

where $noinf_i$ for the ith neuron is a tag analogous to $ininf_k$ for the kth input component.

Using eqns. (2.45), (3.59), and (7.32)–(7.34) [15], we obtain

$$conf_i = \begin{cases} \left|\frac{\eta_i}{unden_i}\right| & \text{if } noinf_i = 1 \\ \eta_i & \text{otherwise.} \end{cases} \tag{7.35}$$

Let neurons $p1'$ and $p2'$ generate the highest and second highest output responses η_{f_p} and η_{s_p}, respectively, for pattern p with input vector x. If neither $noinf_{p1'} = 1$ nor $noinf_{p2'} = 1$, then the system finalizes the decision inferred, irrespective of whether the input information is complete or partial.

Decide that η_{f_p} and η_{s_p} are in favor of classes $C_{k1'}$ and $C_{k2'}$, respectively, when

$$m_{(p1')(3n+k1')} = \max_k \left[m_{(p1')(3n+k)} \right]$$
$$m_{(p2')(3n+k2')} = \max_k \left[m_{(p2')(3n+k)} \right], \tag{7.36}$$

where $k = 1, \ldots, l$.

The inferred highest and second highest output memberships $\mu_{k_1}(\eta)$ and $\mu_{k_2}(\eta)$, to classes C_{k_1} and C_{k_2}, respectively, are given [see eqns. (3.67)–(3.68)]

$$\mu_{k_1}(\eta) = \frac{m_{(p1')(3n+k1')}}{s}$$
$$\mu_{k_2}(\eta) = \frac{m_{(p2')(3n+k2')}}{s} * \frac{\eta_{s_p}}{\eta_{f_p}}, \tag{7.37}$$

with $p_1 = p1'$, $p_2 = p2'$, $k_1 = k1'$, $k_2 = k2'$, if $m_{(p1')(3n+k1')} \geq m_{(p2')(3n+k2')} * (\eta_{s_p}/\eta_{f_p})$. Otherwise

$$\mu_{k_1}(\eta) = \frac{m_{(p2')(3n+k2')}}{s} * \frac{\eta_{s_p}}{\eta_{f_p}}$$
$$\mu_{k_2}(\eta) = \frac{m_{(p1')(3n+k1')}}{s}, \tag{7.38}$$

where $p_1 = p2'$, $p_2 = p1'$, $k_1 = k2'$, and $k_2 = k1'$. Here p_1 and p_2 refer to the neurons inferred to be generating the highest and second highest membership values to classes C_{k_1} and C_{k_2}, respectively, and s is the scaling factor from eqn. (3.55).

A certainty measure for the neuron p_1 is defined as [15]

$$bel_{p_1}^{k_1} = \frac{1}{s} * \left[m_{(p_1)(3n+k_1)} - \sum_{k=1}^{l} m_{(p_1)(3n+k)} \right], \qquad (7.39)$$

where $k \neq k_1$ and $bel_{p_1}^{k_1} \leq 1$. Here k_1 and p_1 are obtained from eqns. (7.37)–(7.38).

7.5.2   Querying

If either $noinf_{p_1} = 1$ or $noinf_{p_2} = 1$ by eqn. (7.34), where p_1 and p_2 are obtained from eqns. (7.37)–(7.38), the querying phase begins. The *unknown* output neuron i_1 is selected from among the (p_1)th and/or (p_2)th neuron(s) with $noinf_{p_1} = 1$ and/or $noinf_{p_2} = 1$, such that $conf_{i_1}$ by eqn. (7.35) (among them) is maximum.

Then the path from neuron i_1 is pursued to find the *ambiguous* input feature vector component x_{k_1} with the greatest absolute influence on neuron i_1. For this, $k = k_1$ is selected such that [15]

$$|m_{i_1 k_1} * x_{k_1}| = \max_k |m_{i_1 k} * x_k|, \text{ where } ininf_k = 1. \qquad (7.40)$$

The model queries the user for the value of the corresponding input feature j_1 such that

$$j_1 = (k_1 - 1) \bmod 3 + 1, \qquad (7.41)$$

where $1 \leq j_1 \leq n$ and n is the dimension of the input pattern vector. Note that here only the $3n$-dimensional input feature information vector x' of eqn. (3.54) is under consideration.

If a *missing* input variable (as represented by eqn. (7.12)) is found to be missing once again, it is then tagged as *unobtainable*. The inferencing mechanism treats such variables as *known* with values $x_{k_1} = x_{k_1+1} = x_{k_1+2} = 0.5$, but having $ininf_{k_1} = ininf_{k_1+1} = ininf_{k_1+2} = 0$. On completion of this phase, one has $noinf_{p_1} = noinf_{p_2} = 0$ by eqn. (7.34).

7.5.3   Justification

Let the user request justification for a conclusion regarding class C_{k_1} at neuron p_1. Starting from neuron p_1, the process reasons *backward* to the input vector along the *maximum weighted* paths. Those input feature vector components x_k that have a significant positive impact on the conclusion reached at neuron p_1 are selected.

Input feature vector component x_k is chosen if

$$x_k > 0.5, \qquad (7.42)$$

where $0 \leq k \leq 3n$. Let the set of h components selected be $\{x_{k_1}, x_{k_2}, \ldots, x_{k_h}\}$ and their corresponding link weights to neuron p_1 be $\{m_{p_1 k_1}, m_{p_1 k_2}, \ldots, m_{p_1 k_h}\}$, respectively.

The chosen input components are arranged in the decreasing order of their *net impacts*, where *net impact*$_k = x_k * m_{p_1 k}$. Then the clauses for an IF–THEN rule are generated from this ordered list (by a procedure analogous to that described in Section 7.3.4 for the fuzzy MLP) until

$$\sum_{k_s} m_{p_1 k_s} > 2 \sum_{k_n} m_{p_1 k_n}, \tag{7.43}$$

where k_s indicates the input components selected for the clauses and k_n denotes the input components remaining from the set $\{x_{k_1}, x_{k_2}, \ldots, x_{k_h}\}$ such that $|k_s| + |k_n| = h$.

For an input component $x_{k_{s_1}}$, selected for clause generation, the corresponding input feature j_{s_1} is obtained as in eqn. (7.41), such that $1 \leq j_{s_1} \leq n$ and $1 \leq k_{s_1} \leq 3n$. The antecedent of the rule is given in linguistic form, where the linguistic property is determined from eqn. (7.24) (as described for the fuzzy MLP).

The consequent part of the rule can be stated in quantitative form as membership value $\mu_{k_1}(\eta)$ to class C_{k_1} by eqns. (7.37)–(7.38). However, a more *natural* form of decision (analogous to that discussed for the fuzzy MLP) can also be provided, considering the value of $bel_{p_1}^{k_1}$ of eqn. (7.39).

Table 7.22 Inferred output response on *vowel* data, with fuzzy Kohonen network

Sr.	Input features			First choice		Second choice		
no.	F_1	F_2	F_3	C_{k_1}	$\mu_{k_1}(\eta)$	C_{k_2}	$\mu_{k_2}(\eta)$	$bel_{p_1}^{k_1}$
1	700	1000	*Missing*	a	0.84	a	0.81	.80
2	700	1000	2600	a	0.83	a	0.67	.45
3	700	*Missing*	*Unobt*	a	0.66	∂	0.38	−.55
4	400	*Unobt*	*Missing*	e	0.59	e	0.48	.30
5	300	900	*Missing*	u	0.87	u	0.76	.65
6	450	2400	*Missing*	e	0.92	e	0.91	.85
7	700	2300	*Missing*	e	0.89	e	0.75	.65
8	900	1400	*Missing*	a	0.78	a	0.67	.45
9	*High*	*Mol low*	*Missing*	a	0.80	a	0.67	.45
10	*Between* *500 and 600*	1600	*Missing*	∂	0.62	e	0.48	.30
11	*Greater* *than 650*	*High*	*Missing*	e	0.75	∂	0.37	.65

Table 7.23 Querying on *vowel* data, with fuzzy Kohonen network

Serial	Input features			Query
no.	F_1	F_2	F_3	for
1	700	*Missing*	*Missing*	F_3
2	*About* 350	*Missing*	*Missing*	F_2
3	400	*Missing*	*Missing*	F_2
4	· *Missing*	1000	*Missing*	F_3

7.5.4 Results

Some results corresponding to the vowel data (Fig. 3.4) and the three sets (A, B, C) of synthetic (linearly nonseparable) pattern classes (Figs. 3.5–3.7) are provided here.

Table 7.24 Rules generated on *vowel* data, with fuzzy Kohonen network

Serial	Input features			Justification/rule generation	
no.	F_1	F_2	F_3	IF clause	THEN part
1	300	900	*Missing*	F_2 *very low*	*Likely* class *u*
2	700	1000	2600	F_2 *very low,* F_1 *Mol high*	*Mol likely* class *a*
3	700	2300	*Missing*	F_2 *very high,* F_1 *very med.*	*Likely* class *e*
4	450	2400	*Missing*	F_2 *very high,* F_1 *very med.*	*Very likely* class *e*
5	900	1400	*Missing*	F_2 *Mol low,* F_1 *very high*	*Mol likely* class *a*
6	*High*	*Mol low*	*Missing*	F_2 *Mol low,* F_1 *high*	*Mol likely* class *a*
7	*Between* 500 and 600	1600	*Missing*	F_2 and F_1 *very medium*	*Not unlikely* class ∂
8	*Greater than* 650	*High*	*Missing*	F_1 *very med.,* F_2 *high*	*Likely* class *e*

7.5.4.1 Vowel data Tables 7.22–7.24 demonstrate the inferencing, querying, and rule generation by a 10×10 fuzzy Kohonen network (with *cdenom* = 100) trained using 10% samples of vowel data. The results may be verified, as before, by comparison with Fig. 3.4. Entries 3 and 4 of Table 7.24 are observed to generate slightly different consequent parts for a rule with the same antecedent clauses. This is because different pattern points are used to

obtain the two justifications. Entries 5 and 6 are found to generate the same
rules from numeric and linguistic input specifications, respectively.

7.5.4.2 Synthetic data (A, B, C)

In the following paragraphs and in Tables 7.25–7.33 we provide sample results corresponding to a fuzzy Kohonen
network of size 14×14 for pattern set A, and size 16×16 for pattern sets B
and C (with 50% training data). Tables 7.25, 7.28, and 7.31 demonstrate the
inferred output responses of the network on some partial and complete input
feature vectors. Tables 7.26, 7.29, and 7.32 show the querying phase, where in
some cases the missing feature information is *necessary* for inferring a decision
and hence queried for. Tables 7.27, 7.30, and 7.33 illustrate the generation
of a few rules from the three *knowledge bases*. Verification regarding these
tables may be made, as before, by examining the original patterns given in
Figs. 3.5–3.7.

Table 7.25 Inferred output response on pattern set A, with fuzzy Kohonen network

Serial	Input features		First choice		Second choice		Certainty
no.	F_1	F_2	C_{k_1}	$\mu_{k_1}(\eta)$	C_{k_2}	$\mu_{k_2}(\eta)$	$bel_{p_1}^{k_1}$
1	*Missing*	*Low*	2	0.90	2	0.77	0.79
2	*Not low*	*Missing*	*None*	0.99	*None*	0.99	0.99
3	*Mol medium*	*Missing*	*None*	0.93	*None*	0.90	0.79
4	*Not medium*	*Low*	1	0.90	1	0.59	0.17
5	*Very high*	*Missing*	*None*	0.99	*None*	0.99	0.99
6	*Low*	*Low*	*None*	0.94	*None*	0.82	0.88
7	*Medium*	*Low*	2	0.90	2	0.77	0.79
8	*Medium*	*Medium*	*None*	0.93	*None*	0.90	0.79
9	*Medium*	*High*	2	0.96	2	0.82	0.91

Table 7.26 Querying on pattern set A, with fuzzy Kohonen network

Serial	Input features		Query
no.	F_1	F_2	for
1	*Not low*	*Missing*	–
2	*Mol medium*	*Missing*	–
3	*Not medium*	*Missing*	F_2
4	*High*	*Missing*	–

Entries 2 and 5 of Table 7.27 correspond to the same antecedent clause
generating two consequent parts as justifications to two separate inferences,

Table 7.27 Rules generated on pattern set A, with fuzzy Kohonen network

Serial	Input features		Justification/rule generation	
no.	F_1	F_2	IF clause	THEN part
1	Very low	Missing	F_1 very low	Very likely no class
2	Missing	Low	F_2 low	Likely class 2
3	Not low	Missing	F_1 very high	Very likely no class
4	Mol medium	Missing	F_1 Mol medium	Likely no class
5	Not medium	Low	F_2 low	Not unlikely class 1
6	Very high	Missing	F_1 very high	Very likely no class
7	Medium	Low	F_1 medium, F_2 low	Likely class 2

Table 7.28 Inferred output response on pattern set B, with fuzzy Kohonen network

Serial	Input features		First choice		Second choice		Certainty
no.	F_1	F_2	C_{k_1}	$\mu_{k_1}(\eta)$	C_{k_2}	$\mu_{k_2}(\eta)$	$bel_{p_1}^{k_1}$ or $bel_{p_1}^{k_2}$
1	Mol low	Missing	None	0.81	2	0.65	(0.30)
2	Medium	Missing	None	0.78	None	0.67	0.56
3	Mol high	Missing	1	0.99	1	0.99	0.99
4	Low	Medium	2	0.86	2	0.82	0.73
5	Medium	Medium	None	0.78	None	0.67	0.34
6	High	High	1	0.89	None	0.77	0.54

Table 7.29 Querying on pattern set B, with fuzzy Kohonen network

Serial	Input features		Query
no.	F_1	F_2	for
1	Medium	Missing	–
2	Not medium	Missing	F_2
3	Mol high	Missing	–
4	Not high	Missing	–

Table 7.30 Rules generated on pattern set B, with fuzzy Kohonen network

Serial	Input features		Justification/rule generation	
no.	F_1	F_2	IF clause	THEN part
1	*Mol low*	*Missing*	F_1 *very medium*	*Not unlikely* class 2
2	*Medium*	*Missing*	F_1 *medium*	*Not unlikely* no class
3	*Not medium*	*Low*	F_2 *low*	*Not unlikely* no class
4	*Mol high*	*Missing*	F_1 *Mol high*	*Very likely* class 1
5	*Low*	*Medium*	F_2 *medium*, F_1 *low*	*Likely* class 2
6	*Medium*	*Low*	F_1 *medium*, F_2 *low*	*Very likely* no class
7	*Medium*	*Medium*	F_1 *medium*, F_2 *medium*	*Not unlikely* no class
8	*High*	*High*	F_2 and F_1 *high*	*Mol likely* class 1

Table 7.31 Inferred output response on pattern set C, with fuzzy Kohonen network

Serial	Input features		First choice		Second choice		Certainty
no.	F_1	F_2	C_{k_1}	$\mu_{k_1}(\eta)$	C_{k_2}	$\mu_{k_2}(\eta)$	$bel_{p_1}^{k_1}$
1	*Low*	*Missing*	1	0.93	1	0.59	0.87
2	*Mol low*	*Missing*	*None*	0.67	*None*	0.54	0.07
3	*Not low*	*Missing*	1	0.99	1	0.98	0.97
4	*Medium*	*Missing*	1	0.60	1	0.56	0.11
5	*Not medium*	*Low*	1	1.0	1	0.99	1.0
6	*High*	*Missing*	1	0.99	1	0.98	0.97
7	*Not high*	*Missing*	1	0.94	1	0.58	0.87
8	*Low*	*Low*	*None*	0.97	*None*	0.76	0.95
9	*Low*	*Medium*	1	0.94	*None*	0.53	0.87
10	*Medium*	*Medium*	1	0.95	1	0.60	0.20
11	*High*	*Low*	*None*	0.98	*None*	0.95	0.97
12	*High*	*Medium*	1	0.99	1	0.98	0.97

Table 7.32 Querying on pattern set C, with fuzzy Kohonen network

Serial	Input features		Query
no.	F_1	F_2	for
1	*Low*	*Missing*	−
2	*Mol low*	*Missing*	−
3	*Medium*	*Missing*	−
4	*Not medium*	*Missing*	F_2
5	*High*	*Missing*	−
6	*Not high*	*Missing*	−

Table 7.33 Rules generated on pattern set C, with fuzzy Kohonen network

Serial	Input features		Justification/Rule generation	
no.	F_1	F_2	IF clause	THEN part
1	*Low*	*Missing*	F_1 *low*	*Very likely* class 1
2	*Mol low*	*Missing*	F_1 *Mol low*	*Unable to recognize*
3	*Not low*	*Missing*	F_1 *very high*	*Very likely* class 1
4	*Medium*	*Missing*	F_1 *medium*	*Mol likely* class 1
5	*Not medium*	*Low*	F_2 *low*	*Very likely* class 1
6	*High*	*Missing*	F_1 *high*	*Very likely* class 1
7	*Not high*	*Missing*	F_1 *very low*	*Very likely* class 1
8	*Low*	*Low*	F_1 *and* F_2 *low*	*Very likely no class*
9	*Low*	*Medium*	F_2 *medium,* F_1 *low*	*Very likely* class 1
10	*Low*	*High*	F_1 *low,* F_2 *high*	*Very likely no class*
11	*Medium*	*Low*	F_1 *medium,* F_2 *low*	*Likely no class*
12	*Medium*	*Medium*	F_2 *and* F_1 *medium*	*Not unlikely* class 1
13	*High*	*Low*	F_1 *high,* F_2 *low*	*Very likely no class*
14	*High*	*Medium*	F_2 *medium,* F_1 *high*	*Very likely* class 1

obtained from entries 1 and 4 in Table 7.25. Both entries have the same F_2 value and hence can be used to generate separate but individually valid rules, although with different certainty measures. The certainty value within parentheses (entry 1) in Table 7.28 indicates belief more in favor of the decision of second choice (*i.e.*, class C_{k_2}) as compared to the first choice (*i.e.*, class C_{k_1}). This is obtained from the connection weight values as given by eqn. (7.39). Here the decision is *ambiguous* and in favor of class 2, as observed from the certainty measure (although class *none* generates the highest response followed by class 2). As F_1 changes to *medium* (in entry 2), the decision becomes *more certain* in favor of class *none*, while for $F_1 = Mol\ high$ (entry 3) the decision is *certainly* in favor of class 1. Note that the value of the certainty measures, and not the output membership values, determines the *ambiguity* in a decision. It is observed from Table 7.33 that the entry 2 is unable to infer any positive decision, *i.e.*, *unable to recognize*. This is due to the extremely low certainty measure in the corresponding entry 2 in Table 7.31.   ♣

As in Chapter 3, the performance (inferencing and rule generation capability) of the fully supervised fuzzy MLP has been observed here to be better than that of the partially supervised fuzzy Kohonen network. For both these models, the rules generated for the vowel data have been found to be more complete and/or accurate compared to those for the three sets of linearly nonseparable patterns. This is due to the *difficult* nature of the class separability in these nonconvex pattern sets.

REFERENCES

1. E. Charniak and D. McDermott, *Introduction to Artificial Intelligence*. Cambridge, MA: Addison-Wesley, 1985.

2. F. Hayes-Roth, D. A. Waterman, and D. B. Lenat, *Building Expert Systems*. London: Addison-Wesley, 1983.

3. D. A. Waterman, *A Guide to Expert Systems*. London: Addison-Wesley, 1985.

4. S. I. Gallant, "Connectionist expert systems," *Communications of the Association for Computing Machinery*, vol. 31, pp. 152–169, 1988.

5. K. Saito and R. Nakano, "Medical diagnostic expert system based on PDP model," in *Proceedings of IEEE International Conference on Neural Networks* (San Diego, USA), pp. I.255–I.262, 1988.

6. I. Taha and J. Ghosh, "Evaluation and ordering of rules extracted from feedforward networks," in *Proceedings of IEEE International Conference on Neural Networks* (Houston, USA), pp. 408–413, 1997.

7. R. Poli, S. Cagnoni, R. Livi, G. Coppini, and G. Valli, "A neural network expert system for diagnosing and treating hypertension," *IEEE Computer*, pp. 64–71, March 1991.

8. C. W. Omlin and C. Lee Giles, "Extraction of rules from discrete-time recurrent neural networks," *Neural Networks*, vol. 9, pp. 41–52, 1996.

9. M. Ishikawa, "Structural learning with forgetting," *Neural Networks*, vol. 9, pp. 509–521, 1996.

10. Y. Hayashi, "Neural expert system using fuzzy teaching input and its application to medical diagnosis," *Information Sciences Applications*, vol. 1, pp. 47–58, 1994.

11. K. Yoshida, Y. Hayashi, A. Imura, and N. Shimada, "Fuzzy neural expert system for diagnosing hepatobiliary disorders," in *Proceedings of the 1990 International Conference on Fuzzy Logic and Neural Networks, Iizuka* (Japan), pp. 539–543, 1990.

12. D. L. Hudson, M. E. Cohen, and M. F. Anderson, "Use of neural network techniques in a medical expert system," *International Journal of Intelligent Systems*, vol. 6, pp. 213–223, 1991.

13. M. Umano, S. Fukunaka, I. Hatono, and H. Tamura, "Acquisition of fuzzy rules using fuzzy neural networks with forgetting," in *Proceedings of IEEE International Conference on Neural Networks* (Houston, USA), pp. 2369–2373, 1997.

14. S. Mitra and S. K. Pal, "Fuzzy multi-layer perceptron, inferencing and rule generation," *IEEE Transactions on Neural Networks*, vol. 6, pp. 51–63, 1995.

15. S. Mitra and S. K. Pal, "Fuzzy self organization, inferencing and rule generation," *IEEE Transactions on Systems, Man and Cybernetics, Part A: Systems and Humans*, vol. 26, pp. 608–620, 1996.

16. J. M. Keller and H. Tahani, "Implementation of conjunctive and disjunctive fuzzy logic rules with neural networks," *International Journal of Approximate Reasoning*, vol. 6, pp. 221–240, 1992.

17. J. M. Keller, R. R. Yager, and H. Tahani, "Neural network implementation of fuzzy logic," *Fuzzy Sets and Systems*, vol. 45, pp. 1–12, 1992.

18. H. Ishibuchi, H. Tanaka, and H. Okada, "Interpolation of fuzzy if-then rules by neural networks," *International Journal of Approximate Reasoning*, vol. 10, pp. 3–27, 1994.

19. H. Ishibuchi, R. Fujioka, and H. Tanaka, "Neural networks that learn from fuzzy If-Then rules," *IEEE Transactions on Fuzzy Systems*, vol. 1, pp. 85–97, 1993.

20. H. Ishibuchi, K. Kwon, and H. Tanaka, "A learning algorithm of fuzzy neural networks with triangular fuzzy weights," *Fuzzy Sets and Systems*, vol. 71, pp. 277–293, 1995.

21. H. Takagi and I. Hayashi, "Artificial neural network driven fuzzy reasoning," *International Journal of Approximate Reasoning*, vol. 5, pp. 191–212, 1991.

22. J. Nie, "Constructing fuzzy model by self-organizing counterpropagation network," *IEEE Transactions on Systems, Man, and Cybernetics*, vol. 25, pp. 963–970, 1995.

23. J. M. Keller, R. Krishnapuram, and F. C. -H. Rhee, "Evidence aggregation networks for fuzzy logic inference," *IEEE Transactions on Neural Networks*, vol. 3, pp. 761–769, 1992.

24. F. C. H. Rhee and R. Krishnapuram, "Fuzzy rule generation methods for high-level computer vision," *Fuzzy Sets and Systems*, vol. 60, pp. 245–258, 1993.

25. J. M. Zurada and A. Lozowski, "Generating linguistic rules from data using neuro-fuzzy framework," in *Proceedings of 4th International Conference on Soft Computing, Iizuka*, (Japan), pp. 618–621, 1996.

26. S. Mitra and S. K. Pal, "Logical operation based fuzzy MLP for classification and rule generation," *Neural Networks*, vol. 7, pp. 353–373, 1994.

27. R. R. Yager, "Modeling and formulating fuzzy knowledge bases using neural networks," *Neural Networks*, vol. 7, pp. 1273–1283, 1994.

28. R. R. Yager, "Implementing fuzzy logic controllers using a neural network framework," *Fuzzy Sets and Systems*, vol. 48, pp. 53–64, 1992.

29. C. Lin and Y. Lu, "A neural fuzzy system with linguistic teaching signals," *IEEE Transactions on Fuzzy Systems*, vol. 3, pp. 169–189, 1995.

30. R. W. Zhou and C. Quek, "POPFNN: A pseudo outer-product based fuzzy neural network," *Neural Networks*, vol. 9, pp. 1569–1581, 1996.

31. S. G. Romaniuk and L. O. Hall, "Decision making on creditworthiness, using a fuzzy connectionist model," *Fuzzy Sets and Systems*, vol. 48, pp. 15–22, 1992.

32. E. Sanchez, "Fuzzy connectionist expert systems," in *Proceedings of the 1990 International Conference on Fuzzy Logic and Neural Networks, Iizuka* (Japan), pp. 31–35, 1990.

33. E. Sanchez and R. Bartolin, "Fuzzy inference and medical diagnosis, a case study," *Biomedical Fuzzy Systems Bulletin*, vol. 1, pp. 4–21, 1990.

34. S. Mitra and S. K. Pal, "Rule generation and inferencing with a layered fuzzy neural network," in *Proceedings of 2nd International Conference on Fuzzy Logic and Neural Networks, Iizuka*, (Japan), pp. 641–644, July 1992.

35. S. Mitra and S. K. Pal, "Fusion of fuzzy sets and layered neural networks at the input, output and neuronal levels," *Indian Journal of Pure and Applied Mathematics*, vol. 24, pp. 121–133, 1994.

36. S. Mitra and S. K. Pal, "Neuro-fuzzy expert systems: Overview with a case study," in *Fuzzy Reasoning in Information, Decision and Control Systems*, S. G. Tzafestas and A. N. Venetsanopoulos, eds., pp. 121–143. Boston/Dordrecht: Kluwer Academic Publishers, 1994.

37. R. P. Lippmann, "An introduction to computing with neural nets," *IEEE Acoustics, Speech and Signal Processing Magazine*, vol. 4, pp. 4–22, 1987.

38. K. Kwon, H. Ishibuchi, and H. Tanaka, "Neural networks with interval weights for nonlinear mapping of interval vectors," *IEICE Transactions on Information and Systems*, vol. E77-D, pp. 409–417, 1994.

39. T. Kohonen, *Self-Organization and Associative Memory*. Berlin: Springer-Verlag, 1989.

40. A. Di Nola, S. Sessa, W. Pedrycz, and E. Sanchez, *Fuzzy Relation Equations and their Applications to Knowledge Engineering*. Dordrecht: Kluwer Academic Publishers, 1989.

41. S. K. Pal and S. Mitra, "Multi-layer perceptron, fuzzy sets and classification," *IEEE Transactions on Neural Networks*, vol. 3, pp. 683–697, 1992.

42. S. K. Pal and D. Dutta Majumder, *Fuzzy Mathematical Approach to Pattern Recognition*. New York: Wiley (Halsted Press), 1986.

43. S. K. Pal and D. P. Mandal, "Linguistic recognition system based on approximate reasoning," *Information Sciences*, vol. 61, pp. 135–161, 1992.

44. Y. Hayashi, personal communication on medical data, 1993.

45. D. K. Biswas, "Study of Kala-azar with special reference to renal function," Master's thesis, School of Tropical Medicine, University of Calcutta, Calcutta, India, 1989.

46. S. Mitra, S. N. Sarbadhikari, and S. K. Pal, "An MLP-based model for identifying qEEG in depression," *International Journal of Biomedical Computing*, vol. 43, pp. 179–187, 1996.

47. S. N. Sarbadhikari, "A neural network confirms that physical exercise reverses EEG changes in depressed rats," *Medical Engineering and Physics*, vol. 17, pp. 579–582, 1995.

48. S. N. Sarbadhikari, S. Dey, and A. K. Ray, "Chronic exercise alters EEG power spectra in an animal model of depression," *Indian Journal of Physiology and Pharmacology*, vol. 40, pp. 47–57, 1996.

49. S. Mitra and S. K. Pal, "Self-organizing neural network as a fuzzy classifier," *IEEE Transactions on Systems, Man and Cybernetics*, vol. 24, no. 3, pp. 385–399, 1994.

$$8$$

Using Knowledge-Based Networks and Fuzzy Sets

8.1 INTRODUCTION

In Chapters 3 and 7 we have described classification and rule generation with reference to various fuzzy neural networks, where fuzziness was incorporated at various stages of ANNs. In this chapter we embark on knowledge-based networks, described in Section 2.6, for performing these tasks. Generally ANNs consider a fixed topology of neurons connected by links in a predefined manner. These connection weights are usually initialized by small random values. Knowledge-based networks [1, 2] constitute a special class of ANNs that consider crude domain knowledge to generate the initial network architecture, which is later refined in the presence of training data. This process helps in reducing the searching space and time while the network traces the optimal solution.

Preexisting symbolic rules, used for initializing a neural network architecture, can not only improve the network learning efficiency but also serve to provide knowledge that is not captured by training cases or that cannot be easily learned. This improves the predictive performance of the system. During learning an MLP searches for the set of weights that corresponds to some local minima. There may be a large number of such minima corresponding to various *good* solutions. The knowledge-based network initially considers these weights so as to be near one such *good* solution. As a result, the searching space is reduced and learning becomes faster.

If the initial knowledge is *complete* then one can simply map it into the neural network. But if this knowledge is *incomplete* or partially correct, ad-

309

ditional hidden units and connections need to be added and the network is to be trained with the data set. This leads to knowledge enhancement or refinement. The number of additional hidden units is usually determined empirically. Growing and pruning of nodes and/or links are done in order to generate the optimal network architecture. Incorporation of the concept of neuro-fuzzy integration at this level can also help in designing more efficient (intelligent) knowledge-based networks.

First we describe, in a review on the existing literature on knowledge-based networks, the nonfuzzy models by Yin and Liang [3], Fu [1], Towell and Shavlik [2, 4], Opitz and Shavlik [5], and Lacher *et al.* [6]. Next we explain the fuzzy knowledge-based models by Masuoka *et al.* [7], Kasabov [8]–[10], Kosko [11], and Mitra *et al.* [12] (under category 1 of neuro-fuzzy integration, Section 2.5.1); and the models by Machado and Rocha [13, 14], Pedrycz and Rocha [15], Hirota and Pedrycz [16], and Tan [17] (under category 3, Section 2.5.1). Finally, the incorporation of genetic algorithms is discussed with reference to the model of Opitz and Shavlik [18].

These are followed by a detailed formulation of the classification and rule generation strategies for a knowledge-based network [12] developed using the fuzzy MLP of Section 3.3. The model is capable of generating both *positive* (indicating the belongingness of a pattern to a class) and *negative* (indicating *not* belongingness of a pattern to a class) rules in linguistic form to justify any decision reached. This is found to be useful for inferencing in ambiguous cases. (Note that the novel concept of negative rules, which was introduced in Ref. [12], has not been considered in the previous chapter). The knowledge encoding procedure, unlike most other methods [1, 2], involves a nonbinary weighting mechanism. The *a priori* class information and the distribution of pattern points in the feature space are taken into account while encoding the crude domain knowledge from the data set among the connection weights. An estimation of the links connecting the output and hidden layers (in terms of the preceding layer link weights and node activations) is provided.

Finally, we describe the performance of the previously mentioned knowledge-based fuzzy MLP for synthetic and real life speech and medical data. Its comparison with the conventional and fuzzy versions of the MLP and fuzzy min–max neural network [19] is also provided. It is found that the classification performance improves appreciably with the encoding of the initial knowledge in the network architecture. The knowledge-based network converges much earlier, and hence more meaningful rules are generated at this stage as compared to the other models.

8.2 VARIOUS MODELS

Here we first describe the conventional knowledge-based networks. These are followed by those involving fuzziness in various stages and using genetic algorithms. Among these models, a few are given more emphasis for the convenience of the readers.

8.2.1 Knowledge-based networks

Let us consider here the models developed by Gallant [20], Fu [1], Shavlik *et al.* [2, 4, 5], Yin and Liang [3], and Lacher *et al.* [6]. The networks, other than that in Ref. [6], involve *crisp* inputs and outputs. The initial domain knowledge, in the form of rules, is mapped into the multilayer feedforward network topology, using binary link weights to maintain the semantics. Note that the rule generation aspect of Gallant's model [20] has already been described in Section 7.2.1 (Chapter 7), as this is one of the seminal works in this direction. The other models are now described.

Yin and Liang [3] have employed a *gradually augmented-node* learning algorithm to incrementally build a dynamic knowledge base capable of both acquiring new knowledge and relearning existing information. The rules are explicitly represented among the *condition nodes, rule nodes*, and *action nodes*, and the algorithm gradually builds the multilayer feedforward network. This connectionist incremental model is used as an *animal identification system* whose network structure is changed dynamically according to the new environment or through human intervention. In Fu's model [1] hidden units and additional connections are introduced appropriately when the network performance stagnates during training using backpropagation. Weight decay, pruning of weights, and clustering of hidden units are incorporated to improve the generalization of the network.

Towell and Shavlik [2] have designed a hybrid learning system for problems of molecular biology. Disjunctive rules are rewritten as multiple conjunctive rules while building the network structure. Nodes and links are incorporated, on instructions from the user, to augment the knowledge-based module. An expansion of the network guided by both the domain theory and training data has been reported by Opitz and Shavlik [5]. Dynamic additions of hidden nodes are made by heuristically searching through the space of possible network topologies, in a manner analogous to the adding of rules and conjuncts to the symbolic rulebase.

A way of using the knowledge of the trained neural model to extract the revised rules for the problem domain is described by Fu [1] and Towell and Shavlik [4]. Let us describe the salient features of the algorithms.

1. Insertion of knowledge through translation of rules into network. Let the rules $R_i, i = 1, \ldots, 4$, be
   $R1 : A = BC$, $R2 : B = H'$, $R3 : B = F'G$, $R4 : C = IJ$.
   For insertion into a neural net, these rules should be rewritten in the disjunctive normal form. This yields
   $A = BC$, $B = H' + F'G$, $C = IJ$.

The other links represent low-weighted connections, allowing subsequent additional refinement.

2. Training through error backpropagation.

3. Rule extraction after network training and refinement. It is assumed that

    a. The neurons have binary inputs and hard-limiting activation functions.

    b. The method of rule extraction searches for constraints on the inputs of a given neuron such that the weights $> \theta$ (bias).

An exhaustive search for firing conditions follows. Each firing corresponds to a rule under a certain combination of inputs. All combinations are checked, such that the rule search becomes a combinatorial task.

The subset algorithm [1] can be used by the network to improve the search complexity for the combination of firing conditions in step 3. The steps are as follows.

- Step 1: (a) search for any single weight exceeding the bias; (b) rewrite all conditions found in 1.(a) as rules with single input variable.

- Step 2: (a) increase the size of the set to two, and search for any combination of two weights exceeding the bias; (b) rewrite conditions found as rules with two input variables.

The search as in steps 1a–2b continues for increased size of sets until all sets have been explored and possibly rewritten as rules. However, the subset algorithm produces many rules and requires lengthy, exhaustive searches. This method has been further modified in Towell and Shavlik [4] by the M of N algorithm for extracting meaningful rules.

A general rule in this case is of the form: IF (M of the following antecedents are true), THEN ....

The steps of this algorithm are as follows.

1. *Clustering.* Weights of each neuron are clustered into groups of similar values (*i.e.*, within distance 0.25).

2. *Averaging.* Weights of each neuron are set into the average value of each cluster. Equivalence classes are created.

3. *Eliminating.* Low value weights (or their clusters) are eliminated if they have no effect on the sign of the total activation. Methods available are

    - Algorithmic, performing searches through weight sets only (steps 1 and 2 reduce combinatorics of the problem).

- Heuristic, with all actual inputs used for training. Clusters of weights are eliminated as a result of this step and the network becomes pruned.

4. *Optimizing.* Usually performed by freezing the remaining weights and retraining the biases using the backpropagation algorithm. The steepness of the activation function is increased to resemble the binary output neuron.

5. *Extracting.* Rules are formulated that describe the network in an M of N form. Arithmetic is performed such that one searches for all weighted antecedents, which when summed up exceed the threshold value of a given neuron.

6. *Simplifying.* Weights and thresholds are eliminated and M of N rules replace results of arithmetic search in step 5.

Note that the algorithm considers groups of links as equivalence classes, thereby generating a bound on the number of rules rather than establishing a ceiling on the number of antecedents. This approach differs from that of Saito and Nakano [21] (described in Section 7.2.1), where a breadth-first search is employed to exhaustively find those input settings that cause the weighted sum to exceed the bias at a node.

Lacher *et al.* [6] have designed event-driven, acyclic networks of neural objects called *expert networks*. There are regular nodes and operation nodes (for conjunction and negation). Input weights are hard-wired, while the output weights of a node are adaptive. Antecedents of a disjunction in a rule are simplified to generate a set of individual rules before formulating the initial network architecture. Virtual rules are used to create potential connections for learning, in order to overcome situations involving small initial set of rules. The backpropagation algorithm is modified to work in the event-driven environment, where both forward and backward signals propagate in *data-flow* fashion. The form of the rules (coarse knowledge) is tuned with the associated certainty factors (fine knowledge), and the resultant network trained for better performance.

8.2.2 Incorporating fuzziness

A brief survey on the knowledge-based networks involving fuzziness at different stages is provided here, based on several studies [7]–[17]. The first five approaches fall under category 1 of the fusion methodologies described in Section 2.5.1, while the rest can be grouped in category 3.

Knowledge extracted from experts in the form of membership functions and fuzzy rules (in AND–OR form) is used to build and preweight the neural net structure, which is then tuned using training data. The model by Masuoka *et al.* [7] consists of the input variable membership net, the rule net, and the output variable net. Kasabov [8] uses three neural subnets–production memory, working memory, and variable binding space–to encode the production rules, which can later be updated. Fuzzy signed digraph with feedback, termed *fuzzy cognitive map*, has been used by Kosko [11] to represent knowledge. Additive combination of augmented connection matrices are employed to include the views of a number of experts for generating the knowledge network.

Machado and Rocha [13] have used a connectionist knowledge base involving fuzzy numbers at the input layer, fuzzy AND at the hidden layers, and fuzzy OR at the output layer. The hidden layers chunk input evidences into clusters of information for representing regular patterns of the environment. The output layer computes the degree of possibility of each hypothesis. The initial network architecture is generated using *knowledge graphs* elicited from experts by the application of the knowledge acquisition technique [22]. The experts express their knowledge about each hypothesis of the problem domain, by selecting an appropriate set of evidences and building an acyclic weighted AND–OR graph (knowledge graph) to describe how these must be combined to support decision making.

Pedrycz and Rocha [15] have used basic aggregation neurons (AND/OR) and referential processing units (matching, dominance, and inclusion neurons) to design knowledge-based networks. The inhibitory and excitatory characteristics are captured by embodying direct and complemented input signals, and fully supervised learning is employed. Another related approach, by Hirota and Pedrycz [16], has incorporated the use of fuzzy clustering for developing the geometric constructs leading to the design of knowledge-based networks.

Tan [17] has used a generalization of fuzzy ARTMAP [23], called *cascade ARTMAP*. It represents intermediate attributes and rule cascades of rule-based knowledge explicitly, and performs multistep inferencing. A major problem of using MLP to refine rule-based knowledge [1, 4] is the preservation of symbolic knowledge under the weight tuning mechanism of the backpropagation algorithm. Another limitation is that unless the initial rulebase is roughly complete, the initial network architecture may not be sufficiently rich for handling the problem domain. A rule insertion algorithm translates IF–THEN symbolic rules into cascade ARTMAP architecture. This knowledge can be refined and enhanced by the learning algorithm. During learning, new recognition categories (rules) can be created dynamically to cover the deficiency of the domain theory. This is in contrast to the static architecture of the standard slow learning backpropagation networks. Learning in cascade ARTMAP does not wash away existing knowledge and the meanings of units do not shift.

Most of these models are mainly concerned with the encoding of initial knowledge by a fuzzy neural network followed by refinement during training. Extraction of fuzzy rules in this framework has been attempted [7, 8, 13, 17]. Connection weights above a preset threshold determine the *condition* or *action* elements in the extracted rules, along with the corresponding *degrees of importance* and *confidence factors* [9, 10]. Inference, inquiry, and explanation are possible during consultation in Ref. [13]. As the cascade ARTMAP [17] preserves symbolic rule form, the extracted rules can be directly compared with the originally inserted rules. These rules are claimed [17] to be simpler and more accurate than the M of N rules [4]. Besides, each extracted rule is associated with a confidence factor that indicates its importance or usefulness. This allows ranking and evaluation of the extracted knowledge.

Machado and Rocha [14] have also used an interval-based representation for membership grades (MGI) to allow reasoning with different types of uncertainty: vagueness, ignorance, and relevance. The model reported in their 1992 study [13] is used as the building block for developing the facilities of incremental learning, inference, inquiry, censorship of input information, and explanation, as in expert systems. The utility-based inquiry process permits significant reduction of consultation cost or risk and gives the system the common sense property possessed by experts when selecting tests to be performed. The ability to criticize input data when they disrupt a trend of acceptance or rejection observed for a hypothesis mimics the behavior of experts, who are often able to detect suspicious input data and either reject them or ask for their confirmation. Let us now describe these capabilities in some detail.

The neuronal activation is represented as an interval [*current activation* (CA), *potential activation* (PA)], $CA \leq PA$ and both lying in $[0,1]$, such that *ignorance degree* $(IG) = PA - CA$. The consultation process assumes that input data are provided gradually to the system, as and when queried according to its importance. During the *passive* phase the user enters a set of triggering data to form a *consultation focus* involving hypotheses yielding CA larger than a predefined *triggering threshold*. During the *active* phase the system tries to prove or refute the hypotheses belonging to the focus by actively querying the user. Only classes with a possibility degree larger than a predefined *acceptance threshold* (T_{acc}) are presented to the user as the problem solution. The focus may be revised periodically to account for new data. Available input MGIs are propagated in the network through the *current evidential flow* (CEF_{ij}) and *potential evidential flow* (PEF_{ij}) along excitatory connection w_{ij} as

$$CEF_{ij} = CA_i.w_{ij} \ \ \text{and} \ \ PEF_{ij} = PA_i.w_{ij}$$

and along inhibitory connection as

$$CEF_{ij} = (1 - PA_i)\, w_{ij} \ \ \text{and} \ \ PEF_{ij} = (1 - CA_i)\, w_{ij}.$$

In excitatory synapses, the rise of the input signal provides higher support to increase the activation of their postsynaptic neurons, contrasting with inhibitory synapses where the inverse situation prevails. The fuzzy AND and OR neurons aggregate the incoming evidential flows as

$$CA_Y = \min_{i \in R_Y}(CEF_i), \ \ PA_Y = \min_{i \in R_Y}(PEF_i) \tag{8.1}$$

and

$$CA_Y = \max_{i \in R_Y}(CEF_i), \ \ PA_Y = \max_{i \in R_Y}(PEF_i) \tag{8.2}$$

respectively, where R_Y refers to the fan-in of neuron Y.

Maximal activation (MA) is the PA at the beginning of the consultation, and is usually one throughout. At time t, CA represents the support (positive evidence) for hypothesis H, while $MA - PA$ is the available concept refutation (negative evidence). Only those hypotheses yielding $CA \geq T_{acc}$ are accepted by the system as a problem solution; hypotheses yielding $PA < T_{acc}$ are rejected by the system. Hypotheses showing $CA < T_{acc}$ and $PA \geq T_{acc}$ are considered undecided, *i.e.*, requiring additional information before a decision can be made.

The inquiry process has as its goal, the determination of the *best* node from which to select the next user query. This is done corresponding to the *undecided* hypothesis of the focus with the largest ignorance degree at that moment. Then one backtracks by

1. Selecting the set of synapses R reaching hypothesis H, where
   $R = \{i|PEF_i = PA_H\}$ if H is a fuzzy OR node, or
   $R = \{i|CEF_i = CA_H\}$ if H is a fuzzy AND node.

2. Selecting the synapse of R with the largest $(PEF_i - CEF_i)$.

This process is repeated until an input node is reached. This is used for querying the user. The system reduces the number of feature evaluations during a consultation by *inquiry pruning*. This is due to the use of the fuzzy *Or* nodes, which select the largest incoming evidential flow for activation. The property of *early decision* allows termination of the consultation as soon as a decision can be reached.

The system is made sensitive to the costs and/or risks associated with measurement procedures by using a *utility flow* (UF) in the synapses. Then

$$UF_{ij} = NU_i \ . \ s(PA_i - CA_i), \tag{8.3}$$

where $s(u) = 1$ if $u > 0$ and $s(u) = 0$ if $u \leq 0$. Fuzzy AND neurons aggregate cost utilities according to

$$NU_j = \sum_{i \in R_{AND}} UF_{ij},$$

where $R_{AND} = \{i|CEF_{ij} < PA_j\}$. Analogously, for fuzzy OR neurons one has

$$NU_j = \min_{i \in R_{OR}} \{UF_{ij}\},$$

where $R_{OR} = \{i|(PEF_{ij} > T_{acc}) \ and \ (PEF_{ij} > CA_j) \ and \ (PEF_{ij} - CEF_{ij} > 0)\}$. If a new evidence disrupts a firmly established trend for some hypothesis, the system may infer that these new data are possibly faulty and ask either for their confirmation or for a new measurement. It may even select an alternative sensor to replace the one providing suspect evidence.

The explanation algorithm provides responses to queries such as *how* a particular conclusion was reached or *why* a particular question was formulated.

The network forms a set of pathways that compete to send the largest evidential flow to the output neuron representing the hypothesis. The structure of the winning pathway represents a chain of fuzzy pseudoproduction rules, that can be presented to the user either in a graphical format or as English text.

Application of this algorithm has been made to the deforestation monitoring of the Amazon region, using Landsat-V satellite images. The classes considered are forest, savanna, water, deforested area, cloud, and shadow. Eighty two numerical features of spectral, textural, and geometric nature were measured on each image segment (of spectrally homogeneous regions, generated by region growing). Fuzzy classification allows the modeling of complex situations such as transition phenomena (as in the regeneration of forest in a previously burned area) or multiple classification (as in the case of forest overcast by clouds).   ♣

A model by Mitra *et al.* [12], falling under category 1 of the neuro-fuzzy integration scheme (Section 2.5.1), has been developed for classification, inferencing, querying, and rule generation. This is described in detail, with experimental results, in Sections 8.3–8.5.

8.2.3 Incorporating genetic algorithms

As mentioned in Chapter 2 (Section 2.7.2) and Appendix A, genetic algorithms [24, 25] have found various applications in fields like pattern recognition, image processing and neural networks [26]. In the area of ANNs, they have been used in determining the optimal set of connection weights as well as the optimal topology of layered neural networks.

Opitz and Shavlik [18] have used the domain theory of Towell and Shavlik [2, 4], as described in Section 8.2.1, to generate the knowledge-based network structure. Random perturbation is applied to create an initial set of candidate networks or *population*. A node is perturbed by either deleting it or by adding new nodes to it. Next, these networks are trained using backpropagation and placed back into the population. New networks are created by using crossover and mutation operators, specifically designed to function on these networks. The algorithm tries to minimize the destruction of the rule structure of the crossed-over networks, by keeping intact nodes belonging to the same syntactic rule (*i.e.*, the nodes connected by heavilylinked weights). The mutation operator adds diversity to a population, while still maintaining a directed heuristic search technique for choosing where to add nodes. In this manner, the algorithm searches the topology space in order to find suitable networks, which are then trained using backpropagation.

Other methods of incorporating GAs to determine network parameters are described in Refs. [27] and [28], among others. Pal and Bhandari [27] have incorporated a new concept of nonlinear selection for creating mating pools and a weighted error as a fitness function. A fixed topology MLP is used to determine the optimal solution for selecting a decision boundary for pattern recognition problem. Maniezzo [28] has used variable-length chromosomes, incorporating the concept of presence and absence bits, for encoding various topologies of an MLP. A new concept of GA-simplex is also introduced.

8.3   CLASSIFICATION WITH KNOWLEDGE-BASED FUZZY MLP

In this section, we provide in detail the development of a knowledge-based fuzzy MLP for classification and rule generation. First we describe a methodology [12] for encoding *a priori* initial knowledge in the fuzzy MLP, along with an example. The network topology is then refined using the training data. Scope for growing hidden nodes and pruning links, when necessary (as determined by the network performance), enables the generation of a near optimal network architecture with improved classification performance.

8.3.1   Knowledge encoding

Let an interval $[F_{j_1}, F_{j_2}]$ denote the range of feature F_j covered by class C_k. The membership value of the interval is denoted as $\mu([F_{j_1}, F_{j_2}])$ ($= \mu(between\ F_{j_1}\ and\ F_{j_2})$) and computed, using eqn. (7.11), as

$$\mu(between\ F_{j_1}\ and\ F_{j_2}) = \{\mu(greater\ than\ F_{j_1}) * \mu(less\ than\ F_{j_2})\}^{1/2}, \quad (8.4)$$

where

$$\mu(greater\ than\ F_{j_1}) \quad = \quad \{\mu(F_{j_1})\}^{1/2} \quad \text{if } F_{j_1} \leq c_{prop}$$
$$= \quad \{\mu(F_{j_1})\}^{2} \quad \text{otherwise,} \qquad (8.5)$$

and

$$\mu(less\ than\ F_{j_2}) \quad = \quad \{\mu(F_{j_2})\}^{1/2} \quad \text{if } F_{j_2} \geq c_{prop}$$
$$= \quad \{\mu(F_{j_2})\}^{2} \quad \text{otherwise.} \qquad (8.6)$$

As mentioned in Chapter 3, c_{prop} denotes c_{low}, c_{medium}, and c_{high} for each of the three overlapping fuzzy sets *low*, *medium*, and *high* of eqn. (3.30) corresponding to feature F_j. The output membership for the corresponding class C_k is found using eqns. (3.32) and (3.33), where F_{ij} of eqn. (3.32) is replaced by the mean of the interval $[F_{j_1}, F_{j_2}]$ for the jth feature.

The complement of the interval $[F_{j_1}, F_{j_2}]$ of the feature F_j is the region where the class C_k does not lie. This is defined as $[F_{j_1}, F_{j_2}]^c$. The linguistic membership values for $[F_{j_1}, F_{j_2}]^c$ is denoted by $\mu([F_{j_1}, F_{j_2}]^c)$ ($= \mu(not\ between\ F_{j_1}\ and\ F_{j_2})$) and is calculated as [12]

$$\mu(not\ between\ F_{j_1}\ and\ F_{j_2}) = \max\{\mu(less\ than\ F_{j_1}), \mu(greater\ than\ F_{j_2})\}, \quad (8.7)$$

since *not between F_{j_1} and F_{j_2}* $\equiv$ *less than F_{j_1} OR greater than F_{j_2}*.

Let the linguistic membership values for class C_k in interval $[F_{j_1}, F_{j_2}]$, computed by eqns. (8.4)–(8.6), be $\{\mu_L([F_{j_1}, F_{j_2}]), \mu_M([F_{j_1}, F_{j_2}]), \mu_H([F_{j_1}, F_{j_2}])\}$.

Here L, M, H refer to the three overlapping linguistic partitions *low, medium,* and *high* (Fig. 3.2). Similarly for the complement of the interval, using eqn. (8.7), one has
$$\{\mu_L([F_{j_1}, F_{j_2}]^c), \mu_M([F_{j_1}, F_{j_2}]^c), \mu_H([F_{j_1}, F_{j_2}]^c)\}.$$

A fuzzy MLP with only one hidden layer is considered, taking two hidden nodes corresponding to $[F_{j_1}, F_{j_2}]$ and its complement respectively for each of the j input features. In each case, links are introduced between the input nodes $A \in \{L, M, H\}$ and the corresponding nodes in the hidden layer

$$\text{Iff} \quad \mu_A([F_{j_1}, F_{j_2}]) \ or \ \mu_A([F_{j_1}, F_{j_2}]^c) \geq 0.5.$$

The weight $w^0_{k_{\alpha_p} j_m}$ between the k_{α_p} node of the hidden layer (the hidden node corresponding to the interval $[F_{j_1}, F_{j_2}]$ for class C_k) and j_m ($m \in \{first(L),$ $second(M), third(H)\}$)th node of the input layer corresponding to feature F_j is set by

$$w^0_{k_{\alpha_p} j_m} = p_k + \varepsilon, \tag{8.8}$$

where p_k is the *a priori* probability of class C_k and ε is a small random number. This hidden node is designated a *positive* node. A second hidden node k_{α_n} is considered for the complement case and is termed a *negative* node. Its connection weights are initialized as

$$w^0_{k_{\alpha_n} j_m} = (1 - p_k) + \varepsilon. \tag{8.9}$$

Note that the small random number ε is considered to destroy any symmetry among the weights. Thus for an l-class problem domain there are $2l$ nodes in the first hidden layer. The algorithm considers the following two cases:

- *All* connections between these $2l$ hidden nodes and all nodes in the input layer are possible. The other weights are initially set as small random numbers.

- Only those *selected* connection weights initialized by eqns. (8.4)–(8.9) are allowed.

It is to be mentioned that the method described above can suitably handle convex pattern classes only. In the case of concave classes one considers multiple intervals for a feature F_j corresponding to the various convex partitions that may be generated to approximate the given concave decision region. This also holds for the complement of the region in F_j in which a particular class C_k is not included. In such cases *positive* and *negative* hidden nodes are introduced for each of the intervals, where connections are established by eqns. (8.8) and (8.9) for the cases of a class belonging and not belonging to a region, respectively. Note that a concave class may also be subdivided into several convex regions [29].

Let there be $(k_{pos} + k_{neg})$ hidden nodes, where $k_{pos} = \sum_{\alpha_p} k_{\alpha_p}$ and $k_{neg} = \sum_{\alpha_n} k_{\alpha_n}$, generated for class C_k such that $k_{pos} \geq 1$ and $k_{neg} \geq 1$ [12]. Now connections are established between kth output node (for class C_k) and only the corresponding $(k_{pos} + k_{neg})$ hidden nodes. It is assumed that if any feature value (for class C_k) is outside some interval α, the total input received by the corresponding hidden node k_α is zero and this thereby produces an output $y^1_{k_\alpha} = 0.5$ because of the sigmoidal nonlinearity of eqn. (2.38).

The connection weight $w^1_{k k_\alpha}$ between the kth output node and the (k_α)th hidden node is calculated from a series of equations generated as below. For an interval α as input for class C_k, the expression for output y^2_k of the kth output node is given by

$$ y^2_k = f \left(y^1_{k_\alpha} w^1_{k k_\alpha} + \sum_{r \neq \alpha} 0.5 w^1_{k k_r} \right), \qquad (8.10) $$

where $f(.)$ is the sigmoidal function as in eqn. (2.38) and the hidden nodes k_r correspond to the intervals not represented by the convex partition α. Thus for a particular class C_k one has as many equations as the number of intervals (including *not*) used for approximating any concave and/or convex decision region C_k. Thereby, each of the connection weights $w^1_{k k_\alpha}$ $\forall \alpha$ (corresponding to each hidden node k_α and class C_k pair) can be uniquely computed.

The network architecture, so encoded, is then refined by training it on the pattern set supplied as input. In case of "all connections" between input and hidden layers, all the link weights are trained. In case of "selected connections" only the selected link weights are trained, while the other connections are kept clamped at zero. If the network achieves satisfactory performance, the classifier design is complete. Otherwise, the system resorts to node growing or pruning.

8.3.2 Example

Consider the network depicted in Fig. 8.1 [12]. Let the output node k, corresponding to a class C_k, be connected to two hidden nodes k_{α_p} and k_{α_n} via connection weights $w^1_{k k_{\alpha_p}}$ and $w^1_{k k_{\alpha_n}}$. Let class C_k lie in the interval $[F_{j_1}, F_{j_2}]$ of input feature F_j. Then the weights between the input and the hidden layer are initially set from eqns. (8.8)–(8.9) as

$$ w^0_{k_{\alpha_p} j_L} = p_k + \varepsilon_1 , $$

$$ w^0_{k_{\alpha_p} j_H} = p_k + \varepsilon_2 $$

and

$$ w^0_{k_{\alpha_n} j_M} = (1 - p_k) + \varepsilon_3 . $$

In the case of the network with *all connections*, the other weights between the input and the hidden layers (e.g., $w^0_{k_{\alpha_p} j_M}$, $w^0_{k_{\alpha_n} j_L}$, $w^0_{k_{\alpha_n} j_H}$) are initialized by small random values. On the other hand, in the case of the network with *selected connections*, these are not considered at all.

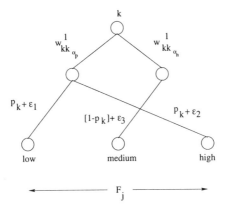

Fig. 8.1 Example demonstrating knowledge encoding

Substituting eqn. (8.10) in eqn. (2.38), one obtains [12]

$$y_k^2 = \frac{1}{1 + \exp\left\{-\left(y_{k_{\alpha_p}}^1 w_{kk_{\alpha_p}}^1 + 0.5 w_{kk_{\alpha_n}}^1\right)\right\}}, \tag{8.11}$$

where y_k^2 is the output of the kth output node and $y_{k_{\alpha_p}}^1$ that of the hidden node, corresponding to the presented interval, connected to the kth output node. This yields

$$y_{k_{\alpha_p}}^1 w_{kk_{\alpha_p}}^1 + 0.5 w_{kk_{\alpha_n}}^1 = \ln \frac{y_k^2}{1 - y_k^2}. \tag{8.12}$$

Similarly, considering the complement interval $[F_{j_1}, F_{j_2}]^c$ of the feature F_j, one can write

$$1 - y_k^2 = \frac{1}{1 + \exp\left\{-\left(0.5 w_{kk_{\alpha_p}}^1 + y_{k_{\alpha_n}}^1 w_{kk_{\alpha_n}}^1\right)\right\}}. \tag{8.13}$$

Solving, one obtains

$$0.5 w_{kk_{\alpha_p}}^1 + y_{k_{\alpha_n}}^1 w_{kk_{\alpha_n}}^1 = \ln \frac{1 - y_k^2}{y_k^2}. \tag{8.14}$$

The outputs $y_{k_{\alpha_p}}^1$ and $y_{k_{\alpha_n}}^1$ are calculated using eqns. (2.37)–(2.38) with appropriate input values. Then from eqns. (8.12) and (8.14) one can evaluate $w_{kk_{\alpha_p}}^1$ and $w_{kk_{\alpha_n}}^1$.

8.3.3 Pruning and growing

The method we are describing here has incorporated link pruning and node growing. A connection weight is pruned if its contribution toward the network output is least significant during the presentation of the training set.

Therefore, the link w_{ji}^h in layer h is pruned if

$$\sum_{trainset} w_{ji}^h y_i^h = \min_{k,m} \left\{ \sum_{trainset} w_{km}^h y_m^h \right\}, \qquad (8.15)$$

where the summation is taken over all the patterns in the training set and the *minimum* is computed over the indices k, m.

When a network with large number of connection weights results in poor classification performance after a certain number of epochs, links between layers $h + 1$ and h, for each h, need to be selected for pruning by eqn. (8.15). The resulting network is retrained for a few more epochs, and this process continues until one obtains a satisfactory recognition score.

Since the number of hidden nodes is initially encoded using domain knowledge, there exists no redundancy in this aspect. Therefore, node pruning is not attempted here. During refinement by training, the growth of some extra links leads to redundancy. These are the ones that may be pruned in order to improve the generalization capability of the network.

Learning methods have also been developed to incrementally change the network structure, once learning fails in a small network. If after a certain number of epochs (experimentally determined) the classifier still does not recognize a certain class C_k well and the network size is not too large, the system resorts to adding a hidden node. Connection weights are established between this new node and all the classes. Links are also introduced from all input nodes to this newly added node. Now training is allowed on these new connection weights for a few epochs (again empirically set) using only those samples that are in class C_k, while keeping all the other links frozen. Then all the links are retrained with the entire training set and the process of adding, freezing, and retraining continues, until all the classes are reasonably well recognized.

8.4 RULE GENERATION WITH KNOWLEDGE-BASED FUZZY MLP

The trained knowledge-based network is used for rule generation in IF-THEN form. These rules describe the extent to which a test pattern belongs or does not belong to one of the classes in terms of antecedent and consequent clauses provided in natural form. Two rule-generation strategies, as developed by Mitra *et al.* [12], are described below. (Note that these algorithms are different from that described in Section 7.3.)

- Treating the network as a blackbox and using the training set input (in numeric and/or linguistic forms) and network output (with confidence factor) to generate the antecedent and consequent parts.

- Backtracking along maximal weighted paths using the trained net and utilizing its input and output activations (with confidence factor) for obtaining the antecedent and consequent clauses.

8.4.1 Numeric and/or linguistic inputs: method 1

In this method an exhaustive set of numeric and/or linguistic inputs are used along with their hedges at the input for antecedent clauses (IF parts). For example, consider a data set with two features F_1 and F_2. The linguistic pattern corresponding to F_1 *low* and F_2 *high* is computed [using eqns. (3.28)–(3.29)] as the six-dimensional vector

$[0.95, \quad \pi(F_1(\text{low}); c_{\text{medium}}, \lambda_{\text{medium}}), \quad \pi(F_1(\text{low}); c_{\text{high}}, \lambda_{\text{high}}),$
$\pi(F_2(\text{high}); c_{\text{low}}, \lambda_{\text{low}}), \quad \pi(F_2(\text{high}); c_{\text{medium}}, \lambda_{\text{medium}}), \quad 0.95],$

where $\pi(F_1(\text{low}); c_{\text{low}}, \lambda_{\text{low}}) = 0.95$ and $\pi(F_2(\text{high}); c_{\text{high}}, \lambda_{\text{high}}) = 0.95$. Here $F_1(\text{low})$ and $F_2(\text{high})$ refer to the feature values for F_1 and F_2 at which $\mu_{\text{low}(F_1)} = 0.95$ and $\mu_{\text{high}(F_2)} = 0.95$, respectively. All the linguistic patterns corresponding to the different hedges [as defined by eqns. (7.5)–(7.7)] are also generated. Thus one obtains an additional 9^n such patterns (corresponding to *very*, *more or less*, and *not* for each of linguistic values *low*, *medium*, and *high* of each feature) for a data set with n features. The linguistic pattern (with or without the hedges) closest to the pth pattern, in terms of distance, determines the antecedent part of the rule.

A *confidence factor (CF)* is defined [30] as

$$CF = \frac{1}{2}[\{y_{\text{max}}^2\}^{f_{\text{max}}} + \frac{1}{l-1}\sum_{j=1}^{l}\{y_{\text{max}}^2 - y_j^2\}], \quad 0 \le CF \le 1, \quad (8.16)$$

where $y_{\text{max}}^2 = \max_{j=1}^{l}\{y_j^2\}$, y_j^2 is the jth component in the output vector $\mathbf{y}^2$ [by eqn. (2.38)] and f_{max} indicates the number of occurrences of y_{max}^2 in $\mathbf{y}^2$. The difficulty in assigning a particular pattern class depends not only on the highest entry in output vector y_{max}^2 but also on its differences from the other entries y_j^2. It is seen that the higher the value of CF, the lower is the difficulty in deciding a class and hence greater is the degree of certainty of the output decision. On the basis of the value of CF, the system makes the following decisions while generating the consequent clause (THEN part) of the rule. Let $y_k^2 = y_{\text{max}}^2$ such that the pattern under consideration belongs to class C_k. We have

1. If $(0.8 \le CF_k \le 1.0)$, then *very likely* class C_k, and there is no second choice.

2. If $(0.6 \le CF_k < 0.8)$, then *likely* class C_k, and there is second choice.

3. If $(0.4 \le CF_k < 0.6)$, then *more or less likely* class C_k, and there is second choice.

4. If $(0.1 \leq CF_k < 0.4)$, then *not unlikely* class C_k, and there is no second choice.

5. If $(CF_k < 0.1)$, then *unable to recognize* class C_k, and there is no second choice.

To obtain a second choice corresponding to a pattern class C_{k_2} (say), the *confidence factor* CF_{k_2} is computed for the second highest entry $y_{k_2}^2$ in the output vector using eqn. (8.16). There may be some cases where there are multiple entries with the highest value y_{max}^2 in the output vector. In that case, there will not be a second choice of pattern class. Instead, the form of the consequent will be "*likely* class C_k *or* C_j" where the output values corresponding to classes C_k and C_j both have the highest value y_{max}^2.
Identical rules, if any, are discarded from the generated rule set.

8.4.2 Backtracking along trained connection weights: method 2

An input pattern $\mathbf{F}_p$ from the training set is presented to the input of the trained network and its output computed. The consequent part of the corresponding IF-THEN rule is generated by eqn. (8.16) as described in Section 8.4.1. To find the antecedent clauses of the rule, one may backtrack from the output layer to the input through the maximal weighted links. The path from node k in the output layer to node i_A in the input layer through node j in the hidden layer is maximal if

$$w_{kj}^1 y_j^1 + w_{ji_A}^0 y_{i_A}^0 = \max_m \left\{ w_{km}^1 y_m^1 + w_{mi_A}^0 y_{i_A}^0 \right\}, \qquad (8.17)$$

provided $y_j^1 \geq 0.5$, $y_{i_A}^0 > 0.5$ and the *maximum* is computed over the index m. Here the path length from node k in the output layer to node j in the hidden layer is $w_{kj}^1 y_j^1$, and not w_{kj}^1 as described in Section 7.3.4 (for the fuzzy MLP). Besides, the *confidence factor* of eqn. (8.16) is also different and in certain ways better than the *belief* used there. Only one node i_A corresponding to the three linguistic values of each feature F_i is considered so that

$$w_{ji_A}^0 y_{i_A}^0 = \max_{B \in \{L,M,H\}} w_{ji_B}^0 y_{i_B}^0, \qquad (8.18)$$

where A and B correspond to *low* (L), *medium* (M), or *high* (H). The three-dimensional linguistic pattern vector of eqn. (3.29) with or without hedges defined by eqns. (7.5)–(7.7) [corresponding to the linguistic feature F_{i_A} computed by eqn. (8.18)], which is closest to the relevant three-dimensional part of pattern $\mathbf{F}_p$, is selected as the antecedent clause. This is done for all input features to which a path may be found by eqn. (8.17). The complete IF part of the rule is obtained by ANDing clauses corresponding to each of the features, *e.g.*,

If F_1 is *more or less* A and F_2 is *not* A and ... and F_n is *very* A.

8.4.2.1 Negative rules It may sometimes happen that we are unable to classify a test pattern directly with the help of the *positive* rules (concerning its belonging to a class) derived by any of the above two methods. In such cases, one proceeds by discarding some classes that are unlikely to contain the pattern, and thereby arrive at the class(es) to which the pattern possibly belongs. In other words, in the absence of positive information regarding the belonging of pattern $\mathbf{F}_p$ to class C_k, the complementary information about the pattern $\mathbf{F}_p$ not belonging to class $C_{k'}$ is used. To handle such situations, *negative* rules are generated with the consequent part of the form *not in class $C_{k'}$* by backtracking from the output layer through the trained connection weights. Note that for a *positive* rule one traverses the hidden node k_{α_p} while for a *negative* rule the hidden node k_{α_n} is used.

Let an input pattern $\mathbf{F}_p$ from the training set be presented to the input layer of the trained network such that the output of the node in the output layer corresponding to the class $C_{k'}$ is minimum, *i.e.*, $y_{k'}^2 = \min_l \{y_l^2\}$. Therefore, one is certain that the pattern is (possibly) not included in the class $C_{k'}$. Hence, the consequent part of the corresponding rule becomes *not in class $C_{k'}$*. The antecedent part of the rule is obtained by backtracking from the output node k' through the maximal path of eqn. (8.17) with a restriction considering only the absolute values of the individual product terms. The corresponding rule, so obtained, is of the form

> If F_1 is *more or less A* and ... and F_n is *very A*,
> then the pattern is *not* in class $C_{k'}$.

Note that the approach in Section 7.3.4 did not consider such negative rules. It is worth mentioning that the rule generation techniques described above can also handle the feature information F_j in set form: (1) $F_j \geq F_{j_1}$, some lower bound, (2) $F_j \leq F_{j_2}$, some upper bound, or (3) in some interval $[F_{j_1}, F_{j_2}]$ such that F_j lies between F_{j_1} and F_{j_2}.

8.4.2.2 Example Consider a knowledge-based network as in Fig. 8.2, demonstrating the rule generation technique. Let feature F_j be the input. Classes C_k and $C_{k'}$, with maximum and minimum outputs, respectively, have been considered for the generation of *positive* and *negative* rules. The hidden nodes 1 and 2 correspond to two convex segments of the region represented by class C_k (*positive* nodes), and 3 corresponds to the region complement to class C_k (*negative* node). Similarly *positive* hidden node 4 refers to the region of class $C_{k'}$ while *negative* nodes 5, 6 correspond to the region other than class $C_{k'}$.

Let a pattern with linguistic values *low (L)* = 0.6, *medium (M)* = 0.8, and *high (H)* = 0.2 of feature F_j be presented at the input. Assume that the activations of the output nodes corresponding to the classes C_k and $C_{k'}$ are 0.9 and 0.1, respectively. Backtracking starts from the output node corresponding to class C_k and searches for the maximal path through hidden nodes 1 and 2 only (if their activations are at least 0.5) for *positive* rule generation. Similarly, for *negative* rule generation, it starts from the output node corresponding to

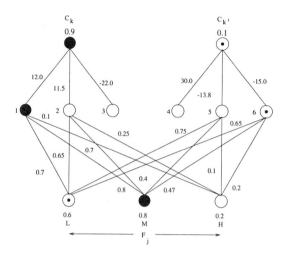

Fig. 8.2 Example demonstrating *positive* and *negative* rule generation

class $C_{k'}$ and searches for the maximal path through hidden nodes 5 and 6 only. The links with weights as shown in the figure are obtained during training. For clarity of representation, the links through hidden nodes 3 and 4 are not provided.

Let the path length [eqn. (8.17)] from the hidden node j to the input node i be denoted by $path^0_{ji}$, and that from the output node k to the hidden node j by $path^1_{kj}$. The path length from the output node k to the input node i via hidden node j is denoted by $path_{kji}$. Therefore, from Fig. 8.2 we have $path^0_{1L} = 0.7 * 0.6 = 0.42$, $path^0_{1M} = 0.8 * 0.8 = 0.64$, $path^0_{2L} = 0.39$ and $path^0_{2M} = 0.56$. Note that $path^0_{1H}$ and $path^0_{2H}$ have not been considered, as the activation of the input node H is less than 0.5. The activations of hidden nodes 1 and 2 are found to be $y^1_1 = 0.75$ and $y^1_2 = 0.73$, resulting in $path^1_{k1} = 9.0$ and $path^1_{k2} = 8.4$. The total path lengths are found to be $path_{k1L} = 9.42$, $path_{k1M} = 9.64$, $path_{k2L} = 8.79$, $path_{k2M} = 8.96$. Hence, the maximal path from the output node corresponding to the class C_k is obtained as the path via the hidden node 1 to the input node M (the selected path consists of the links joining the nodes indicated by solid circles in Fig. 8.2). The antecedent clause corresponding to the feature F_j is "F_j is *more or less medium*" and is obtained by finding the closest match of the three-dimensional vector corresponding to the feature F_j, to the respective linguistic pattern (with/without hedges) given by eqns. (3.29), and (7.5)–(7.7). The consequent part of the rule is *very likely class C_k*, as obtained from eqn. (8.16).

For the generation of *negative* rule, one computes the path lengths $path^0_{5L} = 0.45$, $path^0_{5M} = 0.32$, $path^0_{6L} = 0.39$, and $path^0_{6M} = 0.38$. The activations at hidden nodes 5 and 6 are $y^1_5 = 0.69$ and $y^1_6 = 0.69$. This leads to $path^1_{k'5} = 9.52$ and $path^1_{k'6} = 10.35$. The total path lengths are $path_{k'5L} = 9.97$, $path_{k'5M} = $

9.84, $path_{k'6L} = 10.74$, and $path_{k'6M} = 10.73$. Hence, the maximal path from the output node corresponding to the class $C_{k'}$ is obtained as the path via the hidden node 6 to the input node L (the path consisting of the links joining the nodes indicated by circles with dots inside in Fig. 8.2). The extracted *negative* rule is

If F_j is *more or less low*, then the pattern is *not* in class $C_{k'}$.

8.5   RESULTS

The following tables and graphs compare the performance of the knowledge-based fuzzy MLP [12] with that of the conventional and fuzzy versions of the MLP (Sections 3.3 and 7.3), and the fuzzy min–max neural network [19], both on synthetic and real life (speech and medical) data. The two-dimensional synthetic data in pattern set A of Fig. 3.5 are considered here with 557 points from the two classes (1 and 2). As the class structures are concave, the sets of intervals of the features where each pattern class lies (or does not lie) are determined approximately (by inspection). Note that here the background region, represented by class *none* in Sections 3.3.4 and 7.3.5, has been omitted to simplify the representation of the knowledge encoding procedure for the concave classes. The speech data *vowel* of Fig. 3.4 consists of six convex pattern classes and three input features. In both cases, the networks are trained with 10% of the original data while the remaining 90% data constitutes the test set.

The medical data *hepato*, consisting of nine input features and four pattern classes, deals with various *hepatobiliary disorders* of 536 patients and has been described in Section 4.2.1. Here, 30% of the original data set comprises the *training* set while the remaining 70% data forms the *test* set. The pattern classes are assumed to be convex as it is otherwise very difficult to visualize the exact nature of the nine-dimensional feature space.

The different knowledge-based models used in the experiment include

All connections with not: model AN
All connections without not: model A
Selected connections with not: model SN
Selected connections without not: model S

Note that terms "all" and "selected" correspond to the two broad categories of knowledge encoding mentioned in Section 8.3.1. The term "with/without not" refers to the inclusion/exclusion of negative hidden nodes, as mentioned in Section 8.3.1.

The performance of these models is compared with that of the

Fuzzy MLP: model F
Conventional MLP: model C
Fuzzy min–max network: model FMM [19]

The number of links required in each case is appropriately indicated (within parentheses) in the tables.

8.5.1 Classification

Table 8.1 depicts the result obtained with pattern set A. A total of six intervals (*i.e.*, six hidden nodes) for the two features is found to be sufficient to characterize the classes, if one does not consider the intervals in which any of the classes is *not included*. This is termed as the *without not* case. Otherwise, one requires a total of 10 intervals (*i.e.*, 10 hidden nodes), for the *with not* case. It is observed that models A and SN give 100% recognition score in just 600 epochs (sweeps). The other models (AN and S) have not been able to recognize class 2 at this stage. In model AN, perhaps the large number of interconnections encode too much redundant information thereby not enabling the classifier to recognize class 2. On the other hand, model S provides poor result probably due to under-information. The performance of F and C, being found to be the same as that of AN and S, are not included in the table.

Table 8.1 Performance of different models on pattern set A

Model	Class	Recognition score (%)	
		Training	Testing
AN (82)	1	100.0	100.0
	2	0.0	0.0
	Overall	83.64	82.47
A (47)	1	100.0	100.0
	2	100.0	100.0
	Overall	100.0	100.0
SN (≤ 82)	1	100.0	100.0
	2	100.0	100.0
	Overall	100.0	100.0
S (≤ 47)	1	100.0	100.0
	2	0.0	0.0
	Overall	83.64	82.47
FMM (84)	1	100.0	100 0
	2	100.0	84.09
	Overall	100.0	97.21
FMM (48)	1	100.0	100.0
	2	55.56	48.86
	Overall	92.73	91.04

Let us now discuss the pruning of models AN and F and growing of hidden nodes in models S, F, and C, using pattern set A. The links were pruned from 600 epochs at intervals of 10 epochs, up to 750 epochs, and then the networks (AN, F) were trained till 900 epochs. Pruning model AN resulted in 100% recognition scores for both the training and test sets.

Table 8.2 Performance of different models on *vowel* data

Model	Class	Recognition score (%)	
		Training	Testing
AN (138)	∂	42.86	27.69
	a	87.5	86.42
	i	94.12	87.74
	u	100.0	82.35
	e	90.0	69.52
	o	100.0	93.83
	Overall	90.59	78.63
SN (≤ 138)	∂	0.0	0.0
	a	62.5	58.02
	i	94.12	87.74
	u	100.0	82.35
	e	85.0	68.45
	o	94.44	93.21
	Overall	82.35	73.79
FMM (504)	∂	71.43	30.77
	a	100.0	80.25
	i	100.0	91.61
	u	86.67	72.06
	e	95.0	62.57
	o	88.89	85.80
	Overall	91.76	73.92
FMM (198)	∂	71.43	75.38
	a	50.0	41.98
	i	76.47	74.19
	u	33.33	43.38
	e	65.0	68.98
	o	44.44	35.19
	Overall	56.47	56.36

However, model F could recognize only around 20% of the patterns from class 2 at this stage. In the case of growing, it is found that after only 100 epochs model S provides overall recognition score of 100% on the training set and 99.8% on the test set. This demonstrates a remarkable improvement in performance. Hidden nodes were also added to models C and F at the same stage, but the performance was found to be poor (0% recognition for class 2).

Table 8.2 shows the results obtained with *vowel* data. Since all the classes in the feature space are convex, two hidden nodes are used for each of the

Table 8.3 Effect of adding hidden node on the performance of various knowledge-based models, for *vowel* data

| Model | Class | Recognition score (%) | |
		Training	Testing
AN	∂	42.86	23.08
	a	87.5	88.89
	i	94.12	87.74
	u	100.0	82.35
	e	90.0	70.05
	o	100.0	93.83
	Overall	90.59	78.63
SN	∂	14.29	1.54
	a	62.5	58.02
	i	94.12	92.26
	u	100.0	84.56
	e	85.0	66.84
	o	94.44	93.83
	Overall	83.53	74.17

classes for the *with not* models resulting in a total of 12 hidden nodes. It is seen that model AN gives acceptably good performance in just 200 epochs whereas model SN cannot do the same due to underinformation. Note that the *vowel* classes are overlapping and fuzzy, thereby generating fuzzy output class membership values that require storage of more information than in case of crisp class membership values. Perhaps this accounts for the better performance of the model AN (with more connections). Models C and F are *unable to recognize* classes ∂, a, and u, and fare the worst (overall recognition score during training and testing at 42.35% and 39.19% for model C and 55.29% and 52.93% for model F).

As model AN performed reasonably well for all classes initially (before growing), the incorporation of additional hidden nodes did not improve the results in this case. When model SN was augmented, it could recognize 14.29% of class ∂ during training and 1.54% during testing after 350 epochs. The overall scores rose to 83.53% and 74.17% for the training and testing sets, respectively. The results are depicted in Table 8.3.

Table 8.4 demonstrates the classification performance for the medical data *hepato* where classes 1, 2, 3, and 4 correspond to the four disease classes ALD, PH, LC, and C, respectively (Section 4.2.1). It is assumed that the classes are convex, so that eight hidden nodes are required for the four classes. As in the case of *vowel*, only the *with not* models AN and SN have been used. Model SN, which uses only those links that are encoded with the initial knowledge, performs rather poorly. Perhaps it would require more nodes and links than were available under the convex-classes assumption. However model AN, which is allowed to grow extra links, is found to have solved this problem. Its performance is considerably better than models SN and F in just 500 epochs (Table 8.4).

Table 8.4 Performance of different models on *hepato* data

Model	Class	Recognition score (%)	
		Training	Testing
F (260)	1	41.18	37.80
	2	90.57	89.60
	3	2.70	9.20
	4	91.43	92.77
	Overall	59.75	60.48
AN (236)	1	61.76	52.44
	2	84.91	77.60
	3	59.46	43.68
	4	91.43	86.75
	Overall	75.47	66.31
SN (≤ 236)	1	0.0	0.0
	2	98.11	100.0
	3	0.0	0.0
	4	0.0	0.0
	Overall	32.70	33.16
FMM (2068)	1	76.47	32.93
	2	90.57	60.0
	3	48.65	2.30
	4	82.86	55.42
	Overall	76.10	39.79
FMM (236)	1	8.82	0.0
	2	100.0	100.0
	3	18.92	0.0
	4	0.0	0.0
	Overall	39.62	33.16

   Tables 8.1, 8.2, and 8.4 also show the classification performance of the fuzzy min–max neural network (model FMM) [19] on the three data sets. In this model, the number of links can be varied by altering some of the parameters. The results for two different configurations are shown, providing more or less the (1) same overall recognition score (on training sets) and (2) same number of links, as the knowledge-based networks. Model A for pattern set A (Table 8.1), and model AN for both *vowel* and *hepato* (Tables 8.2 and 8.4) have been compared for this purpose, as they perform the best. It is clear that the model FMM requires more links to get more or less the same overall recognition score. Similarly, with more or less the same number of links, the

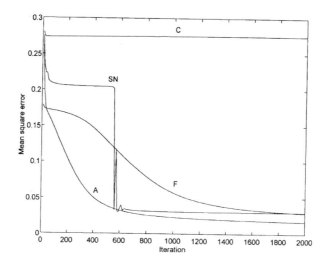

Fig. 8.3 Variation of mean square error with number of sweeps for pattern set A

model FMM performs poorer for all the data sets. Note that conventional and fuzzy versions of the MLP consider empirically determined fixed architecture, whereas the knowledge-based models automatically determine it. The fuzzy min–max network [19], on the other hand, generates hidden nodes from some empirically determined parameter values.

Figures 8.3 and 8.4 depict the variation of *mean square error* with the number of sweeps or iterations for pattern set A and *vowel*, respectively. It is observed that model C has the worst performance. Model A (for pattern set A) and model AN (for *vowel*) behave the best. Model SN is better than model F in the beginning and converges to a good solution very fast (in about 600 sweeps in Fig. 8.3) for pattern set A, while model F requires about twice to thrice this time to reach the same level of performance. In contrast, for *vowel* data model F surpasses model SN at around 500 sweeps (as seen from Fig. 8.4). However, model AN or A is always the best perhaps due to the presence of less redundancy (than model F) along with more knowledge (than model SN). Note that Tables 8.1 and 8.2 depict the performance of the knowledge-based models at 600 and 200 sweeps (epochs), respectively. This accounts for the relatively poor performance of model F, whereas it fares better with longer training time (as is evident from the figures).

8.5.2   Rule generation

Tables 8.5 and 8.6 compare the rules generated for pattern set A and *vowel* data, respectively, by the methods described in Section 8.4, using the various knowledge-based models and the fuzzy MLP (Section 7.3). The rules generated by the various models are not identical because of the different amounts

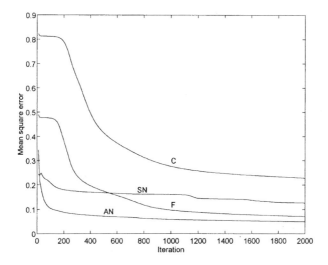

Fig. 8.4 Variation of mean square error with number of sweeps for *vowel* data

of redundancy inherent in them and the difference in the encoding of their architectures. The method of Section 8.4.2, *viz.*, method 2, often produces different results (as compared to that of Section 8.4.1, *viz.*, method 1, where only the input and output of the network are considered). This is because the trained connection weight magnitudes are utilized during the tracing of the maximal weighted paths, thereby using the encoded and refined domain knowledge along with the test case feature values. It is observed that the less redundant knowledge-based models yield better rules much earlier.

Table 8.5 Rules obtained by different models on pattern set *A*

Model	Antecedent	Consequent	
		Method 1	Method 2
A	F_1 *low*, F_2 *high*	*Likely* class 1, but *unable to recognize* 2	*Very likely* class 1
	F_1 and F_2 *Mol medium*	*Mol likely* class 2, but *unable to recognize* 1	*Likely* class 2, but *unable to recognize* 1
SN	F_1 *low*, F_2 *high*	*Very likely* class 1	*Very likely* class 1
	F_1 and F_2 *Mol medium*	*Likely* class 2, but *unable to recognize* 1	*Very likely* class 2
F	F_1 *low*, F_2 *high*	*Very likely* class 1	*Very likely* class 1
	F_1 and F_2 *Mol medium*	*Likely* class 2, but *unable to recognize* 1	*Likely* class 2, but *unable to recognize* 1

8.5.2.1 Negative rules Let us consider the trained connection weights $w^1_{kk_\alpha}$ of the knowledge-based network in the case of pattern set A to explain the generation of *negative* rules. It is interesting to note that the weights $w^1_{kk_{\alpha_n}}$ connecting k_{α_n} nodes in the hidden layer with the corresponding kth output node are found to be negative, whereas those connecting k_{α_p} nodes are positive for each of the classes C_k. Therefore, when a pattern belonging to class $C_{k'}$ is presented to the input layer of the network, the output produced by the k_{α_n} hidden nodes is greater than those by k_{α_p} hidden nodes (or sometimes comparable in magnitude, when the weights $w^1_{kk_{\alpha_p}}$ and $w^1_{kk_{\alpha_n}}$ are also comparable). But in such cases, the output produced by the k'_{α_p} nodes is always found to be greater than those by k'_{α_n} nodes.

Table 8.6 Rules obtained by the knowledge-based and fuzzy MLP on *vowel* data

Model	Antecedent	Consequent	
		Method 1	Method 2
AN	F_1 *medium*, F_2 and F_3 *low*	*Very likely* class o	*Very likely* class u
	F_1 *low*, F_2 *high*, F_3 *Mol medium*	*Very likely* class i	*Very likely* class i
	F_1 and F_2 *low*, F_3 *high*	*Not unlikely* class o	*Mol likely* class o, but *unable to recognize u*
	F_1 *high*, F_2 *medium*, F_3 *very low*	*Mol likely* class ∂, but *unable to recognize a*	*Not unlikely* class ∂
	F_1 *very high*, F_2 *low*, F_3 *very medium*	*Mol likely* class a, but *unable to recognize e*	*Mol likely* class a, but *unable to recognize e*
	F_1 and F_2 *high*, F_3 *medium*	*Likely* class e, but *unable to recognize i*	*Very likely* class e
F	F_1 *medium*, F_2 and F_3 *low*	*Very likely* class o	*Very likely* class u
	F_1 *low*, F_2 *high*, F_3 *Mol medium*	*Likely* class i, but *not unlikely e*	*Likely* class i, but *unable to recognize e*
	F_1 and F_2 *low*, F_3 *high*	*Mol likely* class o, but *unable to recognize u*	*Mol likely* class o, but *unable to recognize u*
	F_1 *high*, F_2 *medium*, F_3 *very low*	*Likely* class ∂, but *unable to recognize a*	*Likely* class ∂, but *unable to recognize a*
	F_1 *very high*, F_2 *low*, F_3 *very medium*	*Mol likely* class a, but *unable to recognize ∂*	*Mol likely* class a, but *not unlikely ∂*
	F_1 and F_2 *high*, F_3 *medium*	*Likely* class e, but *unable to recognize i*	*Very likely* class e

The hidden nodes 1, 2, 3, and 4 correspond to the intervals to which class 1 belongs, while node 5 refers to the interval in which class 1 does not lie. Hidden nodes 6 and 7 correspond to the intervals to which class 2 belongs, while nodes 8, 9, and 10 are indicative of the region where class 2 is not included. The connection weights from nodes 1, 2, 3, and 4 to class 1 and nodes 6 and 7 to class 2 are 8.24, 13.47, 13.29, and 8.41, and 16.49 and 16.46, respectively. Similarly, the connection weights from nodes 5 to class 1 and 8, 9, and 10 to class 2 are -43.49, -9.28, -14.06, and -9.12 respectively. Hence one backtracks along k'_{α_n} nodes while determining a rule about a pattern not belonging to class $C_{k'}$, and generates that path having the maximal value for the magnitude of the product term.

Two sample *negative* rules obtained using the *AN* and *F* models for *vowel* data are provided below. This also serves as a comparative study. Note that the AND terms, connecting the different IF clauses, are replaced by *commas* for reducing clutter.

Using model AN:

- If F_1 is *Mol low*, F_2 is *medium*, F_3 is *very low*, then the pattern is *not in* class *u*.

- If F_1 is *very high*, F_2 is *Mol medium*, F_3 is *very medium*, then the pattern is *not in* class *i*.

Using model F:

- If F_1 is *high*, F_2 is *medium*, F_3 is *high*, then the pattern is *not in* class *u*.

- If F_1 is *very high*, F_2 is *Mol medium*, F_3 is *very medium*, then the pattern is *not in* class *i*.

It is seen that *negative* rules offer an useful solution in cases where no suitable *positive* rule can be found. Note that model *F* (Section 7.3) does not have k_{α_p} or k_{α_n} nodes encoded in its structure. Hence the negative rules are generated in this case by simply backtracking along the maximal magnitude paths from the class producing the minimal output. A sample *negative* rule generated by the *AN* and *F* models for the medical data *hepato* is also provided below.

Using model AN:

- If F_1 is *low*, F_2 is *low*, F_3 is *very medium*, F_4 is *low*, F_5 is *low*, F_6 is *medium*, F_7 is *Mol medium*, F_8 is *low*, F_9 is *very medium*, then the pattern is *not in* class 1.

Using model F:

- If F_1 is *low*, F_2 is *low*, F_3 is *very medium*, F_4 is *low*, F_5 is *Mol medium*, F_6 is *medium*, F_7 is *Mol medium*, F_8 is *Mol low*, F_9 is *very medium*, then the pattern is *not in* class 1. ♣

In this chapter, we have described how the concept of neuro-fuzzy integration can be incorporated in designing knowledge-based network for classification and rule generation. In the next chapter we introduce a different scheme of generating a knowledge-based fuzzy MLP. The model, which is based on rough set theoretic concepts, is termed as *rough–fuzzy MLP*. This also demonstrates an example of *rough–neuro-fuzzy* hybridization in the soft computing framework.

REFERENCES

1. L. M. Fu, "Knowledge-based connectionism for revising domain theories," *IEEE Transactions on Systems, Man, and Cybernetics*, vol. 23, pp. 173–182, 1993.

2. G. G. Towell and J. W. Shavlik, "Knowledge-based artificial neural networks," *Artificial Intelligence*, vol. 70, pp. 119–165, 1994.

3. H. F. Yin and P. Liang, "A connectionist incremental expert system combining production systems and associative memory," *International Journal of Pattern Recognition and Artificial Intelligence*, vol. 5, pp. 523–544, 1991.

4. G. G. Towell and J. W. Shavlik, "Extracting refined rules from knowledge-based neural networks," *Machine Learning*, vol. 13, pp. 71–101, 1993.

5. D. W. Opitz and J. W. Shavlik, "Heuristically expanding knowledge-based neural networks," in *Proceedings of 13th International Joint Conference on Artificial Intelligence (IJCAI-93)* (Chambery, France), pp. 1360–1365, 1993.

6. R. C. Lacher, S. I. Hruska, and D. C. Kuncicky, "Back-propagation learning in expert networks," *IEEE Transactions on Neural Networks*, vol. 3, pp. 62–72, 1992.

7. R. Masuoka, N. Watanabe, A. Kawamura, Y. Owada, and K. Asakawa, "Neurofuzzy system–fuzzy inference using a structured neural network," in *Proceedings of the 1990 International Conference on Fuzzy Logic and Neural Networks, Iizuka* (Japan), pp. 173–177, 1990.

8. N. K. Kasabov, "Adaptable neuro production systems," *Neurocomputing*, vol. 13, pp. 95–117, 1996.

9. N. Kasabov, "Learning fuzzy rules and approximate reasoning in fuzzy neural networks and hybrid systems," *Fuzzy Sets and Systems*, vol. 82, pp. 135–149, 1996.

10. N. K. Kasabov, "Fuzzy rules extraction, reasoning and rules adaptation in fuzzy neural networks," in *Proceedings of IEEE International Conference on Neural Networks* (Houston, USA), pp. 2380–2383, 1997.

11. B. Kosko, "Hidden patterns in combined and adaptive knowledge networks," *International Journal of Approximate Reasoning*, vol. 2, pp. 377–393, 1988.

12. S. Mitra, R. K. De, and S. K. Pal, "Knowledge-based fuzzy MLP for classification and rule generation," *IEEE Transactions on Neural Networks*, vol. 8, pp. 1338–1350, 1997.

13. R. J. Machado and A. F. Rocha, "A hybrid architecture for fuzzy connectionist expert systems," in *Intelligent Hybrid Systems*, A. Kandel and G. Langholz, eds., pp. 136–152. Boca Raton, FL: CRC Press, 1992.

14. R. J. Machado and A. F. da Rocha, "Inference, inquiry, evidence censorship, and explanation in connectionist expert systems," *IEEE Transactions on Fuzzy Systems*, vol. 5, pp. 443–459, 1997.

15. W. Pedrycz and A. F. Rocha, "Fuzzy-set based models of neurons and knowledge-based networks," *IEEE Transactions on Fuzzy Systems*, vol. 1, pp. 254–266, 1993.

16. K. Hirota and W. Pedrycz, "Knowledge-based networks in classification problems," *Fuzzy Sets and Systems*, vol. 59, pp. 271–279, 1993.

17. A. H. Tan, "Cascade ARTMAP: Integrating neural computation and symbolic knowledge processing," *IEEE Transactions on Neural Networks*, vol. 8, pp. 237–250, 1997.

18. D. W. Opitz and J. W. Shavlik, "Connectionist theory refinement: Genetically searching the space of network topologies," *Journal of Artificial Intelligence Research*, vol. 6, pp. 177–209, 1997.

19. P. K. Simpson, "Fuzzy min-max neural networks: 1. Classification," *IEEE Transactions on Neural Networks*, vol. 3, pp. 776–786, 1992.

20. S. I. Gallant, "Connectionist expert systems," *Communications of the Association for Computing Machinery*, vol. 31, pp. 152–169, 1988.

21. K. Saito and R. Nakano, "Medical diagnostic expert system based on PDP model," in *Proceedings of IEEE International Conference on Neural Networks* (San Diego, USA), pp. I.255–I.262, 1988.

22. B. F. Leao and A. F. Rocha, "Proposed methodology for knowledge acquisition: A study on congenital heart disease diagnosis," *Methods of Information in Medicine*, vol. 29, pp. 30–40, 1990.

23. G. A. Carpenter, S. Grossberg, N. Markuzon, J. H. Reynolds, and D. B. Rosen, "Fuzzy ARTMAP: A neural network architecture for incremental supervised learning of analog multidimensional maps," *IEEE Transactions on Neural Networks*, vol. 3, pp. 698–713, 1992.

24. D. E. Goldberg, *Genetic Algorithms in Search, Optimization and Machine Learning.* Reading, MA: Addison-Wesley, 1989.

25. Z. Michalewicz, *Genetic Algorithms + Data Structures = Evolutionary Programs.* Berlin: Springer Verlag, 1994.

26. S. K. Pal and P. P. Wang, eds., *Genetic Algorithms for Pattern Recognition.* Boca Raton, FL: CRC Press, 1996.

27. S. K. Pal and D. Bhandari, "Selection of optimum set of weights in a layered network using genetic algorithms," *Information Sciences*, vol. 80, pp. 213–234, 1994.

28. V. Maniezzo, "Genetic evolution of the topology and weight distribution of neural networks," *IEEE Transactions on Neural Networks*, vol. 5, pp. 39–53, 1994.

29. D. P. Mandal, C. A. Murthy, and S. K. Pal, "Determining the shape of a pattern class from sampled points in R^2," *International Journal of General Systems*, vol. 20, pp. 307–339, 1992.

30. S. K. Pal and D. P. Mandal, "Linguistic recognition system based on approximate reasoning," *Information Sciences*, vol. 61, pp. 135–161, 1992.

9

Rough–Fuzzy Knowledge-Based Networks

9.1 INTRODUCTION

The theory of rough sets, introduced by Pawlak [1], provides another approach to reasoning with vagueness and uncertainty. Its underlying assumption is that knowledge has granular structure caused by the situation when some objects of interest cannot be distinguished from each other; *i.e.*, they are indiscernible. The effectiveness of the theory of rough sets has been investigated in the domain of artificial intelligence and cognitive sciences, especially for representation of and reasoning with vague and/or imprecise knowledge, data classification and analysis, machine learning, and knowledge discovery [2]–[4]. The focus of rough set theory is on the ambiguity caused by limited discernibility of objects in the domain of discourse. The intention is to approximate a *rough* (imprecise) concept in the domain of discourse by a pair of *exact* concepts, called the lower and upper approximations. These exact concepts are determined by an *indiscernibility* relation on the domain, which, in turn, may be induced by a given set of *attributes* ascribed to the objects of the domain. The lower approximation is the set of objects definitely belonging to the vague concept, whereas the upper approximation is the set of objects possibly belonging to the same. The boundary region of the vague concept is the difference between its upper and lower approximations. These approximations are used to define the notions of *discernibility matrices, dis-*

cernibility functions [5], *reducts*, and *dependency factors* [1], all of which play a fundamental role in the reduction of knowledge.

In this chapter we demonstrate a way of integrating rough sets and fuzzy–neural network for designing a knowledge-based system where the theory of rough sets is utilized for extracting domain knowledge. First of all, we provide some mathematical preliminaries of rough set theory. This is followed by a short description of the models of Yasdi [6] and Czyzewski and Kaczmarek [7], which have used rough sets for the design of knowledge-based networks in the rough-neuro framework.

The formulation of a rough–fuzzy MLP [8]–[11] is then described in detail. Here, the extracted crude domain knowledge is encoded among the connection weights. This helps one to automatically generate an appropriate network architecture in terms of hidden nodes and links. Methods are derived to model (1) convex decision regions with single-object representatives, and (2) arbitrary decision regions with multiple-object representatives. These knowledge encoding algorithms are radically different from the model described in the previous chapter. As in Section 8.3, a three-layered fuzzy MLP is considered where the feature space gives the condition attributes and the output classes the decision attributes, so as to result in a decision table. This table may be transformed, keeping the complexity of the network to be constructed in mind. Rules are then generated from the (transformed) table by computing relative reducts. The dependency factors of these rules are encoded as the initial connection weights of the fuzzy MLP.

Finally, some results of the said rough–fuzzy MLP are presented. This includes classification performance of the system and its comparison with the conventional and fuzzy versions of the MLP, when implemented on the synthetic and real life speech data (of Section 3.3.4). Note that the knowledge encoding procedure described in Section 9.4, unlike most other methods [12, 13], involves a nonbinary weighting mechanism based on a detailed and systematic estimation of the available domain information. Moreover, the appropriate number of hidden nodes is automatically determined here.

9.2   ROUGH SET CHARACTERISTICS

Let us present here some requisite preliminaries of rough set theory. For details one may refer to Pawlak [1] and Skowron and Rauszer [5].

An *information system* is a pair $S = < U, A >$, where U is a nonempty finite set called the *universe* and A a nonempty finite set of *attributes*. An attribute a can be regarded as a function from the domain U to some value set V_a.

An information system may be represented as an *attribute-value table*, in which rows are labeled by objects of the universe and columns by the attributes.

With every subset of attributes $B \subseteq A$, one can easily associate an equivalence relation I_B on U:

$$I_B = \{(x, y) \in U : \text{for every } a \in B, \ a(x) = a(y)\}.$$

Then $I_B = \bigcap_{a \in B} I_a$.

If $X \subseteq U$, the sets $\{x \in U : [x]_B \subseteq X\}$ and $\{x \in U : [x]_B \cap X \neq \emptyset\}$, where $[x]_B$ denotes the equivalence class of the object $x \in U$ relative to I_B, are called the B-*lower* and B-*upper approximations* of X in S and denoted $\underline{B}X$ and $\overline{B}X$, respectively.

$X(\subseteq U)$ is B-*exact* or B-*definable* in S if $\underline{B}X = \overline{B}X$. It may be observed that $\underline{B}X$ is the greatest B-definable set contained in X, and $\overline{B}X$ is the smallest B-definable set containing X.

Let us consider, for example, an *information system* $< U, \{a\} >$ where the domain U consists of the students of a school, and there is a single attribute a–that of "belonging to a class." Then U is partitioned by the classes of the school.

Now consider the situation when an infectious disease has spread in the school, and the authorities take the two following steps.

1. If at least one student of a class is infected, all the students of that class are vaccinated. Let $\overline{B}$ denote the union of such classes.

2. If every student of a class is infected, the class is temporarily suspended. Let $\underline{B}$ denote the union of such classes.

Then $\underline{B} \subseteq \overline{B}$. Given this information, let the following problem be posed:
• *Identify the collection of infected students.* Clearly, there cannot be a unique answer. But any set I that is given as an answer, must contain $\underline{B}$ *and* at least one student from each class comprising $\overline{B}$. In other words, it must have $\underline{B}$ as its *lower approximation* and $\overline{B}$ as its *upper approximation*.
• I is then a *rough* concept or set in the information system $< U, \{a\} >$. Further, it may be observed that any set I' given as another answer, is *roughly equal* to I, in the sense that both are represented (characterized) by $\overline{B}$ and $\underline{B}$.

We now define the notions relevant to knowledge reduction. The aim is to obtain irreducible but essential parts of the knowledge encoded by the given information system–these would constitute *reducts* of the system. So one is, in effect, looking for *maximal* sets of attributes taken from the initial set (A, say), which induce the *same* partition on the domain as A. In other words, the essence of the information remains intact, and superfluous attributes are removed. Reducts have been nicely characterized in another study [5] by *discernibility matrices* and *discernibility functions*. A principal task in our proposed methods will be to compute reducts relative to a particular kind of information system, and relativised versions of these matrices and functions shall be the basic tools used in the computation.

Let $U = \{x_1, ..., x_n\}$ and $A = \{a_1, ..., a_m\}$ in the information system $S =< U, A >$. By the discernibility matrix [denoted $\mathbf{M}(S)$] of S is meant an

$n \times n$-matrix such that

$$c_{ij} = \{a \in A : a(x_i) \neq a(x_j)\}, \ i,j = 1, ..., n. \tag{9.1}$$

A discernibility function f_S is a Boolean function of m Boolean variables $\bar{a}_1, ..., \bar{a}_m$ corresponding to the attributes $a_1, ..., a_m$, respectively, and defined as follows:

$$f_S(\bar{a}_1, ..., \bar{a}_m) = \bigwedge \{\bigvee (c_{ij}) : 1 \leq j < i \leq n, \ c_{ij} \neq \emptyset\}, \tag{9.2}$$

where $\bigvee(c_{ij})$ is the disjunction of all variables $\bar{a}$ with $a \in c_{ij}$.

It is seen in another work [5] that $\{a_{i_1}, \cdots, a_{i_p}\}$ is a reduct in S if and only if $a_{i_1} \wedge ... \wedge a_{i_p}$ is a prime implicant (constituent of the disjunctive normal form) of f_S.

The next concept required during rule generation is that of the *dependency factor*. It may well happen for $B, C \subseteq A$, that C depends on B, viz., $I_B \subseteq I_C$, so that information because of the attributes in C is derivable from that due to the attributes in B. This dependency can be partial, in which case one introduces a dependency factor df, $0 \leq df \leq 1$:

$$df = \frac{card(POS_B(C))}{card(U)}, \tag{9.3}$$

where $POS_B(C) = \bigcup_{X \in I_C} \underline{B}X$, and $card$ denotes cardinality of the set.

We are concerned with a specific type of information system $S = < U, A >$, called a *decision table*. The attributes in such a system are distinguished into two parts: *condition* and *decision* attributes. Classification of the domain due to decision attributes could be thought of as that given by an expert. One may now want to deal with *consistent* decision tables, such that a decision attribute does not assign more than one value to an object, or for that matter, to objects indiscernible from each other with respect to the given (condition) attributes. Formally, one has the following.

Let $C, D \subseteq A$ be the sets of condition and decision attributes of S, respectively. The *rank* of a decision attribute $d \in D, r(d)$, is the cardinality of the image $d(U)$ of the function d on the value set V_d. One can then assume that $V_d = \{1, ..., r(d)\}$. The *generalized decision* in S corresponding to d is then defined as a function $\partial_S : U \rightarrow \mathcal{P}(\{1, ..., r(d)\})$ such that $\partial_S(x) = \{i : \exists x' \in [x]_C \text{ and } d(x') = i\}$, $\mathcal{P}$ denoting the power set. A decision table S with $D = \{d\}$ is called *consistent* (*deterministic*) if $card(\partial_S(x)) = 1$ for any $x \in U$, or equivalently, if and only if $POS_C(d) = U$. Otherwise, S is *inconsistent* (*nondeterministic*).

Knowledge reduction now consists of eliminating superfluous values of the condition attributes by computing their reducts, and we come to the notion of a *relative reduct*.

An attribute $b \in B(\subseteq C)$ is *D-dispensable* in B, if $POS_B(D) = POS_{B \setminus \{b\}}(D)$; otherwise b is *D-indispensable* in B.

If every attribute from B is D-indispensable in B, B is D-*independent* in S. A subset B of C is a D-*reduct* in S if B is D-independent in S and $POS_C(D) = POS_B(D)$.

Relative reducts can be computed by using a D-*discernibility matrix*. If $U = \{x_1, ..., x_n\}$, it is an $n \times n$ matrix [denoted $\mathbf{M}_D(S)$], the (ij)th component of which has the form

$$c_{ij} = \{a \in C : a(x_i) \neq a(x_j) \text{ and } (x_i, x_j) \notin I_D\} \tag{9.4}$$

for $i, j = 1, ..., n$.

Relative discernibility function f_D is constructed from the D-discernibility matrix in an analogous way as f_S is computed from the discernibility matrix of S [cf. eqns. (9.1) and (9.2)]. It is once more observed that [5] $\{a_{i_1}, ..., a_{i_p}\}$ is a D-reduct in S if and only if $a_{i_1} \wedge ... \wedge a_{i_p}$ is a prime implicant of f_D.

9.3 KNOWLEDGE ENCODING USING ROUGH SETS

The relevance of rough sets to the design of knowledge-based networks has been described in Section 2.7.2. As mentioned there, the literature on various approaches in this line is scarce as compared to that of neuro-fuzzy systems. We provide here some of the attempts recently reported in this area.

Many have looked into the implementation of decision rules extracted from operation data using rough set formalism, especially in problems of machine learning from examples, and control theory [2]. In the context of neural networks, an attempt of such implementation has been made by Yasdi [6]. The intention is to use rough sets as a tool for structuring the neural networks. The methodology consists of generating rules from training examples by rough set learning, and mapping them into a single layer of connection weights of a four-layered neural network. Attributes appearing as rule antecedents (consequents) become the input (output) nodes, while the dependency factors become the weight of the adjoining links in the hidden layer. The input and output layers involve non-adjustable binary weights. *Max, min* and OR operators are modeled at the hidden nodes, based on the syntax of the rules. The backpropagation algorithm is slightly modified. However, the network has not been tested on any real life problem and no comparative study is provided to bring out the effectiveness of this hybrid approach.

Application of rough sets in neurocomputing has also been made [7]. However, in this method, rough sets are used for knowledge discovery at the level of data acquisition, (*viz.*, in preprocessing of the feature vectors), and not for structuring the network. Sarkar and Yegnanarayana [14] have used a fuzzy–rough set theoretic approach to determine the importance of different subsets of incomplete information sources, which are used by several small feedforward subnetworks. The individual solutions are then combined to obtain the final classification result.

9.4   CONFIGURATION OF ROUGH–FUZZY MLP FOR CLASSIFICATION

Here we describe the formulation of two methods [8, 9] for rule generation and knowledge encoding, for configuring a rough–fuzzy MLP. Method 1 works on the assumption that each object of the domain of discourse corresponds to a single decision attribute. On the other hand, method 2 is able to deal with multiple objects corresponding to one decision attribute. From the perspective of pattern recognition, this implies using a single prototype to model a (convex) decision region in case of method 1. For method 2, this means using multiple prototypes to serve as representatives of any arbitrary decision region.

The crude domain knowledge, so extracted, is encoded among the connection weights, leading to the design of a knowledge-based network. Such a network is found to be more efficient than the conventional version, as explained in Section 8.1. The architecture of the network becomes simpler, due to the inherent reduction of the redundancy among the connection weights. A block diagram in Fig. 9.1 illustrates the entire procedure for both the methods.

9.4.1   Method 1

Let $S = < U, A >$ be a decision table, with C and D its sets of condition and decision attributes, respectively. In this method it is assumed that there is a decision attribute $d_i \in D$ corresponding to each object $x_i \in U$, in the sense that all objects other than x_i are indiscernible with respect to d_i.

9.4.1.1 Rule generation For each D-reduct $B = \{b_1, ..., b_k\}$ (say), a discernibility matrix [denoted $\mathbf{M}_D(B)$] from the D-discernibility matrix [given by eqn. (9.4)] is defined as follows:

$$c_{ij} = \{a \in B : a(x_i) \neq a(x_j)\}, \tag{9.5}$$

for $i, j = 1, ..., n$.

Now for each object x_i of U, the discernibility function $f_D^{x_i}$ is defined as

$$f_D^{x_i} = \bigwedge \{\bigvee (c_{ij}) : 1 \leq i, j \leq n, \ j \neq i, \ c_{ij} \neq \emptyset\}, \tag{9.6}$$

where $\bigvee (c_{ij})$ is the disjunction of all members of c_{ij}; $f_D^{x_i}$ is brought to its conjunctive normal form (cnf) P_i. For $i = 1, ..., n$, $f_D^{x_i}$ then gives rise to a dependency rule r_i, viz. $P_i \rightarrow d_i$, where $d_i \in D$ corresponds to the object x_i.

It may be noticed that each component of P_i induces an equivalence relation on U as follows. If a component is a single attribute b, the relation I_b is taken. If a component of the cnf is a disjunct of attributes, say $b_{i_1}, ..., b_{i_p} \in B$, the

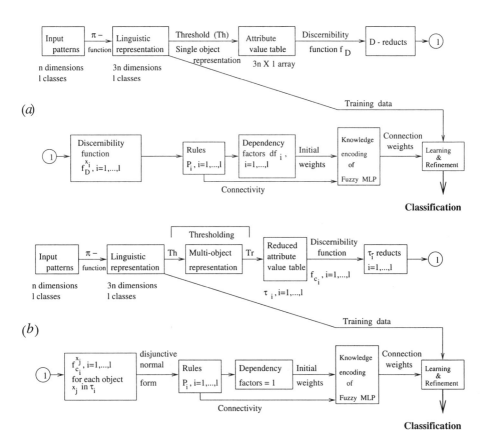

Fig. 9.1 Block diagram of rough–fuzzy MLP: (*a*) method 1; (*b*) method 2

transitive closure of the union of the relations $I_{b_{i_1}}, ..., I_{b_{i_p}}$ is considered. Let I_i denote the intersection of all these equivalence relations.

The dependency factor df_i for r_i is then given by

$$df_i = \frac{card(POS_i(d_i))}{card(U)}, \tag{9.7}$$

where $POS_i(d_i) = \bigcup_{X \in I_{d_i}} lw_i(X)$, and $lw_i(X)$ is the lower approximation of X with respect to I_i.

9.4.1.2 Knowledge encoding   Here we describe a methodology [8] for encoding initial knowledge in the fuzzy MLP (Section 3.3), in terms of the dependency rules and dependency factors, generated by the aforesaid algorithm. Let us consider the case of feature F_j for the kth class in the l-class problem domain. The inputs for the ith representative sample $\mathbf{F_i}$ are mapped to the corresponding 3D feature space of $\mu_{\text{low}(F_{ij})}(\mathbf{F_i})$, $\mu_{\text{medium}(F_{ij})}(\mathbf{F_i})$ and $\mu_{\text{high}(F_{ij})}(\mathbf{F_i})$, by eqn. (3.28). Let these be represented by L_j, M_j, and H_j, respectively. Then consider only those attributes that have a numerical value greater than some threshold Th ($0.5 \le Th < 1$). This implies clamping those features demonstrating high membership values with one, while the others are fixed at zero. In this manner an $l \times 3n$-dimensional attribute-value (decision) table can be generated from the n-dimensional data set. The antecedent parts of the l dependency rules therefore contain a subset of the $3n$ attributes.

The input layer of the fuzzy MLP consists of the $3n$ attribute values while the output layer is represented by the l classes. The hidden layer nodes model the disjuncts ($\vee$) in the antecedents of the dependency rules. For each disjunct, corresponding to one output class (one dependency rule), one hidden node is dedicated. Only those input attributes that appear in a disjunct are connected to the appropriate hidden node, which in turn is connected to the corresponding output node. Each conjunct ($\wedge$) is modeled at the output layer by joining the corresponding hidden nodes. Note that a single attribute (involving no disjuncts) is directly connected to the appropriate output node via a hidden node.

Let the dependency factor for a particular dependency rule for the kth class be α by eqn. (9.7). The weight w_{ki}^1 between a hidden node i and output node k is set at $(\alpha/fac) + \varepsilon$, where fac refers to the number of conjunctions in the antecedent of the rule and ε is a small random number taken to destroy any symmetry among the weights. Note that $fac \ge 1$ and each hidden node is connected to only one output node. Let the initial weight so clamped at a hidden node be denoted as β. The weight $w_{ia_j}^0$ between an attribute a_j [where a corresponds to *low* (L), *medium* (M), or *high* (H)] and hidden node i is set to $(\beta/facd) + \varepsilon$, such that $facd$ is the number of attributes connected by the corresponding disjunct. Note that $facd \ge 1$. The sign of the weight is set to positive (negative) if the corresponding entry in row k, and column a_j is 1 (0). Thus for an l-class problem domain there are at least l hidden nodes. All other possible connections in the resulting fuzzy MLP are set as small random numbers. It is to be mentioned that the number of hidden nodes is determined from the dependency rules.

The connection weights, so encoded, are then refined by training the network on the pattern set supplied as input.

9.4.2   Method 2

Let $S =< U, A >$ be a decision table, with C and $D = \{d_1, ..., d_l\}$ its sets of condition and decision attributes respectively.

9.4.2.1   Rule generation

Divide the decision table $S =< U, A >$ into l tables $S_i =< U_i, A_i >, i = 1, ..., l$, corresponding to the l decision attributes $d_1, ..., d_l$, where $U = U_1 \cup ... \cup U_l$ and $A_i = C \cup \{d_i\}$.

The size of each S_i $(i = 1, ..., l)$ is first reduced with the help of a threshold on the number of occurrences of the same pattern of attribute values. This will be elicited in the sequel. Let the reduced decision table be denoted by $\mathcal{T}_i$, and $\{x_{i1}, ..., x_{ip}\}$ be the set of those objects of U_i that occur in $\mathcal{T}_i, i = 1, ..., l$.

Using eqns. (9.5) and (9.6), for each d_i-reduct B (say), one may define the discernibility matrix $(\mathbf{M}_{d_i}(B))$ and for every object $x_j \in \{x_{i1}, ..., x_{ip}\}$, the discernibility function $f_{d_i}^{x_j}$. Then $f_{d_i}^{x_j}$ is brought to its conjunctive normal form. One thus obtains a dependency rule r_i, viz., $P_i \rightarrow d_i$, where P_i is the disjunctive normal form (dnf) of $f_{d_i}^{x_j}, j \in \{i_1, ..., i_p\}$. It may then be noticed that the dependency factor df_i for each r_i is one [by eqn. (9.7)].

9.4.2.2   Knowledge encoding

The knowledge encoding scheme [9] is similar to that described in Section 9.4.1. As this method considers multiple objects in a class (unlike method 1), a separate $n_k \times 3n$-dimensional attribute-value table is generated for each class (where n_k indicates the number of objects in the kth class).

Let there be m sets $O_1, ..., O_m$ of objects in the table having identical attribute values, and $card(O_i) = n_{k_i}, i = 1, ..., m$, such that $n_{k_1} \geq ... \geq n_{k_m}$ and $\sum_{i=1}^{m} n_{k_i} = n_k$. The attribute-value table can now be represented as an $m \times 3n$ array. Let $n_{k_1'}, n_{k_2'}, ..., n_{k_m'}$ denote the distinct elements among $n_{k_1}, ..., n_{k_m}$ such that $n_{k_1'} > n_{k_2'} > ... > n_{k_m'}$. Let a heuristic threshold function be defined as

$$Tr = \left\lceil \frac{\sum_{i=1}^{m} \frac{1}{n_{k_i'} - n_{k_{i+1}'}}}{Th} \right\rceil, \tag{9.8}$$

so that all entries having frequency less than Tr are eliminated from the table, resulting in the reduced attribute-value table. Note that the main motive of introducing this threshold function lies in reducing the size of the resulting network. One attempts to eliminate noisy pattern representatives (having lower values of n_{k_i}) from the reduced attribute-value table. The whole approach is, therefore, data-dependent. The dependency rule for each class is obtained by considering the corresponding reduced attribute-value table. A smaller table leads to a simpler rule in terms of conjunctions and disjunctions, which is then translated into a network having fewer hidden nodes. The objective is to strike a balance by reducing the network complexity and reaching a *good* solution, perhaps at the expense of not achieving the *best* performance.

While designing the initial structure of the fuzzy MLP, the union of the rules of the l classes is considered. Here the hidden layer nodes model the first level (innermost) operator in the antecedent part of a rule, which can be either a conjunct or a disjunct. The output layer nodes model the outer level operator, which can again be either a conjunct or a disjunct. As mentioned earlier, the dependency factor of any rule is one in this method. The initial weight encoding procedure is the same as described before. Since each class has multiple objects, the sign of the weight is set randomly.

9.5   RESULTS

Here we provide some of the results [8, 9] of these methods on real life (*vowel* of Fig. 3.4) and artificial (pattern set C of Fig. 3.7) data. The initial weight encoding scheme is demonstrated and recognition scores presented. The six overlapping vowel classes and the three linearly nonseparable classes of pattern set C are denoted by $c_1, \ldots, c_6$, and c_1, c_2, c_3, respectively, in the sequel.

The training set considered 50% of the data selected randomly from each of the pattern classes. The remaining 50% data constituted the test set. It is found that the knowledge-based model converges to a good solution with a small number of training epochs (iterations) in both cases. Note that the *vowel* data consist of convex classes that may be modeled by single representative points (objects). On the other hand, pattern set C consists of concave and disjoint classes that can be modeled only by multiple representative points (objects). As method 1 considers single-object classes only, the synthetic data could not be used there, whereas both data sets are used in method 2, which considers multiple objects in a class.

9.5.1   Method 1

The rough set theoretic technique is applied on the vowel data to extract some knowledge that is initially encoded among the connection weights of the fuzzy MLP. The data is first transformed into the $3n$-dimensional linguistic space of eqn. (3.28). A threshold of $Th = 0.8$ is imposed on the resultant input components such that $y_i^0 = 1$ if $y_i^0 \geq 0.8$ and $y_i^0 = 0$ otherwise. The resulting information is represented in the form of a decision table $\mathcal{S} =< U, A >$ as in Table 9.1.

Let us explain this transformation by an example. Let a sample pattern from class c_1 have numerical components $F_1 = 600$, $F_2 = 1500$, $F_3 = 1200$. This is mapped to the nine-dimensional linguistic space with components $L_1 = 0.4$, $M_1 = 0.85$, $H_1 = 0.7$, $L_2 = 0.8$, $M_2 = 0.9$, $H_2 = 0.4$, $L_3 = 0.82$, $M_3 = 0.7$, $H_3 = 0.4$. Application of Th yields a nine-dimensional vector $(0,1,0,1,1,0,1,0,0)$. Let class c_1 consist of n_1 pattern vectors. Each of them is transformed to this nine-dimensional form with binary components. We select the most representative template, $i.e.$, the one with the maximum number of occurrences, from this set of n_1 templates to serve as object x_1.

U consists of six objects $x_1, \ldots, x_6$, the condition attributes are L_1, L_2, L_3, M_1, M_2, M_3, H_1, H_2, H_3 and the decision attribute set D consists of the six vowel classes $c_1, \ldots, c_6$. Each entry in row j, column i corresponds to the input y_i^0 for class c_j. Note that these inputs are used only for the knowledge encoding procedure. During the refinement phase, the network learns from the original $3n$-dimensional training set with $0 \le y_i^0 \le 1$ [eqn. (3.28)].

The decision table is abbreviated by putting all the decision attributes in one column [this does not result in any ambiguity, as the object x_i is assumed to correspond to the decision attribute c_i only ($i = 1, \ldots, 6$)].

Table 9.1   Attribute-value table of *vowel* data

	L_1	M_1	H_1	L_2	M_2	H_2	L_3	M_3	H_3	D
x_1	0	1	0	1	1	0	1	0	0	c_1
x_2	0	0	1	1	0	0	1	1	0	c_2
x_3	1	0	0	0	0	1	0	0	1	c_3
x_4	1	0	0	1	0	0	0	1	0	c_4
x_5	1	1	0	0	0	1	0	1	0	c_5
x_6	1	1	0	1	0	0	1	0	0	c_6

The D-reducts obtained are as follows:
$(L_1 \wedge M_1 \wedge L_2), (L_1 \wedge L_2 \wedge M_3), (L_1 \wedge M_1 \wedge H_2), (L_1 \wedge H_2 \wedge M_3), (L_1 \wedge M_1 \wedge M_3),$
$(L_1 \wedge M_1 \wedge L_3 \wedge H_3), (M_1 \wedge H_1 \wedge L_2 \wedge M_2), (H_1 \wedge L_2 \wedge M_2 \wedge M_3),$
$(M_1 \wedge H_1 \wedge M_2 \wedge H_2), (H_1 \wedge M_2 \wedge H_2 \wedge M_3), (M_1 \wedge H_1 \wedge M_2 \wedge M_3),$
$(M_1 \wedge L_2 \wedge M_2 \wedge L_3), (L_2 \wedge M_2 \wedge L_3 \wedge M_3), (M_1 \wedge M_2 \wedge H_2 \wedge L_3),$
$(M_2 \wedge H_2 \wedge L_3 \wedge M_3), (M_1 \wedge M_2 \wedge L_3 \wedge M_3), (M_1 \wedge M_2 \wedge L_3 \wedge H_3),$
$(L_1 \wedge H_1 \wedge L_2 \wedge L_3 \wedge H_3), (L_1 \wedge L_2 \wedge M_2 \wedge L_3 \wedge H_3),$
$(L_1 \wedge H_1 \wedge H_2 \wedge L_3 \wedge H_3), (L_1 \wedge M_2 \wedge H_2 \wedge L_3 \wedge H_3),$
$(H_1 \wedge L_2 \wedge M_2 \wedge L_3 \wedge H_3), (H_1 \wedge M_2 \wedge H_2 \wedge L_3 \wedge H_3),$
$(M_1 \wedge H_1 \wedge M_2 \wedge L_3 \wedge H_3).$

Let us consider the reduct set $B = (L_1 \wedge M_1 \wedge M_3)$. Then the discernibility function $f_D^{x_i}$ (in cnf) for $i = 1, \ldots, 6$, obtained from the discernibility matrix $\mathbf{M}_D(B)$ [using eqns. (9.5) and (9.6)], are
$f_D^{x_1} = L_1 \wedge (M_1 \vee M_3)$, $f_D^{x_2} = L_1 \wedge (M_1 \vee M_3)$, $f_D^{x_3} = M_1 \wedge M_3$,
$f_D^{x_4} = L_1 \wedge M_1 \wedge M_3$, $f_D^{x_5} = M_1 \wedge M_3$, $f_D^{x_6} = L_1 \wedge M_1 \wedge M_3$.

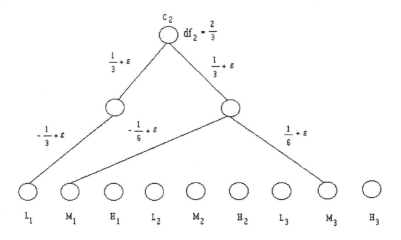

Fig. 9.2 Initial weight encoding for class c_2, using method 1; remaining weights initialized to small random values

The dependency factors df_i for the resulting rules $r_i, i = 1, \ldots, 6$ are $\frac{2}{3}$, $\frac{2}{3}$, 1, 1, 1, 1, using eqn. (9.7).

In the same way one may consider the remaining D-reducts and find the corresponding rules and their dependency factors. These factors are encoded as the initial connection weights of the fuzzy MLP. Let us now explain the process with an example. Consider the rule r_2, *viz.*, $L_1 \wedge (M_1 \vee M_3) \to c_2$ with dependency factor $df_2 = 2/3$. Here one needs two hidden nodes corresponding to class c_2 to model the operator $\wedge$. The two links from the output node representing class c_2 to these two hidden nodes are assigned weights of $(df_2/2)$ to keep the weights equally distributed. From Table 9.1 it is seen that the entries for L_1, M_1, M_3 in case of class c_2 are 0,0,1, respectively. The attributes M_1 and M_3, connected by the operator $\vee$, are combined at one hidden node with link weights of $-(df_2/4)$, $(df_2/4)$ respectively, while the link weight for attribute L_1 is clamped to $-(df_2/2)$ (since there is no further bifurcation). All other connection weights are assigned very small random weights ε, lying in the range $[-0.005, +0.005]$. The resultant network is finally refined during training, using a training set. Performance of the network is validated on the test set. Figure 9.2 illustrates the weight encoding procedure for class c_2.

Table 9.2 shows the results obtained with a three-layered knowledge-based network whose connection weights are initially encoded as explained earlier. It is observed that this method functions more efficiently with a smaller network. Therefore, we demonstrate the results corresponding to six hidden nodes (the lower bound in this case) only. The performance is compared with those of the conventional and fuzzy MLP (Section 3.3), having the same number of hidden nodes but with no initial knowledge encoding. It was seen that the conventional MLP with six hidden nodes is unable to classify the data.

Hence this is not included in the table. It may be noticed that this method generated D-reducts of different sizes. In the table, R_n indicates a collection of D-reducts with n components (attributes).

Table 9.2 Percent correct recognition scores on *vowel* data, using method 1

Attributes	Fuzzy MLP	Rough–fuzzy MLP						
		R_5		R_4			R_3	
		$L_1, M_2,$ $H_2,$ L_3, H_3	$L_1, H_1,$ $L_2,$ L_3, H_3	$M_1, M_2,$ L_3, H_3	$H_1, M_2,$ H_2, M_3	$M_1, H_1,$ L_2, M_2	$L_1,$ $M_1,$ L_2	$L_1,$ $M_1,$ H_2
b	80.9	83.2	80.0	83.4	82.3	79.5	80.7	83.9
∂	21.6	62.2	27.0	45.9	54.1	29.7	27.0	40.5
a	82.2	82.2	88.9	84.4	86.7	88.9	88.9	84.4
i	94.1	82.4	95.3	94.1	85.9	94.1	82.4	84.7
u	87.8	87.8	87.8	87.8	87.8	87.8	87.8	90.2
e	88.7	90.6	87.7	90.6	94.3	90.5	97.2	96.2
o	95.1	95.1	95.1	93.9	95.1	93.9	95.1	93.9
Net	84.4	86.0	85.6	87.0	87.2	85.8	85.4	86.5

9.5.2 Method 2

This method is applied to both *vowel* and pattern set C. A threshold of $Th = 0.8$ was used for the *vowel* data. It can be observed from Fig. 3.7 that the synthetic data set is uniformly distributed over the entire feature space. Therefore, setting a threshold greater than 0.5 caused problems here, such that for certain objects all three input components corresponding to a feature became clamped at zero. To circumvent this, $Th = 0.5$ for pattern set C.

9.5.2.1 Vowel data Each class had a separate attribute-value table consisting of multiple objects. Let us consider class c_6 as an example. The first column of Table 9.3 corresponds to the objects whose attribute values are indicated in the respective rows. Observe that the rows correspond to 20, 9, 7, 5, 4, 4, 2, 2, 1, 1, and 1 objects, respectively.

After applying the threshold Tr of eqn. (9.8), objects $x_{42} - x_{56}$ are eliminated from the table. Hence the reduced attribute-value table (Table 9.4) now consists of four rows only.

The discernibility matrix for class c_6 is

Table 9.3   Attribute-value table for class c_6 of *vowel* data

	L_1	M_1	H_1	L_2	M_2	H_2	L_3	M_3	H_3
$x_1 - x_{20}$	1	0	0	1	0	0	1	0	0
$x_{21} - x_{29}$	1	1	0	1	0	0	1	0	0
$x_{30} - x_{36}$	1	1	0	1	0	0	0	0	1
$x_{37} - x_{41}$	1	1	0	1	0	0	0	1	0
$x_{42} - x_{45}$	1	1	0	1	0	0	0	1	1
$x_{46} - x_{49}$	1	0	0	1	0	0	0	1	1
$x_{50} - x_{51}$	0	1	0	1	0	0	0	1	1
$x_{52} - x_{53}$	0	1	0	1	0	0	1	0	0
x_{54}	1	0	0	1	0	0	1	1	0
x_{55}	0	1	0	1	0	0	0	0	1
x_{56}	1	0	0	1	0	0	0	0	1

Table 9.4   Reduced attribute-value table for class c_6 of *vowel* data

	L_1	M_1	H_1	L_2	M_2	H_2	L_3	M_3	H_3
$x_1 - x_{20} : (y_1)$	1	0	0	1	0	0	1	0	0
$x_{21} - x_{29} : (y_2)$	1	1	0	1	0	0	1	0	0
$x_{30} - x_{36} : (y_3)$	1	1	0	1	0	0	0	0	1
$x_{37} - x_{41} : (y_4)$	1	1	0	1	0	0	0	1	0

	y_1	y_2	y_3	y_4
y_1	ϕ			
y_2	$\{M_1\}$	ϕ		
y_3	$\{M_1, L_3, H_3\}$	$\{L_3, H_3\}$	ϕ	
y_4	$\{M_1, L_3, M_3\}$	$\{L_3, M_3\}$	$\{M_3, H_3\}$	ϕ

The discernibility function f for c_6 is

$$M_1 \wedge (M_1 \vee L_3 \vee H_3) \wedge (L_3 \vee H_3) \wedge (M_1 \vee L_3 \vee M_3) \wedge (L_3 \vee M_3) \wedge (M_3 \vee H_3)$$

$$= M_1 \wedge (L_3 \vee H_3) \wedge (L_3 \vee M_3) \wedge (M_3 \vee H_3).$$

The disjunctive normal form of f is

$$(M_1 \wedge L_3 \wedge M_3) \vee (M_1 \wedge L_3 \wedge H_3) \vee (M_1 \wedge M_3 \wedge H_3) \vee (M_1 \wedge L_3 \wedge M_3 \wedge H_3).$$

The resultant reducts are

$$M_1 \wedge L_3 \wedge M_3, \quad M_1 \wedge L_3 \wedge H_3, \quad M_1 \wedge M_3 \wedge H_3.$$

The reduced attribute-value table for reduct $M_1 \wedge L_3 \wedge M_3$ is

	M_1	L_3	M_3
y_1	0	1	0
y_2	1	1	0
y_3	1	0	0
y_4	1	0	1

The reduced discernibility matrix for $M_1 \wedge L_3 \wedge M_3$ is

	y_1	y_2	y_3	y_4
y_1	ϕ			
y_2	$\{M_1\}$	ϕ		
y_3	$\{M_1, L_3\}$	$\{L_3\}$	ϕ	
y_4	$\{M_1, L_3, M_3\}$	$\{L_3, M_3\}$	$\{M_3\}$	ϕ

The discernibility functions f_{y_i} for each object y_i, $i = 1, 2, 3, 4$ are

$$\begin{aligned}
f_{y_1} &= M_1 \wedge (M_1 \vee L_3) \wedge (M_1 \vee L_3 \vee M_3) &&= M_1 \\
f_{y_2} &= M_1 \wedge L_3 \wedge (L_3 \vee M_3) &&= M_1 \wedge L_3 \\
f_{y_3} &= (M_1 \vee L_3) \wedge L_3 \wedge M_3 &&= M_3 \wedge L_3 \\
f_{y_4} &= (M_1 \vee L_3 \vee M_3) \wedge (L_3 \vee M_3) \wedge M_3 &&= M_3.
\end{aligned}$$

A dependency rule thus generated for class c_6 is

$$M_1 \vee (M_1 \wedge L_3) \vee (M_3 \wedge L_3) \vee M_3 \rightarrow c_6,$$

$$i.e., \quad M_1 \vee M_3 \rightarrow c_6.$$

The other rules for c_6 are

$$M_1 \ \lor \ H_3 \ \to \ c_6,$$

and

$$M_1 \ \lor \ M_3 \ \lor \ H_3 \ \to \ c_6.$$

Similarly, one can obtain 1,2,1,1,2 dependency rules for the classes c_1, c_2, c_3, c_4, c_5, respectively. The dependency factor for each rule is one. So, considering all possible combinations one generates 12 sets of rules for the six classes. Therefore, this leads to 12 possible network encodings.

A sample set of dependency rules generated for the six classes is
$H_1 \land L_2 \land L_3 \to c_1$, $M_1 \lor L_3 \to c_2$, $M_3 \lor H_3 \to c_3$, $M_3 \lor H_3 \to c_4$, $M_3 \to c_5$, $M_1 \lor M_3 \to c_6$.
This corresponds to the network represented in column 1 (of rough–fuzzy MLP) in Table 9.5.

Table 9.5 Percent correct recognition scores of *vowel* data, using method 2

Attr. for	Rough–fuzzy MLP					
c_1, c_3, c_4	$H_1 \land L_2 \land L_3$;		$M_3 \lor H_3$;		$M_3 \lor H_3$	
c_2	$M_1 \lor L_3$		$M_1 \lor M_3$			
c_5	M_3				H_3	
c_6	$M_1 \lor M_3$	$M_1 \lor M_3$ $\lor H_3$	$M_1 \lor M_3$	$M_1 \lor H_3$	$M_1 \lor M_3$	$M_1 \lor M_3$ $\lor H_3$
b	85.48	80.65	81.11	80.19	83.18	82.72
∂	51.4	21.6	56.8	43.2	54.1	59.5
a	84.4	88.9	82.2	88.9	82.2	75.6
i	94.1	85.9	95.3	85.9	94.1	87.1
u	90.2	86.6	87.8	87.8	90.2	87.8
e	84.0	97.2	78.3	93.4	82.1	84.9
o	93.9	93.9	95.1	93.9	93.9	93.9
Net	86.27	85.13	85.13	86.27	85.81	84.44

To encode the rule for class c_6, one hidden node is required for modeling the conjunct. The corresponding output node is connected to the hidden node with an initial link weight of $df_6 = 1$. Then the input attribute pair (M_1, M_3) is connected to this hidden node with link weights $df_6/2 \ (= 0.5)$. All other connection weights are assigned very small random weights ε, lying in the range $[-0.005, +0.005]$. The resultant network is finally refined during training, using a training set. The performance of the network is tested on the remaining test set. A sample network is illustrated in Fig. 9.3.

Table 9.5 demonstrates sample results obtained using the three-layered knowledge-based network. Unlike method 1, in all cases method 2 constructed

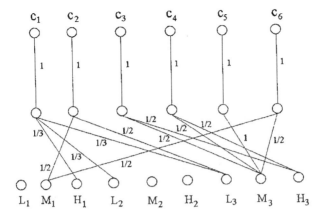

Fig. 9.3 ınitial weight encoding for a sample network, using method 2; remaining weights initialized to small random values

networks with six hidden nodes. Its performance improves over that of the fuzzy and conventional versions of the MLP (as observed from Table 9.2).

9.5.2.2 Synthetic data The attribute-value table for class c_2 is depicted in Table 9.6. The rows correspond to 16,12,9,8,3,2,1 objects, respectively. Application of eqn. (9.8) results in the elimination of objects $x_{46} - x_{51}$. The D-reducts generated are
$L_1 \wedge L_2, H_1 \wedge L_2, H_1 \wedge H_2, L_1 \wedge H_2$.
Similarly, one obtains four D-reducts for each of the other two classes. Considering all possible combinations, 64 sets of rules are generated for the three classes. Therefore, this results in 64 possible network encodings.

Table 9.6 Attribute-value table for class c_2 of pattern set C

	L_1	M_1	H_1	L_2	M_2	H_2
$x_1 - x_{16}$	1	1	0	1	1	0
$x_{17} - x_{28}$	1	1	0	0	1	1
$x_{29} - x_{37}$	0	1	1	1	1	0
$x_{38} - x_{45}$	0	1	1	0	1	1
$x_{46} - x_{48}$	1	1	0	0	0	1
$x_{49} - x_{50}$	0	1	1	0	0	1
x_{51}	1	1	0	1	0	0

A sample set of dependency rules for the three classes is
$(L_1 \wedge M_2 \wedge H_2) \vee (L_1 \wedge M_1 \wedge H_2) \to c_1$, $H_1 \wedge H_2 \to c_2$,
$(M_1 \wedge H_1) \vee (H_1 \wedge M_2 \wedge H_2) \vee (M_1 \wedge M_2 \wedge H_2) \to c_3$.
This corresponds to column 3 of Table 9.7.

Table 9.7   Percent correct recognition scores of pattern set C, using method 2

		Rough–fuzzy MLP		
c_1		$(L_1 \wedge M_2 \wedge H_2)$ $\vee(L_1 \wedge M_1 \wedge H_2)$	$(H_1 \wedge M_2 \wedge H_2)$ $\vee(M_1 \wedge M_2 \wedge H_2)$	$(H_1 \wedge L_2 \wedge M_2)$ $\vee(M_1 \wedge H_1 \wedge L_2)$
c_2		$H_1 \wedge H_2$	$L_1 \wedge H_2$	$H_1 \wedge H_2$
c_3		$(M_1 \wedge H_1)$	$(L_1 \wedge M_1)$	$(M_1 \wedge H_1)$
	Fuzzy	$\vee(H_1 \wedge M_2 \wedge H_2)$	$\vee(L_1 \wedge L_2 \wedge M_2)$	$\vee(H_1 \wedge L_2 \wedge M_2)$
	MLP	$\vee(M_1 \wedge M_2 \wedge H_2)$	$\vee(M_1 \wedge L_2 \wedge M_2)$	$\vee(M_1 \wedge L_2 \wedge M_2)$
b	82.0	84.05	80.87	83.83
1	88.08	93.08	84.23	91.54
2	69.23	69.23	65.38	57.69
3	68.39	68.39	81.94	67.1
Net	80.05	82.99	82.31	80.95

The subnetwork for class c_3 consists of three hidden nodes, each with initial output link weight of $df_3/3$ ($= 0.33$). The input attribute pair (M_1, H_1) is connected to the first of these hidden nodes with link weights $df_3/6$ ($= 0.17$). The remaining attributes (H_1, M_2, H_2) and (M_1, M_2, H_2) are connected to the next two hidden nodes with link weights $df_3/9$ ($= 0.11$). Table 9.7 provides a sample set of results obtained by a three-layered knowledge-based network.

Note that in all the 64 encodings the algorithm generated networks with six hidden nodes. The performance was compared with that of the conventional and the fuzzy MLP. The conventional MLP failed to recognize class c_2 (e.g., the scores for classes c_1, c_2, and c_3 were 87.1, 0.0, and 51.6, respectively, for the test set). The rough–fuzzy MLP is found to generalize better than the fuzzy MLP for the test patterns, considering both overall and classwise scores. Banerjee et al. further compared the rough–fuzzy MLP with other related techniques [9].   ♣

Remarks

1. Method 1 is based on the assumption that there is one decision attribute corresponding to each object, i.e., the classes are considered to be convex with single representative points. This method is not a special case of method 2, although the latter deals with multiple representative points for each class.

2. The decision table (constructed from the initial data) is transformed by dividing it into subtables, each corresponding to a decision attribute of

the given system. The initial table gave rise to discernibility functions [computed by eqn. (9.6)] with too large a number of components and hence a network with a huge number of hidden nodes. The computational complexity of such a network was not considered to be feasible. On the contrary, the subtables resulted in the generation of discernibility functions with less components and thus finally, a less cumbersome (more efficient) network.

3. Each decision table considered so far is clearly consistent.

4. Any comparative study of the performance of the model should consider the fact that here the appropriate number of hidden nodes is automatically generated by the rough set theoretic knowledge encoding procedure. On the other hand, both the fuzzy and conventional versions of the MLP are required to empirically generate a suitable size of the hidden layer(s). Hence this can be considered to be an added advantage.

5. Unlike other hybrid approaches involving rough sets (as mentioned in Section 9.3), the rough–fuzzy MLP considers an integration of the three soft computing paradigms: neural nets, rough sets, and fuzzy sets. The network has adaptive weights in all the layers. The process of rule generation and mapping of the dependency factors to the connection weight values is novel to this approach.

REFERENCES

1. Z. Pawlak, *Rough Sets, Theoretical Aspects of Reasoning about Data.* Dordrecht: Kluwer Academic, 1991.

2. R. Slowiński, ed., *Intelligent Decision Support, Handbook of Applications and Advances of the Rough Sets Theory.* Dordrecht: Kluwer Academic, 1992.

3. S. K. Pal and A. Skowron, eds., *Rough-Fuzzy Hybridization: New Trends in Decision Making.* Singapore: Springer-Verlag, 1999.

4. E. Orlowska, ed., *Incomplete Information: Rough Set Analysis.* Heidelberg: Physica Verlag, 1998.

5. A. Skowron and C. Rauszer, "The discernibility matrices and functions in information systems," in *Intelligent Decision Support, Handbook of Applications and Advances of the Rough Sets Theory,* R. Slowiński, ed., pp. 331–362. Dordrecht: Kluwer Academic, 1992.

6. R. Yasdi, "Combining rough sets learning and neural learning method to deal with uncertain and imprecise information," *Neurocomputing,* vol. 7, pp. 61–84, 1995.

7. A. Czyzewski and A. Kaczmarek, "Speech recognition systems based on rough sets and neural networks," in *Proceedings of Third Workshop on Rough Sets and Soft Computing (RSSC'94)*, (San Jose, USA), pp. 97–100, 1994.

8. S. Mitra, M. Banerjee, and S. K. Pal, "Rough knowledge-based network, fuzziness and classification," *Neural Computing and Applications*, vol. 7, pp. 17–25, 1998.

9. M. Banerjee, S. Mitra, and S. K. Pal, "Rough fuzzy MLP: Knowledge encoding and classification," *IEEE Transactions on Neural Networks*, vol. 9, pp. 1203–1216, 1998.

10. S. Mitra and M. Banerjee, "Knowledge-based neural net with rough sets," in *Proceedings of 4th International Conf. on Soft Computing, Iizuka* (Japan), pp. 213–216, October 1996.

11. M. Banerjee, S. Mitra, and S. K. Pal, "Knowledge-based fuzzy MLP with rough sets," in *Proceedings of IEEE International Conference on Neural Networks* (Houston, USA), pp. 499–504, June 1997.

12. L. M. Fu, "Knowledge-based connectionism for revising domain theories," *IEEE Transactions on Systems, Man, and Cybernetics*, vol. 23, pp. 173–182, 1993.

13. G. G. Towell and J. W. Shavlik, "Knowledge-based artificial neural networks," *Artificial Intelligence*, vol. 70, pp. 119–165, 1994.

14. M. Sarkar and B. Yegnanarayana, "Fuzzy-rough sets and fuzzy integrals in modular neural networks," in *Rough-Fuzzy Hybridization: New Trends in Decision Making*, S. K. Pal and A. Skowron, eds., Singapore: Springer-Verlag, 1999.

Appendix A
Genetic Algorithms: Basic Principles, Features

One of the major ingredients of soft computing (Section 2.7 of Chapter 2) is genetic algorithms (GAs). These are also used in a neuro-fuzzy–genetic hybridization described in Section 5.3 of Chapter 5. Therefore, let us mention here the basic characteristics and operators of GAs, to enable a clearer understanding of this book.

Genetic algorithms [1]–[4] (GAs) are adaptive computational procedures modeled on the mechanics of natural genetic systems. They express their ability by efficiently exploiting the historical information to speculate on new offspring with expected improved performance [3]. GAs are executed iteratively on a set of coded solutions, called *population,* with three basic operators: *selection–reproduction, crossover,* and *mutation.* They use only the payoff (objective function) information and probabilistic transition rules for moving to the next iteration. They are different from most of the normal optimization and search procedures in four ways:

- GAs work with the coding of the parameter set, not with the parameter themselves.

- GAs work simultaneously with multiple points, and not a single point.

- GAs search via sampling (a blind search) using only the payoff information.

- GAs search using stochastic operators, not deterministic rules.

Since a GA works simultaneously on a set of coded solutions, it has very little chance to get stuck at local optima when used as an optimization technique. Again, it does not need any sort of auxiliary information, such as a derivative of the optimizing function. Moreover, the resolution of the possible search space is increased by operating on coded (possible) solutions and not on the solutions themselves. Further, this search space need not be continuous.

GAs are intended to mimic some of the processes observed in natural evolution. The evolution starts from a set of individuals (assumed solution set for the function to be optimized) and proceeds from generation to generation through genetic operations. Replacement of an old population with a new one is known as *generation* when a generational replacement technique (replace all the members of old population with the new ones) is used. Another reproduction technique, called *steady-state-reproduction*, replaces one or more individuals at a time instead of the whole population [2]. GAs require only a suitable objective function that acts as the environment in order to evaluate the suitability of the derived solutions (chromosomes).

Although there are many variants, the basic mechanism of GAs (conventional GAs) consists of the following steps:

1. Start with an initial population (a set of strings or chromosomes)

2. Evaluation of fitness of every string and selection of appropriate candidate strings to form the mating pool

3. Crossover and mutation

4. Repetition of steps 2 and 3 until the system ceases to improve, or some stopping criterion is reached

A GA typically consists of the following components:

- A population of binary strings or coded possible solutions (biologically referred to as *chromosomes*)

- A mechanism to encode a possible solution (mostly as a binary string)

- Objective function and associated fitness evaluation techniques

- Selection–reproduction procedure

- Genetic operators (crossover and mutation)

- Probabilities to perform genetic operations

Let us briefly describe these components

Population   To solve an optimization problem, GAs start with the chromosomal (structural) representation of a parameter set $\{x_1, x_2, \ldots, x_p\}$. The parameter set is to be coded as a finite-length string over an alphabet of finite length. Usually, the chromosomes are strings of zeros and ones. For example, let $\{a_1, a_2, \ldots, a_p\}$ be a realization of the parameter set and the binary representation of a_1, a_2, ..., a_p be 10110, 00100, ..., 11001, respectively. Then the string 10110 00100 ... 11001 is a chromosomal representation of the parameter set. It is evident that the number of different chromosomes (strings) is 2^l, where l is the string length. Each chromosome actually refers to a coded possible solution. A set of such chromosomes in a generation is called a *population*. The size of a population may vary from one generation to another, or it can be constant. Usually, the initial population is chosen randomly.

Encoding/decoding mechanism   This mechanism converts the parameter values of a possible solution into binary strings resulting in chromosomal representation. If the solution of a problem depends on p parameters and if we want to encode each parameter with a binary string of length q, then the length of each chromosome will be $p \times q$. Decoding is just the reverse of encoding.

Objective function and associated fitness evaluation techniques
The fitness or objective function is chosen depending on the problem. It is chosen in a way such that highly fitted strings (possible solutions) have high fitness values. It is the only index to select a chromosome to reproduce for the next generation.

Selection–reproduction procedure   The selection–reproduction process copies individual strings (called *parent chromosomes*) into a tentative new population (known as *mating pool*) for genetic operations. The number of copies reproduced for the next generation by an individual is expected to be directly proportional to its fitness value, thereby mimicking the natural selection procedure to some extent. Roulette wheel parent selection [3] and linear selection [2] are the most frequently used selection procedures.

Genetic operators are applied on parent chromosomes, and new chromosomes (called *offspring*) are generated. Frequently used genetic operators are described below.

Crossover   The main purpose of crossover is to exchange information between randomly selected parent chromosomes by recombining parts of their corresponding strings. Actually, it recombines genetic material of two parent chromosomes to produce offspring for the next generation. The crossover may proceed in two steps: (1) members of the reproduced strings in the mating pool are mated at random, and (2) each pair of strings undergoes crossing over when an integer position k is selected uniformly at random between 1 and $l - 1$, where l is the string length greater than 1. Two new strings are created by swapping all characters from position $(k + 1)$ to l. Let

$$a = 11000\ 10101\ 01000 \ldots 01111\ 10001$$
$$b = 10001\ 01110\ 11101 \ldots 00110\ 10100$$

be two strings (parents) selected for the crossing-over operation and the generated random number be 11 (eleven). Then the newly produced offspring (swapping all characters after position 11) will be

$$a' = 11000\ 10101\ 01101 \ldots 00110\ 10100$$
$$b' = 10001\ 01110\ 11000 \ldots 01111\ 10001.$$

Some common crossover techniques are one-point crossover, multiple-point crossover, shuffle-exchange crossover, and uniform crossover [2].

Mutation The main aim of mutation is to introduce genetic diversity into the population. Sometimes, it helps to regain the information lost in earlier generations. In case of binary representation, it negates the bit value and is known as *bit mutation*. Like natural genetic systems, mutation in GAs also occurs occasionally. A random bit position of a random string is selected and is replaced by an another character from the alphabet. For example, let the third bit of string a, given above, be selected for mutation. Then the transformed string after mutation will be

$$11100\ 10101\ 01000 \ldots 01111\ 10001.$$

Mutation is not always worth performing. A high mutation rate can lead the genetic search to a random one. It may change the value of an important bit, and thereby affect the fast convergence to a good solution. Moreover, it may slow down the process of convergence at the final stage of GAs.

Probabilities to perform genetic operations The probability to perform crossover operation is chosen in such a way that recombination of potential strings (highly fitted chromosomes) increases without any disruption. Generally, the crossover probability lies in between 0.6 and 0.9 [2, 3]. Since mutation occurs occasionally, it is clear that the probability of performing mutation operation will be very low. Typically the value lies between 0.001 to 0.01 [2, 3].

Elitism In standard GA (SGA) we do not preserve the best possible solution obtained so far, thereby increasing the chance of losing the obtainable best possible solution. *Elitist* strategy overcomes this problem by copying the best member of each generation into the next one. Although this strategy may increase the speed of dominance of a population by a potential string (string with high fitness value), it enhances the performance of a GA using generational replacement.   ♣

Concepts of distributed GAs and parallel GAs have also been introduced [5, 6]. Recent studies on the convergence of GAs can be found elsewhere in the literature [7, 8].

REFERENCES

1. L. Davis, ed., *Genetic Algorithms and Simulated Annealing*. Los Altos: Morgan-Kaufmann, 1987.

2. L. Davis, *Handbook of Genetic Algorithms*. New York: Van Nostrand Reinhold, 1991.

3. D. E. Goldberg, *Genetic Algorithms in Search, Optimization and Machine Learning*. Reading, MA: Addison-Wesley, 1989.

4. Z. Michalewicz, *Genetic Algorithms + Data Structures = Evolutionary Programs*. Berlin: Springer-Verlag, 1994.

5. D. Whitley, T. Starkweather, and C. Bogart, "Genetic algorithms and neural networks: Optimizing connections and connectivity," *Parallel Computing*, vol. 14, pp. 347–361, 1990.

6. V. Maniezzo, "Genetic evolution of the topology and weight distribution of neural networks," *IEEE Transactions on Neural Networks*, vol. 5, pp. 39–53, 1994.

7. C. A. Murthy, D. Bhandari, and S. K. Pal, "ε-optimal stopping time for genetic algorithms," *Fundamenta Informaticae*, vol. 35, pp. 91–111, 1998.

8. D. Bhandari, C. A. Murthy, and S. K. Pal, "Genetic algorithm with elitist model and its convergence," *International Journal of Pattern Recognition and Artificial Intelligence*, vol. 10, pp. 731–747, 1996.

Appendix B
Derivation of the
Expression for $\mathcal{E}(E)$

In this appendix we derive eqn. (6.37) (from Chapter 6.
For a pattern $\mathbf{x} \in C_k$,

$$\frac{\mu_k(1-\mu_k)\alpha_k}{\frac{1}{2}\sum_{k'\neq k}[\mu_k \times (1-\mu_{k'}) + \mu_{k'} \times (1-\mu_k)]} = \frac{\mu_k(1-\mu_k)\alpha_k}{\frac{1}{2}\sum_{k'\neq k}[\mu_k + \mu_{k'} - 2\mu_k\mu_{k'}]}$$

$$= \frac{\mu_k(1-\mu_k)\alpha_k}{\frac{1}{2}\mu_k\sum_{k'\neq k}[1 - (2 - \frac{1}{\mu_k})\mu_{k'}]}$$

$$= \frac{(1-\mu_k)\alpha_k}{\frac{1}{2}[(l-1) - (2 - \frac{1}{\mu_k})\sum_{k'\neq k}\mu_{k'}]}$$

$$= \frac{(1-\mu_k)\alpha_k}{\frac{1}{2}(l-1)[1 - (2 - \frac{1}{\mu_k})\frac{\sum_{k'\neq k}\mu_{k'}}{l-1}]}$$

$$\approx \frac{2(1-\mu_k)\alpha_k}{(l-1)}\left[1 + (2 - \frac{1}{\mu_k})\frac{\sum_{k'\neq k}\mu_{k'}}{l-1}\right]$$

as $(2 - \frac{1}{\mu_k})(\frac{\sum\limits_{k' \neq k} \mu_{k'}}{l-1}) < 1.$

Thus $\dfrac{\mu_k(1-\mu_k)\alpha_k}{\frac{1}{2}\sum\limits_{k' \neq k}[\mu_k \times (1-\mu_{k'})+\mu_{k'} \times (1-\mu_k)]} = $

$$\frac{2\alpha_k}{l-1}\left(1 - \mu_k + \left(3 - 2\mu_k - \frac{1}{\mu_k}\right)\frac{\sum\limits_{k' \neq k}\mu_{k'}}{l-1}\right).$$

Therefore, using eqn. (6.38),

$$\mathcal{E}\left(\frac{\mu_k(1-\mu_k)\alpha_k}{\frac{1}{2}\sum\limits_{k' \neq k}[\mu_k \times (1-\mu_{k'})+\mu_{k'} \times (1-\mu_k)]}\right)$$

is given by $\mathcal{E}\left(\dfrac{\mu_k(1-\mu_k)\alpha_k}{\frac{1}{2}\sum\limits_{k' \neq k}[\mu_k \times (1-\mu_{k'})+\mu_{k'} \times (1-\mu_k)]}\right) = $

$$\int_{\mathbf{x} \in C_k}\frac{\mu_k(1-\mu_k)\alpha_k}{\frac{1}{2}\sum\limits_{k' \neq k}[\mu_k \times (1-\mu_{k'})+\mu_{k'} \times (1-\mu_k)]}\mathcal{P}(\mathbf{x})d\mathbf{x} \approx$$

$$\int_{x_1=-\infty}^{\infty}\cdots\int_{x_n=-\infty}^{\infty}\frac{2\alpha_k}{l-1}\left(1 - \mu_k + (3 - 2\mu_k - \frac{1}{\mu_k})\frac{\sum\limits_{k' \neq k}\mu_{k'}}{l-1}\right)p_k\mathcal{P}(\mathbf{x}|C_k)dx_1$$

$\ldots dx_n.$ Let J_k

$$= \int_{x_1=-\infty}^{\infty}\cdots\int_{x_n=-\infty}^{\infty}(1-\mu_k)p_k\frac{1}{(\sqrt{2\pi}\sigma)^n}\exp\left(-\sum_i\frac{(x_i-m_{ki})^2}{2\sigma^2}\right)dx_1\ldots dx_n$$

$$= p_k - p_k\int_{x_1=-\infty}^{\infty}\cdots\int_{x_n=-\infty}^{\infty}\mu_k\frac{1}{(\sqrt{2\pi}\sigma)^n}\exp\left(-\sum_i\frac{(x_i-m_{ki})^2}{2\sigma^2}\right)dx_1\ldots dx_n$$

$$= p_k - p_kJ_{k1},$$

where $J_{k1} = \displaystyle\int_{x_1=-\infty}^{\infty}\cdots\int_{x_n=-\infty}^{\infty}\mu_k\frac{1}{(\sqrt{2\pi}\sigma)^n}\exp\left(-\sum_i\frac{(x_i-m_{ki})^2}{2\sigma^2}\right)dx_1$

$\ldots dx_n.$ Also let $J_{k2} = $

$$\int_{x_1=-\infty}^{\infty}\cdots\int_{x_n=-\infty}^{\infty}(3-2\mu_k-\frac{1}{\mu_k})\sum\limits_{k' \neq k}\mu_{k'}p_k\frac{1}{\sqrt{2\pi}\sigma}\exp\left(-\sum_i\frac{(x_i-m_{ki})^2}{2\sigma^2}\right)dx_1$$

$\ldots dx_n = p_k\sum\limits_{k' \neq k}(3J_{kk'1} - 2J_{kk'2} - J_{kk'3}),$ where

$$J_{kk'1} = \int_{x_1=-\infty}^{\infty}\cdots\int_{x_n=-\infty}^{\infty}\frac{\mu_{k'}}{l-1}\frac{1}{(\sqrt{2\pi}\sigma)^n}\exp\left(-\sum_i\frac{(x_i-m_{ki})^2}{2\sigma^2}\right)dx_1\ldots dx_n,$$

$$J_{kk'2} = \int_{x_1=-\infty}^{\infty} \cdots \int_{x_n=-\infty}^{\infty} \mu_k \frac{\mu_{k'}}{l-1} \frac{1}{(\sqrt{2\pi}\sigma)^n} \exp\left(-\sum_i \frac{(x_i - m_{ki})^2}{2\sigma^2}\right) dx_1 \ldots dx_n,$$

$$J_{kk'3} = \int_{x_1=-\infty}^{\infty} \cdots \int_{x_n=-\infty}^{\infty} \frac{1}{\mu_k} \frac{\mu_{k'}}{l-1} \frac{1}{(\sqrt{2\pi}\sigma)^n} \exp\left(-\sum_i \frac{(x_i - m_{ki})^2}{2\sigma^2}\right) dx_1 \ldots dx_n.$$

Therefore

$$\mathcal{E}\left(\frac{\mu_k(1 - \mu_k)\alpha_k}{\frac{1}{2}\sum_{k' \neq k}[\mu_k \times (1 - \mu_{k'}) + \mu_{k'} \times (1 - \mu_k)]}\right) = \frac{\alpha_k}{l-1}(J_k + J_{k2}). \qquad \text{(B.1)}$$

Also assume that

$$J_{k1i} = \int_{x_i=-\infty}^{\infty} \frac{1}{\sqrt{2\pi}\sigma} \exp\left[-\frac{(x_i - m_{ki})^2}{2\sigma^2} - \frac{(x_i - m_{ki})^2 w_i^2}{2\lambda^2}\right] dx_i,$$

$$J_{kk'1i} = \int_{x_i=-\infty}^{\infty} \frac{1}{\sqrt{2\pi}\sigma} \exp\left[-\frac{(x_i - m_{ki})^2}{2\sigma^2} - \frac{(x_i - m_{k'i})^2 w_i^2}{\lambda^2}\right] dx_i,$$

$$J_{kk'2i} = \int_{x_i=-\infty}^{\infty} \frac{1}{\sqrt{2\pi}\sigma} \exp\left[-\frac{(x_i - m_{ki})^2}{2\sigma^2} - \frac{(x_i - m_{k'i})^2 w_i^2}{2\lambda^2} - \frac{(x_i - m_{ki})^2 w_i^2}{2\lambda^2}\right] dx_i,$$

$$J_{kk'3i} = \int_{x_i=-\infty}^{\infty} \frac{1}{\sqrt{2\pi}\sigma} exp\left[-\frac{(x_i - m_{ki})^2}{2\sigma^2} - \frac{(x_i - m_{k'i})^2 w_i^2}{\lambda^2} + \frac{(x_i - m_{ki})^2 w_i^2}{\lambda^2}\right] dx_i,$$

so that

$$J_k = p_k(1 - J_{k1}) = p_k\left(1 - \prod_i J_{k1i}\right)$$

and

$$J_{k2} = p_k \sum_{k' \neq k}\left(3\prod_i J_{kk'1i} - 2\prod_i J_{kk'2i} - \prod_i J_{kk'3i}\right).$$

Therefore, from eqn. (B.1) one has

$$\mathcal{E}\left(\frac{\mu_k(1 - \mu_k)\alpha_k}{\frac{1}{2}\sum_{k' \neq k}[\mu_k \times (1 - \mu_{k'}) + \mu_{k'} \times (1 - \mu_k)]}\right) = \left(\frac{\alpha_k}{l-1}\right)\left(J_k + \frac{J_{k2}}{l-1}\right).$$

$$\text{(B.2)}$$

For evaluating the integrals J_{k1i}, $J_{kk'1i}$, $J_{kk'2i}$ and $J_{kk'3i}$ one uses the result of the integral

$$J = \int_{-\infty}^{\infty} e^{-(\alpha x^2 + \beta x + \gamma)} dx.$$

Now

$$\begin{aligned} J &= \int_{-\infty}^{\infty} e^{-\alpha(x^2 + 2x\frac{\beta}{2\alpha} + \frac{\beta^2}{4\alpha^2}) + (\frac{\beta^2}{4\alpha} - \gamma)} dx \\ &= e^{(\frac{\beta^2}{4\alpha} - \gamma)} \int_{-\infty}^{\infty} e^{-\alpha(x + \frac{\beta}{2\alpha})^2} dx \\ &= e^{(\frac{\beta^2}{4\alpha} - \gamma)} \int_{-\infty}^{\infty} e^{-\alpha y^2} dy, \end{aligned}$$

where

$$y = x + \frac{\beta}{2\alpha}.$$

Therefore

$$
\begin{aligned}
J &= 2 \, \exp(\tfrac{\beta^2 - 4\alpha\gamma}{4\alpha}) \int_0^\infty e^{-\alpha y^2} \, dy \\
&= 2 \, \exp(\tfrac{\beta^2 - 4\alpha\gamma}{4\alpha}) \int_0^\infty \tfrac{1}{2\sqrt{\alpha}} e^{-z} z^{-(1/2)} \, dz,
\end{aligned}
$$

where $z = \alpha y^2$.

Hence

$$J = \frac{\exp(\tfrac{\beta^2 - 4\alpha\gamma}{4\alpha})\sqrt{\pi}}{\sqrt{\alpha}}. \tag{B.3}$$

One can use the following transformation for evaluating J_{k1i}, $J_{kk'1i}$, $J_{kk'2i}$, and $J_{kk'3i}$.

$$
\begin{aligned}
y_i &= \left(\frac{x_i - m_{ki}}{\sqrt{2}\lambda}\right) w_i, \\
dx_i &= \frac{\sqrt{2}\lambda}{w_i} dy_i.
\end{aligned}
$$

Then $\left[\frac{(x_i - m_{ki})^2 w_i^2}{2\lambda^2} + \frac{(x_i - m_{ki})^2}{2\sigma^2}\right] = y_i^2 + \frac{\rho^2}{w_i^2} y_i^2 = \left(1 + \frac{\rho^2}{w_i^2}\right) y_i^2$,

$$
\begin{aligned}
\left[\frac{(x_i - m_{k'i})^2 w_i^2}{2\lambda^2} + \frac{(x_i - m_{ki})^2}{2\sigma^2}\right] &= y_i^2 + \frac{\sqrt{2} w_i c_{kk'i}}{\lambda} y_i + \frac{c_{kk'i}^2 w_i^2}{2\lambda^2} \frac{\rho^2}{w_i^2} y_i^2 \\
&= \left(1 + \frac{\rho^2}{w_i^2}\right) y_i^2 + \frac{\sqrt{2} w_i c_{kk'i}}{\lambda} y_i + \frac{c_{kk'i}^2 w_i^2}{2\lambda^2},
\end{aligned}
$$

$$
\left[\frac{(x_i - m_{ki})^2 w_i^2}{2\lambda^2} + \frac{(x_i - m_{k'i})^2 w_i^2}{2\lambda^2} + \frac{(x_i - m_{ki})^2}{2\sigma^2}\right] = \left(2 + \frac{\rho^2}{w_i^2}\right) y_i^2 + \frac{\sqrt{2} w_i c_{kk'i}}{\lambda} y_i + \frac{c_{kk'i}^2 w_i^2}{2\lambda^2},
$$

$$
\left[-\frac{(x_i - m_{ki})^2 w_i^2}{2\lambda^2} + \frac{(x_i - m_{k'i})^2 w_i^2}{2\lambda^2} + \frac{(x_i - m_{ki})^2}{2\sigma^2}\right] = \frac{\rho^2}{w_i^2} y_i^2 + \frac{\sqrt{2} w_i c_{kk'i}}{\lambda} y_i + \frac{c_{kk'i}^2 w_i^2}{2\lambda^2}.
$$

Therefore, using the result of J [eqn. (B.3)], one has

$$
\begin{aligned}
J_{k1i} &= \frac{1}{\sqrt{2\pi}\sigma} \frac{\sqrt{2}\lambda}{w_i} \frac{1}{\left(1 + \frac{\rho^2}{w_i^2}\right)^{1/2}} \sqrt{\pi} \\
&= \frac{\rho}{(w_i^2 + \rho^2)^{1/2}},
\end{aligned}
$$

where $\alpha = (1 + \rho^2/w_i^2)$, $\beta = 0$, and $\gamma = 0$. Similarly, the expressions for $J_{kk'1i}$, $J_{kk'2i}$, and $J_{kk'3i}$ are obtained as follows.

$$
\begin{aligned}
J_{kk'1i} &= \frac{1}{\sqrt{2\pi}\sigma} \frac{\sqrt{2}\lambda}{w_i} \frac{1}{\left(1 + \frac{\rho^2}{w_i^2}\right)^{1/2}} \exp\left\{-\left[\frac{c_{kk'i}^2}{2\sigma^2\left(1 + \frac{\rho^2}{w_i^2}\right)}\right]\right\} \sqrt{\pi} \\
&= \rho \frac{\exp\left\{-\left[\frac{c_{kk'i}^2}{2\sigma^2\left(1 + \frac{\rho^2}{w_i^2}\right)}\right]\right\}}{(\rho^2 + w_i^2)^{1/2}},
\end{aligned}
$$

where $\alpha = (1 + \frac{\rho^2}{w_i^2})$, $\beta = \frac{\sqrt{2}w_i c_{kk'i}}{\lambda}$, and $\gamma = \frac{c_{kk'i}^2 w_i^2}{2\lambda^2}$.

$$J_{kk'2i} \;=\; \rho\,\frac{\exp\left\{-\left[\dfrac{c_{kk'i}^2\left(1+\frac{\rho^2}{w_i^2}\right)w_i^2}{2\sigma^2\left(2+\frac{\rho^2}{w_i^2}\right)}\right]\right\}}{(\rho^2+w_i^2)^{1/2}},$$

where $\alpha = (2 + \frac{\rho^2}{w_i^2})$, $\beta = \frac{\sqrt{2}w_i c_{kk'i}}{\lambda}$, and $\gamma = \frac{c_{kk'i}^2 w_i^2}{2\lambda^2}$.

$$J_{kk'3i} \;=\; \exp\left\{-\left[\dfrac{c_{kk'i}^2\left(1-\frac{w_i^2}{\rho^2}\right)w_i^2}{2\sigma^2}\right]\right\},$$

where $\alpha = \frac{\rho^2}{w_i^2}$, $\beta = \frac{\sqrt{2}w_i c_{kk'i}}{\lambda}$, and $\gamma = \frac{c_{kk'i}^2 w_i^2}{2\lambda^2}$.

Therefore, from eqn. (B.2), one has

$$\mathcal{E}\left(\frac{\mu_k(1-\mu_k)\alpha_k}{\frac{1}{2}\displaystyle\sum_{k'\neq k}[\mu_k\times(1-\mu_{k'})+\mu_{k'}\times(1-\mu_k)]}\right)$$

$$= \frac{\alpha_k p_k}{l-1}\left(\left[1-\prod_i\frac{\rho}{(w_i^2+\rho^2)^{1/2}}\right] + \sum_{k'\neq k}[3\prod_i\rho\,\frac{\exp\left\{-\left[\dfrac{c_{kk'i}^2}{2\sigma^2\left(1+\frac{\rho^2}{w_i^2}\right)}\right]\right\}}{(\rho^2+w_i^2)^{1/2}}\right.$$

$$-2\prod_i\rho\,\frac{\exp\left\{-\left[\dfrac{c_{kk'i}^2\left(1+\frac{\rho^2}{w_i^2}\right)w_i^2}{2\sigma^2\left(2+\frac{\rho^2}{w_i^2}\right)}\right]\right\}}{(\rho^2+w_i^2)^{1/2}} - \prod_i\exp\left\{-\left[\dfrac{c_{kk'i}^2\left(1-\frac{w_i^2}{\rho^2}\right)w_i^2}{2\sigma^2}\right]\right\}])$$

$$\approx \frac{\alpha_k p_k}{l-1}\left(\left[1-\prod_i\frac{\rho}{(w_i^2+\rho^2)^{1/2}}\right] + \sum_{k'\neq k}[3\prod_i\rho\,\frac{\exp\left\{-\left[\dfrac{c_{kk'i}^2}{2\sigma^2\left(1+\frac{\rho^2}{w_i^2}\right)}\right]\right\}}{(\rho^2+w_i^2)^{1/2}}\right.$$

$$-2\prod_i\rho\,\frac{\exp\left\{-\left[\dfrac{c_{kk'i}^2}{2\sigma^2\left(1+\frac{\rho^2}{w_i^2}\right)}\right]\right\}}{(\rho^2+2w_i^2)^{1/2}} - \prod_i\exp\left\{-\left[\dfrac{c_{kk'i}^2}{2\sigma^2\left(1+\frac{\rho^2}{w_i^2}\right)}\right]\right\}]). \qquad (B.4)$$

Now

$$\prod_i\frac{\rho}{(w_i^2+\rho^2)^{1/2}} = \prod_i\frac{\rho}{\rho\left(1+\frac{w_i^2}{\rho^2}\right)^{1/2}} = \prod_i\left(1+\frac{w_i^2}{\rho^2}\right)^{-(1/2)} = \prod_i\left(1-\frac{w_i^2}{2\rho^2}\right)$$

$$= \left(1 - \frac{\sum_i w_i^2}{2\rho^2}\right), \text{ as } \frac{w_i}{\rho} \ll 1. \text{ Similarly}$$

$$
\begin{aligned}
\prod_i \frac{\rho}{(2w_i^2 + \rho^2)^{1/2}} &= \prod_i \frac{\rho}{\rho\left(1 + \frac{2w_i^2}{\rho^2}\right)^{1/2}} \\
&= \prod_i \left(1 + \frac{2w_i^2}{\rho^2}\right)^{-(1/2)} \\
&= \prod_i \left(1 - \frac{w_i^2}{\rho^2}\right) \\
&= \left(1 - \frac{\sum_i w_i^2}{\rho^2}\right).
\end{aligned}
$$

Therefore

$$\mathcal{E}(E) \approx \sum_k \frac{\alpha_k p_k}{l-1} \frac{\sum_i w_i^2}{2\rho^2} \left(1 + \sum_{k' \neq k} \exp\left\{-\left[\sum_i \frac{c_{kk'i}^2}{2\sigma^2 \left(1 + \frac{\rho^2}{w_i^2}\right)}\right]\right\}\right). \quad \text{(B.5)}$$

Index

About the Authors

Sankar K. Pal is a *Distinguished Scientist,* and *Founding Head* of Machine Intelligence Unit, at the Indian Statistical Institute, Calcutta. He received the M. Tech. and Ph.D. degrees in Radio Physics and Electronics in 1974 and 1979 respectively, from the University of Calcutta. In 1982 he received another Ph.D. in Electrical Engineering along with DIC from Imperial College, University of London. He worked at the University of California, Berkeley and the University of Maryland, College Park during 1986-87 as a *Fulbright Post-doctoral Visiting Fellow;* at the NASA Johnson Space Center, Houston, Texas during 1990-92 and 1994 as a *Guest Investigator* under the *NRC-NASA Senior Research Associateship Program;* and at the Hong Kong Polytechnic University, Hong Kong in 1999 as a *Visiting Professor.* He was appointed a *Distinguished Visitor of IEEE Computer Society (USA)* for the *Asia-Pacific Region* for 1997-99.

Prof. Pal is a *Fellow* of the IEEE, USA, Third World Academy of Sciences, Italy, Indian National Science Academy, Indian Academy of Sciences, National Academy of Sciences, India, and the Indian National Academy of Engineering. He has been regularly contributing in the areas of Pattern Recognition, Image Processing, Soft Computing, Neural Nets, Genetic Algorithms, and Fuzzy Systems. He is a co-author of the book *Fuzzy Mathematical Approach* to *Pattern Recognition,* John Wiley & Sons (Halsted), N.Y., 1986 and a co-editor of four books: *Fuzzy Models for Pattern Recognition,* IEEE Press, N.Y., 1992, *Genetic Algorithms for Pattern Recognition,* CRC Press, Boca Raton, 1996, *Rough Fuzzy Hybridization: A New Trend in Decision-Making,* Springer

Verlag, Singapore, 1999 and *Soft Computing for Image Processing*, Physica Verlag, Heidelberg, 1999.

He has received several prizes/awards in India and USA including the *1990 Shanti Swarup Bhatnagar Prize in Engineering Sciences* (which is the most coveted award for a scientist in India), *1993 Jawaharlal Nehru Fellowship*, *1993 Vikram Sarabhai Research Award*, *1993 NASA Tech Brief Award*, *1994 IEEE Transactions on Neural Networks Outstanding Paper Award*, *1995 NASA Patent Application Award*, *1997 IETE - Ram Lal Wadhwa Gold Medal* and the *1998 Om Bhasin Foundation Award for Science & Technology.*

Prof. Pal is an *Associate Editor*, IEEE Trans. Neural Networks, Pattern Recognition Letters, Neurocomputing, Applied Intelligence, Information Sciences, Fuzzy Sets and Systems, Fundamenta Informaticae and Far-East Journal of Mathematical Sciences; and a *Member, Executive Advisory Editorial Board*, IEEE Trans. Fuzzy Systems and International Journal of Approximate Reasoning. He was also the *Guest Editor* of IEEE Computer special issue on Neural Networks: Theory and Practice, March 1996, JIETE special issue on Neural Networks, July-October, 1996 and Fundamenta Informaticae special issue on Soft Computing, January, 1999.

Sushmita Mitra obtained her B. Sc. (Hons.) in Physics and B. Tech and M. Tech. in Computer Science from the University of Calcutta in 1984, 1987, and 1989, respectively. She was awarded a Ph.D. in Computer Science by the Indian Statistical Institute, Calcutta in 1995.

Since 1995 she has been an *Associate Professor* at the Indian Statistical Institute, Calcutta, where she joined in 1989. From 1978 to 1983, she was a recipient of the *National Talent Search Scholarship* from the National Council for Educational Research and Training, India. From 1992 to 1994 she was in the European Laboratory for Intelligent Techniques Engineering (RWTH), Aachen, as a *German Academic Exchange Service (DAAD) Fellowship* holder. She was awarded the *IEEE Transactions on Neural Networks Outstanding Paper Award* in 1994. She worked in Meiji University, Japan as a *Visiting Professor* in 1999. Her research interests include pattern recognition, fuzzy sets, artificial intelligence, neural networks and soft computing.